APPETITE FOR DEFINITION

APPETITE FOR DEFINITION

An A–Z Guide to Rock Genres

IAN KING

HARPER PERENNIAL

NEW YORK • LONDON • TORONTO • SYDNEY • NEW DELHI • AUCKLAND

HARPER ● PERENNIAL

HarperCollins books may be purchased for educational, business, or sales promotional use. For information, please email the Special Markets Department at SPsales
@harpercollins.com.

FIRST EDITION

Designed by Jamie Lynn Kerner and Jen Ouerstreet

Library of Congress Cataloging-in-Publication Data has been applied for.

ISBN 978-0-06-268888-0 (pbk.)

18 19 20 21 22   LSC   10 9 8 7 6 5 4 3 2 1

For Jessica and Elliott

CONTENTS

GENRES

||||||||||||||||||||||||||||||||||||||||||||||||||||||||||||||||||||||||||||||||||||||||||||||||||||||||||||||||||

APPETITE FOR DEFINITION

PREFACE

A young boy and his parents stand quietly before three stage costumes once worn by David Bowie that bookend his creative prime. On the left is a glinting red bodysuit with the silver and blue lightning bolt down the back designed by Freddie Burretti for the 1972 tour for *The Rise and Fall of Ziggy Stardust and the Spiders from Mars*. On the right, a mannequin wears the grey one-button suit with a crescent moon breast pocket that Peter Hall crafted for the Serious Moonlight tour in 1983. In between is another memento from the Ziggy Stardust tour, a flowing yellow, red, and purple top both new-agey and out of this world. The tweenager turns to his mother and asks, *"Are all musicians really small?"*

It is a Saturday morning in late March at the Rock & Roll Hall of Fame. The day before was an unseasonably warm seventy-three degrees and the only clouds in the sky were contrails, but today's weather is closer to what one would expect in Cleveland this time of year. I. M. Pei's black glass pyramid rests starkly against a grey sky and a grey Lake Erie. The ring of engraved paving bricks in front of the entrance is filled with hundreds of tributes, sentiments and shout-outs: "WHO ARE THE BRAIN POLICE?," "ONLY UFO CAN ROCK ME!," "SLADE, SWEET, T REX THE BEST," "SKYNYRD'S IN THE HOUSE!," and well over a dozen various

puns on Pink Floyd's "Another Brick in the Wall." Every short rock-
and-roll slogan you could come up with has been immortalized here
by fans and charter members. There is a real, heartening affection
emanating from the ground.

Patti Smith's "Gloria" begins to play over the outside PA, the
quiet piano chords leaning in the wind gusting in off the water, and
even after forty years the opening line, "Jesus died for somebody's
sins but not mine," still feels a bit risqué at this volume in a public
setting. Inside, the escalator leads down to the ticket lines, which
are already filling with people wearing old band T-shirts, except for
the Pittsburghers who all identify themselves with black-and-yellow
football and hockey jerseys. Given the nature of a pyramid's shape,
the most square-footage is of course found at the bottom, so the history of rock and roll lies in the basement of King Tut's spaceship.

Stepping through the first door, "Rock and roll is a form of
popular music" are practically the first words you read. The origins
are laid out in detail. There are the first uses of "rock" in song titles:
Trixie Smith's "My Daddy Rocks Me," where the term was first used
as slang for sex, as well as Duke Ellington's "Rockin' in Rhythm"
and Wynonie Harris' "Good Rockin' Tonight." Muddy Waters' guitar, nicknamed "the Hoss," is encased in glass with other legendary
axes. The blues, gospel, and country music are all given their due for
contributing to the genesis of rock and roll.

Then comes a hallway with a ramp that leads down to four
separate booths with touchscreen displays where visitors can search
through the big, basic rock and pop music categories, jumping from
the roots to "The Beat Goes On" with no moment in between where
it all crystallized into one "rock 'n' roll." The sequence of exhibits
seems to be almost an admission that a single definition is too difficult and elusive. However, at the end of the "Don't Knock the Rock"
hallway, which is lined with stories about moral outrage directed
toward early rock-and-roll music that illustrate how far the line has

been pushed forward since the 1950s, comes a unifying answer in big red capital letters: ELVIS. *"Elvis is the undisputed king of rock 'n' roll"* states the wall placard near the screen showing a short film about his life. However you personally feel about this assertion, as general rock wisdom it is likely only to get more ingrained with the passage of time.

The lesson turns to geography in the "Cities" exhibit that comes next, leading visitors through the scenes in places like Memphis, Detroit, London and Liverpool (lumped together, surely to the mild dismay of visitors from both), San Francisco, Los Angeles, and Seattle. The section is not without a few somewhat morbid artifacts: pieces of the plane Otis Redding died in, a copy of Kurt Cobain's death certificate. The mood lightens up in the next room over, where visitors can take a gander at bric-a-brac such as those David Bowie outfits, Jimi Hendrix's family couch, Paul Weller's punk-rock trading card, Liz Phair's Tascam recorder, a relatively modest Flavor Flav neck clock, and a nondescript hat worn by a guy from the indie rock band Cloud Nothings.

From recordings of old blues singles to bits of apparel worn by modern pop stars, it is an admirably curated stroll through a chaotic story written simultaneously by thousands of people in hundreds of places. Keeping the chronology safe and tidy behind glass cases gives the Hall an impression of authority over what was once the sound of youthful rebellion. The truth, however, is more unsettling. No one is really in charge. Those at the top of the music industry ladder can and will keep honoring their own, but they'll always have to deal with widespread griping every time they continue to pass up the Smiths, Iron Maiden, King Crimson, and probably one of your personal favorites. They may have control over the coronations, but the conversation is well out of their hands.

INTRODUCTION

When rock and roll grew from fringe youth interest to mainstream commercial and cultural force in the 1950s, it was essentially one straightforward, if also new and therefore vaguely defined, style of music. In the 1960s, different branches would sprout and shoot off in myriad directions: towards folk music, back through the blues, into psychedelic sounds, and the roots of heavy metal. It only became more complicated from there. The 1970s saw the rise of not just more new genres but reactionary genres: the prog-rock poison and the punk antidote.

Ten years later, genres multiplied as artists came up with more ways to reconfigure their tastes, influences, wardrobes and hairstyles. Music writers and fans alike were also becoming increasingly creative as they strove to discover and classify every new trend. Genres were often a combination of organic creative growth and music-press manufacturing.

Today, dozens upon dozens of genres, some with more to substantiate them than others, have worked their way into the rock dialogue. There are scores of music websites and blogs—and even some print magazines left—fueled by trend-seeking writers who delight in coming up with new names for new sounds or new names for old sounds, if they decide that history didn't get it right the first time.

Some of these labels merely linger as passing fads while others become recognized as genuine movements—even if those movements might last for only a summer or are carried out by just a few like-minded bands. Other genres are tied less to a time and place and carry on even today. The names they have been given (or stuck with) can sometimes be maddeningly vague, or oddly specific. Some subcategories have their own subcategories. More kinds of metal exist than you can shake a skull at.

"There's obviously purists with every genre," says Brandon Stosuy, editor in chief at Kickstarter's The Creative Independent and a music curator. "But I feel with metal there's a real splitting of hairs that goes beyond maybe other genres, where people will say, 'Yeah, this is black metal,' or 'this is black-into-death metal,' or 'this is crust punk or crusty doom' or whatever." Stosuy understands how a listener could be into classic doom metal but not any other metal genre, though at the same time feels that the micro-level of niche that metal taxonomy reaches can get a little ridiculous. "Before the Internet, maybe you'd get your copy of *Maximum Rocknroll* or *Metal Edge*, then next month you'd get another one, but it wasn't a daily update. Now you can update things daily, it's just such a quicker moving thing, and I think that's really a huge part of why there are so many genre divisions now. Sometimes people will even say something offhandedly and then it gets coined a new subgenre."

Dates and definitions can be slippery when tracing the rapid evolution of rock music across six decades. The term "rock and roll" had come into common use by 1956, the same year that Elvis Presley left Sun Records and signed with RCA. It had been kicking around for a little while before that, however, and in its beginning was essentially interchangeable with "rhythm and blues." Discussing the differences in how Bill Haley & His Comets and Big Joe Turner performed the song "Shake, Rattle and Roll" in his book *How the Beatles Destroyed*

Rock 'n' Roll, writer Elijah Wald observes, "I have no problem with historians who consider those differences a musical dividing line between R&B and rock 'n' roll. But that semantic distinction was not made in the 1950s."[1]

The blues, country, jazz and gospel served as the primary colors of the popular music palette in America in the 1950s, and the parallel pop styles that developed out of them in the late 1950s and early 1960s—rock 'n' roll, R&B, soul, rockabilly—were all mixtures of two or more of those original hues in different proportions, blended together with different compositional and technological innovations. The nature of open exchange between musicians working in modern-minded milieus meant that these new forms were free to borrow and learn from one another. The Beatles were as fond of covering Motown songs like the Marvelettes' "Please Mr. Postman" as they were of performing country songs like Buck Owens' "Act Naturally." At a point when American rock and roll seemed to have already forgotten about its blues roots, English groups like the Rolling Stones arrived as a friendly reminder.

With the beat boom, folk rock and blues rock (not commonly known by that term at the time) all making inroads in the early- to mid-1960s, rock and roll as a template was clearly offering more and more possibilities for experimentation. Advancements in electrical instrumentation and studio technology accelerated these developments. In 1965 and 1966, the first traces of psychedelic rock started to appear in places as far apart as London, San Francisco, and Austin, Texas. Hard rock, and what would become known as heavy metal, took hold in 1968 with groups like Black Sabbath, Deep Purple and Iron Butterfly. The Moody Blues released *Days of Future Passed*, one of the first progressive rock albums, in 1967, around the same time that other major prog rock groups—Jethro Tull, Yes, Genesis, and others—were firing up their Mellotrons, polishing their flutes and starching their wizard hats.

If rock and roll and rhythm and blues (R&B) had grown apart after the 1950s, the two reconnected in the influence that psychedelic rock would have on funk and soul music in the 1960s and 1970s. In particular, the differences between rock and funk can be slim: the prominence of rhythm over melody and the greater or lesser role of the guitar produces different results, but the two forms have regularly conversed with each other over the years, naturally melding to make genres like funk rock and funk metal. Soul, funk, and their subgenres would continue to grow with disco, electronic dance music, and hip-hop and rap, but artists have routinely found ways to overlap with rock and roll—like Prince, rest his soul.

What led to the explosion of rock genres in the 1960s? There was no single fuse. Like so much of human history, the truth lies somewhere under a messy confluence of events. Once rock and roll had gained a foothold in youth culture, ongoing advances in media and technology aided its delivery to bored teenagers in California and Kansas alike. Just like the invention of the electric guitar made rock and roll possible in the first place, new gear opened new doors in music recording capability, live performance, and the breadth of sounds a musician could make to confound the previous generation and irritate parents everywhere.

More and more newcomers brought their own ideas and influences to the table. Sometimes the chain reactions caused by one musician influencing another made music history. One of the most famous examples of that is the back-and-forth between the Beatles and the Beach Boys, where one-upmanship drove the creative leaps and bounds from *Rubber Soul* to *Pet Sounds* to *Revolver*. The normalization and influence of recreational drugs, too, had an effect. Indeed, it played no small role in the creation of those three landmark albums.

Those genres that first appeared in the 1960s continued to develop and reach wider audiences in the early 1970s, and new genres kept popping up and captured the public's imagination. The UK delivered another groundbreaking genre with glam rock, as David Bowie, T. Rex, Roxy Music and more offered up a bit of androgyny and a flair for glittery fashion. The US had a grimier kind of glam with artists like the New York Dolls. As the Byrds carried on through the 1960s they struck upon country rock. As with R&B, the line between country and rock music had long been blurry, but, along with the Byrds, other artists like Gram Parsons and the Flying Burrito Brothers and Buffalo Springfield brought the two together in a new way.

While the 1960s saw the first explosion of rock genres, the 1970s saw the first reactionary rock genres. In Britain, the stylistic and sartorial excesses of progressive rock and glam rock didn't quite manage to win everyone over. The briefly lived phenomenon of pub rock came around in the early- to mid-1970s to fight back, with bands like Dr. Feelgood and Kilburn and the High Roads dressing down and playing simple, fuzzed-out guitar riffs. Pub rock was, in the UK at least, the casual older brother of the punk rock brat that would spit and sneer its way into the spotlight by 1976. Like pub rock, punk was not so much a new style as it was a back-to-basics rock genre, albeit with a more prickly personality and a wardrobe to match.

Rock and roll was an American invention, but from the moment the Beatles stepped off their plane in New York, an ongoing exchange of ideas was established among rock musicians on both sides of the Atlantic that would spur on the development of rock music for at least the next thirty years. In his memoir, *Going Deaf for a Living*, longtime BBC Radio DJ Steve Lamacq describes the history of punk as "a huge game of trans-Atlantic tennis," concluding that "the evolution of punk and then hardcore music has always relied on Britain and America taking a sound or a scene and then refining it into a new image."[2] *Sound of the Beast* author Ian Christe characterizes heavy metal's development in the 1980s in much the same way, writing that "by 1985 heavy metal had become a giant terrifying red ball, bouncing across the Atlantic and back, transplanting ideas between distant nations."[3]

No matter which side of the ocean a rock genre starts in, it often ends up becoming a joint concern. San Francisco may have been the first major scene for psychedelic rock, but London quickly became an important place for it as well—significant enough that Jimi Hendrix chose to launch his career there. (The Stray Cats and the Strokes would do much the same in their own eras.) Progressive rock, with all of its European classical aspirations, was largely a British concern, but the United States offered up Frank Zappa, Styx and Kansas, at least. This unique pop culture relationship shapes the perspective of this book's narrative, though of course many other countries—English speaking and otherwise—have made major contributions to rock music that are also recognized here both in individual entries and in the Translations section: Japan with Group Sounds, Norway with black metal, France and Belgium with cold wave, Turkey with Anadolu Pop, Canada with CanRock, and many more.

The 1980s and 1990s were a fruitful time for movements and new genres springing up throughout America, the UK, and beyond. Rapid advancement in communication technology meant word about such scenes, or pseudo-scenes, comprising little more than a few musicians, could spread wider and faster than ever before. Recognition from journalists and listeners could then quickly cement their presence. This was a golden age for branding rock music with curious names: the Paisley Underground, C86, baggy, shoegaze, grunge, grebo, riot grrrl.

The speed and access of connectivity from the 2000s onward would take genre proliferation to a whole new level. As blogs replaced photocopied fanzines and websites began to take over the role of breaking new artists from traditional music publications, the race was on to generate hype and page views. The Internet created an endless appetite for anything new, and a practically risk-free space for linguistic experimentation. Genres could live in the imagination of a writer for the length of one single article, or they might take hold for a little while.

It may be true that today's youth, with their unlimited access to all music at all times, don't feel the same level of social pressure to align their personal identities with one particular scene. At the same time, however, the use of labels in rock music is more prevalent than ever. Music websites make a habit of preceding a band name with their most identifiable genre (e.g., "blues rock duo the Black Keys"). Customers who used to encounter a handful of different sections at record stores—the long-gone Tower Records that was once on Mercer Street in Seattle, for example, used to put classical music in its own back room—are now confronted with playlists that cater to their every possible mood.

In his book *This Will End in Tears*, Adam Brent Houghtaling observes that, "As the public conversation becomes decentralized with the decline of 800-pound tastemakers such as *Rolling Stone* and MTV, the disappearance of record stores, the postmodern cut-and-paste approach to the creation of new music, and the rise of blogs, niche websites, social networking, and Internet radio, genres are not solidified with the certainty that they once were."[4] Nowhere is this truer than on streaming music services, which are now constantly churning out their own new sub-subgenre terms that break down existing genres into brain-frying specifics and pull others that have been heretofore unheard of out of thin air. An entire website, Every Noise at Once, is run by Spotify data analyst Glenn McDonald simply to keep tabs on the 1,500-plus music genres that listeners can encounter on the service. "I'm cheerfully unrigorous about what a genre can be," McDonald told the website PopMatters in early 2017.

"Some of them are musicological, some are historical, and others are regional themes. A genre can be any listening mode I think people might want."[5]

An ever-growing list of hyper-specific styles is perhaps a computer-simulated endgame to the music-genre conversation, a visually appealing manifestation of what Houghtaling gets at with the assertion that "the act of classification has become simultaneously more and less relevant."[6] An endless array of sorting and marketing tags—from the real (hard rock) to the real-ish (psychedelic doom), from the seemingly contradictory "deep melodic death metal" to odd concepts like "sleaze rock," "orgcore," and "fallen angel"—is entertaining to look at and good for an afternoon of cruising, but does it help people get a better understanding of the music itself, who and where it comes from, and what inspired it?

This book, then, is intended not to be an alternate endpoint, but another way into the history, discussion and debate surrounding rock and roll and the multiplying offspring that is has produced over the past sixty years. Collecting and elaborating on the great diversity of styles that have sprouted from what began as a relatively simple sound, this book will go branch by branch up and around the sprawling, knotty family tree of rock music. Its many limbs have a habit of crisscrossing, overlapping or entwining, but the tree still grows and the fruit remains nourishing.

HOW TO USE THIS BOOK

When you think of rock and roll, you might think of the Beatles, Led Zeppelin, or Metallica. Perhaps the Clash, Foo Fighters, or Arcade Fire first comes to mind. The beauty and complexity of rock music is that, basically, whatever you think of, you are right. There are some rock classifications, however, that won't be found in the table of contents here. For instance, you won't see classic rock because, as beloved a "genre" as it is, it's ultimately more of a broad radio format (like AOR, album-oriented rock) than one distinct style of music. In the 1980s and 1990s, "classic rock" could be all of the hard, soft, progressive, psychedelic rock (all covered here) from twenty years before, and now that we're twenty years beyond those decades, classic rock can include the likes of heartland rock, alternative rock, and grunge as well. The book also bypasses certain revisionist concepts, some genre terms that are too new to really substantiate, and the more agonized hair-splitting that runs rampant in the modern inventory of metal, but overall the intent is to be largely inclusionary with its definition of what qualifies as a genre.

Just as there is no single right way to hear rock music, there is no single right way to read this book. This book is designed to work in different ways, and however you choose to dive, wade or dip a toe into these waters is the correct approach. Start to finish, this is an alphabetical expedition through rock music, with a focus on the conversation surrounding it and the ongoing pursuit (however fool-hardy) to understand and define it. Zigging and zagging across the past six decades in this way shows, among other things, how similar the development and experience of different music scenes has been. You can also flip the book open to any random entry, and that is a fine way to enter this story as well.

The A-to-Z format allows for ease of use as a reference tool. This way, when you come across a new artist on your favorite music web-site, and read that they are the foremost purveyors of a new hybrid style called "ambient crust pop," "death wave blues" or "doom twee," you can quickly look up the pieces that have been put together to create this puzzling new genre. This will give you the context to understand *what* is being created, even if it's still unclear *why* it is being created.

Intended to facilitate discovery, at the end of each genre entry are lists of "key players" and "crossover tracks." Key players are pioneers in a genre and/or artists whose music best exemplifies the sound of it. This doesn't mean that every song in a key player's back catalogue is indicative of one genre—the Byrds' sound, for example, quickly evolved from folk rock to psychedelic rock to country rock—but these musicians have made records that are crucial to understanding the genre. Of course, a genre hasn't truly hit the big time until it has proliferated beyond the control of such instigators. To that end, a bank of Spotify playlists has been created to dig deeper into many of the genres in this book, providing a soundtrack to read along with. Those playlists can be accessed via the Spotify page ianfking1.

Crossover tracks serve as bridges from one genre into another. These songs have been chosen as notable examples of how genres in-tersect and overlap. If you don't think college rock and rockabilly have much in common, give the Replacements' "I Will Dare" a listen and reconsider. Musicians don't tend to have the same use for stylistic borders that audiences have. Though some of the more dedicated strains of metal have stuck to their own path, there are few rock music genres that don't rub up against half a dozen others. These crossover tracks are a jumping off point to go genre hopping, a sort of "Choose Your Own Adventure" approach to navigating the book, albeit one without any bad endings.

Staggered in between the individual entries are five sections that cover many genres together. This was not done merely for narrative expediency—though, really, there isn't all that much to say about acoustic black metal—but to illustrate how genres can connect beyond the merit of what they sound like. "America, America" surveys a range of US-born rock, styles tied to geographical locales from California to the Jersey Shore, and also deriving from distinct American perspectives, such as Afro-punk and Taqwacore. "Dressing Up" covers artists who go above and beyond the call of duty to fashion, whose musical identities are tied to their characteristic appearance.

"Have a Sense of Humor" is concerned with less-than-serious rock genre nicknames (be they affectionate, observant or mocking) that have worked their way into the pop lexicon, or even come to be recognized as a legit style of music. "Micro-genres" are the creations of lone wolves, or at most a den of two or three, who demand their own categorization. The "Translations" section visits different kinds of rock from countries around the globe that are not sung in the English language, some of which have stylistic counterparts in the US and/or UK, and some of which are very much unique to their environment.

Any old way you choose to use it, the hope is that this book will lead you somewhere new in rock and roll music, or remind you of what first made you excited about it. To paraphrase something that John Richards, DJ at Seattle radio station KEXP, once said years ago on the air during a breathless pledge drive speech, there is no other feeling like finding out about a band for the first time and realizing how many great new records you suddenly have to look forward to. (Richards was speaking about a teenager discovering the Cure, though he might not have been thinking specifically about *Wild Mood Swings*.) This experience is by nature more likely to occur in the newness of youth, but it can happen at any point in life. There is simply too much music out there to hear everything in one lifetime, and that's a great problem to have.

GENRES

2 Tone

A rare genre, 2 Tone, like Motown, was named after a single record label that came up with its own in-house sound. As the *Two Tone Britain* documentary from 2004 sums it up, 2 Tone was the "energy of punk fused with reggae's ancestor, ska."[1] The unlikely birthplace of the socially significant scene in the late 1970s was the city of Coventry, located roughly halfway between the UK's punk capitals, Manchester and London. At the heart of the movement was the band the Specials, and at the heart of that band was Jerry Dammers, founder of 2 Tone Records. Nicking the name from a style of suit worn by mods and skinheads, it also denoted the Specials' mix of black and white musicians, significant in a time of heightened racial tensions in the country.[2]

Dammers played in few different local bands—including his own, a punky reggae prototype called the Automatics—as the lineup for the Specials came together piece by piece. Not fully content with the way punk and reggae were coming together in their music, Dammers and the renamed the Special A.K.A. turned to ska, which a generation prior had been favored by mods.[3]

Like 4AD, 2 Tone was one of the first UK labels to grasp the value of "brand image" before that idea became universal. On stage the Special A.K.A. band members wore tonic suits and pork pie hats. The band's record sleeves became adorned with bits of black-and-white checkerboard pattern and an illustrated mascot named Walt Jabsco.

2 Tone Records became a reality when the fan buzz around the Special A.K.A. and their single "Gangsters" grew so loud that the

major labels couldn't ignore it. Roy Eldridge from Chrysalis Records saw them play at the Moonlight Club in London in May of 1979 and signed Dammers to a five-album deal by giving 2 Tone a distribution deal as part of the package, allowing them to sign and release records by other groups.

The Specials' landmark self-titled debut arrived in October of that year. 2 Tone, meanwhile, had already released Madness' "The Prince" and the Selecter's "On My Radio," and would soon put out singles by the Beat (called the English Beat in North America), the Body Snatchers, and even a one-off single from Elvis Costello, "I Can't Stand Up for Falling Down." 2 Tone bands may have technically been signed to Chrysalis, but curation of the label, and thus essentially the scene itself, was left to Dammers and the Specials.[4] The Beat and Madness in particular would go on to considerable success in the early '80s; Madness scored a big hit in the US as well as the UK in 1982 with "Our House," and the Beat's "Save It for Later" and "Mirror in the Bathroom" are staples of any new wave playlist.

That scene moved fast, and though *The Specials* had turned the spirit of unity and tension of social unrest into something new and danceable, their second album, *More Specials*, in 1980, lost some of their momentum. They recaptured the zeitgeist the following year with "Ghost Town," a hit single that addressed the hard times being faced in post-industrial British cities. Between the band succumbing to internal conflicts and the label's lack of business acumen, 2 Tone wasn't quite what it had been after "Ghost Town," but within a few years the genre's ripple effect would start to be felt across the pond in America with the first signs of ska punk.

Key Tracks: Bad Manners–"Special Brew," the Beat–"Mirror in the Bathroom," Madness–"One Step Beyond," the Selecter–"On My Radio," the Specials–"Gangsters" and "Ghost Town"

CROSSOVER TRACKS

POST-PUNK

The Pop Group–"She is Beyond Good and Evil," the Slits–
"Typical Girls," Scritti Politti–"The Sweetest Girl"

REGGAE ROCK

The Police–"Walking on the Moon," UB40–"Red Red Wine"

SKA PUNK

Dance Hall Crashers–"Go," Fishbone–"Party at Ground Zero,"
Operation Ivy–"Sound System"

Acid Rock

On a Friday in April of 1943, Albert Hoffman, a Swiss chemist working at Sandoz Laboratories accidentally came into contact with the lysergic acid diethylamide he was experimenting with and stumbled into his first acid trip.[1] Two decades later, the mind-expanding chemical was moving into a central role in American counterculture, and found one champion in Ken Kesey, whose transition from off-beat writer to LSD figurehead culminated in the Acid Tests—small social gatherings centered around attendees trying out the new psychedelic drug—he held in 1965 and 1966.

A group from the San Francisco area that had recently changed its name from the Warlocks to the Grateful Dead would become Acid Test regulars. They weren't alone in their zeal for mixing rock music with enlightened states of mind. In Austin, Texas, the 13th Floor Elevators were also devising their mission "to musically 'play the acid' and carry the word," as author Jesse Jarnow points out in *Heads*.[2]

Acid rock is, basically, psychedelic rock. The two terms are generally interchangeable, but for some time it has been commonplace to use "acid rock" to denote the darker, aggressive side of psych rock. The spirit of acid rock is in the extended guitar 'freak out,' in distorted heavy blues jams that wander off course, in the lava lamp you stare at while sinking into your bean bag chair, Iron Butterfly on the hi-fi. It also works when applied to rock music that isn't heavy but was made under the influence of LSD, like Pink Floyd's first album, The Piper at the Gates of Dawn, or music and bands that overtly reference acid—Eric Burdon & the Animals' "A Girl Named Sandoz," or Japanese legends Acid Mothers Temple.

Pioneer Tracks: The 13th Floor Elevators—"Slip Inside This House," Eric Burdon & the Animals—"A Girl Named Sandoz," the Beatles—"Lucy in the Sky with Diamonds," Grateful Dead—"Alligator," Pink Floyd—"Interstellar Overdrive"

CROSSOVER TRACKS

ALTERNATIVE ROCK

The Flaming Lips—"One Million Billionth of a Millisecond on a Sunday Morning," Primal Scream—"Slip Inside This House" (the 13th Floor Elevators), Smashing Pumpkins—"A Girl Named Sandoz" (Eric Burdon & the Animals)

BAGGY

Flowered Up—"Weekender," Happy Mondays—"Hallelujah," the Stone Roses—"Don't Stop"

KRAUTROCK

Amon Düül II—"Eye-Shaking King," Can—"Yoo Doo Right," Faust—"Why Don't You Eat Carrots?"

Alternative Country

"I should say first that I'm not sure 'alt-country' is really a thing these days," begins Kim Ruehl, writer, singer/songwriter, and current editor of *No Depression*, the "journal of roots music" that was once synonymous with alternative country. *No Depression* was also the title of the 1990 debut album from Illinois band Uncle Tupelo, the first of four records they released in quick succession, after which founders Jeff Tweedy and Jay Farrar split to form Wilco and Son Volt, respectively—the most visible groups among a growing alt-country field.

Ruehl explains that the reason *No Depression* founders Grant Alden and Peter Blackstock started the magazine was because they weren't seeing anyone taking alternative country seriously as a legitimate style and musical movement. "They wanted to chronicle the scene and tell the artists' stories and clue fans into the fact that, if you like the Bottle Rockets, there are actually bands like that playing all over the US."

Country music, Ruehl observes, had been the home of artists like Merle Haggard, Johnny Cash, Loretta Lynn and Tammy Wynette. "But then Garth Brooks happened, and I think the recording industry figured out that it could make a *ton* of money if it made pop music dressed up in country clothes. Suddenly, artists that were continuing the line of Merle and Johnny and Kris [Kristofferson] and Hank [Williams] didn't fit on country radio. So alt-country was the way that went. It gave audiences a chance to connect with that line of country music, and outlaw country especially, without having to sit through songs like 'Boot Scootin' Boogie.'"

If it didn't take over the world, by most any measure the crossover can be considered a success. Son Volt's 1995 debut, *Trace*, made its way into unexpected places like the top of the year-end best albums list in Seattle's former biweekly music paper, *The Rocket,* and the tour van of Milwaukee emo band the Promise Ring.[1] Wilco upped the ante with every release until the band that made *A. M.* was practically unrecognizable next to the one that made *A Ghost is Born* a decade later.

As the originators of alt-country built on and redirected their music, the genre became something of an outdated idea. "I think what was once considered alt-country has since been swallowed up by Americana," Ruehl reasons. "You could probably trace a line from Hank Williams to Johnny Cash to Lucinda Williams to Margo Price and Jason Isbell, which might make you inclined to call this new generation alt-country, but I think Americana is more fitting."

Pioneer Tracks: Cowboy Junkies–"Misguided Angel," Giant Sand–"Thin Line Man," Jason and the Scorchers–"Last Time Around," the Jayhawks–"Five Cups of Coffee," Uncle Tupelo–"Factory Belt"

Key Players: The Bottle Rockets, the Jayhawks, Old 97's, Son Volt, Whiskeytown, Wilco

CROSSOVER TRACKS

ALTERNATIVE ROCK

Big Head Todd and the Monsters–"Broken Hearted Savior," the Lemonheads–"Big Gay Heart," Toad the Wet Sprocket–"Nanci"

INDIE ROCK

Blitzen Trapper–"Furr," My Morning Jacket–"Golden," Okkervil River–"Kansas City"

PAISLEY UNDERGROUND

Danny & Dusty–"The Word Is Out," Green on Red–"Good Patient Woman," the Long Ryders–"Final Wild Son"

Alternative Metal

As with alternative rock, the idea with alternative metal was to catch as many fish outside the mainstream as possible with one hip-yet-inclusive net. Alternative metal can be any manner of alt-rock that incorporates metal techniques or influences; examples include Faith No More and Soundgarden. It can also be metal that incorporates alternative rock influences, or just even has some artistic outsider appeal that speaks to rock fans who don't like Megadeth, such as White Zombie and Ministry.

Alice in Chains started out as a young suburban metal band before being introduced to a less showy scene in Seattle[1], and flashes of that background still gleam through the grime on their debut album, *Facelift*. From the other side of Lake Washington came Queensrÿche, who earned their place in progressive metal history with one of the best-named concept albums of all time, *Operation: Mindcrime*. Their next opus, the double album *Empire*, featured "Jet City Woman" and the power ballad "Silent Lucidity," which established a presence on commercial radio and MTV, and between their artsier inclinations and ability to write big hooks they arrived at alternative metal from the other direction.[2]

Alternative metal can also include bands who are just different, like Voivod from Montreal.[3] "When I first got into music I was, of course, always searching for something more and more extreme," says John Haughm, founder of the former genre-crossing metal band Agalloch, currently with the group Pillorian. "Extremity was not inclusive to heaviness though and I liked finding bands who were also extremely unique. Voivod was huge for me in this way."

Key Tracks: Alice in Chains–"Man in the Box," Faith No More–"Midlife Crisis," Living Colour–"Cult of Personality," Tool–"Sober," Voivod–"Clouds in My House"

|||||||||||||||||||||||||||||||||||||||||||||||||||||||||||||||||||||||||||

CROSSOVER TRACKS

|||||||||||||||||||||||||||||||||||||||||||||||||||||||||||||||||||||||||||

INDUSTRIAL ROCK

Filter–"Hey Man Nice Shot," Ministry–"Jesus Built My Hotrod," Nine Inch Nails–"Wish"

POST-HARDCORE

Helmet–"In the Meantime," Quicksand–"Freezing Process," Thrice–"Identity Crisis"

PROGRESSIVE METAL

Dream Theater–"Pull Me Under," King's X–"Black Flag," Queensrÿche–"Spreading the Disease"

Alternative Rock

||||||||||||||||||||||||||||||||||||||||||||||||||||||||||||||||||||||||||||||||||||||||||||||||||||||||||||||||||||||||||||||||||||||||||||||||

The dreadful state of mainstream music in the late 1980s has been reiterated time and again, but the fact is that "alternative" would not have happened the way it did if audiences weren't in need of it. Just take a quick peek at Billboard's Hot 100 singles of 1989. *Four* Milli Vanilli songs in the top thirty. Debbie Gibson and New Kids on the Block were electrifying the youth. Paula Abdul and Richard Marx were right there waiting for you. Roxette were inexplicably huge, a guitar-and-hairspray-happy link in the Swedish pop lineage from ABBA to Ace of Base. It wasn't a completely barren wasteland, but if you were older than fourteen, younger than forty, and didn't like rock bands who wore leather pants, you had to look elsewhere.

"I think the 'alternative' thing probably raised its ugly head for the first time toward the middle of the '80s," recalls Marco Collins, who in the heyday and aftermath of grunge was the music director and leading voice on Seattle's major alternative rock station, 107.7.

"Commercial stations don't launch without tons of research done on whether or not the audience for that market is ready for a station that is much further to the left than most of them," says Collins. 107.7 The End, whose bumper stickers would soon be ubiquitous around Seattle, happened for that reason. At its core, the term "alternative" doesn't signify anything more specific than "not mainstream." That was the intention, anyway. The modern use of "alt-rock" is a narrowing of a genre that was formerly defined in a loose sense by what it *wasn't*.

"As the term 'alternative rock' has moved steadily toward utter meaningless, it's become increasingly prevalent in the mainstream media vocabulary, basically as a banner for any contemporary music that's not old-line corporate rock (even if it's only pretending not to be old-line corporate rock),"[1] writes Scott Schinder in his introduction to *Rolling Stone's Alt-Rock-A-Rama*. In that same book, writer James Marshall asserts hyperbolically that "much of what occurs in the name of Alternative Rock is an outgrowth—or, perhaps more accurately, a re-hash–of what the Stooges and the Velvet Underground had achieved in the late sixties and early seventies."[2]

Back in the 1990s, if MTV VJs Kennedy and Matt Pinfield had taken the time in every interview they conducted on Alternative Nation and 120 Minutes to ask artists, "Do you or do you not own records by the Stooges and the Velvet Underground?", there's a good chance that many would answer affirmatively. There's also a good chance that even more of them would own records by the Beatles.

Even if certain critics failed to be impressed, the market validated its worth. For a time it seemed as if every other popular rock band was branded as "alternative." The Cure, R.E.M., Jane's Addiction, Red Hot Chili Peppers, Nine Inch Nails and Nirvana are all associated with other genres found in this book, and at the same time coexist in the alternative rock camp. Numerous others all sold millions of albums, yet were still afforded a semblance of outsider status because they weren't Bon Jovi or Aerosmith. These bands may have started in small clubs, but they were now shifting major units at chain stores. In 1993, Pearl Jam's second album, *Vs.*, famously sold over 900,000 copies in less than a week of its release.

One thing that Collins finds interesting about the rise of alternative radio stations in the 1990s is how they affected smaller stations, possibly for the better. "I think that the word 'alternative' kind of stole a little bit of the thunder from indie and college radio, just because everything was so left of center. It's probably driven indie rock and/or college rock to be even more challenging, to go way further to the left."

As the 1990s wore on and alternative wore out, radio stations started looking elsewhere. Collins was an early supporter of Oasis in the United States, having first read about them in the *New Musical Express* (*NME*), the weekly UK music paper. Not long after the rise of Britpop, he traveled to London and sampled the dance club culture there firsthand. "I remember being in the middle of this crowd and . . . getting a chill. I thought, 'Oh my god, this feels like the same energy as being in a Nirvana pit. That feeling of your heart jumping through your chest. I was like, 'This is it, and it could work with those same kids.'"

Back at home, Collins faced some resistance trying to introduce what was then called "electronica" into rotation on KNDD. "*The Seattle Times* did a column all about me trying to force this sound onto the radio," he remembers, colorfully dismissing what was then the paper's stodgy position. "The electronic thing worked. It didn't take off like grunge did, but we played and broke a lot of really great bands. The Chemical Brothers, Fatboy Slim. We flew the Prodigy out to an Endfest, and that was probably one of my favorite moments in my career."

Endfest was the radio station's annual summer music festival, an event that a lot of people from the industry came from around the country to attend, so Collins knew it would be important for the Prodigy to make a big impression. The End flew them in from the UK to do the one show. Describing the night more than twenty years later, Collins is still audibly energized by how it all went down. "No Doubt got done, and I saw this mass exodus." Collins got hold of a live mic from a sound guy. "I remember going, 'Stop, stop right now, you people walking to your cars, and listen to me for one moment. What you're about to see is something that everybody's going to be talking about in the next couple of weeks. If you leave right now, you're going to be the guy that left before they played.'"

Collins persuaded half of those leaving to return. "It just went off. It was the first time I'd seen [electronica] work with grunge kids. It was an amazing moment for these kids who all of a sudden don't know what to do . . . they're going to mosh because they don't really know how to dance, and the Prodigy played into it." The Prodigy may not fit the modern perception of alternative rock, but, as Collins' experience illustrates, the energy was moving in their direction. Though they began in the early 1990s on a straight-up techno vibe, by that point they were dressing and raging like punks.

Alternative rockers would soon begin abandoning ship anyway. Even Billy Corgan, an alt-rock posterboy, started flirting with electronica on Smashing Pumpkins' 1998 album, *Adore*. Alternative rock, with all of its eclectic intentions and corporate cash infusions, became a concept frozen in time as indie rock burrowed back underground and commercial radio and record labels looked to post-grunge and nu metal for guitar rock. The term still finds use as an adjective, though the notion of a popular music movement that wanted to appear as if it wasn't popular seems a little quaint these days.

Pioneer Tracks: The Cure–"Just Like Heaven," Pixies–"Gigantic," R.E.M.–"The One I Love," the Smiths–"How Soon is Now?," Sonic Youth–"Teen Age Riot"

Key Players: Beck, the Breeders, Dinosaur Jr., the Flaming Lips, Garbage, Goo Goo Dolls, Hole, Jane's Addiction, the Lemonheads, Nirvana, PJ Harvey, Pearl Jam, Radiohead, Red Hot Chili Peppers, Soul Asylum, Smashing Pumpkins, Soundgarden, Weezer

CROSSOVER TRACKS

ALTERNATIVE COUNTRY

The Jayhawks–"Take Me with You (When You Go)," Son Volt–"Drown," Wilco–"Box Full of Letters"

POST-HARDCORE

Fugazi–"Do You Like Me?" Jawbox–"Cornflake Girl" (Tori Amos), Shudder to Think–"Red House"

PROTO-PUNK

The Modern Lovers–"Pablo Picasso," the Stooges–"T.V. Eye," the Velvet Underground–"Sweet Jane"

Ambient Rock

The built-in contradiction in the idea of ambient rock is glaring. However, since at least as far back as progressive rock in the 1970s, there have been ambient passages in rock songs. There is the extended quiet parts of Pink Floyd's "Echoes," from their album *Meddle*, with its sonar-like ping. There's also David Bowie's Berlin Triptych. In more recent years, the Nashville-based guitarists Andrew Thompson and Marc Byrd formed Hammock and floated toward the ambient end of post-rock.

Prime examples of ambient rock can be found on the early records of Icelandic band Sigur Rós and San Diego musician Jimmy LaValle's long-running solo project, the Album Leaf (both of whom are also regularly categorized as post-rock). Both released in the United States in 2001, the Album Leaf's *One Day I'll Be on Time* and Sigur Rós' breakthrough *Ágætis byrjun* wield the power of passivity. Unsurprisingly, the two artists gravitated toward each other not long after those discs came out, and began touring and recording together in the early 2000s.

Key Tracks: The Album Leaf–"The MP," David Bowie–"Subterraneans," Hammock–"Then the Quiet Explosion," Papa M–"I Am Not Lonely with Cricket," Pink Floyd–"Echoes"

CROSSOVER TRACKS

DRONE METAL

Earth–"Teeth of Lions Rule the Divine," Nadja–"Now I Am Become Death, the Destroyer of Worlds," Sunn O)))–"Aghartha"

KRAUTROCK

Cluster–"15:33," Popol Vuh–"In den Gärten Pharaos," Tangerine Dream–"Ashes to Ashes"

POST-ROCK

Fly Pan Am–"L'espace au sol est redessiné par d'immenses panneaux bleus," Mogwai–"Superheroes of BMX," Sigur Rós–"Svefn-g-englar"

Anarcho Punk

Anarcho punk may be defined first and foremost by the social and personal politics that populate its lyrics, but its rough-hewn musicianship and collectivist agit-rhythms set apart its sound. Johnny Rotten may have declared "Anarchy in the UK," and for some punks it was a real principle. The scene's lack of interest in working for the Man's money allowed it to practice chaos.[1]

Radical Essex idealists[2] Crass remain the model example of anarcho punk. Pulling themselves up in the late 1970s after the UK's initial punk boom, Crass spoke up for liberation in the form of feminism and vegetarianism, and they put out albums like *The Feeding of the 5000* and *Stations of the Crass* that would take the rough shape of basic punk and tatter it up even more. Driven by a military drum roll on speed, their "Do They Owe Us a Living?" might not be the most tuneful flagship song, but it gets the message across.

The anarcho punk scene in the UK at this time seemed to be full of either friends of Crass, like Poison Girls and Rubella Ballet, or bands who were featured on one of Crass' *Bullshit Detector* compilations, such as Amebix and Chumbawamba.[3] Yes, *that* Chumbawamba. It is one of anarcho punk's worst kept secrets that the folks who wrote "Tubthumping" once had real punk cred. Anarcho punk wasn't just an English concern: there was the Ex from the Netherlands, and American bands like Anti-Flag picked up on it later.[4] Though less musically unified as it spread across borders and years, anarcho punk's spirit nonetheless carries on in bands that espouse peace and self-reliance . . . and have cool black-and-white logo patches.

Key Tracks: Amebix–"No Gods, No Masters," Chumbawamba–"Revolution," Crass–"Do They Owe Us a Living?" Poison Girls–"Ideologically Unsound," Subhumans–"Dying World"

‖‖‖

CROSSOVER TRACKS

‖‖‖

CROSSOVER THRASH

The Accüsed–"Martha Splatterhead," Iron Reagan–"Tyranny of Will"

HARDCORE PUNK

Black Flag–"Rise Above," Dead Kennedys–"Kill the Poor"

POWERVIOLENCE

Crossed Out–"He-Man," Man Is the Bastard–"Existence Decay"

Art Punk

The term "art punk" acknowledges that a band fits within the punk milieu, but either some or all of the members went to art school, or at least have a creative vision for their music beyond bashing out pogo fodder. Calling some punk music "art" may seem a bit insulting to others, but some of *those* punks probably see "art" as a term of derision.

Television in the US and Wire in the UK are examples of early art-punk bands. But, in its own way, isn't what the Ramones did art, too? Certainly. You can be art punk by accident as well as on purpose. It's art; anything goes as long as it has some kind of an edge.

Though "art" and "avant garde" invoke similar connotations when applied to music, art punk is not the same thing as "avant-punk," which is a term Robert Christgau came up with in 1977 to classify bands from the late 1960s and early 1970s that are now commonly referred to as proto-punk: the Velvet Underground, the Stooges, MC5, the Modern Lovers, Patti Smith, and so on.[1]

Key Tracks: The Fall–"It's the New Thing," Pere Ubu–"Non-alignment Pact," the Raincoats–"Adventures Close to Home #1," Television–"Little Johnny Jewel," Wire–"12XU"

CROSSOVER TRACKS

ART ROCK

Roxy Music–"Virginia Plain," the Velvet Underground–"White Light/White Heat"

NEW WAVE

Devo–"Mongoloid," Talking Heads–"New Feeling," XTC–"Science Friction"

NOISE ROCK

Flipper–"Sex Bomb," No Age–"Cappo," Times New Viking–"No Time, No Hope"

Art Rock

Art rock can't afford to be too precious. With visual art, some is intended for galleries and some for commercial purposes, but mass production is the point of the recording industry, and art-rock records are mass produced like any of the others. One can go online and buy a pack of socks or a copy of King Crimson's *In the Court of the Crimson King* for roughly the same price. Recording artists don't put out a single copy of an album and sell it to some obnoxious wealthy buyer for $2 million unless they are the Wu-Tang Clan, who purportedly did just that when Martin Shkreli bought the lone copy of *Once Upon a Time in Shaolin* in 2015, a big-time art-rock stunt for the Staten Island crew.[1]

The creative accomplishments of rock music's maturation in the late 1960s are apparent. The Mothers of Invention's 1968 album, *We're Only in It for the Money*, is surely more intellectually stimulating than many other rock records made by many other bands who actually *were* only in it for the money. With all of its pretensions, aspirations, and wildly detailed album covers, prog rock would reach for high-art credibility. Punk, too, had its share of art-school students, so when the post-punks arrived and prog faded it was one kind of art rock taking over for another. Art rock can be about costumes and song lengths, but it can also be driven by quirk, subverting expectations, or playing your instruments poorly on purpose.

Key Tracks: Captain Beefheart & His Magic Band–"Moonlight on Vermont," King Crimson–"Pictures of a City," the Mothers of

Invention–"Who Are the Brain Police?" Pink Floyd–"Careful with that Axe, Eugene"

CROSSOVER TRACKS

GLAM ROCK
Roxy Music–"The Bob (Medley)," Sparks–"This Town Ain't Big Enough for Both of Us"

POST-PUNK
Pere Ubu–"Sentimental Journey," Talking Heads–"No Compassion," Wire–"A Touching Display"

PROGRESSIVE ROCK
Genesis–"Firth of Fifth," Yes–"Close to the Edge"

AMERICA, AMERICA

Afro-Punk, Americana, California Sound, Chicano Rock, Cosmic American Music, Cowpunk, Heartland Rock, Jersey Shore Sound, New Weird America, Swamp Rock, Taqwacore, Tropical Rock, Tulsa Sound

AFRO-PUNK

Afro-punk isn't necessarily beholden to US borders, but the discussion about its importance began in punk scenes across the country. "Being caught in a system that you can't identify with, that you don't support, and, like, just being contrary . . . that's the true energy of what punk is,"[1] says Brooklyn resident Tamar-kali Brown early on in the 2003 documentary *Afro-Punk*. Directed by James Spooner, the hour-long film explores the experiences of African American punk musicians and fans in punk communities and their relationship with punk and hardcore culture. Through interviews with people like D. H. Peligro from the Dead Kennedys, Angelo Moore from Fishbone, Kyp Malone from TV on the Radio, and Carley Coma from Candiria, *Afro-Punk* points out the pull of underground music and counterculture: the sense of community, the importance of the DIY spirit, the appeal of letting out aggression, and the connection to positive politics and awareness.

It also brings to light what it is like to navigate the contrasting experiences between people of different races in the same music scene and how people can relate to the same music, even the same concert, so differently. Afro-punk refers to a community and a perspective, but not a *genre* of punk rock that is distinguished by musical differences. As far as "punk" goes, at this point, it has much to do with the energy that Brown referred to, not just three-chord thrash. The Afropunk music festival, growing in size and scope since its first year in 2005, began with a focus on punk but now includes artists from all across the musical spectrum.

AMERICANA ||||||||||||||||||||||||||||||||||||||||||||||||||||||||||||||||||||||||||||||||||||||||||

"Mainstream country these days gets you through the party, and roots music—or Americana, if you prefer commercial terms—will get you through the hangover," says Kim Reuhl. As it applies to music, the idea of Americana means different things to different people, and though there are some basic parameters, there is no one right way to look at it. Americana covers musical territory as broad as the diverse expanse of soil that it is named for. Music writer Amanda Petrusich notes in her book on modern American music, *It Still Moves*, that, "Loosely, Americana music is traditional folk music, a symbiotic swirl of folk, bluegrass, country, gospel, blues, and classic guitar-and-vocals emoting,"[2] and that in more recent times it has "evolved to include rock and roll, Nashville country, alternative country, indie-folk"[3] and more.

CALIFORNIA SOUND ||||||||||||||||||||||||||||||||||||||||||||||||||||||||||||||||||||||||||||||||||

Almost every major city or state in America that has produced notable music—from Memphis to New Orleans to Seattle to Texas—has been declared to have its own "sound," but rarely are these sounds easily definable or limitable by genre, and that goes for those tied to rock and roll as well. The sound of Detroit is Motown *and* garage rock. Minneapolis gave the world Prince, but also the Replacements and Hüsker Dü. Could there really be one identifiable sound for the most populous state in the country? The idea of a California Sound supposes so.

"Between the years 1960 and 1965 a remarkable shift occurred," writes Barney Hoskyns. "The sound and image of Southern California began to take over, replacing Manhattan as the hub of American pop music."[4] As it became understood, the California sound was really about Southern California: the Beach Boys and surf rock. It was as much about imagery and espousing a beach-bound carefree lifestyle as it was about musical characteristics. But that only takes you to 1965, after which point California became a place where folk rock, psychedelic rock, and country rock, all three of which the Byrds had run through in that order before the 1960s, were out. By the 1970s, when people imagined California, they didn't hear the music of Brian Wilson in their heads, but that of the many artists who called Laurel Canyon home at one point or another, including the Eagles, whose early single, "Take It Easy," as Hoskyns writes, "seemed to encapsulate the freewheeling dream of Southern California."[5]

CHICANO ROCK

A complete picture of Californian rock and roll also has to include Chicano Rock. In their book, *Land of a Thousand Dances*, authors David Reyes and Tom Waldman tell the story of rock and roll from the 1950s up through the 1980s as it happened in the Mexican-American communities of Southern California, and East Los Angeles in particular. Describing Chicano rock as "a classic immigrant's tale: assimilation, followed by a return to old country roots, followed again by a synthesis of the two,"[6] Reyes and Waldman trace it back to artists like Bobby Rey and the Armenta Brothers, who arrived a little bit before the fast rise and tragic end of Ritchie Valens in 1959.[7]

Garage groups of the 1960s like Thee Midniters and Cannibal and the Headhunters eventually gave way to more technically proficient, eclectic bands like Yaqui, Tango, and El Chicano, whose music displayed "two prevailing trends in Chicano rock 'n' roll of the late 1960s—references to Mexican culture and improved musicianship."[8] Everything seemed to come together in Los Lobos, who went from a side project hosted in humble living room jam sessions in the mid-1970s to being recognized everywhere for their accomplished border-straddling roots rock a decade later with their major label debut, *How Will the Wolf Survive*. After *Land of a Thousand Dances* was published in the late 1990s, punk rock has played an increasingly large role in the Chicano rock story, as the documentary about East LA's DIY backyard punk scene, *Los Punks*, brought to light in 2016.[9]

COSMIC AMERICAN MUSIC

If the scope of Americana presented by Amanda Petrusich somehow isn't eclectic enough for you, then you might be in search of Cosmic American Music. This was a concept in the imagination of Gram Parsons, a musician at the vanguard of country rock in the late 1960s and early 1970s until his death at the age of twenty-six in 1973. A student at Harvard when he began the International Submarine Band in 1966, Parsons then flitted around from the Byrds to the Flying Burrito Brothers to his own solo work with a promising new vocalist named Emmylou Harris. In those restless years, Parsons developed his idea for a Cosmic American Music, which Parsons biographer David N. Meyer characterizes as a "synthesis of American roots"[10] that brings together "gospel, soul, folk, Appalachia, R&B, country, bluegrass, blues, rockabilly, and honky-tonk."[11]

Parsons' own attempts to capture this ambitious amalgamation can be heard on his two solo albums, *GP* from early 1973 and *Grievous Angel*, released in 1974 several months after his death in Joshua Tree, California. Does Cosmic American Music exist outside of the records Parsons directly touched? Meyer makes the argument that, in comparison to the superficial American roots music approach of the Eagles, the Rolling Stones' 1972 double album *Exile on Main Street* proved the existence of Cosmic American Music[12] (Parsons was famously pals with Keith Richards), which means that it actually doesn't have to be made by Americans or even mostly in America. (Much of the Stones' album was recorded in France, where the band was living in tax exile.) The music just has to have American music in the forefront of its subject.

COWPUNK

As music writer Peter Doggett notes, there has been a "difficult relationship between punk and country"[13] since the two first met, but meet they did, and "Most of the new wave bands who displayed blatant country influences were dubbed 'cowpunks.'"[14] Cowpunk is a fairly straightforward combination of country, rockabilly, and punk style. In the early 1980s, guitarist Billy Zoom from X gave the Los Angeles band a rockabilly flair, and the brothers Phil and Dave Alvin took the LA punk energy down country and blues backroads. Los Angeles was also home to Blood on the Saddle, the Knitters, Tex and the Horseheads, while Austin claimed Rank and File (featuring former members of punk band the Dils) and the True Believers. Nashville produced Jason and the Scorchers, who were noted for their authentic country roots.[15]

HEARTLAND ROCK

In July of 1982, John Mellencamp, then going by the name John Cougar, released a single called "Jack & Diane," a little ditty about two American kids growing up in the heartland. Two years later, Bruce Springsteen released "Born in the U.S.A.," one of the most famously misunderstood songs in all of rock history. But it would be another few years yet before *New York Times* writer Jon Pareles belatedly declared the genre Heartland Rock. "The music is basic— three chords and a back beat," he began his piece in August of 1987. "The tone is earnest, plain-spoken, just folks. The verses are short stories, terse sketches of characters trying to get by. And the choruses, ready-made for sing-alongs, are about 'hard times'." These artists were writing about "factories and farms" instead of "penthouses and limousines" and were "aiming for 'authenticity' rather than state-of-the-art sound."[16]

JERSEY SHORE SOUND

Central to the notion of heartland rock was Bruce Springsteen, who is also central to the notion of another one of those regional scenes, the Jersey Shore Sound, which ties together decades of music from one place, ranging from what has also been described as "Italo-American Rock," exemplified by such vocal groups as Frankie Valli & the Four Seasons, to Springsteen and Southside Johnny, to more recent rock groups like the Bouncing Souls and the Gaslight Anthem. The music website Consequence of Sound took a shot at characterizing all of this in 2009, describing the Jersey Shore Sound as "usually rootsy rock 'n' roll with a greater emphasis on danceable melodies and R&B" and "also characterized by carnival production touches at the center of its otherwise straightforward rock songs"[17] (this latter quality owing to the influence of the amusement park ambience of the boardwalk town Asbury Park).

NEW WEIRD AMERICA

A different kind of circus was in town in Brattleboro, Vermont, when music writer David Keenan came up with the term New Weird America, which plays on the concept of "Old Weird America" posited by Greil Marcus in his book *Invisible Republic*, about Bob Dylan's *Basement Tapes*.[18] There for the Brattleboro Free Folk Festival in 2003, Keenan's new concept became the cover line for the August issue of modern music magazine *The Wire*, which beckoned readers to find out about the band Sunburned Hand of the Man and "the free folk explosion." Petrusich observes that "Following Keenan's article, most of the artists and albums included in his piece were tucked under the umbrella of 'New Weird America,' which flowed into the slightly more descriptive 'free-folk,' which became 'freak-folk.'"[19] New Weird America may have been more folk than rock, but Sunburned Hand of the Man and a few others tied to the idea had at least some rock influences.

SWAMP ROCK

In rock and roll, you don't have to sound like where you're from, as long as you're good at sounding like somewhere else. Case in point: Creedence Clearwater Revival. John Fogerty and his band were from El Cerrito, California, in the Bay Area, but their wildly popular records in the late 1960s were what Martin C. Strong calls "swamp R&B of the rootsiest pedigree, utilizing a simple but stunningly effective hybrid of raw rock 'n' roll, country, and blues."[20] The entire notion of Swamp Rock seems to have been born in the lyrics to "Born on the Bayou" and reinforced by other humid hits like "Run Through the Jungle." Creedence Clearwater Revival didn't pull their sound out of thick air; their first charting single was a cover of the 1957 Southern rockabilly tune "Susie Q," by Louisiana-born Dale Hawkins. Also from Louisiana was Tony Joe White, whose 1969 hit "Polk Salad Annie" was swamp rock from the source.

TAQWACORE

The source of Taqwacore was not a specific place, but a specific, modern cross-cultural experience. Coined by an American writer who converted to Islam in his teenage years named Michael Muhammad Knight, the genre made its way from the pages of Knight's 2003 novel, *The Taqwacores*, into the lives of real Muslim musicians from the United States and other Western nations who wanted to make punk rock that spoke directly to matters of culture, religion, and other issues that affected their lives and their unique place in American society. The Kominas, Sagg Taqwacore Syndicate, and Vote Hezbollah were some of the first such bands to identify with the forward-thinking challenge to certain entrenched beliefs that Knight's book had put forth. The scene gathered the most momentum in the second half of the 2000s, culminating in the release of the documentary film *Taqwacore: The Birth of Punk Islam* in 2009, after which it began to fizzle out.[21]

TROPICAL ROCK

Cruising away from the swamps of Louisiana around the Gulf Coast down to Florida, one will find tropical rock. According to the Trop Rock Music Association's website, tropical rock is "a genre of popular music that incorporates elements and influences of Rock and Roll, Country, and Caribbean themes with an island style that represents a laid-back way of life. Instrumentation is usually acoustic guitar–based, and often includes steel drum[s], congas, marimbas, vibes, or other percussion instruments."[22] As much as swamp rock belongs to Creedence Clearwater Revival, even more so does tropical rock belong to one single artist: Jimmy Buffett, the "Pop of Trop Rock," writer of the immortal hymn to sun-soaked escapism, "Margaritaville." Still, other artists affiliated with this ultimate lifestyle music include Zac Brown Band and Kenny Chesney.

TULSA SOUND

A different kind of mellow came out of the inland musical hotbed of Tulsa, Oklahoma, in the 1960s. An unhurried amalgam of country, blues, and rock and roll, the Tulsa Sound came from two of the city's most renowned musicians from the era: J. J. Cale and Leon Russell. Cale would later develop reclusive tendencies, but in the 1960s, he made enough of a name for himself that his songs would eventually be covered by a wide range of rock artists—most famously his acolyte Eric Clapton, whose covers of Cale's "After Midnight" (1970) and "Cocaine" (1977) both became radio staples. Russell built his reputation as a star session player, working with the Rolling Stones, Bob Dylan, and

Joe Cocker and playing on a number of Phil Spector hits. Defined in part by its subtlety, the influence of the Tulsa Sound isn't always easy to spot, but it can be clearly heard on Dire Straits' "Sultans of Swing."

AMERICA, AMERICA PLAYLIST

AFRO-PUNK	Death–"Politicians in My Eyes" Bad Brains–"I Against I" Fishbone–"Swim"
AMERICANA	The Band–"Up on Cripple Creek" Steve Earle–"Copperhead Road" Hurray for the Riff Raff–"St. Roch Blues"
CALIFORNIA SOUND	The Beach Boys–"California Girls" The Mamas and the Papas–"California Dreamin'" The Eagles–"Hotel California"
CHICANO ROCK	Ritchie Valens–"La Bamba" Cannibal and the Headhunters–"Land of 1,000 Dances" Los Lobos–"Will the Wolf Survive?"
COSMIC AMERICAN MUSIC	The International Submarine Band–"Blue Eyes" The Flying Burrito Brothers–"Wheels" Gram Parsons and Emmylou Harris–"In My Hour of Darkness"
COWPUNK	The Blasters–"Border Radio" Rank and File–"Amanda Ruth" Jason and the Scorchers–"White Lies"
HEARTLAND ROCK	John Mellencamp (John Cougar)–"Jack & Diane" Bruce Springsteen–"The River" Bon Jovi–"Livin' on a Prayer"

JERSEY SHORE SOUND	Frankie Valli & the Four Seasons–"Walk Like a Man" Southside Johnny and the Asbury Jukes–"I Don't Want to Go Home" The Gaslight Anthem–"The '59 Sound"
NEW WEIRD AMERICA	Sunburned Hand of the Man–"No Magic Man" Charalambides–"Voice Within" MV & EE with the Bummer Road–"East Mountain Joint"
SWAMP ROCK	Dale Hawkins–"Susie Q" Creedence Clearwater Revival–"Born on the Bayou" Tony Joe White–"Polk Salad Annie"
TAQWACORE	The Kominas–"Sharia Law in the USA" Sagg Taqwacore Syndicate–"Afghani Wishes" Vote Hezbollah–"Poppy Fields"
TROPICAL ROCK	Jimmy Buffett–"Margaritaville" Kenny Chesney–"Flora-Bama" Zac Brown Band–"Castaway"
TULSA SOUND	J. J. Cale–"Call Me the Breeze" Leon Russell–"Tight Rope" Eric Clapton–"Cocaine"

Baggy and Madchester

The history of baggy begins somewhere in Manchester called Some-wear in Manchester: a clothing stall run by local Phil Saxe in the early 1980s in the center of Northern England's music capital.[1] At some point, Saxe came in to a cache of bell-bottoms at a rock-bottom price. Among those who used to hang around the stall were Shaun and Paul Ryder, brothers from Salford in a fledgling band called Happy Mondays. The Ryders began sporting the flares, and others soon followed their lead. "To a generation reared on tight-trousered orthodoxy, it was an outrage,"[2] writes John Robb. The counter-intuitive clobber caught on with the fashionable kids. Saxe himself would soon go from selling the Mondays their jeans to managing their career.

"Madchester," meanwhile, had been simmering for some time before boiling over in the pop vernacular in 1989. Manchester's music scene, from Joy Division and Factory Records in the late 1970s to the Smiths in the 1980s, was a ten-year span of rock music that ranged from bleak to bleakly humorous. Great bands, all of them, but you can't fight the dreary Northern weather. Unless you were indoors and on drugs, that is, which is where the legendary Haçienda nightclub and the increasing availability of Ecstasy in the late 1980s came in. Kept alive by New Order's money for fifteen against-the-odds years, the Haçienda was crucial in bringing American acid house and techno music to the UK and Europe.

All of the happy pills and upbeat music going around town had an effect on the indie bands. Happy Mondays had been working on their own stiff, slang-heavy "scallydelic" funk mostly unnoticed, until their second album, *Bummed,* finally caught them a wider audience in 1988. The Stone Roses, who were to be the Madchester Beatles to the Mondays' Rolling Stones, began with a dour and serrated rock sound before switching it up with their second single, "Sally Cinnamon." Even more out-there at first were the amiable Inspiral Carpets, who actually started out as a kind of experimental noise group, described once by keyboardist Clint Boon as "like Einstürzende Neubauten, but a more psychedelic version."[3]

Those three bands were all at the height of their powers in 1989, a year whose extended sunny season is known in the UK as the Second Summer of Love. That November, Happy Mondays gave the order to keep the good times rolling with the *Madchester Rave On* EP, securing the name of the movement even if that wasn't their intent. Writing about the EP in his memoir, *Twisting My Melon*, Shaun Ryder recalls that video makers Keith Jobling and Phil Shotton, who called themselves the Bailey Brothers, came up with the term "as a bit of a joke, but we were like, 'Great, yeah, go with it,' because Manchester *was* [mad] at that time. . . . No one used the term in Manchester, unless they were a prick, but it quickly became adopted by the media, who lapped it up."[4]

Everyone could see that something special was happening up north, but not all were in agreement on what exactly that was. Many thought the real Madchester was the city's club scene, its budding-celebrity DJs, and the house and techno records they spun.[5] However, as Dave Haslam, himself one of those DJs, writes, Manchester wasn't really *making* its own dance records, so the guitar bands filled that need. "Thus was born the 'Madchester' sound, indie dance, the sound of young guitar bands with their roots in rock music but their hearts won over by the energy of house, their sense of rhythm unlocked, and their creativity liberated by immersion in E culture."[6]

Even if the guitar bands were siphoning off some of the club culture's fuel, it showed that those DJs were actually making a difference outside of their usual sphere. In his memoir on the Haçienda, former Joy Division and New Order bassist Peter Hook observes, "With the movement placed in a rock context, and thus easily understood and reviewed by the indie press, indie kids had yet another entry point into dance music."[7] If the influence wasn't reciprocal, the benefit of success was still mutual. Happy Mondays' "Sly Stone meets the Velvet Underground"[8] stance and the Stone Roses' extended grooves would be a gateway drug into other dance music for many.

It is that "indie dance" sound that came to be referred to as "baggy." As a genre, then, it began as part of the greater Madchester movement. Bands throughout the UK were soon latching onto indie dance as fans donned cavernous blue jeans and roomy Joe Bloggs-brand T-shirts, topping it off with a floppy bucket hat like the one frequently seen on the head of the Stone Roses drummer Reni. Baggy thus became an isle-wide concern.

Despite the history and the hierarchies of Madchester and the indie dance movement being relatively compact and easy to grasp, mainstream America somehow got it all wrong. The central figures, the Stone Roses and Happy Mondays, had their contingents in New York and LA and would get picked up by major record labels and college radio stations. The peripheral characters, though, were the ones who made a splash on commercial radio and MTV, typically just for one hit. Jesus Jones had "Right Here, Right Now"; EMF had "Unbelievable." The Soup Dragons managed two with "I'm Free" and "Divine Thing." Perhaps the Stone Roses' "Fools Gold" was too spaced out, the Happy Mondays' "Kinky Afro" too clever, but at the very least the Charlatans, with the foolproof "The Only One I Know" in their pocket, should have hit the jackpot.

The Charlatans formed just south of Manchester in Northwich, and their debut album, *Some Friendly*, stood them at the head of what some saw as Madchester's second wave, along with Northside, Paris Angels, and the Mock Turtles. Nearby, Liverpool offered the Real People and the Farm. London, meanwhile, tried its best with Flowered Up.

Another new band from London, Blur, turned up just in time to hitch a ride on the tail end of baggy with their second single, "There's No Other Way." By then it was the spring of 1991, two years on from the Second Summer of Love. The Haçienda remained a fixture of Manchester nightlife until it closed in 1997, but the Madchester moment had passed and the city's mood had altered again. When the Stone Roses returned from nearly five years of reclusion in late 1994, followed by Shaun Ryder and his post-Mondays outfit, Black Grape, they walked into a Britpop world where some of the bands who had once followed them were now near the head of the pack.

Pioneer Tracks: 808 State–"Pacific," Happy Mondays–"Freaky Dancin'," Inspiral Carpets–"Joe," James–"Come Home," the Stone Roses–"Elephant Stone"

Key Players: Blur (*Leisure*), the Charlatans (*Some Friendly*), EMF, the Farm, Flowered Up, the High, Jesus Jones, the Mock Turtles, Northside, Paris Angels, the Soup Dragons

CROSSOVER TRACKS

C86
The Railway Children–"Brighter," the Wedding Present–"My Favourite Dress"

DANCE PUNK

A Certain Ratio–"Shack Up," ESG–"UFO," New Order–
"Everything's Gone Green"

SHOEGAZE

Catherine Wheel–"Balloon," My Bloody Valentine–"Soon," Ride–
"Vapour Trail"

Baroque Pop

Baroque pop is the precursor to the more dramatic and expansive chamber pop of the 1990s. "In the UK, baroque's starting point was the Zombies' 'She's Not There,' which didn't feature any oboes but stuck out rather dramatically in 1964,"[1] writes Bob Stanley in the *Guardian* in 2007, who has himself been credited with coining the term "English Baroque."[2] The following year, the Beatles—pioneers of everything even when by accident—pushed baroque pop forward with "In My Life," even if, famously, that classic "harpsichord" solo is actually producer George Martin's piano sped up on tape.[3]

In 1965, the first fruits of the friendly creative rivalry between the Beatles and the Beach Boys grew. *The Beach Boys Today!*, already the young band's eighth album, moved on from their surf-rock origins. Andrew Grant Jackson notes in his book *1965* that, led by Brian Wilson and aided by the famous group of LA session musicians known as the Wrecking Crew, the combo "now laid their gorgeous vocal harmonies over . . . everything from mandolins, English and French horns, saxophones, and harmonicas; to organs, harpsichords, and accordions; to timbales, congas, vibraphones, xylophones, and sleigh bells."[4]

But 1966 was the year baroque broke. The Beach Boys released *Pet Sounds*, the budding genre's crowning achievement. It was also the year of "Eleanor Rigby" and two classic singles from the Left Banke, New York City's response to the stately rock trend. "Walk Away Renee" and "Pretty Ballerina" were the Left Banke's first and most successful singles. "Pretty Ballerina" has been covered by artists ranging from shock rock pioneer Alice Cooper to Britpop survivors the Bluetones. The Beatles' *Sgt. Pepper's Lonely Hearts Club Band* may have been the genre's climax, but English baroque pop records continued to be made into the early 1970s, as, according to Stanley, "the harpsichord trickle-down took its time to reach the provinces."[5]

Key Tracks: The Beach Boys–"God Only Knows," the Beatles–"In My Life," the Left Banke–"Walk Away Renee," the Walker Brothers–"Make it Easy on Yourself," the Zombies–"She's Not There"

CROSSOVER TRACKS

CHAMBER POP
Belle & Sebastian–"The State I'm In," the Divine Comedy–"Songs of Love," My Life Story–"Girl A, Girl B, Boy C"

INDIE FOLK
Fleet Foxes–"English House," Joanna Newsom–"Emily," Sufjan Stevens–"Say Yes! To M!ch!gan!"

INDIE ROCK
Carissa's Wierd–"A Loose Hair Falls into a Glass of Water Without Ice," Elliott Smith–"Bottle Up and Explode!," Ra Ra Riot–"Each Year"

Beat Boom

"It's an often-forgotten fact," writes Gareth Murphy in *Cowboys and Indies*, his history of the record industry, "that the British invasion of America in 1964 began as a Northern invasion of London in 1963."[1] The same campaign by two different names, like the Revolutionary War and the American War of Independence, the beat boom referred to the bands who would soon follow the Beatles in their conquest of the United States.

The Beatles' hometown of Liverpool, flooded with local groups, was central to the beat boom, providing the movement with an alternate title taken from its river, Merseybeat. *Mersey Beat* also served as the name of journalist Bill Harry's weekly music paper that covered the city's scene. A revved up version of the 4/4 backbeat drove the music, which was a graduation from the scrappy skiffle craze, upgrading with elements of rock and R&B combined with a pop sensibility.

Notable beat boomers include Gerry and the Pacemakers, Herman's Hermits, the Hollies, the Searchers, and Freddie and the Dreamers, all of whom were from either Liverpool or nearby Manchester—Freddie and the Dreamers even pushed their own "Manchester Beat."[2] London's the Dave Clark Five make for a notable exception and were assumed by many a Yankee to also be from Liverpool. This surely irked the city's beat groups, who already had to contend with a London-based music industry that loved having an act of their own to trumpet in the face of what was mostly a Northern phenomenon.

Key Tracks: The Beatles–"She Loves You," Gerry and the Pacemakers–"How Do You Do It?," the Merseybeats–"I Think of You," the Mojos–"Everything's Alright," the Searchers–"Needles and Pins"

|||||||||||||||||||||||||||||||||||||||||||||||||||||||||||||||||||||||||||||||||
CROSSOVER TRACKS
|||||||||||||||||||||||||||||||||||||||||||||||||||||||||||||||||||||||||||||||||

BRITISH INVASION
The Dave Clark Five–"Glad All Over," the Kinks–"You Really Got Me," the Who–"My Generation"

GARAGE ROCK
The Kingsmen–"Louie Louie," Paul Revere and the Raiders–"Just Like Me"

ROCKABILLY
Buddy Holly–"That'll Be the Day," Gene Vincent–"Be-Bop-A-Lula"

Black Metal

In 1982, *Black Metal* was the title of the sophomore album from a marginal metal band from Newcastle, England. A decade later, black metal was fast becoming a matter of life and death for a cadre of young and disaffected Norwegians.

Not always taken seriously in their day, Venom are now credited with birthing a whole genre. *Black Metal*, with its Satan-goatface cover art, found the unholy trio reaching for extremes of speed and, especially, lyrical subject matter. These guys were all in on hell, describing it like a preferred vacation spot on songs like "Leave Me in Hell," "To Hell and Back," and the title track of their first album, "Welcome to Hell." Writers and musicians snorted, but impressionable fans were intrigued.[1] As the history of rock and roll has proven time and again, it only takes a generation for a joke to be taken seriously.

Venom weren't the only metal band toying with dark forces in the early 1980s. Bathory in Sweden, Mercyful Fate in Denmark, Celtic Frost in Switzerland, and Slayer in Los Angeles were some of the first to rep for the goat on their record covers, which also incorporated crazy skulls, demons, and pseudo-pentagrams. Those bands are all well regarded and considered innovators today, but that wasn't always the case.

Somewhere between Venom's unbridled fondness for Beelzebub and Danish heavy metal monarch and King Diamond's, Mercyful Fate's frontman, patented black-and-white face paint, black metal, as it came to be known in the 1990s, was reborn in Norway. The wave began in the mid-1980s with the Oslo band Mayhem, led by Oystein

Aarseth, a teenager who called himself Euronymous. All the kids in the relatively small black metal scene there took on such nicknames as Dead and Count Grishnackh.

Euronymous, Dead, and Count Grishnackh met respective fates of murder, suicide, and jail (for the said murder). Famously, historic Christian churches would burn at the hands of people in the scene who wanted to symbolically vanquish the religion that had violently invaded Norway in the previous millenium.[2] To metalheads elsewhere in the world who heard about these acts as news trickled out of Norway (or read about them later in the 1998 book *Lords of Chaos*), the stories had lurid appeal. These bands crossed a very real line when they went from dressing up in big cloaks and holding axes for photos to attempting to instigate a return to Viking-era pre-Christianity, but some metal fans connected to that realness.

Mayhem, Darkthrone, Burzum, Emperor, Immortal, and Satyricon played the part. The album covers and unintelligible shrieking lyrics payed tribute to nature and Nordic mythology. Other artists such as Mortiis, a former member of Emperor, and the group Ulver from Oslo began pulling the dark energy of black metal into more exploratory and ambient places.

"Black metal is very different than death metal, so you can very well be into black metal and not care about death metal," says Brandon Stosuy. "Their concerns are different, the subject matter is generally different, the way the people look to perform it, the way they present themselves in photos, the band names."

In recent years, black metal has been susceptible to what Stosuy describes as a kind of laboratory approach to the genre, whereby musicians experiment by combining whichever sounds appeal to them instead of being a part of a scene's organic growth over time. As an example of this process proving successful, he cites the San Francisco band Deafheaven, who connect distant dots such as black metal (including the short-lived 1990s San Francisco band Weakling), shoegaze, and Johnny Marr-esque guitar melodies. Deafheaven's collagist sound has inspired new terms like "blackgaze" and "post-black metal" to describe it.

Welcome to Hell: Bathory—"In Conspiracy with Satan," Celtic Frost—"The Usurper," Mayhem—"Deathcrush," Mercyful Fate—"Night of the Unborn," Venom—"Black Metal"

Leave Me in Hell: Ancient, Burzum, Carpathian Forest, Darkthrone, Emperor, Gehenna, Gorgoroth, Immortal, Mayhem, Marduk, Satyricon

CROSSOVER TRACKS

GOTH METAL

Cradle of Filth—"The Principle of Evil Made Flesh," Type O Negative—"Der Untermensch"

POST-METAL

Agalloch—"Limbs," Deafheaven—"Brought to the Water"

THRASH METAL

Exodus—"Deliver Us to Evil," Metallica—"Am I Evil?" (Diamond Head), Slayer—"Evil Has No Boundaries"

Blues Rock

||||||||||||||||||||||||||||||||||||||||||||||||||||||||||||||||||||||||||||||||||||||||||||||||||||||||||||||||||||||||||||||||||||||||||||||||||||||||

The blues and rock and roll were born in bars, back rooms, and recording studios in locations with exotic names like the Mississippi Delta and Memphis, Tennessee. The birthplace of blues rock? Dartford railway station, in the county of Kent, England.

It was there on a December morning in 1961 that Keith Richards ran into his former neighbor, Mick Jagger. The two had once been students at Wentworth Primary School, but their families had long since moved to different parts of Dartford.[1] Now here they were, on the London-bound platform. Richards was heading to Sidcup Art College, and Jagger was on his way to the London School of Economics. Jagger was carrying an armload of records that included Chuck Berry and Muddy Waters, and the two got to talking about music.[2]

The bad boy image they would adopt in the Rolling Stones was for the benefit of media attention[3], but their love of the blues and R&B was genuine. Jagger and Richards' reignited friendship was based as much on nerding out about imported blues records as it was on trying to actually play music.[4]

The son of a lawyer, Paul Butterfield made an early name for himself playing blues harmonica on the South Side of Chicago.[5] Butterfield eventually met Michael Bloomfield, another young white blues enthusiast in the city, who joined him as the guitarist in the Paul Butterfield Blues Band. Elektra Records put out their self-titled debut album in the fall of 1965, only a few months after the release of the Rolling Stones' first number one album in the United States, *Out of Our Heads*.

Rock and roll is a descendant of the blues, and so it would seem that blues rock wouldn't so much combine two genres as dial up an already present element. At the start of the 1960s, though, the blues seemed to have seeped out of rock and roll. The originators from the 1950s had largely moved on, and the teen idols had moved in. Groups like the Beach Boys and the Beatles helped revive rock, but theirs were more pop-oriented approaches. It took the Rolling Stones, the Paul Butterfield Blues Band, and others to reactivate the blues influence.

Eric Clapton was another British blues devotee coming up around the same time as the Stones. *Slowhand* established his career, channeling the spirit of American blues as he spent the 1960s moving on from one group to the next: the Yardbirds, John Mayall & the Blues Breakers, Cream, Blind Faith, and Derek and the Dominos.[6] It wasn't only the more straightforward likes of Johnny Winter and Peter Green's Fleetwood Mac that brought it back; Jimi Hendrix, Janis Joplin, and many other psychedelic rock acts felt the blues as well.

Every decade in rock and roll since then has had some manner of awakening to the blues. In the late 1970s and early 1980s, Jimmie and Stevie Ray Vaughan became the most famous Texas blues brothers since Johnny and Edgar Winter. In the 1990s, the Jon Spencer Blues Explosion made the blues cool for the indie and alternative crowds with their downtown New York eclecticism and self-awareness. In the modern era of social media–enabled pop music feuds, blues rock even got in on the action with a simmering rivalry between Jack White of the White Stripes and Dan Auerbach of the Black Keys.[7]

Pioneer Tracks: The Animals—"Boom Boom," Canned Heat—"Rollin' and Tumblin'," the Paul Butterfield Blues Band—"Shake Your Money-Maker," the Rolling Stones—"(I Can't Get No) Satisfaction," the Yardbirds—"I Wish You Would"

Key Players: Big Brother and the Holding Company, Blind Faith, Cream, Derek and the Dominoes, the Fabulous Thunderbirds, Free, Fleetwood Mac (with Peter Green), Hot Tuna, Jeff Beck Group, Jethro Tull (*This Was*), Savoy Brown, Stevie Ray Vaughan and Double Trouble, Wishbone Ash

CROSSOVER TRACKS

BOOGIE ROCK
Foghat–"I Just Want to Make Love to You," ZZ Top–"La Grange."

ALTERNATIVE ROCK
The Black Crowes–"A Conspiracy," the Jon Spencer Blues Explosion–"Wail"

GARAGE ROCK REVIVAL
The Black Keys–"Girl Is on My Mind," the White Stripes–"Screwdriver"

Boogie Rock

Boogie-woogie, history's best-named music genre, achieved widespread popularity in the 1920s. A cheerful, piano-based contemporary of the blues, the style took its name from a slang term for the kind of rent party where it would provide the soundtrack.[1] Boogie rock, its counterpart-in-name that emerged in the late 1960s and came into its own in the 1970s, is fun-time party music, too, though in execution it borrows more from John Lee Hooker's 1948 song "Boogie Chillun" than from boogie-woogie itself.

Finding its groove in the path of blues rock, boogie rock shuffled its way through the 1970s on both sides of the Atlantic. American boogie rock has a lot in common with Southern rock, so much so that boogie rock's primary distinction might be that it can come from either side of the Mason-Dixon line. The UK, meanwhile, gave the world Status Quo and Foghat, whose "Slow Ride" is a signature tune in the genre.

Boogie rock doesn't move its feet to a traditional boogie-woogie rhythm, and a piano isn't always involved, though Humble Pie's "Natural Born Bugie," Status Quo's "Rockin' All Over the World," and Electric Light Orchestra's "Don't Bring Me Down" all tickle the ivories. It can also be spare and rootsy like Cactus' "Big Mama Boogie, Parts 1 and 2." Recent iterations include the more 1970s-eclectic approach of Endless Boogie.

Key Tracks: Cactus–"Big Mama Boogie, Parts 1 and 2," Foghat–"Slow Ride," Humble Pie–"Natural Born Bugie," T. Rex–"Born to Boogie," ZZ Top–"Tush"

CROSSOVER TRACKS

DESERT ROCK
Fu Manchu–"Boogie Van," Kyuss–"Supa Scoopa and Mighty Scoop"

FUNK ROCK
Funkadelic–"Hit It and Quit It," Sly and the Family Stone–"I Want to Take You Higher"

SOUTHERN ROCK
38 Special–"I'm a Fool for You," Lynyrd Skynyrd–"Call Me the Breeze"

British Invasion

‖‖‖

Is it really fair to either side to call it the British *Invasion*? Surely it was more a retaliatory strike, a delayed response to the United States entering their waters with rock and roll in the first place. It went beyond music as well. *Mersey Beat* creator Bill Harry recalls, "there was a degree of American popular culture domination in Britain"[1] at the turn of the 1960s. The British were not purely the aggressors.

It also makes the United States sound like defenseless victims. Yes, America was caught with her guard down, while mourning the assassination of President John F. Kennedy, but she had put up quite a fight until that point. "I Want to Hold Your Hand" was not the first Beatles single released in the United States; it was the *fourth*. Capitol Records had spent most of 1963 snubbing their own UK parent company, EMI, by refusing to put out the band's records. Of their three prior singles released on minor labels in 1963, "Please Please Me" (February), "From Me to You" (May), and "She Loves You" (September), only "From Me to You" notched any chart appearance (and it was a lowly one).[2]

The Beatles' persistence paid off when a perfect storm finally broke in 1964. Ed Sullivan had seen Beatlemania firsthand in London and arrangements were made to have the band on his immensely popular television show in early February.[3] Concerts at Carnegie Hall were booked by an aspiring promoter in New York, and Capitol Records finally relented just in time to look smart for releasing "I Want to Hold Your Hand," which at the time became the fastest-selling single in history.[4]

The British Invasion was not a single siege but a sustained campaign that went on throughout the 1960s. Because of this, and because trends come and go faster in Britain than in the United States, the British Invasion was not limited to one single style of rock music, though the term is sometimes used as a genre. Musically, the first wave was the beat boom, and as the beat-boom troops grew tired and depleted in the mid 1960s, a battalion of blues rock bands followed with the Rolling Stones at the fore.

Through periods of greater and lesser activity, the British Invasion has never come to a full end and has the potential to be a forever war. America has had a few deserters who returned home as heroes, like one-time Army paratrooper Jimi Hendrix in the 1960s and the Stray Cats in the 1980s. There have been times when the two nations were on the same page, such as with progressive rock and new wave, and others when they weren't even reading the same book, as was the case in the era of grunge and Britpop.

Though it may seem quiet on the Western front as of late, nearly two decades of sustained commercial success in America for Coldplay shows that defeat has yet to be conceded.

Pioneer Tracks: The Animals—"House of the Rising Sun," the Beatles— "I Want to Hold Your Hand," Herman's Hermits—"I'm into Something Good," the Kinks—"You Really Got Me," the Who—"My Generation"

Key Players: Petula Clark, the Dave Clark Five, Freddie and the Dreamers, Gerry and the Pacemakers, the Hollies, the Nashville Teens, Peter and Gordon, the Rolling Stones, the Spencer Davis Group, the Troggs, the Yardbirds, the Zombies

CROSSOVER TRACKS

BLUES ROCK

Cream–"I Feel Free," Jeff Beck Group–"Hi Ho Silver Lining,"
Status Quo–"Pictures of Matchstick Men"

BRITPOP

The Bluetones–"Are You Blue or Are You Blind?," Cast–"Alright,"
Supergrass–"Alright"

GLAM ROCK

David Bowie–*Pin Ups*, Suzi Quatro–"48 Crash," Slade–"Far Far
Away"

Britpop

Britpop often was, and occasionally still is, characterized as being in thrall to the 1960s; the classic tunes of the British Invasion, and the zeitgeist buzz on Swinging London's streets. And though that is part of it, but not all of it—Britpop repurposed the best of UK rock music from the 1970s and 1980s, too. There was even room leftover for innovation, if not wholesale reinvention. It was the victory lap the nation had earned after three decades of producing once-in-a-generation artists, from the Beatles to David Bowie to the Smiths.

In April of 1963, the launch of the British Invasion still almost a year away, the Beatles went to go check out their future chart rivals the Rolling Stones for the first time at the Crawdaddy Club in Richmond, in Greater London.[1] Thirty years later, in April 1993, Brett Anderson of Suede bared his midriff in front of a Union Jack on the cover of *Select* magazine. This wasn't an aggressive flag planting, but a defensive "Battle for Britain," with Suede and their streamlined glam joined on the front lines by Saint Etienne, Denim, Pulp, and the Auteurs. How could the ongoing American alt-rock assault stand a chance? This motley regiment didn't quite resemble the massed troops to come, but the rise of Suede and the long overdue success of Pulp were accurately predicted.

It is curious that Blur were not included on that same magazine cover, given that they would become, along with Oasis, one of Britpop's two flagship bands. The genre-dabblers had even recently adopted a loosely Mod-ish look with musical influences to match. After a brief but impactful post-Madchester fall from media grace, Blur rebooted with the horn-blaring "Popscene" single in 1992 and the album *Modern Life is Rubbish* in 1993. In hindsight, both records are now considered crucial to the Britpop movement, though for all the Kinks and music hall of *Modern Life*, guitarist Graham Coxon's love of heavier noise was also clear on "Oily Water" and "Pressure on Julian."

Luke Haines, leader of the Auteurs, writes about his band's role in the scene's early days and presents the following timeline: "*Modern Life is Rubbish* by Blur is often cited as the first Britpop album. Not so. Suede were without doubt the first Britpop band. Their first single 'The Drowners' was released in May '92. The Auteurs' first album was released some months before *Modern Life* . . . and a few weeks before Suede's debut."[2] Haines posits that lyrically his band's 1993 debut LP, *New Wave*, didn't fit the still-forming mold, and thus, "If you possess the wrong kind of ambition it can be easy to fall between the cracks."

It was early 1993 when the UK music press started cooking up their boldest feast yet, but there had already been some that struck the same vintage-future chords that would characterize Britpop. In one notable radio interview with Steve Lamacq in 1997, Noel Gallagher declared the 1990 debut LP from Liverpool band the La's to be the first Britpop album.[3] A few years before that, even, the Stone Roses transitioned from moody rock to their Madchester years with "Sally Cinnamon," a stand-alone single built on singer Ian Brown's romantic nostalgia and guitarist John Squire's simple but magnetic hooks. To label *The La's* or "Sally Cinnamon" as proto-Britpop might be speculative dot-connecting, but *Live Forever*, the BBC's 2003 documentary on the whole thing, does start with the Roses' legendary Spike Island concert in 1990.[4]

In May of 1994, a year after that *Select* cover, Blur knocked Pink Floyd's *The Division Bell* off the number one spot on the UK albums chart with *Parklife*. The acclaim and adoration that met such a distinctly British guitar-pop record solidified the notion that something was in the air. Describing the context of the times in the nation's capital, Blur bassist Alex James writes that, "Whole swathes of the city were in a redevelopment boom. Social and cultural interest was rejuvenating; something was stirring in the art world; a new government was looking increasingly likely. Blur weren't part of a movement . . . but we were part of London's almost instantaneous rebirth as the world's hippest city."[5]

Synonymous with Britpop was "Cool Britannia," a phrase that came to capture the hipness and optimism of the moment. The music had already peaked by the time *Vanity Fair* drew the world's attention to London's renaissance in March of 1997, but that mattered little given that Cool Britannia was just as much about film (*Trainspotting*), art (Damien Hirst), fashion (Ozwald Boateng), literature (Irvine Welsh and Nick Hornby), and anything else people spend their spare income on. On the cover of that issue of *Vanity Fair*, reposing in a Union Jack–bedecked bed next to then-fiancee Patsy Kensit, was Oasis lead singer Liam Gallagher.

The Manchester band's debut single, "Supersonic," had come out the same month as *Parklife*, and days after Kurt Cobain's death, making April 1994 one of the crucial turning points in the movement's timeline, up there with the infamous and ultimately unhelpful chart showdown between Blur and Oasis sixteen months later in August 1995, a battle between singles that were hardly the best effort of either group. (The *real* single of the year, Pulp's "Common People," had arrived earlier that summer.) By the time of the *Vanity Fair* cover, three years after "Supersonic," Oasis had gone from being a little-known bunch led by a former roadie for Inspiral Carpets to the biggest rock band in Britain by a mile. Oasis came out of the gate prolific in a way that few bands do today. After "Supersonic," Oasis released a new single, backed by two or three B-sides that were actually worth owning, every two to three months. They paused a whole four months after their Christmas 1994 singalong "Whatever" before putting out

"Some Might Say," their first UK number one single, in April 1995. In the middle of that run, they released their debut album, *Definitely Maybe*, in August 1994, immediately winning over legions of fans and critics alike. This made their absence from BBC2's *Britpop Now* special in 1995 somewhat conspicuous, but by then they were already big enough not to need the endorsement.

Hosted by Blur frontman Damon Albarn, *Britpop Now* collected live studio performances from bands from the class of 1994–95: Elastica, Supergrass, Echobelly, Gene, Sleeper, Menswear, Powder, Marion, and a few older guard groups to round things out: Blur themselves, shoegaze survivors the Boo Radleys, new wave misfits Pulp, and, curiously, PJ Harvey.[6]

Not everyone was a fan of the program, not even everyone who was in it. Some, like Sleeper frontwoman Louise Wener, were ambivalent. In her memoir, *Just for One Day*, she recalls of 1995, "The most popular question I'm asked this summer is, do Sleeper mind being called a Britpop band? I'm not in the habit of objecting . . . but I can't protest now even if I wanted to, because we've just been on a program called *Britpop Now*."[7] Pulp frontman Jarvis Cocker recalled in a 1999 interview, "I remember watching *Britpop Now* presented by Damon Albarn in his plus fours thinking, 'This is poor.' It's like Merseybeat. In the early '60s that was a generic sound because of the explosion of the Beatles, and Oasis' success dredged up a lot of stuff that was piss-poor."[8]

America was mostly spared the Oasis-imitator phenomenon, and to this day records by such bands are known in the United States only by dedicated anglophiles. Also filtered out of the experience as it was packaged and delivered to US audiences was the laddism— the ironic-but-not, *Maxim*-reading, anti-New-Man posturing that became attached to the scene in the UK. Oasis themselves, though, laddish swagger and all, were a different story.

"If the Britpop moment was bound up with rejecting the

dominance of the American grunge groups," writes journalist John Harris in his book on the music and times, "the fact that Oasis had apparently managed to take the fight to their home turf surely represented a new, dizzying phase of the story."[9] The commercial success of Oasis' second album, *(What's the Story) Morning Glory?*, in the United States was exceptional, but it also proved to be an exception. Only a few would follow them into the mainstream.

Elastica connected with the alt-crowd, their simple and sexy post-punk-pop far more tuned in to American rock sensibilities than bouncy choruses and nuanced character sketches. One of the first to the Britpop shindig, a reinvented Blur sang about the "Death of a Party" coming as no surprise before it was even over, and their "Song 2" was played everywhere, including sporting events. Then there was the Verve, who in 1995 released *A Northern Soul*, a stunning album of emotional psychedelic rock, only to implode right as the gravy train pulled up. Fortunately, the band patched things up in early 1997 long enough to make *Urban Hymns* and serenade Britpop on its way out the door.

Overexposure is always damaging, and it certainly happened here, but other factors were also at play. Some pointed to the diminishing quality of the music, which others in part blamed on the influence of, and shifting appetites for, drugs. Oasis' third album, *Be Here Now*, arriving as it did at the end of summer in 1997 either bloated or just misunderstood, has received its share of the blame. The music press wasn't much help; as much as they were the vehicle by which these bands were delivered to national attention, they were also often the means by which such bands were shoved aside.

Stuart Murdoch, singer and songwriter behind the Glasgow, Scotland, band Belle & Sebastian was aware of how it all worked and wary of how a beast currently feasting on Oasis imitators would take to his band's quiet, soulful, orchestrated indie pop. "They really kind of moved like a pack," he says. "They liked to think that not only were they where the party was, but they were actually creating the party, and Britpop was very much their thing. Like most great pop music, lots of good stuff came out of that and it was commercial and funny and tuneful. But we were very much on the flip side."

Then there were those attached to the scene that had seen it all before. The Charlatans had come out of the Manchester area at the height of baggy-mania, hitting heights in the record charts in 1990 that they had a hard time replicating over the next few years. So many British rock groups come and go with one media cycle, but the Charlatans stuck it out long enough to get an artistic second wind that stood them well alongside the new crop. "The Charlatans were as much a part of Britpop as we were of Baggy—we didn't ask to be included, but it certainly helped us as TV executives and excitable journalists were falling over themselves for bands,"[10] writes the band's lead singer Tim Burgess.

Pioneer Tracks: The Auteurs—"Show Girl," Blur—"For Tomorrow," Denim—"Middle of the Road," Pulp—"Babies," Suede—"The Drowners"

Key Players: Ash, the Bluetones, the Boo Radleys, Cast, the Charlatans, Dodgy, Echobelly, Gene, Heavy Stereo, Kula Shaker, Mansun, Menswear, Oasis, Ocean Colour Scene, Shed Seven, Sleeper, Super Furry Animals (early), Supergrass

CROSSOVER TRACKS

BRITISH INVASION

The Kinks—"Waterloo Sunset," the Small Faces—"Itchycoo Park," the Who—"I Can See for Miles"

GLAM ROCK

Mott the Hoople–"All the Young Dudes," Roxy Music–"Do the Strand," T. Rex–"Bang a Gong (Get it On)"

INDIE POP

Comet Gain–"Hideaway," Heavenly–"Our Love is Heavenly," Saint Etienne–"Hobart Paving"

C86

Rock genres are often at least in part the product of a music journalist's imagination, but C86 is the only genre named after a *physical* product created by a music magazine.

In 1981, *NME* put out a mail-order mixtape in the UK called *C81*. Assembled in partnership with Rough Trade, the compilation's track list featured the Specials, Buzzcocks, the Raincoats, Cabaret Voltaire, and pretty much the whole roster of the short-lived Scottish label Postcard Records. The tape was successful enough that they released another compilation five years later. The second time around, *NME* put writers Neil Taylor and Roy Carr to work collecting tracks from a wider range of record labels[1], but the music on *C86* would prove more consistent in tone and style than *C81*. Still, the track list is a bit more diverse than it gets credit for.

Primal Scream claimed the first slot on the tape, and it is easy to hear how their contribution might have set up the snap judgment about the other twenty-one songs that followed. "Velocity Girl" was the B-side on their second single, "Crystal Crescent," but it grew more popular than the A-side.[2] In the four combined minutes of "Crystal Crescent" and "Velocity Girl," Primal Scream had nailed the essence of indie jangle pop in one 7" record so precisely that it was best to quit while they were ahead, though changing up their sound right away put off some of their new fans.

C86 was unfussy rock music that had learned its post-punk lessons but still loved its Byrds albums. The term is entwined with "indie pop" and "jangle pop," though of course it denotes a very specific era. A band today can have a C86 *aesthetic*, but only those actually from the period are C86 *bands*, whether they like it or not. A number of the artists included on the tape, or connected with the genre, have had mixed feelings about it.[3]

Where some UK music writers championed the idea of a scene, others saw fit to tear it down, irrationally irritated by the notion of rock music that was jovial and not revolutionary. Simply being "indie" became a slur to some in a way that wouldn't happen in America for some time to come. Though much of that stigma has been washed away with time and critically acclaimed reissues, there are surely still some that have their reservations about being on the little cassette that could.

Pioneer Tracks: Primal Scream–"Velocity Girl," all the other songs on the tape

Key Players: The Bodines, the Mighty Lemon Drops, the Pastels, Shop Assistants, the Wedding Present

CROSSOVER TRACKS

ALTERNATIVE ROCK
R.E.M.–"Laughing," the Smiths–"Cemetry Gates," the Sundays–"Here's Where the Story Ends"

BRITPOP
Cottonmouth–"Shirts & Skins," the Weekenders–"Inelegantly Wasted in Papa's Penthouse Pad in Belgravia"

PAISLEY UNDERGROUND
The Bangles–"Going Down to Liverpool," the Dream Syndicate–"Tell Me When It's Over," the Rain Parade–"Talking In My Sleep"

Canterbury Sound

As is the case with so many regionally named *sounds*, the diversity of influences and output between all of the bands credited with being a part of this scene in Canterbury, England, in the 1960s and early 1970s undermines its application as a stand-alone style of music, which is a less-structured strain of early progressive rock.

The groups affiliated with this style, starting with Soft Machine and Caravan, tend to be classified as progressive rock, and so the Canterbury Sound is, too. Those two groups split off from the mid-1960s R&B group the Wilde Flowers, who existed before the advent of progressive rock. As they split off, swapped members, gained new ones, and regrouped to form different creative alliances, the influences, from folk to blues to jazz, piled up.[1] A tinge of psychedelia is one distinction people use to define the Canterbury Sound apart from progressive rock, as is the players' proclivity for improvisation, which would seem to run counter to the notion of prog rock being a very composed and precise music.

Key Players: Caravan, Gong, Soft Machine, the Wilde Flowers

CROSSOVER GENRES

JAZZ ROCK
Colosseum, Henry Cow

PSYCHEDELIC ROCK
Kevin Ayers (solo), Syd Barrett (solo)

Celtic Punk

Before he became famous for his rousing poetic lyricism, and legendary for his states of inebriation, Shane MacGowan was known in London as Shane O'Hooligan, frontman for a band called the Nipple Erectors in the late 1970s that played catchy punk tunes like "King of the Bop." Neither MacGowan nor the other three original members of the Pogues—Peter "Spider" Stacy, James Fearnley, and Jem Finer—had found real success in punk rock, but it was in punk's DIY spirit that in 1982 they picked up banjos, whistles, and accordions and started bashing out a rollicking modernized take on folk music imbued with Irish themes.

From today's distance, it might seem like the Pogues, who in their early days were called Pogue Mahone (translation: "kiss my arse"), were operating in isolation, but Fearnley recalls in his memoir, *Here Comes Everybody*, that many others in London at the time were on a similar trip: "The release in 1982 of Dexys Midnight Runners' *Too-Rye-Ay* seemed to have spawned all manner of bands across London playing with acoustic instruments—violins, banjos, and accordions. There were skiffle bands playing homemade music with tea-chest basses, washboards, and zob sticks. There were country bands with western shirts, bolo ties, cowboy hats, and beehives playing upright basses and acoustic guitars."[1]

Fearnley names peers that are much lesser known now: Boothill Foot-Tappers, Hackney Five-O, the Shillelagh Sisters, and Skiff Skats. The Pogues would later welcome the Scottish folk-punk duo Nyah Fearties into their circle in the mid-1980s.

Of all the artists that crossed folk and punk in different ways in the 1980s, the Pogues were the most "Celtic" among them, and so remain the model for the genre all the way up until the late 1990s, when the Dropkick Murphys and Flogging Molly came along. Both bands take their Irish-American identities to heart. Coming as they do from Boston's punk scene, the Dropkick Murphys offer a much more rock-based take on the idea of Celtic punk, though they make sure the violins, accordions, and whistles can be heard above the din. Flogging Molly, from Los Angeles, split the difference between the Pogues and the Dropkick Murphys, when they came on the scene in the early 1990s, ably weaving between folk and heavier rock approaches.

Blood or Whiskey, who formed in the early 1990s, are actually *from* Ireland, unlike many others in the genre. The Dublin band plays a mix of traditional and rock instruments, and cites the 1960s folk band the Dubliners and the famous punk band the Clash as influences. They have also played shows with the Pogues, the Dropkick Murphys, and Flogging Molly and might in fact be the closest thing to Celtic punk of the bunch.

Key Artists: Blood or Whiskey, Dropkick Murphys, Flogging Molly, Greenland Whalefishers, Shane MacGowan and the Popes, the Men They Couldn't Hang, the Pogues, the Real McKenzies, Roaring Jack, the Tossers

CROSSOVER TRACKS

ALTERNATIVE ROCK

Big Country–"In a Big Country," the Levellers–"One Way," the Waterboys–"Be My Enemy"

CELTIC ROCK

Runrig–"Breaking the Chains," Tempest–"The Soul Cages,"
Wolfstone–"Cleveland Park"

FOLK PUNK

AJJ–"Bad Bad Things," Billy Bragg–"To Have and to Have Not,"
This Bike Is a Pipe Bomb–"This is What I Want"

Chamber Pop

||||||||||||||||||||||||||||||||||||||||||||||||||||||||||||||||||||||||||||||||||||||||||||||||||||||||||||||||||||||

"You'll never get a complete answer," says Stuart Murdoch, considering the question of a musician's influences, "but, I think, often musicians are too coy about that sort of thing, while they sort out in their minds what's gonna make them look cool." Murdoch concedes that the sum of his own influences would include classical music, church music, and every pop record he's ever heard tossed in, but there were specific signpost records that led to the formation of Belle & Sebastian. In the early and mid-1990s, Murdoch was turning to a lot of what he loved growing up in the 1970s: middle-of-the-road hits like "Sugar, Sugar" by the Archies, and Northern soul—a DJ-led phenomenon that took place in clubs and venues in the north of England in the late 1960s and early 1970s, which placed value on obscurity, favoring lesser known records of Motown and other American soul music.

Murdoch also points to the Left Banke and the Zombies, noting their place in Baroque pop. "I loved the fact that it wasn't just rock as guitars that were leading the way, and there was poetry involved, and there was space for orchestra instruments to be heard." It seems like a left turn when he next brings up his love of 1970s TV themes, but listen to some of the examples that Murdoch cites—in particular "Eye Level," the theme from the Dutch detective series *Van der Valk* and played by the Simon Park Orchestra, which was a hit in the UK in 1973—and the orchestral connection is clear.

A student ensemble called the Kintyre Keynotes was Murdoch's first band, and though they weren't even teenagers yet, the Keynotes line-up was almost identical to who would be in Belle & Sebastian.

Murdoch's ideas about songwriting were starting to coalesce around making symphonies in miniature, and he clearly wasn't alone in this, as Belle & Sebastian became part of a unique generation of groups in the 1990s that made what is referred to as chamber pop. These bands often retained the core rock music instruments of guitar, bass, and drums, but equal emphasis was placed on piano, brass, and strings. They may have sometimes been guided by the vision of one leader, but the ambition of the music necessitated larger-than-normal member rosters. (Some also use the term "orchestral pop," but the membership of these bands was typically closer to that of a chamber ensemble than an orchestra.)

Belle & Sebastian emerged with what felt like a fully realized debut with *Tigermilk*, but Murdoch recalls them initially being a disparate bunch coming from different musical backgrounds, with nothing that really galvanized them at first. Guitarist Stevie Jackson's tastes were rooted in the 1960s and early 1970s, and cellist and singer Isobel Campbell, who left the band in 2002, was into, among other things, folk music. Keyboardist Chris Geddes had a thing for heavy metal. As for himself, Murdoch mentions in particular another touchstone of 1990s chamber pop: Nottingham, England's Tindersticks. "In fact, I can remember feeling, I must admit, pangs of jealousy when they brought out the first couple records. I so admired them, and it was already something in that kind of area that I wanted to get into . . . the delicacy and the strings. I thought their first two LPs were great."

Tindersticks marked the arrival of a chamber pop mini-movement that would grow in stature through the 1990s. Their self-titled debut remains one of the most mysterious, anomalous, and gorgeous records of the decade. Stuart Staples, singer and founding member, could be almost indecipherable at times as he delivered lyrics in a low mumble, but his voice was always magnetic. Refined, filled out, and also self-titled, their second album in 1995 was every bit an equal achievement.

If it seemed like chamber pop was having a moment in the middle of the decade, that idea was reinforced when *Mojo* magazine published their "100 Greatest Albums Ever Made" issue in the fall of 1995, which put the Beach Boys' *Pet Sounds*, the proto-chamber pop landmark, at the very top of its list. The real rage in the UK at the time was Britpop, but chamber pop managed to have some crossover appeal. Neil Hannon had been making music as the Divine Comedy for years before his album *Casanova* broke through in 1996 thanks to the Britpop-friendly singles "Becoming More Like Alfie" and "Something for the Weekend." London songwriter Jake Shillingford's group My Life Story, which at times included as many as a dozen members, also broke through with orchestral aplomb in 1996 with their single "12 Reasons Why I Love Her." Also based in London was Sean O'Hagan, whose band the High Llamas had a similar sound to Brian Wilson's California Sound–pop symphonies.

America also caught the bug. Eric Matthews began in a chamber pop duo called Cardinal before releasing his first solo album, *It's Heavy in Here*, on Sub Pop in 1995. That label was reaching in a number of directions after grunge began to recede, and they also released another, quite unexpected contributor to the style in 1996: Jeremy Enigk's *Return of the Frog Queen*, another lush-yet-intimate solo debut. Up to that point, Enigk had been the singer-guitarist in the band Sunny Day Real Estate, whose emo-innovating rock offered little hint that he might take such a stately turn so soon.

This mid-1990s moment for orchestral indie rock was receding from the spotlight by the end of the decade, as Belle & Sebastian and certain other chamber-pop players pushed themselves in different directions. "We did love to get out and dance, and we wanted to imagine that our records might be played at the sort of clubs that we loved, as well," says Murdoch of the expansion of his band's sound at the time. All the same, chamber pop never quite went overground in the same way as grunge or electronica, which means it never had to deal with being declared over.

Pioneer Tracks: Cardinal–"If You Believe in Christmas Trees," the Divine Comedy–"Your Daddy's Car," the High Llamas–"Giddy and Gay," Lambchop–"Soaky in the Pooper," Tindersticks–"The Not Knowing"

Key Players: Belle & Sebastian, the Divine Comedy, Eric Matthews, the High Llamas, Jack, Jeremy Enigk (solo), Lambchop, My Life Story, Tindersticks

CROSSOVER TRACKS

ALTERNATIVE ROCK
Nirvana–"Dumb," R.E.M.–"Everybody Hurts," Smashing Pumpkins–"Disarm"

BRITPOP
Blur–"The Universal," Gene–"Olympian," Oasis–"The Masterplan"

POST-ROCK
Bell Orchestre–"Throw It on a Fire," Godspeed You! Black Emperor–"Lift Yr. Skinny Fists, Like Antennas to Heaven . . ." Rachel's–"Rhine & Courtesan"

Chillwave

The stories behind how rock genres got their names are often prone to conjecture and conflicting testimony, but the origin of the term "chillwave" is pretty clear. Its coining has been traced back to the blog *Hipster Runoff*, which was begun in 2007 by Texas native Carlos Perez, who wrote it under the name Carles. "I just threw a bunch of pretty silly names on a blog post and saw which one stuck,"[1] was the explanation that Carles gave to *Wired* magazine in 2011 for how he accidentally came up with the term "chillwave" to describe a trend toward ethereal, mellow vibes that many on the Internet were noticing in certain corners of indie rock and electronic music in the late 2000s.

In his "Chillin' in Plain Sight" autopsy for Pitchfork in 2011, writer Nitsuh Abebe argues that "something that could pass for today's 'chillwave' has existed, in wide and steady circulation, at just about every moment for twenty years,"[2] pointing to dream pop, and specifically Slowdive, as an influence. In fact, use of the term "dream pop" itself seems to have received a lasting boost from the chillwave bubble that burst in 2011. The music's soft reverb and delay are no longer niche but rather common textures in indie rock.

Chillwave's relationship to rock and roll has more to do with its before and after than its season in the sun. Some rock-based music was a result, but many of the central chillwave texts are bedroom electropop records made by solo artists such as Washed Out (Ernest Greene), Neon Indian (Alan Palomo), Toro Y Moi (Chaz Bundick), and early Tycho (Scott Hansen). The chillwave wading pool was deepened with the inclusion of bands who would easily slip into the dream-pop stream when the buzz died down, bands like Wild Nothing, a solo project started by Jack Tatum in 2009, and Memory-house, the duo of Evan Abeele and Denise Nouvion from Guelph, Ontario, who also began that same year.

Had it not been under the microscope of a million Tumblr readers from day one, chillwave might have developed into the next step in the evolution of dream pop. Yes, the cheesy, accidental name didn't help its case, but how much did it really hold the music back? Its two words conjoined create no sillier an image than "shoegaze." Interestingly, insinuations that chillwave was middle-class[3] music reflected similar misplaced complaints about shoegaze twenty years prior.

Also notable is the parallel between chillwave and the music trend with a completely opposite demeanor that it followed, new rave. Both were tongue-in-cheek inventions that spun out of control, and, being digital-age trends, both had visual components that were significant to the construction of their identities. With chill-wave, the central theme of borrowed and repurposed memories was introduced before a note was played via hazy-filtered images of warm, empty skies and oceans. The implied zen was such a consistent accompaniment that it felt like a reaction to, if not a direct rebuke of, the proto-Internet nostalgia dumpster fire that new rave projected. Chillwave looked into the MDMA-blasted pupils of new rave and said it's time to mop up all this unicorn vomit and take it easy.

Key Players: Memory Tapes, Memoryhouse, Neon Indian, Real Estate, Small Black, Toro Y Moi, Twin Sister/Mr. Twin Sister, Washed Out, Wild Nothing, Youth Lagoon

CROSSOVER TRACKS

DREAM POP
Beach House–"Walk in the Park," DIIV–"How Long Have You Known"

HYPNOGOGIC POP
Ariel Pink–"Fright Night (Nevermore)," Pocahaunted–"Ashes is White"

SLOWCORE
Bedhead–"Roman Candle," Low–"Shame"

Christian Metal

Heavy metal was an unstoppable force in the 1980s. And while many in moral America spent the decade demonizing it, others saw it as a means to get their message across. The first Christian metal band to have a major impact was Stryper. Glam for God, the soldiers under command from Orange County, dressed in spandex bumblebee outfits and burned through hair product with the best of them.

Soon they were joined by the Oregon band Saint, who had a sound closer to Judas Priest, albeit simplified and with a limited vocal range (as opposed to Stryper frontman Michael Sweet, who could hit the high notes). Messiah Prophet from Pennsylvania took a straightforward party metal sound—minus the partying, presumably. Illinois band Whitecross sounded like Ratt but carried a positive message. In that same year, Seattle's Bloodgood stomped and soloed through *Rock in a Hard Place*, and Kentucky's Bride introduced the genre to the double bass drum pedal.

The recorded output of this first generation gives the impression that Christian metal wasn't willing to adopt the levels of speed and aggression that secular metal was reaching, but that doesn't account for the contentious "unblack metal" of certain early 1990s bands like Horde from Australia and Admonish from Sweden, who slayed for Jesus with the fastest of them. The marginal unblack metal scene carried on (mostly unnoticed), but Christian metal took the same hit that every other hair band did when grunge arrived in the 1990s.

Doug Van Pelt, founder of the Christian rock magazine *HM*, remembers, "I shortened my magazine from *Heaven's Metal*, which was the name from '85 to '95, to *HM* because in '95 metal was kind of a bad word and entire record labels and radio stations and all the sorts of things, they dropped their metal sections entirely overnight." Van Pelt added the subtitle "Your Hard Music Authority" to clarify the acronym and indicate the magazine was branching out to alternative rock and other genres. Christian hard music continued to keep up with trends in metal. P.O.D. found fame with nu metal, and the ADD-suffering hybrid metalcore of the late 2000s proved curiously popular with young Christian rockers with full sleeve tattoos like Underoath and the Devil Wears Prada.

Pioneer Tracks: Bride–"Evil that Men Do," Messiah Prophet–"Master of the Metal," Saint–"Warriors of the Son," Stryper–"Soldiers Under Command," Whitecross–"Enough Is Enough"

Key Players: August Burns Red, Bloodgood, Demon Hunter, Haste the Day, For Today, P.O.D., Stryper, the Devil Wears Prada, Underoath, Whitecross

CROSSOVER TRACKS

GRUNGE

Pearl Jam–"Tremor Christ," Soundgarden–"Jesus Christ Pose," Mother Love Bone–"Chloe Dancer/Crown of Thorns"

HARD ROCK

Black Sabbath–"After Forever," Norman Greenbaum–"Spirit in the Sky," Queen–"Jesus"

METALCORE

Norma Jean–"Memphis Will Be Laid to Waste," Shai Hulud–"Set Your Body Ablaze," We Came as Romans–"To Plant a Seed"

Christian Punk

The roots of Christian punk go back further, but its heyday starts in the 1990s when pop punk was taking off in mainstream. One record label at the center of it was Tooth & Nail, which was started by a pastor's son named Brandon Ebel, who cut his teeth at Frontline Records in California working with groups like the Altar Boys, one of the earliest Christian punk bands. Tooth & Nail got off the ground in 1993, releasing records by a small but diverse roster that included the Crucified and Starflyer 59. The label's first big success story came in 1995 with *Pokinatcha*, the debut album from MxPx.[1]

Noting the similarity between the 100,000-unit-selling *Pokinatcha* and the California pop punk that was all the rage that year, Andrew Beaujon explains in his book on Christian rock, *Body Piercing Saved My Life*, that the Bremerton, Washington, band led by Mike Herrera "also pulled off a trick that's eluded so many of their peers—they managed to come off as a rock band full of Christians rather than a Christian rock band."[2] This is probably the characteristic that set Christian punk apart from its predecessors—more so than the 1980s Christian rock and metal groups, these bands seemed more content to just *be* Christian than to preach it. This remained the case throughout the genre's boom years in the late 1990s and early 2000s with groups like Relient K, Slick Shoes, FM Static, and Ninety Pound Wuss, many of whom were also on Tooth & Nail.

Key Players: FM Static, Ghoti Hook, MxPx, Ninety Pound Wuss, the O.C. Supertones, Slick Shoes

CROSSOVER GENRES

CHRISTIAN ROCK
House of Heroes, Number One Gun, Poor Old Lu

POP PUNK
All Time Low, New Found Glory

Christian Rock

Doug Van Pelt has a few different definitions for what Christian rock is. "I used to think it was three, but I guess there's four." As the founder of *HM* Magazine, which began as a fanzine called *Heaven's Metal* in the 1980s and grew into the leading Christian alternative rock and metal (*Hard Music*) magazine of the 1990s and 2000s, he has certainly had plenty of opportunities to think about such things.

Of his four, which also include "it's made by Christians, therefore it is Christian rock" and "whatever Christians *consider* to be Christian rock," the most narrow definition is one in which each song includes the message of the gospel, the story of Christianity. "That there is a God, there is man, there's a problem of sin and separation from God, and Jesus came and paid the price and penalty for sin," Van Pelt details. "If the song has that story in its entirety or in pieces, then it's considered Christian rock because that song in and of itself proclaims the 'Christian message.'"

Van Pelt brings up one of the most famous examples of a band in a Christian rock grey area. "Young Christian kids, including me and my friends, would debate the band U2. Are they a Christian band?" In the band's early days, Bono, the Edge, and Larry Mullen Jr. attended the Shalom Fellowship in Dublin. In his memoir, *Killing Bono*, Neil McCormick, a childhood friend of the singer, remembers that after the release of their debut album, *Boy*, Bono was "all too aware that rumors about the band's Christian commitments were flying around, and fearful that this was an association that could damage them in the eyes of self-consciously cool rock commentators and consumers."[1]

The blues and country music might be rock and roll's biological parents, but Van Pelt makes the point that Christian music had a hand in raising it as well. "Rock and roll itself came from the church," he says. The blues has roots in spirituals. Elvis recorded dozens of gospel songs. Yet, by the 1960s, the influence of religious music on rock and roll had receded. Christians were still interested in the music, however, and when the evangelical Jesus Movement caught on in the late 1960s, many of the growing flock were ex-hippies whose preferred mode of musical communication was rock.

Christian rock's first major formative event happened at Explo '72, an evangelism conference put on by the Campus Crusade for Christ in Dallas in June of that year. Explo '72 was capped off by an all-day Christian music festival that is sometimes called the "religious Woodstock."[2] Van Pelt, then nine years old and living in a Dallas suburb, was there with his family, taking in performances from Johnny Cash and Kris Kristofferson, the California band Love Song, and singer/songwriter Larry Norman. He estimates the crowd to have been 100,000 strong.

Older churchgoing folk who were suspicious of rock music watched as thousands of longhairs came to Jesus. Begrudgingly, they accepted Christian rock because it did have some undeniably good values, and it was a useful method to reach the new generation.

As Christian rock grew in popularity, a chasm emerged between one camp that saw Christian rock as a ministry and one that saw it as a vocation in and of itself. The former had been the working model for a long time, up to and including Stryper frontman Michael Sweet's habit of tossing bibles into the audience at shows.[3] The new model saw Christian musicians having their art accepted on its own terms, message or not.

The latter model became successful in the 1990s to the point that "kids in that generation," says Van Pelt, "when they were in high school, they were looking up to bands like MxPx, Switchfoot,

P.O.D., and even King's X." These were renaissance years for the subtle side of Christian rock. Jars of Clay hit mainstream alternative airwaves in 1995 with "Flood," and most people didn't notice they were Christian. Sixpence None the Richer hit the jackpot in 1998 with "Kiss Me," and, again, their religious affiliation wasn't an issue or even noted much.

Even more overtly Christian acts were achieving commercial success. Virginia trio dc Talk, who deserve some credit for being early to recognize the potential in fusing hip-hop with rock music even if the results weren't exactly spectacular, went platinum with their 1995 album, *Jesus Freak*.[4] San Diego band P.O.D. rode the nu metal wave to MTV and millions in sales.

Despite all of those breakthroughs, the Christian rock scene that was thriving in the 1990s and early 2000s doesn't exist like it once did. The economic downturn had an impact on Christian retail and media. Many of the harder Christian bands signed to secular records labels, which affected the Christian labels. After fighting these forces for years, Van Pelt shuttered *HM* in 2011. "Christian rock's been a funny beast because the older generation didn't support it, and Christian rock didn't make money because the numbers weren't the same as the counterpart in the world. Christian rock was never really accepted on Christian radio or Christian television because most of those mediums were charities."

Adding to all of that, the listening habits of young Christian music fans have developed more or less the same as secular demographics. Record labels such as Tooth & Nail and Facedown Records in California still exist and have their audiences, but the divisions between fans of different styles of music are more porous. "The younger generation didn't grow up like I did in the '70s," says Van Pelt, "where disco sucks and rock and roll rules. Kids now, they like music if it's good."

Pioneer Tracks: Barnabas–"Savior," Larry Norman–"You Can't Take Away the Lord," Petra–"Walkin' in the Light," Randy Stonehill–"Keep Me Runnin'," Resurrection Band–"Colours"

Key Players: The 77s, dc Talk, Delirious?, Evanescence, Jars of Clay, Jerusalem, P.O.D., Relient K, Sixpence None the Richer, Switchfoot

‖‖‖

CROSSOVER TRACKS

‖‖‖

ALTERNATIVE ROCK

Collective Soul–"Shine," Creed–"What's This Life For," Sunny Day Real Estate–"5/4"

FOLK ROCK

Simon & Garfunkel–"Bridge Over Troubled Water," Sufjan Stevens–"He Woke Me Up Again," Violent Femmes–"Jesus Walking on the Water"

SOFT ROCK

Bob Dylan–"Gotta Serve Somebody," the Doobie Brothers–"Jesus Is Just Alright," Joan Osborne–"One of Us"

College Rock

‖‖‖

The 1991 MTV Video Music Awards belonged to R.E.M., and Michael Stipe's acceptance speech for the Video of the Year award was a memorable one. On stage at the Universal Amphitheatre in Los Angeles that September night, Stipe accepted the Moonman trophy for "Losing My Religion" with bandmates Mike Mills and Bill Berry. One by one, Stipe peeled off five T-shirts with all-caps slogans printed on them as he went through a long thank-you list: WEAR A CONDOM, CHOICE, ALTERNATIVE ENERGY NOW, THE RIGHT TO VOTE, and, finally, HANDGUN CONTROL. Before concluding with gratitude for the fans, he gave a heartfelt shout-out to a crucial resource: "We'd like to especially thank college radio for supporting us all these years and putting us here tonight."[1]

It was a defining moment for college rock, a loose categorization of semi-underground music in the 1980s. College rock was a realm in which R.E.M. were undisputed kings.

The genre grew as student-staffed college radio stations proliferated in the late 1970s and early 1980s, often the only outlet in a given city where one could hear certain kinds of artists on the airwaves. Indeed, pretty much the only factor for what qualified as college rock was whether a band was picked up by college radio but left alone by the big leagues. Pixies, the Replacements, Hüsker Dü, the Smiths, Violent Femmes, 10,000 Maniacs, Camper Van Beethoven, XTC, the Smithereens . . . a long list of now revered bands.

"When I first starting hearing college radio was when I lived in Northern California and I was sixteen years old," recalls Marco Collins. "I remember thinking that they play punk rock, this whole rebellious sound that a sixteen-year-old wants to hear. I remember loving the concept of it. I hated the fact that commercial radio wouldn't embrace some of these artists until they got big and signed major label deals."

Collins had still grown up on commercial radio and had a love for it, and he looked for a middle ground between the two when he moved up to Seattle to become a music director at 107.7 The End. "When we started that station, my ideal was to do college radio on a commercial station. My boss disagreed with that, and the two of us coming together really worked. I was the idealist, the kid bringing in all these records, and he was used to dealing with major labels, who are very pushy."

The hand-off from college rock to alternative rock was symbolized in the first song played on The End: R.E.M.'s "It's the End of the World As We Know It (And I Feel Fine)," although the song was probably chosen more for its title. On 107.7 and other alternative rock stations around the country, the midday "flashback lunch" was started, an hour or two of a transplanted 1980s college radio playlist. In part, it was in those playlists that today's conception of the sound of college rock hardened. Such programming, in a sense, also rewrote the past in favor of the outcasts. Songs like the Smiths' "How Soon Is Now?" were now staples, a flick of the dial from the classic rock establishment but with more hip cred.

If it was all an elaborate trick to get big audiences listening to indie music, it worked. Collins says The End became the first station of its kind in the country to go number one in the ratings 12+, meaning all demographics together, ages twelve through eighty—normally a position held by a pop or Top 40 station that appeals to parents and their kids listening in the car together. "A friend of mine said, 'The reason that your show was number one, and the reason that this station succeeded, was because you have a program director that knew how to program radio, and then you had this idealistic college radio kid that wanted to change the world and thought he could.' It just came together, man."

Thankfully, college radio still exists. Its idealism also still thrives on stations like KEXP in Seattle, which began life in the early 1970s as KCMU at the University of Washington, a student operation run out of the communications building. Like college radio, KEXP's programming is diverse, but during the rock-centric hours, the odds of hearing R.E.M., or even Ned's Atomic Dustbin, are still pretty good.

Spirit of the Radio: The Clash–"This is Radio Clash," Elvis Costello–"Radio, Radio," R.E.M.–"Radio Free Europe," the Replacements–"Left of the Dial," Wall of Voodoo–"Mexican Radio"

Key Players: 10,000 Maniacs, Camper Van Beethoven, the Dead Milkmen, Hoodoo Gurus, Love and Rockets, Pixies, the Smithereens, the Smiths, Sonic Youth, the The, They Might Be Giants, Throwing Muses, Violent Femmes, XTC

||||||||||||||||||||||||||||||||||||||||||||||||||||||||||||||||||||||||

CROSSOVER TRACKS

||||||||||||||||||||||||||||||||||||||||||||||||||||||||||||||||||||||||

ALTERNATIVE ROCK

Cracker–"Low," Dinosaur Jr.–"Start Choppin," Jane's Addiction–"Jane Says"

INDIE ROCK

Archers of Loaf–"Web in Front," Pavement–"Summer Babe," Yo La Tengo–"Tom Courtenay"

POST-PUNK

Echo and the Bunnymen–"The Killing Moon," New Order–"Love Vigilantes," the Psychedelic Furs–"Pretty in Pink"

Comedy Rock

The groundbreaking mockumentary *This Is Spinal Tap* was released in 1984 and was so successful that Christopher Guest, Harry Shearer, and Michael McKean (playing the characters Nigel Tufnel, Derek Smalls, and David St. Hubbins, respectively) started performing actual gigs as the hapless metal band Spinal Tap. In addition to the film's soundtrack, they released two other real albums over the years, which earned better reviews than their fictional *Shark Sandwich*. Spinal Tap have even had an effect on legitimate rock bands. Not only did Soundgarden do a mean cover of "Big Bottom" in their early years, but they also let their own sense of humor loose on songs like "Full on Kevin's Mom" from their 1989 album, *Louder Than Love*.

There is a difference between rock bands who lean on a sense of humor and those who make music defined by its comedic values first. But the line can be blurry. For instance, Tenacious D are both funnier *and* better musicians than the Bloodhound Gang.

The Bonzo Dog Doo-Dah Band (whose 1967 song "Death Cab for Cutie" would be used thirty years later for the name of an indie rock band) hammed it up on episodes of the British television show *Do Not Adjust Your Set*, but their music was legitimately catchy on its own. In his book on 1960s rock-and-roll eccentrics, *Urban Spacemen and Wayfaring Strangers*, Richie Unterberger compares them to Frank Zappa's the Mothers of Invention for their wackiness and aptitude for pop parody. Though they lacked the Mothers' cynicism, "they offered a more whimsical, surreal take on the absurd that was in some ways more sonically versatile, encompassing not just rock but also prewar music hall, jazz, and spoken word."[1]

Satire is a reliable mode for comedy rock. There's Weird Al Yankovic's direct style of parody, but you also have the slightly more impressionistic parody of New Zealand duo Flight of the Conchords. It is clear when watching the video for "Inner City Pressure" that the song is meant to evoke Pet Shop Boys' "West End Girls," but the music, even though similar in tone and rhythm, is the creation of Bret McKenzie and Jemaine Clement.

Key Players: The Bonzo Dog Doo-Dah Band, Flight of the Conchords, the Rutles, Spinal Tap, Tenacious D, Weird Al Yankovic

CROSSOVER GENRES

ALTERNATIVE ROCK
King Missile, Ween

ART ROCK
Captain Beefheart & His Magic Band, Frank Zappa and the Mothers of Invention

SHOCK ROCK
Alice Cooper, GWAR

Country Rock

The complicated relationship between country music and rock and roll resembles that between a hard-headed father and his rebellious son. The two have had difficulties seeing past their differences despite their unmistakably similar features.

Elvis, the King of Rock and Roll, started his recording career by stumbling into a sound closer to what's called rockabilly today, the first country rock. So how could the two be so seemingly at odds in the early years? Even in the late 1960s, when artists coming from the rock scene were offering olive branches with their new hybrid creation, country rock, the country music establishment was having none of it. Their stance was epitomized by country star Merle Haggard's back-to-back hippie-bashing singles, "Okie From Muskogee" and "The Fightin' Side of Me" at the end of the decade, as if flower power hadn't already been stomped into the ground enough at that point.

By today's standards, the records from the mid-to-late 1960s that established the genre sound more country than rock, but that wasn't the perception back then. The International Submarine Band's *Safe at Home*, the Byrds' *Sweetheart of the Rodeo,* or even large bites of the Flying Burrito Brothers' *The Gilded Palace of Sin* show what these bands were up against in even attempting to appease country music purists. The hard-to-please hardly stopped those in the rock and pop world who wanted to express their fondness for country music. Bakersfield, California, songwriter Buck Owens was a notable favorite whose songs inspired covers by no less than the Beatles ("Act Naturally" in 1965) and Ray Charles ("Together Again" in 1966).[1]

Around the time that Owens was getting his due, the Byrds' bassist, Chris Hillman, was still holding back his country inclinations, but that was soon to change.[2] Though it is *Sweetheart of the Rodeo* from late 1968 that gets all the credit for the Byrds' contribution to country rock, Hillman was already nudging the band in that direction by the end of 1966 when he had bluegrass guitarist Clarence White come down to the studio to play country guitar on two tracks for their new album, *Younger Than Yesterday*. The most equal rationing of country and rock (among other influences) on any Byrds album may be on *The Notorious Byrd Brothers*, which came a mere eight months before *Rodeo*.

Prolific and forever in flux, the Byrds were a natural landing place for Gram Parsons. A restless catalyst of country rock, Parsons had his sights set higher than a mere hybrid, he wanted it all: country, rock, R&B, soul, gospel, folk, and the kitchen sink all lifted up together in his concept of "Cosmic American Music." Floridian by birth, Parsons set a course for country rock with his International Submarine Band, which he founded in 1966 up in Boston where he had moved to attend Harvard.

By the time their lone album, *Safe at Home*, was released, the International Submarine Band had broken up and Parsons had joined the Byrds. Though only with them for a matter of months, Parsons is seen as an important force behind the direction of *Sweetheart of the Rodeo*. After a detour to hang out with Keith Richards of the Rolling Stones, Parsons then got Hillman to join *his* new band, the Flying Burrito Brothers. This was all, of course, before his own two solo albums, *GP* (1973) and the posthumous *Grievous Angel* (1974), which added a new dimension to both country rock and Parsons' own vision and also brought the rising country vocalist Emmylou Harris to wider attention.

Bob Dylan, too, had already done the rock-goes-country thing by this point, first with *John Wesley Harding* in 1967 and then even more overtly in 1969 with *Nashville Skyline*. Dylan's anonymously monikered former backing group, the Band, also made a name for themselves with their own kind of roots-tugging Americana in 1968 with *Music from Big Pink* and the following year with the Civil War–themed *The Band*. Many others didn't commit but still dabbled, as the Rolling Stones did on *Beggar's Banquet* and *Let it Bleed*. Country rock was a way to wear salt-of-the-earth grit at a time when psychedelic rock was burning out.

When country rock embedded itself in the mainstream a few years later, however, it had washed off much of that grit. This smoothing over of country rock's rough edges is embodied by the Eagles, simultaneously one of the biggest rock bands of all time, if you're counting sales figures, and one of those most responsible for everything wrong with rock in the 1970s, if you're reading the critics. For some, like writer Peter Doggett, the Eagles "epitomized the individualism which inevitably succeeded the doomed collectivism of sixties counter-culture."[3] Country music has remained an important influence on rock and roll, but the 1970s era of the Eagles, Linda Ronstadt, John Denver, and other mellow stars still stands as the commercial peak for the merger.

The 1980s and 1990s saw rock and roll rediscover country music in rawer, underground forms like cowpunk and alt-country. At the same time, country music itself (though it had rock-leaning outliers like Little Texas, Confederate Railroad, and the Kentucky Headhunters)[4] was moving unabashedly toward pop music, a transition epitomized by the outlandish success of Garth Brooks, who was once such an unstoppable money-making machine that no one talked him out of releasing an album in 1999 by his soul-patched rock alter ego, Chris Gaines. Country has since then walked on both sides of the pop-rock divide, with the more commercial artists unafraid to embrace modern pop tropes and technology, while the more "alt"-inclined acts find more audience crossover with indie crowds.

Pioneer Tracks: The Beatles–"Act Naturally," Bob Dylan–"I'll Be Your Baby Tonight," the Byrds–"Wasn't Born to Follow," the Flying Burrito Brothers–"Christine's Tune," the International Submarine Band–"Blue Eyes"

Key Artists: The Eagles, Emmylou Harris, Mike Nesmith, New Riders of the Purple Sage, the Nitty Gritty Dirt Band, Gram Parsons (solo), Poco, Pure Prairie League, Linda Ronstadt

CROSSOVER TRACKS

ALTERNATIVE COUNTRY

Neko Case–"Bowling Green," Uncle Tupelo–"John Hardy," Whiskeytown–"Too Drunk to Dream"

FOLK ROCK

The Beau Brummels–"Oh, Lonesome Me," Tim Hardin–"Reason to Believe," Buffalo Springfield–"Kind Woman"

SOUTHERN ROCK

The Ozark Mountain Daredevils–"Country Girl," the Marshall Tucker Band–"Losing You," Hank Williams Jr.–"Whiskey Bent and Hell Bound"

Crossover Thrash

"Back in the '80s, you were a metal band or you were a punk band . . . one or the other," remembers Jon Bolling, founder of *Shredding Material*, a Maryland-based zine that covered punk and post-hardcore in the 1990s. "You didn't cross into each other's *neighborhood*. When thrash came out, the metal heads and the punk rockers were like, 'Well, I can listen to thrash, and you can listen to thrash . . . maybe we have some commonality there.'"

The level of animosity that existed between punks and metalheads in the 1980s seems odd and antiquated now. From an outside perspective, at least, the two camps had far more similarities than differences. The gist of the rift, as music writer Steven Blush puts it in the documentary *Get Thrashed*, is that the punks thought the metallers looked dumb, and the metallers didn't grasp the nuances of punk.[1] If that doesn't sound like enough to come to blows over, look up the footage of Anthrax's set at Olympic Auditorium in Los Angeles on April 26, 1986, which was rife with interfaction fighting in the audience, including a brawl that broke out on stage toward the end of the gig.

The advent of crossover thrash helped bring a detente in this hard-rock Balkanization. Musicians from both sides were already less inclined to mind the borders, and crossover thrash was where they met in the middle and even switched sides. Crossover pioneers Suicidal Tendencies, from Venice, California, weren't afraid of mashing up flashy metal solos and three-chord bashes on songs like "Two Sided Politics" on their self-titled debut in 1983. By their third album in 1988, *How Will I Laugh Tomorrow When I Can't Even Smile*

Today, they took the concept further and fully crossed over to become a thrash metal band.

There is a perception that crossover thrash was a result of punks going metal once they learned how to play their instruments, and looking at the creative trajectories of notable crossover bands like Agnostic Front, Cro-Mags, and Corrosion of Conformity, it does seem there are more bands who started punk and went thrash, rather than the other way around.

Pioneer Tracks: Corrosion of Conformity—"Consumed," Discharge— "Hear Nothing, See Nothing, Say Nothing," D.R.I.—"Tear It Down," Nuclear Assault—"Sin," Stormtroopers of Death—"March of the S.O.D."

Key Players: The Accüsed, Agnostic Front (*Liberty and Justice For . . . , One Voice*), Cro-Mags (*Best Wishes*), Hogan's Heroes, Iron Reagan, Municipal Waste, Suicidal Tendencies

CROSSOVER GENRES

HARDCORE:
Bad Brains, Verbal Abuse, Void

THRASH METAL:
Anthrax, Overkill, Slayer (*Undisputed Attitude*)

Crust Punk

For an outsider, it's easier to spot crust punk by sight than by sound. Severely studded, severely ripped, and sometimes severely uncombed, the fashion ethos associated with the genre is its most immediately identifiable element. It is a protective outer shell of metalhead- and biker-influenced apparel, sometimes topped with a helmet of dreadlocks, hence referring to fans as crust punks. Stemming from the UK punk scene of the early 1980s, crust punk for many has since become almost a way of life connected to a style of music but not wholly dependent on it.

The term comes from the first demo made by the Newcastle band Hellbastard. "'Rippercrust' is widely regarded as the first time the word 'crust' was used in the punk context," writes Ian Glasper, "and hence the specific starting point of the whole crustcore genre, although some would attribute that accolade to the likes of Disorder, Chaos UK, and Amebix several years earlier."[1] Hellbastard guitarist Malcolm "Scruff" Lewty told Glasper that "crusty" was a word he came up with to describe the sound of his guitar being played through a dying distortion pedal.

Hellbastard and other crust punk bands like Amebix arrived at a punk-metal crossover sound before it became more widely accepted. Glasper writes of Amebix, "Musically they owed as much to heavy metal and hard rock as they did to punk and hardcore,"[2] and indeed the sound of their 1985 debut album, *Arise*, has as much in the way of big, echoing drums and metal riffs that chug and slash as it does snarling punk attitude.

Key Players: Amebix, Chaos UK, Disorder, Doom, Dystopia, Hellbastard, His Hero Is Gone, Nausea

CROSSOVER GENRES

ANARCHO PUNK
Antisect, Crass

POWERVIOLENCE
Capitalist Casualties, Man Is the Bastard

Cuddlecore

||||||||||||||||||||||||||||||||||||||||||||||||||||||||||||||||||||||||||||||||||||||||||||||||

"Welcome to cuddle core," wrote reporter Rose Apodaca Jones in her 1995 piece "Cute. Real Cute" for the *Los Angeles Times*. "It's a scene that cozily balances the cuddly cute of infantile fashion and punk's hard-core ethic."[1] The term is one of the many by-products of the "core" explosion of the 1990s. Jones' piece positioned cuddlecore as a poppy outgrowth of the riot grrrl movement. It also tied it to Hello Kitty materialism and fixation on youth.

As for the music, Jones first names the long-running Japanese trio Shonen Knife before going on to lump together alt-rockers Juliana Hatfield and Veruca Salt, UK riot grrrl representatives Huggy Bear, and post-C86'ers the Pooh Sticks.[2] None of those last four often come to mind today when thinking about cuddlecore, though the Pooh Sticks' ramshackle indie pop comes closest. By the time of their third album, *Box of Hair*, the Vancouver, BC, band Cub had become the most commonly cited example of cuddlecore, likely due to their name and cute album art.

Key Players: Cub, the Softies, Tiger Trap, Tsunami, Tullycraft

CROSSOVER GENRES

INDIE POP
Bunnygrunt, the Crabs

RIOT GRRRL
Bratmobile, Tattle Tale

D-Beat

D-Beat is an entire subgenre of hardcore punk from the early 1980s defined by one very fast drum beat.

"The style has kinda gotten a bit distorted," explains Brian Roe, drummer for English hardcore band the Varukers, in a short video tutorial on his YouTube page that teaches how to play D-Beat. "People saying it's . . . double bass drums and hi-hats and stuff like that. It's not."[1] Right, none of that frilly stuff. Find your cymbal, bass drum, snare drum, and flail away.

Does the rest of the band have to do anything in particular to play D-Beat? Well, it helps to sound like English hardcore and thrash metal innovators Discharge.[2] As Roe remembers it, he and his childhood pal Garry Maloney—who was the drummer for the Varukers before Roe, and who joined Discharge after original drummer Terence "Tezz" Roberts left—were two of the originators. Indeed, it is said that the "D" in D-Beat stands for Discharge. It did not stand for Denmark, but, interestingly, in its heyday the subgenre was particularly popular in Scandinavia.

Key Players: Anti Cimex, Discharge, Doom, Mob 47, the Varukers

CROSSOVER GENRES

GRINDCORE
Extreme Noise Terror, Napalm Death

STREET PUNK
The Exploited, GBH

Dance Punk

Writing for the *Village Voice* in March of 1980, Lester Bangs was feeling bullish about the new Public Image Ltd album, *Second Edition*, also known as *Metal Box*. "This is a real ensemble making passionate music out of noise and sonic scraps. Quote me: 'the first music of the Eighties.'"[1] It's hard to believe now, but *Metal Box* wasn't always as universally revered as it is today. In the 1990s, fans were used to John Lydon's increasingly smoothed-over PiL and were excited to get Johnny Rotten back with the Sex Pistols' *Filthy Lucre* reunion. It took until the 2000s for the full influence of the "loping almost-funk"[2] of "Albatross" and "Swan Lake" (the latter released in single form under the title "Death Disco") to set in.

Though the term is open enough to allow in danceable punk rock from any era, when people refer to dance punk, they are typically speaking about one of two particular periods: the post-punk bands who began dabbling in disco-like rhythms at the end of the 1970s, and the cluster of bands who sprung up in the early 2000s and clearly admired the former. James Murphy of LCD Soundsystem put it in writing by name-checking some of those groups in "Losing My Edge." The Rapture put it in melody by borrowing a pinch of Public Image Ltd's "Careering" for their own "Echoes."

The part of the post-punk revival of the early 2000s that wasn't the Strokes and Interpol was dominated by post-disco rhythms. New York had the aforementioned LCD Soundsystem and the Rapture, Radio 4, the first Liars album, and Yeah Yeah Yeahs' "Date with the Night." The sound became popular enough to sustain a second wave in 2005 with bands like the Bravery in the United States, and Test

Icicles (whose frontman Devonte Hynes now makes music as Blood Orange) in the UK, who also pushed the limits of goofy band names.

Key Players: !!!, Bush Tetras, ESG, the Faint, Franz Ferdinand, Gang of Four, LCD Soundsystem, Liquid Liquid, Public Image Ltd, Pylon, Radio 4, the Rapture

CROSSOVER TRACKS

ART PUNK

Pere Ubu–"On the Surface," Swell Maps–"The Helicopter Spies"

NEW WAVE

Blondie–"The Hardest Part," Tom Tom Club–"Wordy Rappinghood"

Darkwave

||||||||||||||||||||||||||||||||||||||||||||||||||||||||||||||||||||||||||||||||||||||

Darkwave is the European side of the goth movement that came out of late 1970s punk. It was the continent catching up to a UK scene that by some accounts was starting to lose its inky luster, and at the same time reconstructing the music with synthesizers and drum machines. In modern times, for some, the term "darkwave" has even come to take the place of "goth."[1]

From the early 1980s on, British record label 4AD was home to elegantly melancholic artists such as Cocteau Twins and Dead Can Dance, who would have a notable influence on darkwave bands. The label even signed up a couple: Xmal Deutschland from Germany, and Clan of Xymox from Amsterdam. In the mid 1980s, considering whether or not to sign Clan of Xymox, label founder Ivo Watts-Russell was ultimately won over by their emotional resonance, although he believed that goth was already on its way out. On a one-album contract, Clan of Xymox released their self-titled debut in 1985. Their influences were clear, as on the "Blue Monday"-esque centerpiece, "Stranger," but the lack of musician credits on the record sleeve kept the artists themselves a mystery.[2]

It was the band's own decision to do so, as they anticipated a bias against Dutch bands, and perhaps the strategy might have helped: Clan of Xymox was reviewed well and proved there was still life in dressing like the undead. If goth was running out of steam in its place of origin by the mid-1980s, then it was darkwave that reinvigorated it, swapping standard rock instrumentation for new wave's jerking rhythms and technological instincts, while goth would continue to explore its cold, robotic side as it began to cross over with industrial music later that decade.

Key Players: Clan of Xymox, Cocteau Twins, Dead Can Dance, Pink Turns Blue, Xmal Deutschland

CROSSOVER GENRES

COLDWAVE
Charles de Goal, Die Form

GOTH ROCK
Bauhaus, the Sisters of Mercy

Deathcore

||||||||||||||||||||||||||||||||||||||||||||||||||||||||||||||||||||||||||||||||||||||||||||||||||||||||||||||||||||||||||||

When naming rock genres in the 1980s and 1990s, there were essentially two ways to use "core." The first was to indicate that the music was at least half-rooted in hardcore punk, such as emocore or grindcore. The second, less serious way, though ostensibly aligning the music with punk, really served more to indicate a "core" theme of the music, as in cuddlecore or slowcore. A third way came in the 2000s, when the "core" sometimes didn't stand for hardcore, but *metalcore*. Such is the case for both deathcore (death metal + metalcore) and electronicore (electronic music + metalcore), two of the more popular yet divisive strains of heavy rock in the young millennium.

Metalcore already had a circuitous life through the 1990s before getting mixed up with death metal in the early 2000s. Even trained ears can have a hard time explaining the subtle differences among the styles, beyond deathcore's use of breakdowns—the part in a metalcore song (or other fast, heavy genre) where the beat significantly slows down, the guitarist plays some palm-muted chords, and everything gets low and menacing.

Formed in the early 2000s, Montreal band Despised Icon were fond of both breakdowns and blast beats[1] and have been credited with kicking off deathcore as it is still known today.[2] The band hasn't been too fond of the tag that has followed their career, and the genre itself has been picked on within the metal community. Proclaiming not to mean it as an insult, the website Metal Sucks says that deathcore "is actually really easy to define: it's mallcore kids trying to play death metal, and try as they might, they will never quite get it right."[3]

Key Players: All Shall Perish, Carnifex, Despised Icon, Suicide Silence, Thy Art is Murder, Whitechapel

||||||||||||||||||||||||||||||||||||||||||||||||||||||||||||||||||||||||||
CROSSOVER GENRES
||||||||||||||||||||||||||||||||||||||||||||||||||||||||||||||||||||||||||

DEATH METAL
Decapitated, Dismember

METALCORE
Between the Buried and Me, Bullet for My Valentine

Death Metal

||||||||||||||||||||||||||||||||||||||||||||||||||||||||||||||||||||||||||||||||||||||||||||||||||||||||||||

Rock fans in the 1990s didn't need to hear death metal to understand that it was the most extreme music out there; the name said it all.

Similar to the way that the term "black metal" first appeared as the title of Venom's second album, "Death Metal" was the name of the last song on *Seven Churches,* the first album by Possessed, an early thrash band from the Bay Area. And as with black metal, it took time for the band's dark concept to take on a life of its own. When it did, it had relocated to another bay on the other side of the country: the unlikely death metal hot spot of Tampa, Florida.

Chuck Schuldiner was a high-school student living in a suburb of Orlando when he formed the band Mantas, which would later be renamed Death. He later settled in Tampa alongside another young band who would be one of death metal's pivotal groups, Morbid Angel. The scene solidified with the aid of Morrisound recording studio in nearby Temple Terrace, where resident producer Scott Burns became the in-demand death metal guru. Most every major death metal band would record at Morrisound: the aforementioned Morbid Angel and Death, Sepultura, Cannibal Corpse, Obituary, Deicide, and more.

How is death metal different from speed, thrash, black, et al.? "Death metal is darker and more morbid-sounding than speed metal, and the vocals are usually very deep, guttural, and unintelligible,"[1] writes David Konow. Despite each genre's claims to being distinct from the pack, the most identifiable differences between the heaviest types of metal might be between the vocal techniques. Thrash metal vocalists (such as James Hetfield of Metallica and Dave Mustaine of Megadeth) tend to deliver their lines with a shout or a bark. A meaner beast, death metal vocals growl and roar. Black metal vocalists tend to shriek.

Death metal also stood apart for its use of the blast beat, a drumming technique requiring almost inhuman speed that is also used in grindcore. A significant but nonmusical distinction among these extreme metal categories is imagery and lyrical subject matter. Death metal is, of course, fixated on themes of violence, gore, zombies, and other horror-movie stuff. That can also include Satan, but satanism and paganism is more black metal's territory, as is mystic nature worship. Not that you can understand what either one is yelling about, since the words are typically unintelligible in both. That is probably all for the best, given the repugnant places some have taken their lyrics.

Death metal never really sold out, but it did wane in popularity for a time, weakened by its own ambitions. Against all odds, between Morbid Angel signing to a major label and Cannibal Corpse appearing in *Ace Ventura: Pet Detective*, death metal had attained enough mainstream visibility to open itself up to the most malicious accusation one can make in metal: being a poser.

Pioneer Tracks: Death–"Infernal Death," Kreator–"Total Death," Obituary–"Like the Dead," Possessed–"Death Metal," Slayer–"Angel of Death"

Key Players: Cannibal Corpse, Deicide, Immolation, Morbid Angel, Sepultura, Six Feet Under, Suffocation

CROSSOVER GENRES

BLACK METAL
Emperor, Mayhem, Marduk

GRINDCORE
Carcass, Napalm Death, Repulsion

THRASH METAL
Death Angel, Living Death, Rigor Mortis

Desert Rock

"It's funny, my parents have a condo out in Palm Desert," says Scott Hill, founding guitarist and singer of the Southern California band Fu Manchu. The owners of the place right across the street from Hill's parents? Brant Bjork's parents. Bjork was the original drummer in the foundational desert rock band Kyuss and also played with Fu Manchu in the late 1990s.

Kyuss' desert roots are more than just geographical circumstance. The "generator parties" that went down in the inland valleys when the band was starting out are now the stuff of legend. There were others that made up the desert rock scene, such as the La Quinta-based jammers Yawning Man, but Kyuss made it to farther-out places once they got signed to Elektra Records and released their third album, *Welcome to Sky Valley*. Their reputation ballooned posthumously with the success of Queens of the Stone Age, the band guitarist Josh Homme started after Kyuss broke up. For many, desert rock means "sounds like Kyuss": sun-fried, hazy, highway-bound.

Though the first record Hill ever bought was *Rock and Roll Over* by KISS, a transformational moment came in December of 1980 when a friend played him a cassette of a live Black Flag show. "I remember taking all my rock records—Deep Purple, Blue Cheer, KISS—and putting them in the back of my closet. My friend wanted to take all his rock stuff and skip the vinyl down the street." In November of 1985, Hill went to see the Santa Cruz punk band BL'AST!, whose combination of fast and slow, heavy (but not heavy metal) parts made Hill and his first band, Virulence, rethink their goals of playing ultra-fast all the time. In a sense, those Deep Purple and Blue Cheer records were slowly allowed back out of the closet.

Desert rock, like grunge, is a geographically specific response to the colliding influences of punk and classic psychedelic and hard rock—except it is from sunny California instead of the overcast Pacific Northwest. Fu Manchu kept it simple, heavy, and fuzzy. Aside from Kyuss, Fu Manchu didn't really know what was happening around them locally and identified with other heavy bands like TAD, the Melvins, and Monster Magnet. Hill isn't sure the "desert rock" tag really applies to Fu Manchu, but the bands played a lot of shows and parties together, including, of course, out in the desert. The desert rock scene itself didn't last in the same way beyond the 1990s, but both Fu Manchu and Queens of the Stone Age kept going and have survived the heat of greater success that followed.

Pioneer Tracks: BL'AST!–"Cut Your Teeth," Fu Manchu–"Ojo Rojo," Kyuss–"Katzenjammer," Masters of Reality–"Domino," Monster Magnet–"Pill Shovel"

Key Players: Fu Manchu, Kyuss, Nebula, Queens of the Stone Age, Yawning Man

CROSSOVER TRACKS

GRUNGE

The Melvins–"Oven," Screaming Trees–"Shadow of the Season," TAD–"Jinx"

HEAVY METAL

Black Sabbath–"Paranoid," Blue Cheer–"Summertime Blues,"
Deep Purple–"Burn"

STONER METAL

Bongzilla–"Sacred Smoke," Goatsnake–"Innocent," Sleep–
"Dopesmoker"

Digital Hardcore

Atari Teenage Riot were not a guitar-bass-and-drums rock band, but they were pretty damn punk. The Berlin trio's sound was just as much, if not more, a part of the techno and electronic music realms, but their songs were built with bracing beats and samples of fast, distorted riffs of hardcore. Leader Alec Empire and co. came up in a time when electronica was all the rage and artists like the Chemical Brothers were the new rock stars—not just in their native Europe, but also increasingly in the United States. At the same time, Atari Teenage Riot was founded on anti-Nazi ideals[1], and their political anger set them apart from the feel-good ravers.

Burn, Berlin, Burn! sounded like little else out there when the Beastie Boys' uber-hip Grand Royal label put out the compilation in 1997, and today it sounds simultaneously of-its-time yet still future-minded. Seeing as Empire came up with the term "digital hardcore" and used it as the name of his own record label (which was funded by the sabotaging of a major record deal)[2], it pretty much belongs to Atari Teenage Riot, but a few others from both inside and outside of Germany joined them in their fight.

Key Players: Atari Teenage Riot, Cobra Killer, EC8OR, Sonic Subjunkies

CROSSOVER TRACKS

INDUSTRIAL METAL

KMFDM–"A Drug Against War," Pitchshifter–"Genius"

PUNK ROCK

Dead Kennedys–"Nazi Punks Fuck Off," Namenlos–"Nazis Wieder in Ostberlin"

Doom Metal

||||||||||||||||||||||||||||||||||||||||||||||||||||||||||||||||||||||||||||||||||||||||||||||||||||||||||||||||||||||||||||

"Back then, people used to say that it sounded muffled, and they didn't want to work with us because of that weird sound," explained Dave Chandler to the website Metal Assault in 2012, about how reaction to his distinct guitar tone has changed over time. "But nowadays, people want to get that sound."[1] Chandler's band, Saint Vitus, has gone through intermittent periods of activity since they started gigging in their hometown of Los Angeles in the early 1980s, going on hiatus in the 1990s and the 2000s. So far though, they've always managed to come back, and, at this point, the heft of their influence may match their resilience.

"Throughout every era, there were doom metal counterparts to prevailing trends,"[2] writes Ian Christe, pointing to Lucifer's Friend and Necromandus in the 1970s; Witchfinder General, Pentagram, and the aforementioned Saint Vitus in the 1980s; and Cathedral, Burning Witch, and Sleep in the 1990s, the latter of which are also considered early lords of stoner metal. A moody, mysterious wallflower in those decades, doom metal has long since come into its own, finding an audience not just with the traditional metal base, but also curious thrill seekers who otherwise might be more inclined to read *The New Yorker* than *Revolver*.

There are several slow and heavy metal subgenres that intermingle, notably doom, stoner, sludge, and drone. Among them, doom has the most generalized parameters to qualify—slow, heavy, and foreboding—which makes it retroactively traceable back through eras in which the term didn't exist, giving doom a parental role in the metal genre family tree. Doom also functions as a suffix, which has led to contradictory genres like death-doom, as well as seemingly redundant ones like stoner-doom.

Pioneer Tracks: Black Sabbath–"Black Sabbath," Led Zeppelin–"Dazed and Confused," Lucifer's Friend–"Rose on the Vine," Necromandus–"I've Been Evil," Witchfinder General–"Burning a Sinner"

Key Players: Burning Witch, Candlemass, Cathedral, Pentagram, Saint Vitus, Sleep, Windhand, Yob

CROSSOVER GENRES

DRONE METAL
Earth, Khanate, Sunn O)))

POST-METAL
Isis, Neurosis, Pelican

SLUDGE METAL
Crowbar, Eyehategod, the Melvins

Dream Pop

|||||||||||||||||||||||||||||||||||||||||||||||||||||||||||||||||||||||||||||||||||||||||||||||||||||||||||||||||||||||||||||||||||||||||||||

Dream pop is the lighter side of a coin it splits with shoegaze. Reverb and delay bubble in warm pools, instead of sweeping in on oceanic waves. Less value is placed on epic-ness. "We've been tagged our whole career as playing quiet music," explains Damon Krukowski of Damon & Naomi, the longtime duo he formed with Naomi Yang shortly after their previous band, Galaxie 500, split up in 1991. "It's true and it isn't, 'cause we've always made as much noise as we wanted."

Punk and its aftermath, seen in bands such as the Clash, Joy Division, and early New Order, Mission of Burma, and Pere Ubu, were Krukowski's primary interests when he became a musician. Channeled into Galaxie 500, these influences morphed into music that was urgent and poetically articulate, but any aggression was diffused with hesitant tempos and cold echo. Krukowski and his friend Dean Wareham, since of Luna, were New Yorkers attending Harvard University when they started Galaxie 500 in 1987.

They had a short head start on Britain's shoegazing scene, for a time walking alongside but not within it. Hindsight hears their influential albums *Today* and *On Fire* as dream pop precursors, but Krukowski points out that the groups most frequently associated with the term, the UK bands especially, weren't in their circles and their paths hardly crossed. Galaxie 500 felt themselves part of a more eclectic US scene represented by the Shimmy Disc label, which was run by Galaxie 500's producer Kramer.

On December 1, 1991, mere months after Galaxie 500 dissolved, Simon Reynolds' article "'Dream-Pop' Bands Define the Times in

Britain" appeared in the *New York Times* putting forth an argument for using the term instead of "shoegaze," but the ship was already sailing.[1] By the end of 1991, America was ready to throw down in the pit, not sway back and forth on its heels. Moshing became so common that it even happened at Cranberries' concerts, during "Linger." The Irish band even set aside their folk-ish, dreamy pop long enough to write their grunge-y "Zombie" anthem, appeasing the flanneled masses.

Damon & Naomi's first record, *More Sad Hits*, came in 1992 with a warm, patient indefinability that bridged the not-too-far-apart approaches of Red House Painters and Slowdive. Later in the decade, *Playback Singers* would move into acoustic-driven, textured folk pop songs. Krukowski refutes the dream pop and slowcore tags that have followed his music, noting that freak folk and New Weird America, two genres that sprang up in the 2000s, felt closer to their sensibility, particularly the more psychedelic end like Six Organs of Admittance. Today, the term "shoegaze" denotes a more fixed sound, while dream pop has become a catchall for any music that employs shoegaze elements in light measures. It is used on bands as different as Beach House, the xx, and M83. Interestingly, though shoegaze was what first stuck, dream pop has found wider contemporary favor in an indie sphere where at least a smattering of reverb and delay are *de rigueur*.

Pioneer Tracks: A. R. Kane–"When You're Sad," Cocteau Twins–"Sugar Hiccup," Galaxie 500–"Tugboat," My Bloody Valentine–"Strawberry Wine"

Key Players: A Sunny Day in Glasgow, Asobi Seksu, Beach Fossils, Beach House, Damon & Naomi, DIIV, Fear of Men, Lower Dens, Lush, the Radio Dept., Wild Nothing

|||||||||||||||||||||||||||||||||||||||||||||||||||||||||||||||||||||||||||

CROSSOVER TRACKS

|||||||||||||||||||||||||||||||||||||||||||||||||||||||||||||||||||||||||||

ALTERNATIVE ROCK

Mercury Rev–"Car Wash Hair," the Ocean Blue–"Between Something and Nothing"

INDIE POP

Alvvays–"Archie, Marry Me," Cults–"Go Outside"

SHOEGAZE

Lush–"For Love," Ride–"Like a Daydream"

Drone Metal

Asked to name some favorite subgenres within the wide world of metal, Brandon Stosuy first mentions his appreciation for long, continuous performances and pieces of music. "I like to be pushed to the limit in that way," he says. "I like certain Sunn O))) tracks because of that. Live, I really like Sunn O))) for that reason, just seeing this band who feels completely in control of what they're doing slowly unleash this thing for an hour and a half." Among the varieties of slow metal, including sludge, stoner, and doom, drone may be the slowest and most spare. His appreciation for those kinds of endurance tests aren't limited strictly to metal, but drone metal has gained an almost surprising amount of traction in the twenty-first century.

"There are two schools of playing music: play as many notes as possible, or play fewer notes and make the notes more expressive. I've always striven for the second,"[1] Dylan Carlson told the website Invisible Oranges in 2011, explaining how he tries to "play less with more feeling." Carlson is a guitarist and the central figure behind Earth, who are now regarded as one of drone metal's progenitors, if not the original source. Musically, Earth were an outlier in the Olympia, Washington, scene in the early 1990s, though Carlson was acquainted with the group's closest comparison, nearby metal shapeshifters the Melvins (both groups briefly included bass player Joe Preston, who started his own drone-leaning project Thrones soon afterward).

Earth's second release, *Earth 2: Special Low Frequency Version*, is an abstract storm of guitar feedback cut into three lengthy tracks. Sub Pop put the album out in 1993, as well as Earth's next two,

Phase 3: Thrones and Dominions (1995) and *Pentastar: In the Style of Demons* (1996), which found Carlson already gravitating toward song structures, albeit stoned and circular ones. After a hiatus, Earth returned in the early 2000s to find others, from the medieval cloak–wearing Sunn O))) from Seattle to the intense Toronto duo Nadja, making length and repetition the new extremes to reach in metal.

Key Players: Burning Witch, Black Boned Angel, Earth, Khanate, Locrian, Nadja, Sunn O))), Teeth of Lions Rule the Divine

CROSSOVER GENRES

DOOM METAL
Corrupted, Om

EXPERIMENTAL METAL
Jesu, Neurosis

NOISE ROCK
Boredoms, Swans

Dunedin Sound

"A journalist asked me if there was a Dunedin Sound in about 1980–81. He actually came up with the term, not me! I'm innocent!" So exclaims David Kilgour, who cofounded the Clean with his brother Hamish in 1978. That journalist who pinned a sound to Dunedin, New Zealand, was Gary Steel, who at the time was a writer for the *Evening Post* in Wellington. At that point, Dunedin, one of the South Island's largest cities and the location of New Zealand's first university, hadn't had much of a reputation as a rock music hot spot.

This was about to change: quickly within the country itself, more slowly in the outside world. "Hamish and I were obsessed with catching up with the '60s music we missed while little kids, so there was a lot of scouring of second-hand bins." Musically omnivorous as the brothers were, Kilgour says most influential to them was the early punk movement. They were not alone in their newfound inspiration. Some friends of theirs, including Chris Knox, who would go on to form Tall Dwarfs, were already playing in a punk band called the Enemy when the Clean began. Kilgour has even cited the Enemy as the instigators of the Dunedin scene.[1]

"Most of us were on the dole. There was a lot of downtime, socializing, experimenting, and competition between a lot of us. Dunedin, and generally the South, always seemed less interested in fashion. Punk made an impact here, but not many of us shaved our heads and got Doc Martens." Kilgour says his circle in Dunedin took the spirit and attitude of punk, the feeling of being "up against it," but they didn't have the same kind of image awareness that one would find up north in the Auckland scene, which was taking cues from British magazines. "The Dunedin lot all looked shabby, really."

According to Kilgour, the Clean's initial ambitions as a band were to "get across to people, sell records, pull a crowd, quit work, have a life . . . bulldozer over everything and take no prisoners, and don't follow leaders and question everything." Rounded out with Robert Scott on bass (the late Peter Gutteridge, a school friend of Kilgour's and later a founding member of the Chills, was their first bassist), soon enough the band would achieve those first couple of goals. Though they took a couple of years to release their debut single on a new record label from Christchurch called Flying Nun, when "Tally Ho!" finally met the New Zealand public, it cracked the country's top twenty. Drawing up what writer Marc Masters referred to in *The Pitchfork 500* as "a blueprint for catchy rock created with primitive tools" with their "rough, loose, and polish-free"[2] approach, "Tally Ho!" captures the root elements of what is now known throughout the world as the Dunedin Sound in under three minutes.

Fellow Dunedin bands like the Chills and Tall Dwarfs shared both members and a DIY, often lo-fi aesthetic that would become highly influential on indie rock bands in the US and UK years later. Whereas Kilgour had once been inspired reading about punk scenes abroad in imported music magazines like *New York Rocker*,[3] in 1997, he played host to New York indie rock mainstays Yo La Tengo—huge fans of the Clean and Flying Nun—who were on tour in New Zealand.[4] The intercontinental exchange of ideas had come full circle. Yo La Tengo were particular Dunedin Sound obsessives (apparently going so far as to have a real-size cutout of Tall Dwarfs' Chris Knox in their practice space),[5] but the Clean's emphasis on energy and spontaneity over polish and technical performance can be heard on Pavement's early records and elsewhere across indie rock from the 1990s to now.

Kilgour found out that word of the Clean had spread in the late 1980s, when the band was offered to tour the East Coast in the US, later followed by a month in Germany and the UK. "I was kind of amazed at the crowds," he remembers. "I had no idea. The interest from the USA has sustained us, really, albeit in a small way, but it's never really waned." Playing together again, the band wrote a lot of new music that drove the idea of a reformation, perhaps as more of an experimental, time-to-time thing. The songs they wrote on that tour would become *Vehicle*, their first official full-length album, an achievement long overdue.

The Dunedin Sound remains a steady interest and source of discovery for music fans. "The main thing that still amazes me is the continued interest from around the world," says Kilgour. "You gotta remember when we first reformed I thought, wow, this will never happen again. It seemed like a dream come true, but a lot has happened since then. I've had a charmed life."

Key Players: The Chills, the Clean, the Enemy, the Great Unwashed, Look Blue Go Purple, Sneaky Feelings, Straitjacket Fits, Tall Dwarfs, the Verlaines

‖‖‖

CROSSOVER TRACKS

‖‖‖

GARAGE ROCK

The Bluestars–"Social End Product," the La De Da's–"All Purpose Low," Ray Columbus and the Invaders–"She's a Mod"

INDIE ROCK

The Apples in Stereo–"Tidal Wave," Elf Power–"Jane," Yo La Tengo–"The Cone of Silence"

PUNK ROCK

Radio Birdman–"Burn My Eye," the Saints–"(I'm) Stranded," the Scientists–"Frantic Romantic"

DRESSING UP

Dark Cabaret, Death Rock, Glam Punk, Gothabilly, Horror Punk, Pirate Metal, Steampunk, Visual Kei, Wizard Rock

DARK CABARET

Is there any better place of origin for a kind of music known as Dark Cabaret than a Halloween party? It was at just such a gathering in 2000 that Amanda Palmer and Brian Viglione met. Palmer was schooled in drama and practiced street theater, and Viglione had been a devotee of heavy metal in his youth.[1] The two soon became the Dresden Dolls and somehow found the thespian punk middle ground between their backgrounds. Profiling the Boston duo in 2006, *The Guardian* observed that, "The band's eponymous 2003 debut sounded as if Sylvia Plath had turned to cabaret; their new album, *Yes, Virginia*, adds a healthy dash of Dorothy Parkeresque black humour, as well as a mighty sonic wallop."[2] Dark cabaret has a fashion sensibility that borrows from goth and between-the-wars burlesque and a sound that can wander from gypsy punk (see "Translations") to folk rock to the tongue-in-cheek Misfits-meets-Pogues approach of long-running London trio the Tiger Lillies.

The shadowy underside of sunny Los Angeles has been an ongoing source of inspiration for a number of LA-noir writers from Nathaniel West to James Ellroy, and the shadow of death was also cast over a segment of that city's punk scene in the late 1970s and early 1980s. "There was a whole death rock scene in Los Angeles," Christian Death leader Valor Kand told the *Dallas Observer* in 2013. "It was really just so many different vibes. You had the punk thing not too far from its heyday. There was an emerging new wave scene. You had that whole melodramatic scene from England with bands like the Cure."[3]

DEATH ROCK

Death Rock in the City of Angels was punk with a dark sensibility that was more aggressive than the typical melancholy of goth and also tinted with a bit of the new rockabilly vibe that was introduced by other LA punk bands like X. As a counterpoint to New York's reigning punk ghouls, the Misfits, the death rock scene offered Christian Death, 45 Grave, and Pompeii 99.[4] The Flesh Eaters, another LA punk band, preceded the death rock scene by a couple of years, but their creepy lyrical subject matter helped set the stage.

GLAM PUNK

Between the glam rock movement started by T. Rex and David Bowie in the early 1970s and the glam metal domination of the 1980s, glam punk arrived in the form of the New York Dolls. Though glam punk was not a recognized genre at the time, the Dolls' first two studio albums—their self-titled debut in 1973 and what became their poignantly titled finale (until they reunited in the 2000s), *Too Much Too Soon*, only a year later—set the template before anyone knew it was needed. Dividing glam's glory years into three separate parts threatens to divert attention from the greater meaning of it all as a whole, but it is worth acknowledging the distinct concept of glam punk for two notable differences: its disheveled, almost "anti-" sense of what glamour could be and its lack of regard for putting serious musicianship first, which distinguished it from prevailing rock trends of the era and presaged punk's reclamation of simplicity.

GOTHABILLY

Another in-between genre is gothabilly. Not simply a third wheel among rockabilly and psychobilly, the most unique characteristic that gothabilly brings to the table is its fashion. "The only difference between psychobilly and gothabilly is that while psychobilly is more aggressive, gothabilly adds aspects of the romantic and paranormal,"[5] helpfully explains one video on the genre produced by *Lost Anarchy Magazine* that can be found on YouTube. It's a small subsection of an already small subculture, but, from Australia's now-defunct Zombie Ghost Train to Swiss band the Hillbilly Moon Explosion to Ghoultown from Dallas, the genre's momentum has managed to sustain itself.

HORROR PUNK

If there's a difference between Horror Punk and death rock, it is in the lack of regional identity that death rock initially had in Los Angeles, and the possibility that underneath it all, just maybe, they are having a bit of fun with all the spooky imagery and lyrics and not taking it too seriously.

It only takes one band to start a genre, and as much as the New York Dolls are responsible for the notion of glam punk, another New York band, the Misfits, are responsible for horror punk. "A punk band wearing corpse paint and singing about collecting the heads of little girls sounds brutal, but the Misfits coated it in poppy harmonies and melodies," says *The Pitchfork 500* about their 1979 song "Night of the Living Dead."[6] Aside from being anything Glenn Danzig has touched, horror punk showed up in more recent years in bands like the on-again-off-again Hollywood band the Murderdolls, who stitched together comically morbid subject matter with a sound and sensibility that bridges the gap between glam and black metal.

PIRATE METAL

Metal musicians are known for having high levels of dedication to their craft, be it mastering ways to shred on the guitar or partying as hard as possible. Such rules don't always apply with Pirate Metal, though. "Dude, I could not tell you a single thing about historical pirates."[7] said Alestorm frontman Christopher Bowes to *Guitar World* back in 2011. All the same, the metal band from Perth, Scotland, found themselves at the forefront of pirate metal with the release of their debut album, *Captain Morgan's Revenge*, in 2008.

It is a fortunate thing that the advent of pirate metal coincided with the rise of YouTube, as it is through Alestorm's numerous music videos, viewed by millions, that the band are best enjoyed. The sight of Bowes alternating between steering a pirate ship through a storm and shredding on his Roland keytar in the video for "Keelhauled" or the band thrashing away on acoustic instruments and pillaging a stately home's prim quiet dinner for all its booze in "Drink" make pirate metal a worthy endeavor.

Pirate metal is the rare metal subgenre where the bands are more concerned with having fun than taking themselves and their image too seriously, yet their musicianship is not in doubt, and their dedication to theme is admirable.

STEAMPUNK

Though it has the word "punk" in it, steampunk is not a subgenre of punk, nor is it even primarily a style of music. Steampunk satisfies a curious modern desire to see 1800s Victorian and Wild West fashion and classic science fiction technology thrown together as a kind of dedicated cosplay. The culture has been reinforced throughout the years by both literature and movies—think the 1999 film *Wild Wild West* starring Will Smith or, before that, *Back to the Future Part III*, with Doc's time-travelling flying steam train at the end.

One band who went all in on steampunk was Seattle group Abney Park, who would mix different kinds of folk music instrumentation with their distorted guitars, reminiscent of gypsy punk but set to more steady, sauntering rhythms. If the affiliation wasn't already established with their string of albums in the late 2000s from *Lost Horizons* to *The End of Days*, it was laid out in detail on "Steampunk Revolution," the opening track from their 2012 album, *Ancient World*. Runner up in the steampunk sweepstakes would surely be

San Diego's robotic Steam Powered Giraffe, who are no less visually arresting but play a gentler, family-friendly style of music.

VISUAL KEI

Going all in is exactly what Visual Kei is all about. Japan's answer to glam rock is the awesome, overstimulating circus one would imagine it to be. Visual kei is not defined by one particular style of music so much as it is defined by dedication to image and dramatic performance. The Gazette, from Kanagawa, play accessible nu metal. BORN made manic pop punk metal. Others make Day-Glo electronicore or goth metal. All of them dress to the elevens in an over-the-top fashion that somehow combines the sensibilities of most of the other genres mentioned in this section.

WIZARD ROCK

Perhaps the oddest costume genre of them all is wizard rock. Unlike pirate metal, wizard rock ("wrock" for short) is not a celebration of wizard life in general, but is purely a side effect of the Harry Potter phenomenon. Norwood, Massachusetts, was the birthplace of wizard rock, where brothers Paul and Joe DeGeorge started Harry and the Potters in 2002, a jangly, charmingly unslick tribute to the world J. K. Rowling created. Every genre's Beatles needs a rival Rolling Stones, of course, and a few years after Harry and the Potters came Draco and the Malfoys from nearby Rhode Island, who play "songs about the Harry Potter stories from Draco Malfoy's Perspective."[8] In 2007, ABC News reported that by then there were "nearly 200 Harry Potter–themed bands—including the Hungarian Horntails, the Whomping Willows and the Remus Lupins."[9] and enough momentum to sustain a Wrockstock festival in Missouri for multiple years in the late 2000s.

DRESSING UP PLAYLIST

DARK CABARET	The Tiger Lillies–"Banging in the Nails" The Dresden Dolls–"Coin-Operated Boy" Katzenjammer Kabarett–"Gemini Girly Song"
DEATH ROCK	Christian Death–"Burnt Offerings" 45 Grave–"Evil" Pompeii 99–"The Nothing Song"
GLAM PUNK	Iggy and the Stooges–"Search and Destroy" The New York Dolls–"Trash" Lou Reed–"N.Y. Stars"
GOTHABILLY	Zombie Ghost Train–"Graveyard Queen" Hillbilly Moon Explosion–"My Love For Evermore" Ghoultown–"Drink with the Living Dead"
HORROR PUNK	The Misfits–"Night of the Living Dead" Samhain–"Horror Biz" Murderdolls–"Dead in Hollywood"
PIRATE METAL	Alestorm–"Captain Morgan's Revenge" Swashbuckle–"Cruise Ship Terror" Lagerstein–"Drink the Rum"
STEAMPUNK	Abney Park–"Airship Pirate" The Men That Will Not Be Blamed For Nothing–"Brunel" Steam Powered Giraffe–"Brass Goggles"
VISUAL KEI	The Gazette–"Filth in the Beauty" BORN–"Demons" An Café–"Escapism"
WIZARD ROCK	Harry and the Potters–"Save Ginny Weasley" Draco and the Malfoys–"My Dad is Rich"

Electric Folk

The acoustic guitar that the United States takes for granted as fundamental to its twentieth-century roots music was barely available in the UK until some time after World War II. Rob Young explains in his book *Electric Eden* that "the ubiquitous image of the folkie strumming an acoustic guitar is an invention of the late 1950s and early 1960s." Before that, the guitar was "practically unknown as an accompaniment to European popular and folk song."[1]

This is an important detail to keep in mind when considering the differences between the American and British approaches to merging folk music and rock and roll. In Britain, the mere presence of a guitar in folk music, even an acoustic one, makes it a kind of folk rock. Electric folk, then, became, and remains, the term by which British folk rock is distinguished from American folk rock. Not all electric folk bands in the UK even incorporated rock and roll into their sound aside from guitars. Drums weren't necessarily prominent, if even present.

In his 2010 memoir, *White Bicycles*, Joe Boyd, the American producer who played a key role in the British folk and psychedelic rock scenes in the 1960s, still sounds awed when describing the rapid rise of Scottish folk benders the Incredible String Band. "The Americans regarded them with amazement. . . . When the third LP, *The Hangman's Beautiful Daughter*, was finished in early 1968, I thought it was the best thing I had produced."[2] Though much more folk than rock, they had legions of admirers in both camps, wooed by their earthy untethered melodies and dazzled by the pan-cultural range of instruments they arranged them with.[3] When they finally did start plugging in and using drums in 1970, their critical and commercial wave had already crested.

In the case of the London collective Fairport Convention, rock music was de-emphasized over the course of their first few records. Their self-titled debut album from 1968 was the most like a conventional rock band they would ever sound. The album that followed in 1969, *What We Did on Our Holidays*, marked the arrival of folk singer Sandy Denny on the spare acoustic opener "Fotheringay." That song's traditional feel signaled the direction they would head on the next two albums, *Unhalfbricking* and *Liege & Lief*, that bookmarked a sadly tumultuous time for them but sealed the reputation the musical institution retains well over twenty albums later.

After *Liege & Lief*, Hutchings would go on to form another revolving ensemble, Steeleye Span, to pursue an even more rustic sound on their 1970 debut, *Hark! The Village Wait*. Here begins the minor subgenre of medieval folk rock, weaving electric guitars and a modern mid-tempo rock rhythm section into folk songs that otherwise might as well have been beamed straight in from the middle ages. Few since Steeleye Span have kept the subgenre going, but Ritchie Blackmore, former guitarist for Deep Purple and Rainbow, went medieval on folk rock as well. In the late 1990s he formed Blackmore's Night with singer Candice Night, who plays multiple Renaissance and woodwind instruments when the band performs.[4] Live, their investment in the concept extends beyond the music to their stage sets and wardrobes. The same goes for the London band Circulus, led by Michael Tyack. The band's dedication to the fashion was a hindrance for years until it became an asset, when they finally found some attention and acclaim in the mid-2000s.[5]

The quintet that made up the group Pentangle included members like singer Jacqui McShee and Scottish guitarist/songwriter Bert Jansch who had established folk credentials, but their Aquarian-age approach to mingling it with jazz and blues was enough to raise the hackles of older purists. "As young heirs to the folk tradition," Young notes, "the Pentangle generation's treatment of British folk tunes was severely scrutinised, and often criticised for what seemed like roughshod trampling on a delicate heritage site."[6] That trampling never turned into a stampede, and mainstream popularity for electric folk proved fleeting by the early- to mid-1970s, though some like Fairport Convention continued to tell the tale.

Key Players: The Incredible String Band, Fairport Convention, Pentangle, Steeleye Span

CROSSOVER TRACKS

FOLK ROCK

Shirley Collins and the Albion Country Band–"Murder of Maria Marten," Strawbs–"Witchwood"

PSYCHEDELIC ROCK

The Byrds–"Renaissance Fair," the Grateful Dead–"Morning Dew"

Electronicore

|||||||||||||||||||||||||||||||||||||||||||||||||||||||||||||||||||||||||||||||||||||||||||||||||||||||||||||

Oh sure, we all had a nice, long laugh back in the summer of 2009 when a band from the deepest, darkest heart of Ohio named Attack Attack! unleashed their video for "Stick Stickly" and thrust "crab-core" into that week's Internet conversation. But you know who wasn't laughing? The children. They took that crap seriously. Or did they? That's the crux—or one of them, anyway—at the core of electronicore. The genre is a kind of bad-faith postmodernism run amok, the stuff of nightmares for people who value an earnest awareness of history.

Electronicore is a nihilist bathtub brew consisting of metalcore's heaviness, fondness for breakdowns, and screaming-to-growling vocals, along with seemingly antithetical electronic pop music elements like synthesizers and auto-tuning. Truly a mouthwatering appraisal, but it's only part of the picture. Electronicore is also defined by an ongoing competition between the bands to create music videos that push the boundaries of absurdism while maintaining a straight face.

"Stick Stickly" set the standard: a three-minute horror movie about a girl who just stares at a rickety old house in a field, presumably the same one in which the band practiced their seam-splitting stances for hours on end. Years later, it is still impossible to tell if the band is in on the joke. After that, the game was on to see which electronicore band could make the most nonsensical tribute film.

Sky Eats Airplane went with *The Shining*-meets-Disney's Haunted Mansion for "Numbers." I See Stars scored some molly and took notes while watching *Game of Thrones* and *The Lord of the Rings*.

Best as of late may be from the English band Enter Shikari, who once upon a time wrote one of the more decent tunes to come out of this whole thing, "Sorry You're Not a Winner." Still, as obvious as it seems that the four members raging on their instruments in a tiny boat lost at sea in a video for a song called "Hoodwinker" would be done for a laugh, it isn't safe to assume anything in the wacky world of electronicore.

Key Tracks: Attack Attack!–"Stick Stickly," Enter Shikari–"Sorry You're Not a Winner," I See Stars–"The Common Hours," Sky Eats Airplane–"Numbers"

CROSSOVER TRACKS

DIGITAL HARDCORE
Atari Teenage Riot–"Sick to Death," EC8OR–"Dynamite"

METALCORE
Bring Me the Horizon–"Pray for Plagues," the Devil Wears Prada–"Hey John, What's Your Name Again?"

NINTENDOCORE
Horse the Band–"Seven Tentacles and Eight Flames," Moshing Samurai–"Betrayer of Divinity"

Emo(core)

On a Saturday night in January 2017, a band called American Football took the stage at Terminal 5 in New York City, a 3,000-capacity concert venue near the Hudson River in the Hell's Kitchen neighborhood. This wouldn't be remarkable, except that the band had, until recently, been inactive since the end of the 1990s, when they recorded a self-titled EP and album that both sold modestly upon release. They were led by Mike Kinsella, who had also been in the influential Chicago band Cap'n Jazz with his older brother Tim.[1]

American Football in their original incarnation played about a dozen shows total and then broke up. Over the years that followed, Kinsella built a career performing under the solo act name Owen, while the two American Football CDs slowly took on a life of their own in the bedrooms and chat rooms of indie rock kids too young to catch them the first time around. Nearly twenty years since first picking up their instruments together, American Football were now revered among a new generation of fans, the most unlikely comeback story in the unlikely comeback story of a rock genre called emo. In the beginning, it was emo*core*, a playful but pointed taunt aimed at a handful of Washington, DC, hardcore bands in 1985: primarily Rites of Spring and Embrace, and a few others like Beefeater, Fire Party, and Grey Matter.[2] "It was the way to say you were doing tough music, but you were a little lighter," says Tom Mullen, archivist and tastemaker for the maligned and misunderstood genre and founder of the *Washed Up Emo* website and podcast. The mark that Rites of Spring and Embrace left on DC's hardcore glory days greatly outsized the mere months they were together. This is because their respective leaders, Guy Picciotto and Ian MacKaye (who had already fronted early 1980s hardcore trailblazers Minor Threat), joined forces in Fugazi, a band that sustained a singular career from the late 1980s to the early 2000s despite undercharging for shows and not selling T-shirts.

The difference between "emo" and "emocore" may seem insignificant, but when the term casually drops the "core," it shrugs off the hardcore and post-hardcore scenes that grounded both the centralized first generation and the decentralized second generation. The semantic tweak symbolized and enabled the opening up of a word that was initially meant to poke fun at hardcore punk songs with sensitive lyrics to encompass the acoustic balladry of Dashboard Confessional, the indie rock of Death Cab for Cutie, and Fall Out Boy's referential song titles. However it's written, it must be said that the term "emocore" has never found much favor among any of the artists tagged with it.

The first generation of emocore was comprised of a handful of hardcore bands. The second generation began to take shape in the early 1990s, parallel to what's now called post-hardcore. Here, Fugazi was an influence, but this time MacKaye and Picciotto managed to dodge the tag. Jawbox and Moss Icon, both from the DC area, and Drive Like Jehu from San Diego, were post-hardcore bands with two-guitar interplay, angular lines, and restless stop-start rhythms that also guided the genre's direction. The second generation had a traceable heritage, but, from Jawbreaker's *Bivouac* to Jimmy Eat World's *Clarity*, its identity in the 1990s wasn't nearly as tidy.

This allowed the audience to step in and define what "emocore" meant to them. "If you are asking about the sound," says Mullen, "to me it's euphoria. It's not a catchy chorus, it's not a breakdown, it's putting it all out there. Emo is music that exudes a sense of tension in the song. There are many sounds of emo depending on the time and place, but the root is a sense of euphoria in the music and a notion that the sound, song, and moment could break apart at any moment and any time." Sunny Day Real Estate, for example, built their reputation on intensity. The Seattle band's 1994 debut album, *Diary*, quickly became a foundational document for emocore (that title alone), and their live shows were received as cathartic experiences, not just entertainment.

The year 1995 was pivotal for emocore. Cap'n Jazz broke up, and Jawbreaker put out *Dear You*, their first major label album and unexpected swansong. From across the United States, debut 7"s, EPs, and albums came from the Promise Ring, Texas is the Reason, Braid, and Mineral, while Christie Front Drive released a venerated split 10" with Boys Life. These bands came from Milwaukee, New York, Illinois, Austin, Denver, and Kansas City, Missouri. Emo had long since left DC and become a national underground concern.

Over the next few years, these bands and others would go from sharing 7" singles to releasing albums that make up the second-wave canon, but a number of them, including Texas is the Reason, Boys Life, and Christie Front Drive, didn't make it to 1998. Even though Christie Front Drive didn't last as long as some of their peers, they were an important pin in the middle of the emo map, singer-guitarist Eric Richter in particular. "Eric was a big catalyst in Colorado," Mullen notes. "Christie Front Drive is why Jimmy Eat World got signed." Mineral broke through with *The Power of Failing* in early 1997 but broke up the following year before their second album, *End Serenading*, even came out. Braid delivered their finest hour, *Frame & Canvas*, in 1998 and then hit the brakes with the "Please Drive Faster" 7" in 1999.

As new bands were sprouting up to take their place, those bigger groups that remained changed up their sound. In 1999, the Get Up Kids took emo to the pop punk prom with *Something to Write Home About*, the Promise Ring got happier with *Very Emergency*, and Jimmy Eat World went widescreen with *Clarity*. Many bands who were considered emo remained recognizable as they moved into new territory, but an unforeseen paradigm shift was soon to occur.

"I call it pre–*Bleed American* and post–*Bleed American*," says Mullen, citing Jimmy Eat World's hit album from 2001 as the platinum hinge on which the fortunes of emo swung. Mullen, who had recently started working at TVT Records, suddenly found he had the ear of higher-ups: "The president's calling me down for a meeting . . . pointing to the CMJ chart, asking me if I know the Casket Lottery and can I help them."

Bleed American's pop sensibilities brought emo, a sound and culture forged in the fire of relentless touring, independent distribution, and fanzine conversation, to an audience that had little conception of any of those things. By 2004, "there was a feeding frenzy for all those kinds of bands," Mullen remembers. "Thursday got signed. Taking Back Sunday got a major label deal. Brand New were on the radio." Most from the second generation barely got a taste of the financial windfall they helped stir up.

This is the point where two different tribes of emo fans start to remember things differently. For middle- and high-school kids who had never heard of Fugazi and found My Chemical Romance's lack of subtlety appealing, these were the glory days. For older fans from the 1990s, they were the wilderness years.

In 2007, Mullen turned to the same place so many others were going to at the time to release their futile anger: Blogger. He had witnessed up close the genre he loved being bent into something else, and he didn't see anyone talking about any of the bands he thought should have been remembered.

As Mullen recalls, a couple of years later a sliver of light finally shone through when, of all things, a friend in Russia who he had met online introduced him to a Russian band that sounded like Mineral. Then he started hearing about new bands like Algernon Cadwallader and Snowing, both from Philadelphia, Pennsylvania, and upstart record labels like Count Your Lucky Stars in Michigan, where others like them were congregating. The music was strikingly familiar.

Around this time, many second-generation bands started to get back together for at least a handful of shows, with some even putting out new records. Between all the old bands who were making the rounds and all the new bands who sounded like the old bands, by 2013 the "emo revival" had become a popular subject on music sites across the Internet.

As all of this was happening, terminology once again got a little tricky. Calling it a "revival" works for the reunion element of it, but it wasn't the most fair thing to call those who were making an emotional racket for the first time. Then there's the recent reclamation of emo in connection with aspects of the third wave that lifers like Mullen would rather forget. He has faith that one day emo will be spoken of with the same sense of validity as indie rock, heavy metal, or jazz, and that the music will be gauged by its entire history, not just the few awkward years it spent in the mainstream eye. Ultimately, though, any path that leads to the good stuff is worth taking. "I get emails every day from someone saying 'I loved so-and-so, now I'm listening to this band, now I get it.' Whatever you did, at least you found out that there's a bigger world. That's when I feel okay."

Pioneer Tracks: Cap'n Jazz–"Oh Messy Life," Embrace–"No More Pain," Jawbreaker–"Chesterfield King," Rites of Spring–"Theme (If I Started Crying)," Sunny Day Real Estate–"In Circles"

Key Players: American Football, Boys Life, Braid, Christie Front Drive, Compound Red, Dashboard Confessional, Ethel Meserve, the Get Up Kids, Hot Water Music, Jimmy Eat World, Knapsack, Mineral, the Promise Ring, Rainer Maria, Texas is the Reason, Vitreous Humor

CROSSOVER TRACKS

ALTERNATIVE ROCK

Buffalo Tom–"Taillights Fade," Catherine Wheel–"Pain," Hum–
"Stars"

POP PUNK

Blink 182–"Emo," New Found Glory–"My Friends Over You,"
Screeching Weasel–*Emo*

POST-HARDCORE

At the Drive In–"Alpha Centauri," Quicksand–"Head to Wall,"
Thursday–"Understanding in a Car Crash"

Ethereal Wave

"Of a lightness, delicacy, or refinement that does not appear to belong to this world"[1] is one of the Oxford English Dictionary's definitions of ethereal, though that description could just as easily have come from an old review of any Cocteau Twins album. Hailing from Grangemouth, Scotland[2], and renowned for guitarist Robin Guthrie's rich, reverb-soaked sound and Elizabeth Fraser's choir-in-tongues voice, the band was stalked throughout their career by the word "ethereal." Their record label, 4AD, was, in its original 1980s incarnation, also never found too far from the adjective.

When it comes to substantial documentation, ethereal wave is as elusive as one might expect. The term's most common and practical application is for people to assure themselves, not unreasonably, that the Cocteau Twins were a bit goth, but not full-on goth. Ethereal wave is a gentler parallel of darkwave. Mood-wise, one might say the distinction between the two is "also sad, but not as upset about it." Really, it's the guitars and production, painstakingly arranged layers of wet spiderwebs, that make the difference. Guthrie was known to play through many guitar effects, and the Cocteau Twins' sound would later be cited as a significant influence on genres like shoegaze and dream pop.

Key Players: Black Tape for a Blue Girl, Cocteau Twins, Lycia, This Mortal Coil

CROSSOVER TRACKS

GOTH ROCK

The Cure–"The Funeral Party," Siouxsie and the Banshees–
"Night Shift"

SHOEGAZE

Pale Saints–"Hair Shoes," Slowdive–"Shine"

Experimental Metal

Brandon Stosuy has a theory as to how younger metal bands sometimes stretch the genre's imagination even in a field where there's a classification for everything. "Someone can have a Tumblr page that has an image from a film they like, and then a band, and then their own picture, and some weird quote. It's this nonlinear kind of thing, but it's also often just people pulling from a lot of different areas. I think a lot of music, some metal music being made by younger people now, often feels like a Tumblr page to me. There'll be clean vocals, but then also more grindcore vocals. The music is kind of heavy, but there's a ska part."

Inventing "ska-grind" is but one way to be experimental in metal. Another more tried-and-true way is to absorb lessons from traditional and classical music. A more contrarian way would be to find the value in records that have been written off by the mainstream. For his new band, Pillorian, John Haughm has gone both ways. "Many people are shocked when I say that I am more influenced by '80s–'90s era Rush than their '70s work," he says. "Also, most of the guitar harmonies I write for Pillorian are influenced directly by choral music; especially Arvo Pärt, Veljo Tormis, and Le Mystère des voix Bulgares. That might surprise some people." Each step along the way in the growth of heavy metal was at one point an experiment, but metal was taken to more and more out-there places since it splintered into many subgenres in the 1980s and 1990s.

Key Players: Agalloch, Boris, Fantomas, Kayo Dot, Maudlin of the Well, Meshuggah, Mr. Bungle, Neurosis, Sleepytime Gorilla Museum, Voivod

CROSSOVER GENRES

EXPERIMENTAL ROCK
Butthole Surfers, Primus

PROGRESSIVE METAL
Baroness, Mastodon

Experimental Rock

The period from *Revolver* to *Magical Mystery Tour* was an especially experimental one for the Beatles, as Mark Hertsgaard recounts in *A Day in the Life*. They would record acoustic guitars to sound like electric guitars, play cymbal tracks in reverse, and record drums in hallways. John Lennon once sang through "a plastic bag-encased microphone inside a milk bottle filled with water"[1] to give his vocals an unusual quality. On "Lovely Rita," the *Sgt. Pepper's* tune, "Many of the incidental noises on the song were produced by blowing on combs covered with toilet paper."[2]

Experimental rock is a vast and smoky arena in which rock bands play or even create their own nontraditional instruments and bend the rules of whatever genre—or, even better, *multiple* genres—they are working in. In fact, most rock genres of the 1960s were born out of such tinkering. *Highway 61 Revisited* was the vinegar-and-baking-soda volcano of folk rock. Psychedelic rock, progressive rock, and heavy metal were defined by their experimentation with established, but still relatively new, parameters. As a label, it works nicely because you can swap it out for a number of tags that artists aren't fond of (i.e., post-rock), and it doesn't draw nearly the same amount of ire.

Experimental rock involves any combination of disobeying verse-chorus structure; writing songs that are longer than six minutes; making prominent use of instruments other than guitar, bass, and drums (though keyboards don't count as "experimental" anymore, unless they sound awful); and believing that the Velvet Underground were more important than the Rolling Stones.

Key Players: Animal Collective, the Beatles, Butthole Surfers, the Residents, Silver Apples, Soft Machine, Sonic Youth, This Heat, the Velvet Underground, Frank Zappa

CROSSOVER GENRES

KRAUTROCK
Can, Faust

POST-ROCK
Bark Psychosis, Disco Inferno

PROGRESSIVE ROCK
Henry Cow, King Crimson

Folk Metal

The first stirrings of folk metal came from England and Ireland. Skyclad were a heavy metal band from Newcastle that began their journey in a time when thrash was king. Their 1991 debut, *The Wayward Sons of Mother Earth*, had songs that harked back to pagans and jigs, images of "Moongleam and Meadowsweet," but it was with subsequent albums that folk really began to dance around the fire with metal, introducing instrumentation like pipe and fiddle to give authenticity to the themes and vocal styles they were exploring.

Dublin band Cruachan were watching and decided to weave their own native folklore into black metal on their 1995 debut, *Tuatha na Gael*. Cruachan's music is where the terms "folk metal" and "Celtic metal" intersect, though the "folk" in folk metal isn't limited to Ireland as Celtic metal is. By the 2000s, Northern Europe, Scandinavia in particular, had become the focal point for folk metal. Scandinavian metal's fondness for pre-Christian history had already been well established with black metal. There, too, comes the terminological conflation between folk metal and viking metal.

The folk metal tag followed Portland, Oregon, band Agalloch around from their first album, *Pale Folklore*, which came out in 1999. John Haughm says he still likes a few neofolk bands such as Naervaer from Norway and Michael Cashmore's groups Current 93 and Nature and Organisation, but he is no longer as interested in the genre—a kind of ambient-industrial music anchored by folk instrumentation—as he was in the 1990s and 2000s. Given Agalloch's eclectic sound, most associations with subgenres made sense, but folk metal was the only label that bothered him. "Agalloch was never, ever a fucking folk metal band!"

Key Players: Amorphis, Cruachan, Eluveitie, Finntroll, Heidevolk, Korpiklaani, Skyclad, Subway to Sally

||||||||||||||||||||||||||||||||||||||||||||||||||||||||||||||||||||||||||

CROSSOVER GENRES

||||||||||||||||||||||||||||||||||||||||||||||||||||||||||||||||||||||||||

CELTIC METAL
Primordial, Waylander

VIKING METAL
Amon Amarth, Ásmegin

Folk Punk

The sight of a punk rocker strapping on an acoustic guitar in the 1990s usually meant that a dose of social criticism laced with poignant humor was about to be injected into the room. Playing punk rock solo on an acoustic guitar removes the distortion, but not the passion. The ease of access to a single beaten-up fifty-dollar guitar versus a full band setup also fits in with punk's DIY, "anyone can do it" spirit.

The other side of the genre goes one step further than just playing punk on acoustic instruments and folds the sounds and signifiers of traditional folk music into punk rock. Sitting at the head of that table is the Pogues with their groundbreaking early records like *Rum Sodomy & the Lash*, and Shane MacGowan's clan also heralded the arrival of Celtic punk. Feeling the fiddle but updating the energy and production values are artists like England's Frank Turner or the emo-gone-Americana solo material from Chuck Ragan of Hot Water Music. Intriguing new variations can be heard in groups like Brooklyn's Cult of Youth, who mix folk and punk with a harsher, gothic outlook.

Key Players: Against Me!, Billy Bragg, Cult of Youth, O'Death, Jeff Ott (Crimpshrine, Fifteen), the Pogues, Chuck Ragan, Frank Turner, Violent Femmes

CROSSOVER TRACKS

INDIE FOLK

The Mountain Goats–"No Children," Neutral Milk Hotel–"Holland, 1945"

POP PUNK

Alkaline Trio–*Damnesia*, Green Day–"Good Riddance (Time of Your Life)"

Folk Rock

The image that modern folk rock—"indie folk," as it is now often called—wears is one of getting back to roots. For the musicians who came up with folk rock in the mid-1960s, however, rock and roll was the root they were returning to. Bob Dylan was folk before he went electric, but he was also rock before he went folk, an avowed admirer of Little Richard, Carl Perkins, and Elvis in his high-school days in Minnesota[1], before Woody Guthrie became his hero.

Turning to rock music wasn't actually the cool thing to do at the time. Rock and roll was seen to have gone soft by the end of the 1950s and was no longer the fuel for teenage rebellion it had once been. The folk revival of the early 1960s looks almost quaint from today's distance, but it was, in fact, edgy at the time. As Richie Unterberger writes, "Those raised in subsequent generations of sensory overload may find it hard to comprehend that quiet acoustic folk, which sounds so tame to many twenty-first century listeners, was once considered the counter-cultural music."[2]

The drama of the 1965 Newport Folk Festival gets played up, but the symbolism of Bob Dylan's big folk rock reveal in a set of only three songs is undoubtedly significant. It didn't come without warning, though. Over a month before Dylan and his band took the stage on July 25 in Rhode Island, *Billboard* ran a cover story titled "Folkswinging Wave On—Courtesy of Rock Groups," which covered Dylan, the Byrds, the Animals, the Lovin' Spoonful, the Rising Sons (which featured Ry Cooder and Taj Mahal), the Nashville Teens (who were not from Nashville, but Surrey, England), Sonny

& Cher, and others. In it, Elliot Tiegel used the term "folk-rock" numerous times,[3] a label that Dylan, the Byrds' Roger McGuinn, and others rejected almost immediately.[4] Sonny & Cher, however, latched on to the hype with Sonny Bono's own term, "Folk & Roll," to the chagrin of those who would have rather seen the term "folk rock" go away.[5] Though using such a label risked pigeonholing artists, it was easy enough to see that, after a fallow season of crooners, folk rock was the best shot America had at recapturing its rock-and-roll crown from Britain's beat boom.

Besides, the two at the top of it all, Dylan and the Byrds, were too restless to get stuck in one mode for long. Between the folkie Dylan picking up an electric guitar and the Byrds playing his folk songs with electric instruments, an entire new rock genre had been born, and the two of them would essentially repeat the trick a few years later when their separate journeys both led them to country music. Folk rock may have been partly a creation of hype, but the Byrds, the Lovin' Spoonful, Donovan, and others became stars because fans were ready for what they were doing.

Folk rock also proved to be an important phase of growth for rock music, its first major step toward maturity after years of party tunes and silly love songs. Folk had something important to say, and rock and roll had a huge audience. Still, as much as the folk side of the bargain allowed rock and roll to carry a message, the rock side allowed folk to have fun if it wanted to. It wouldn't last long. As Unterberger points out, "Though still generating headlines and heated debates at the outset of the year, by the end of 1966, folk rock as a phrase had passed out of wide usage."[6]

Folk rock began with the Byrds playing folk songs with rock instruments and wound up being more about playing rock and pop songs with folk (i.e., acoustic) instruments. It also came from two distinct places, springing from two distinct traditions, and developing two distinct sounds and energies. No matter such dualities, the popular perception of folk rock is now narrowed down to Mumford & Sons.

It has been a long time since anyone has flinched at the idea of polluting folk's purity with rock and roll.

As for the revival of folk rock, or indie folk, in this new century, it's hard to imagine a movie soundtrack having a major impact on a whole genre, but the *O Brother, Where Art Thou?* soundtrack, which stuck "I Am a Man of Constant Sorrow" into millions of American brains everywhere in 2001, created a weird period of musical flux. "You had all these weird things happening there for a while," says Kim Ruehl, "where people were starting these twelve-member 'orchestral folk' bands and people who would have, five years earlier, been in the hardcore punk scene were instead discovering old-time music."

She points to the Northwest United States as a melting pot of rootsy music in the 2000s, first with the Decemberists from Portland and then Fleet Foxes from the Seattle area. Then came the wild popularity of Mumford & Sons, as well as others like Sufjan Stevens and Bon Iver. "After Mumford hit, people started moving to Denver and Boulder and doing exciting things with bluegrass instruments and jam band traditions. Now, things have kind of settled back down again, and there's more creativity happening again."

Pioneer Tracks: The Animals—"The House of the Rising Sun," the Byrds—"Mr. Tambourine Man," Bob Dylan—"Subterranean Homesick Blues," the Lovin' Spoonful—"Do You Believe in Magic?"

Key Players: Buffalo Springfield, Crosby, Stills & Nash, Donovan, Fairport Convention, the Mamas and the Papas, the Nashville Teens, Pentangle, Simon & Garfunkel, Sonny & Cher

CROSSOVER TRACKS

COUNTRY ROCK

The Civil Wars–*Barton Hollow*, Poco–*Pickin' Up the Pieces*, Pure Prairie League–*Pure Prairie League*

INDIE FOLK

Great Lake Swimmers–*Ongiara*, Iron & Wine–*The Shepherd's Dog*, Mumford & Sons–*Sigh No More*

PROGRESSIVE ROCK

Gryphon–*Red Queen to Gryphon Three*, Jethro Tull–*Songs from the Wood*, Strawbs–*From the Witchwood*

Freak Folk

America's folk rock and Britain's electric folk were both commercial and artistic successes in the mid- to late-1960s, the only catch being that their success was as quick to fizzle out as it was to spark up. Electric folk dissipated, and folk rock wandered into Laurel Canyon and acquired a Californian country rock accent. Psychedelic folk slipped underground, but, as writer Jeanette Leech shows in her thorough history of the genre, *Seasons They Change*, the spirit stayed alive in corners far removed from the mainstream. Certain indie-level folk artists and groups began to gain recognition in the alternative-minded 1990s, which in turn inspired others to pick up acoustic instruments and get a little weird.

The artists eventually labeled with "freak folk" were not the oddest of the bunch. By the time the term came into use, this new generation of psychedelic folk music was bringing more notoriety to the style than it had received in a long time. If anything, what made those in the scene freaks among other folk wanderers of recent years was how popular their music became. Those who read websites like Pitchfork regularly between, say, 2003 and 2005, will remember the big names well: Animal Collective, Devendra Banhart (a prominent connector in the scene), Joanna Newsom, CocoRosie, Vetiver, and Akron/Family.

"Freak folk has an unclear etymology," writes Leech. "It is likely a bastardisation of free folk; for a short time, the two terms were used somewhat interchangeably. Yet by 2006, the term 'free folk' was no longer in mainstream use. Others were bandied about—alt-folk, nu folk . . . avant folk—but freak folk was the name that endured for progressive or psychedelic acoustic-based music."[1] The wide integration of acoustic and folk sounds into indie rock that was happening around this time meant that freak folk faced a more receptive audience in the mid-2000s than it would have even a few years before. Musically, its relationship to rock was about as peripheral as with any era of psychedelic folk over the years, being most tangibly one of formative influence, except that as some of the artists moved away from freak folk, they began incorporating more rock-oriented instrumentation and structure into their sound.

Animal Collective picked a fortuitous moment to explore their folk side with *Sung Tongs* and the *Prospect Hummer* EP, the latter of which they recorded with the patron saint of freak folk, British songwriter Vashti Bunyan (also a friend of Banhart). In 2005, as Bunyan came out with *Lookaftering* after nearly thirty years of self-imposed retirement, Animal Collective plugged back in on *Feels*. Banhart headed in a more folk rock direction with *What Will We Be* in 2009. Vetiver's album from that same year, *Tight Knit*, had a country rock energy. Brooklyn bands Akron/Family and Grizzly Bear had been an awkward fit for the freak-folk box, and their respective second albums in 2006, *Meek Warrior* and *Yellow House*, would have made further attempts to put them in it more futile had the term not already fallen out of popular use by that point.

Pioneer Tracks: Vashti Bunyan—"Rose Hip November," Comus—"Diana," the Holy Modal Rounders—"Mobile Line," the Incredible String Band—"The Hedgehog's Song," Tyrannosaurus Rex—"Hippy Gumbo"

Key Players: Akron/Family, Animal Collective (*Prospect Hummer* EP and *Sung Tongs*), Devendra Banhart, Brightblack Morning Light, CocoRosie, Espers, Joanna Newsom (*The Milk-Eyed Mender*), Vetiver

CROSSOVER TRACKS

INDIE FOLK

Beirut–"Postcards from Italy," the Dodos–"Horny Hippies," Mount Eerie–"Grave Robbers"

INDIE ROCK

Deer Tick–"Art Isn't Real (City of Sin)," Grizzly Bear–"Deep Sea Diver," Thao & the Get Down Stay Down–"Bag of Hammers"

Freakbeat

The term "freakbeat" is used to describe certain psychedelic rock bands from the 1960s, though no one called it that at the time.[1] Credited with its coining is Philip Lloyd-Smee, who founded the Bam-Caruso label in 1983, which focused on releasing psychedelic and garage rock records.[2] This rip in the rock fabric of the swinging 1960s in the UK and Europe may or may not have been crying out for a new name to distinguish it from those two genres, but it does bring some deserved attention to bands like the Move and the Sorrows, who have often been overshadowed by their more famous contemporaries.

Key Players: The Creation, the Eyes, the Move, the Sorrows

CROSSOVER GENRES

MOD
The Action, the Faces

PSYCHEDELIC ROCK
The 13th Floor Elevators, Shocking Blue

Funk Metal

||||||||||||||||||||||||||||||||||||||||||||||||||||||||||||||||||||||||||||||||||||||||||||||||||||||||||||||||||||||

Born in the Reagan era, funk metal is the gnarly, Body Glove–and-Zubaz-wearing cousin of funk rock. As far as the term goes, *Nu-Metal* author Joel McIver is pretty much on point calling it "a slightly clumsy term applied in the late Eighties to any rock band whose bass player used a slapping style."[1]

Because the Red Hot Chili Peppers mellowed out at the end of the 1990s with *Californication*, it's almost easy to forget that in their early days they were at the vanguard of funk metal. Their self-titled debut album remains an intriguing period piece. The record's unlikely producer, Andy Gill from Gang of Four, gave the band's California party rock a wiry coat of Northern England post-punk anti-polish. Because of this, the album version of "Baby Appeal" answers a question on nobody's mind: What would a mash-up of Joy Division's *Unknown Pleasures* and early 1980s rap sound like?

Funk metal got a shot in the arm with the 1988 release of Living Colour's breakout debut album, *Vivid*. The production dates it a bit, but not as much as some other funk metal discs, and it remains pretty badass. Funk was one of a handful of genres with which Living Colour built their eclectic sound, but its presence was strong enough to spot a connection with the Chili Peppers, Faith No More, and other funk metallers who, as McIver noted, "ranged from the credible, such as Infectious Grooves (a side project of hardcore punks Suicidal Tendencies), to the abysmal, with the Dan Reed Network a best-forgotten example."[2] That judgement might be a little too fair to Infectious Grooves and a bit too harsh on the Dan Reed Network, but at least it puts them both in the conversation.

Key Players: 24-7 Spyz, Faith No More, Infectious Grooves, Living Colour, Mr. Bungle, Rage Against the Machine, Red Hot Chili Peppers

CROSSOVER GENRES

ALTERNATIVE ROCK
311, Incubus

NU METAL
Alien Ant Farm, Korn

Funk Rock

"Somewhere along the way it became clear to me that we had a strong young group of players who were, to us, what the Funk Brothers were to Motown," George Clinton recounts in his memoir about the early days of Funkadelic, "and because we were so deep into psychedelic rock, we started adding the *-delic* to it. . . . White groups had done the blues, and we wanted to head back in the other direction, to be a black rock group playing the loudest, funkiest combination of psychedelic rock and thunderous R&B."[1] There was significant overlap between funk music and rock music in the late 1960s and early 1970s, when funk was coming into its own. So much so that pulling out the parts of it that would be "funk rock" might not be as relevant when considering the first funk voyagers like Sly and the Family Stone and Parliament-Funkadelic, as their earlier records (which are also sometimes classified as psychedelic soul) had a restless foot planted on both sides of the zigzagging line.

Funk didn't remove rock music instrumentation, but it did de-emphasize it and rearrange the pecking order. All those cliched drummer and bass player jokes in rock and roll go out the window with funk. The beat comes first. Built on James Brown's pioneering downbeat, funk's foundation is the groove, and without it the music wouldn't be what it is. As the rhythm section leads the way, the bass guides people's feet. The guitars are still significant, but they spend a lot of time following the rhythm, while keyboards and horns are also given melodic responsibilities.

As funk developed into its own thing, "funk rock" became a way to identify rock bands who were feeling funk's vibe. Some big names borrowed it for a song or two: David Bowie had "Fame," Aerosmith offered "Last Child," and the Rolling Stones came up with the weak "Hot Stuff" and the better "Fingerprint File." For others, like Mother's Finest from Atlanta, Georgia, and Wild Cherry from Ohio, it was a mode they operated in more regularly, though the single genre distinction doesn't capture their range. It certainly didn't capture Prince's range. Funk and rock were both important tools at his disposal, but even early songs like "I Wanna Be Your Lover" aren't as straightforward as they sound at first.

The term did capture what two Los Angeles bands were up to in the 1980s: Fishbone and the aforementioned Red Hot Chili Peppers (who had just enough edge to get called "funk metal" as well). In their early days, both bands actually did something of a service to funk, keeping its flame alight even as the major players and audiences of the 1970s had moved on. Fishbone were also equally enamored with ska, and their first single, "Party at Ground Zero," was the first effective American response to 2 Tone and remains one of their calling cards. Their 1986 debut album, *In Your Face*, bounced back and forth between funk rock and ska, with the two sometimes colliding.

Pioneer Tracks: Funkadelic–"I'll Bet You," Mother's Finest–"Give You All the Love (Inside of Me)," Sly and the Family Stone–"Everyday People," Eric Burdon & War–"Spill the Wine"

Key Players: George Clinton (Parliament, Parliament-Funkadelic), Faith No More, Fishbone, Living Colour, Rage Against the Machine, Red Hot Chili Peppers

CROSSOVER TRACKS

FUNK METAL
Extreme–"Get the Funk Out," Jane's Addiction–"Pigs in Zen"

HARD ROCK
Aerosmith–"Last Child," the Rolling Stones–"Fingerprint File"

NEW WAVE
Ian Dury and the Blockheads–"Sex & Drugs & Rock & Roll,"
Talking Heads–"I Zimbra"

Garage Punk

|||||||||||||||||||||||||||||||||||||||||||||||||||||||||||||||||||||||||||||||||||||||||||||||||||||||||||||||||||||||

A minor taxonomic crisis has been inching up through the dirt of rock terminology that has gone mostly unaddressed. That is, if we continue to rebrand 1960s bands like the Sonics and the Seeds as garage *punk*, what will be left for garage *rock* to call its own?

The use of the term "garage punk"[1] has been traced as far back as the early 1970s (which would put another wrinkle in the timeline of when and how the term "punk" came into use), but it is probably most helpful as a way to delineate between the original garage rock of the 1960s and the later collision of the punk aesthetic with garage's inherent primitivism. It is, for instance, a fair enough way to describe Portland, Oregon, punk trailblazers the Wipers and their first trio of albums, *Is This Real?*, *Youth of America*, and *Over the Edge*. Even more apt is its use in discussing bands from the garage rock revival of the late 1990s who couldn't help but have punk's legacy twisted up in their DNA.

It does not help the current situation, however, to up and take bands like the Electric Prunes and the Litter away from garage rock.[2] If the genre can no longer claim "I Had Too Much to Dream Last Night" and "Action Woman" among its accomplishments, what will be the next to go, and where does it all end? A hundred cover versions of "Louie Louie" playing on shuffle for eternity? Don't even think about taking that one away from garage rock.

Key Players: Dead Moon, Guitar Wolf, New Bomb Turks, Oblivians, Jay Reatard, Ty Segall, Thee Oh Sees, the Wipers

CROSSOVER GENRES

GARAGE ROCK
The Monks, the Sonics

GARAGE ROCK REVIVAL
The Dirtbombs, the Hives

PUNK ROCK (2000s)
The Catheters, Hot Snakes

Garage Rock

Garage rock was an amateur second wave of rock and roll that came in the early 1960s when the music was viewed by some as a fad that had run its course. It is romantic to think that a bunch of impassioned teenagers in different corners of the United States took it upon themselves to rush downstairs to their parents' garages and save rock and roll from an untimely death at the hands of 1960s teenybopper pop singers, yet to some extent that is actually what they did.

"Given that the greatest garage bands could barely play," writes notable garage rock advocate Lester Bangs, "we may assume not only that virtuosity has nothing to do with the form, but also that the utopian dream of everyman [sic] an artist can come true right here, in our suburban land of opportunity—the ultimate proof that rock & roll is the most democratic and all-American of art forms."[1] Garage rock is defined by aspiration, not achievement; not the dream come true but the dream itself. To polish it would be to deface it.

Case in point is "Louie Louie," garage rock's best-known classic. Richard Berry wrote and released the R&B original in 1957, but a few years later, it became a staple of the Pacific Northwest's burgeoning garage rock scene. Most every local band of note would record a cover of it at some point. Rockin' Robin Roberts and the Tacoma, Washington, group the Wailers (also known as the Fabulous Wailers) were the first to have a regional hit with it in 1961—and again briefly in 1962 when Seattle hosted the World's Fair. Then in 1963, two bands based in Portland, Oregon, Paul Revere and the Raiders and the Kingsmen, simultaneously released their own versions. Paul

Revere and the Raiders came out ahead first with a major label record deal, but it is the Kingsmen's belovedly inscrutable rendition that eventually stood out and stood the test of time.[2]

Aside from the unabashed amateurism, many have since noted that garage rock, particularly that which came from Cascadia—such as the Sonics, who formed in Tacoma in 1963—was also notable for its pre-punk aggression. In his book, *Rock and the Pop Narcotic*, Joe Carducci writes that such bands were "less pop in intent"[3] than was usual for the time. "Their music, though a dance music, typically possessed a psychotic male perspective and this led the sound towards a tougher, sardonic approach."[4]

In the second half of the 1960s, garage rock turned on as the fuzz box and wah-wah pedal became standard, as did dropping acid. The 13th Floor Elevators, one of the first psychedelic rock bands, but whose sound was also garage-born, even had an electric jug. Saginaw, Michigan, group ? and the Mysterians were out-there, but played it straight enough to score an early hit single with "96 Tears." Garage rock also spread as it matured, with notable scenes in Los Angeles, Minneapolis, Chicago, and Michigan, where the more potent presence of MC5 and the Stooges led these two bands to later be characterized, like the Sonics, as a precursor to punk rock.

"I'd be remiss if I didn't mention the *Nuggets* compilation that originally came out in the early seventies, which compiled all of what at that time were considered real rarities," says JJ Wandler, cofounder of the Seattle-based punk reissue label Sinister Torch Records. *Nuggets* was compiled by writer and musician Lenny Kaye for Elektra Records in 1972, not long before he started playing regularly with the Patti Smith Group. The double album highlighted a couple dozen bands including The 13th Floor Elevators, Count Five, the Seeds, and the Electric Prunes and is credited with both preserving garage rock's legacy and kick-starting punk.

Punk-rock bands in the 1970s were the first to go back and mine garage rock. "The Cramps were doing covers of songs that were only ten or fifteen years old," Wandler says, "but they were just making them their own and throwing in some rockabilly. In the eighties it seemed like the UK discovered garage rock: Thee Milkshakes, the Guana Batz." Japanese garage rockers Guitar Wolf have been going since the late 1980s, and, well before them the Spiders, from Tokyo in the 1960s, had a bit of garage rock's rough edge on some of their tracks as well. "Japan mined garage rock pretty heavily, and they loved when those bands came through. They were treated like royalty." Australia, too, has a rich garage rock legacy that includes the Saints, the Scientists, Radio Birdman, the Dagoes, and more.

Garage rock transcends borders as well as the 1960s, ebbing and flowing in popularity every decade since. "There's stuff in every country," Wandler says. "I've heard 'Paint It Black' by the Rolling Stones a hundred times, but when a Spanish garage rock band is doing it, it makes it seem fresh again."

Pioneer Tracks: Cannibal and the Headhunters–"Land of 1000 Dances," Paul Revere and the Raiders–"Steppin' Out," the Pretty Things–"Don't Bring Me Down," Rockin' Robin Roberts with the Wailers–"Louie Louie," the Sonics–"The Witch"

Key Players: The 13th Floor Elevators, the Chessmen, Count Five, the Electric Prunes, the Kingsmen, ? and the Mysterians, the Seeds, Them, the Troggs

CROSSOVER TRACKS

GARAGE ROCK REVIVAL

The Dirtbombs–"Stuck in Thee Garage," the Makers–"(Are You on the Inside or the Outside of Your) Pants?," the White Stripes–"You're Pretty Good Looking (For a Girl)"

LO-FI ROCK

Guided by Voices–"Wished I Was a Giant," Sebadoh–"Magnet's Coil"

PUNK ROCK

The Cramps–"Strychnine" (the Sonics), Patti Smith–"Gloria" (Them)

Garage Rock Revival

The Motor City has been one of America's most reliable music manufacturers since its population peaked in the 1950s. No single sound defines Detroit; it was as much "Motown" as "Detroit Rock City" in the 1960s and 1970s. In the 1980s, it moved into groundbreaking techno. In the late 1990s, Eminem became a widely recognized face of its hip-hop scenes, but Detroit's rock reputation was soon revitalized by a collection of bands who brought its garage rock past into the present.

Detroit garage rock was pulled back above ground when the White Stripes toured with Sleater-Kinney in the fall of 2000, shortly after the release of the Stripes' second album, *De Stijl*. "That was when people were calling me and saying, 'What's going on? What is this? Who else do I need to pay attention to?'" remembers Melissa Giannini, former editor in chief at *Nylon* magazine, who was then the new music writer with the *Detroit Metro Times*. "It was like it had sort of woken them up. My phone was starting to ring off the hook with people from New York and everywhere wanting to know more about what was happening in Detroit in that scene." First, it was friends and colleagues curious about the White Stripes, then it was talent scouts looking for recommendations of other bands to check out. Suddenly, Giannini had an active role in the Next Big Thing.

What came to be recognized as the garage rock revival of the early 2000s reached around the globe, from the Hives in Sweden to the Datsuns in New Zealand, but Detroit, home to the White Stripes, the Dirtbombs, the Von Bondies, the Detroit Cobras, and others, was the epicenter. There was a unique dynamic in the scene that made it both creatively open-minded and protective of its legacy. "I always said that the Great Lakes were like this moat that separated us from the rest of the country," says Giannini. "Detroit was a city that was cognizant and respectful of its history, the people there, because the history was so rich. There was a rich garage rock scene in the '60s, but then also this proto-punk scene with the Stooges and MC5, and more obscure bands like Death." In the 1990s and early 2000s, when Detroit was down and out in the public eye, "there was this wistful memory of back in the day when things were cool."

Legacy is meaningful in Detroit, and legacies were carried from band to band as well. From the mid-1980s to the early 1990s, a band called the Gories carried the torch for Detroit garage rock. That trio featured both Mick Collins and Dan Kroha, who would respectively go on to form the Dirtbombs and the Demolition Doll Rods when the Gories split. The 1990s also brought important reissues, including Rhino Records' CD reissue of the famous *Nuggets* compilation in 1998. Before that, in 1994 came a personal favorite of Giannini's, *The History of Michigan Garage Bands in the '60s Volume 1: The Wheels 4 Label Story*, which focused on the small Dearborn-based label. "It was going on for a good decade before it really blew up, and no one cared," says Giannini of the garage rock revival.

Momentum was already building in the late 1990s. From record labels like Sympathy for the Record Industry in California and Estrus Records in Bellingham, Washington, to bands like the Makers in Spokane and the Mooney Suzuki in New York City, garage rock was staging a coast-to-coast comeback, but the moment in Detroit was still unique.

"It was a fertile, collaborative, loose time where everyone was in each other's bands," remembers Giannini. "Everyone was broke, but no one cared because you were having a good time. Expenses were very low. Everyone just wore Mod things that they found from the Salvation Army, and you ate and drank at the restaurants and bars where your friends worked, and rent was cheap. Everyone rented these big old houses, and there was a lot of space to practice. . . . The houses were big, old, and drafty so a lot of times your biggest expense was heating bills, and then car insurance was kind of a gouge because break-ins were common." Giannini recalls that the Club, the classic anti-car-theft device, was something everyone had back then.

Fame was actually something to downplay. Patti Smith and Fred "Sonic" Smith raised their kids in nearby St. Clair Shores, and everyone let them be. Rodriguez, the 1970s songwriter whose story was told in the *Searching for Sugar Man* documentary in 2012, would show up to see Monster Island—a band featuring Carrie Lauren from the 1970s proto-punk band Destroy All Monsters—play at a tiny gallery, and no one would make a fuss about it. "With Jack and Meg [of the White Stripes]," says Giannini, "they could go out to the bar like regular humans, and that was around when they started getting a lot of attention, but if they were to go to New York, they would be swarmed."

Indeed, some of Giannini's friends in New York who were working at places like Spin started calling her to ask, "What's up with this brother and sister?" Giannini didn't give up the secret, finding the White Stripes' manufactured sibling backstory in their early days fun to play along with. A wrinkle came up, however, when she did a cover story on them for the *Metro Times* around the release of their third album, *White Blood Cells*, and, keeping with journalistic integrity, mentioned in a parenthetical that they were formerly married. "He was actually very cool about it, but it wasn't until *Time* magazine found their marriage certificate . . . that sort of blew their cover" she says of *Time*'s "White Lies and the White Stripes" story that came out in June of 2001, a few weeks after her own.[1]

Once the press came flocking, they stuck around, and it wasn't just folks from New York. "I feel like the British press was obsessed with [the] garage rock revival more so than the rest of the country," says Giannini. "I remember any time I would see one of the Detroit bands . . . I'd be sitting down at the table with them, and there would be some guy with a British accent just hanging out. He was probably some reporter doing a story." The garage rock revival was in full swing everywhere by 2002. At that year's MTV Video Music Awards, the White Stripes' LEGO-riffic video for "Fell in Love with a Girl" won multiple awards, and hosts Jimmy Fallon and Kirsten Dunst introduced a miniature battle of the bands between the Hives and the Vines.

By 2006, the scene in Detroit was still going, but it didn't feel as much like the living, breathing thing that it was earlier in the decade. "It was goofy; everyone was just having a good time enjoying themselves. Then when people started paying attention, it got kind of dark: the fist fights, different lawsuits, and things. . . . You know, that little glorious moment in the late '90s and early '00s was really beautiful."

Pioneers: The Demolition Doll Rods, Gas Huffer, the Gories, Thee Headcoats, the Makers, the Mono Men

Key Players: The Black Keys, the Datsuns, the Detroit Cobras, the Dirtbombs, Electric Six, the Fratellis, the Hives, the Mooney Suzuki, the Strokes, the Von Bondies, the White Stripes

CROSSOVER TRACKS

GARAGE ROCK

The Monks–"I Hate You," the Pleasure Seekers–"What a Way To Die"

POST-PUNK REVIVAL

Hot Hot Heat–"Bandages," the Libertines–"Up the Bracket"

PROTO-PUNK (DETROIT)

MC5–"Ramblin' Rose," the Stooges–"Not Right"

Glam Metal

"Our early shows were ridiculous," writes Mötley Crüe drummer Tommy Lee in *Tommyland*. "We had alcohol-burning funny cars, fake blood, mannequin heads, and any other cheap horror props we could think of that would freak people out. We'd walk around all the time, in stiletto heels with makeup on looking like chicks, so we got in fights with people just about everywhere we went. We used to set Nikki on fire while he played his bass by rubbing pyro gel on his legs that Vince would light with a torched sword."[1]

Now synonymous with every ill and indulgence that hair metal havoc wreaked on America in the 1980s, Mötley Crüe had to begin somewhere, and there was nowhere else they could have come from but Los Angeles. Not only did the city have a burgeoning heavy metal scene that needed focus, but, as befitted the great bastion of superficiality, it also had a history with 1970s glam rock. Los Angeles didn't produce many of its own glam bands in the original era, but it did have Rodney Bingenheimer's English Disco, clubhouse to a dedicated cadre of glam fans and groupies until it closed in 1975. That was around the same time that a teenage Nikki Sixx, future founder of the Crüe, rolled into town.

They weren't the only heavy metal band who had found appeal in glam's flash and bang. Twisted Sister were a bridge between UK glam rock and the electrocuted Barbie dolls of Sunset Strip. They came together in the mid-1970s, a bit late for the original scene. Had they thrown in the towel, they also might have been too early for glam metal. Their perseverance paid off with a record deal just in time for the arrival of MTV, where they always belonged.

On the surface, glam metal's attraction to costumes, makeup, and stage props might have appeared more in debt to the shock of Alice Cooper than the subversion of David Bowie, but underneath the heavy metal trappings, the guitar solos, and macho vocals were often big pop hooks. "Bands like Poison ushered metal and hard rock into what could be compared to a bubblegum pop period," writes David Konow in *Bang Your Head*. "Eventually metal magazines began resembling the cover of *Tiger Beat*, with story headlines like, 'Write a Poem and Win Warrant's Hearts!'"[2]

Glam metal offered "real" heavy metal something to rebel against. In the 1980s, the higher the hair and chart positions that the glam metal bands achieved, the more the early speed and thrash metal bands dressed down and played faster. MTV's growth as an influencer saw groups with at least a trace amount of edge cede more and more airtime to the likes of Cinderella and Great White.

Pioneer Tracks: KISS–"God of Thunder," Mötley Crüe–"Live Wire," Queen–"Stone Cold Crazy," Ratt–"Round and Round," Twisted Sister–"Bad Boys (of Rock 'n' Roll)"

Key Players: Autograph, Cinderella, Dokken, Extreme, Lita Ford, Great White, Hanoi Rocks, Poison, Quiet Riot, Skid Row, Vixen, Warrant, Whitesnake, White Lion, Winger

CROSSOVER GENRES

GLAM ROCK
New York Dolls, Slade, Status Quo

HARD ROCK
Bon Jovi, Def Leppard, Van Halen

HEAVY METAL
Judas Priest, Ozzy Osbourne, Rainbow

Glam Rock

|||||||||||||||||||||||||||||||||||||||||||||||||||||||||||||||||||||||||||||||||||||||||||||||||||||||||||||||||||||

Glam, as Simon Reynolds writes, "refers to a cluster of artists and bands who are often connected by relationships of collaboration and shared management, and energised by friendly rivalry with each other."[1] It was a movement in early 1970s rock that had recent influences in powerful rockers who dabbled in dressing up like Little Richard and the Velvet Underground and more distant ones in figures like Oscar Wilde. Among the relatively small number of glam rock bands from the original era in the early to mid-1970s there was more agreement on what glam rock should look like than about how it might actually sound. To the extent that the music the glam rock scene produced can be characterized as a whole, "glam often seems to hark backward and step forward at the same time."[2]

Marc Bolan was half of a mystic-minded hippie folk duo called Tyrannosaurus Rex in the late 1960s before he became the glam rock movement's first electric warrior. As the 1970s arrived, Bolan shortened his band's name to T. Rex, ditched the long album titles as well, plugged in, and let "Ride a White Swan" loose. The single, a playful and buzzing rockabilly boogie, transformed Bolan's career and set the stage for a steady stream of hot-blooded hit singles in the UK from 1971 to 1973. Released in 1971, T. Rex's *Electric Warrior* album was both the reintroduction of Bolan to pop music audiences, and the first significant introduction to the era of newly forming glam rock's pleasures and principles.

"The idea of a larger-than-life style rock figure struck me around the end of 1970,"[3] Bowie wrote about the germination of *The Rise and Fall of Ziggy Stardust and the Spiders From Mars*. This would be around the time that his third LP, *The Man Who Sold the World*, was released, the UK cover for which featured him reclining on a chaise lounge in quite a nice dress. Already trying on glam's androgyny, Bowie found that, "At that moment in time, rock seemed to have wandered into some kind of denim hell. Street life was long hair, beards, leftover beads from the Sixties and, God forbid, flares were still evident (and refused to leave the party for many more years). In fact, all was rather dull attitudinizing with none of the burning ideals of the Sixties."[4]

It was on a promotional trip to the United States in early 1971 that Bowie went to stay with record producer Tom Ayers, who at the moment was working with 1950s rockabilly legend Gene Vincent, who was most famous for "Be-Bop-A-Lula" and would die later that year at the age of thirty-six. Bowie had a few songs from *Ziggy Stardust* already written, and one night he was given the chance to run through "Hang On to Yourself" with Vincent. "I went on to explain that Ziggy wasn't going to be a real rock star and that I would play him," Bowie wrote. "I think they all thought I was talking in terms of a musical. It's possible that I was; it's now hard to remember what direction I had expected him to go."[5]

Bowie finally became a rock star by playing one. Not just in the fake-it-till-you-make-it way, but in a manner akin to real theater, which in turn allowed him to have a real effect on the music of others. Taking on Manhattan with hype man Tony Defries, Bowie would soon rub off on Lou Reed. Bowie and his guitarist Mick Ronson produced and played on Reed's 1972 solo album, *Transformer*, with its piano-led tracks "Satellite of Love" and "Perfect Day." Iggy Pop, too, soon joined the glitter fold, which helped to pull his Stooges out of their early 1970s limbo.

Looking at a certain faction of the mid-1970s glam rock scene today, there's something of a disconnect between their presentation and their records. David Bowie's lithe form and fair complexion fit well in alien fabrics, other styles not so much. The Sweet and Slade wore brash outfits, but their bubblegum blues rock had more in common with the pub rock craze that was just around the corner than the multidirectional artistic paths David Bowie and Roxy Music were setting off on. Perhaps no band looked less natural in glam than KISS, so it's a good thing that the hairy New York quartet opted to become a cartoon version of Alice Cooper's horror-glam rather than try to follow in Ziggy's footsteps. Ace Frehley, in his memoir about his time as the band's lead guitarist, *No Regrets*, describes the pivotal image makeover they went through in 1973. "By this point the costumes had evolved from denim to leather and were on their way to spandex. Sneakers had been replaced by platform shoes. Each of us had refined the hair and facial makeup of his particular character."[6] This was still the early days for KISS, who would need a few more years to grow into a junk merchandise powerhouse.

Queen, on the other hand, whose image and music seemed to line up with the glam ideology, well outlived the genre. Lead singer Freddie Mercury was a natural attention grabber, and the band had so much flash to spare that they wound up making the *Flash Gordon* soundtrack in 1980. As another glam-era singer, Steve Harley of Cockney Rebel, put it to Mercury biographer Lesley-Ann Jones, "The thing is, Queen fronted by Freddie Mercury would have been theatrical in any era. It didn't need that 'glam rock' label to validate it or set it in context."[7]

Glam rock didn't entirely stop in the late 1970s, but, between Bolan's death in 1977, Bowie's evolving personas, Roxy Music's first break up, and waning interest in other lingering glam rockers, it had lost the wider public's imagination. Roxy Music would soon enough return as elder statesmen among the New Romantics, bearing smooth new wave singles like "More Than This." Not known for being the most masculine-minded genre, glam rock would nonetheless echo in American sports arenas for decades, as blasting Queen's "We

Will Rock You" and Gary Glitter's "Rock and Roll, Part 2" became standard ways to get crowds stomping.

Pioneer Tracks: David Bowie–"The Man Who Sold the World," T. Rex–"Ride a White Swan"

Key Players: David Bowie, Mott the Hoople, Mud, New York Dolls, Queen, Lou Reed (*Transformer*), Roxy Music, Slade, Steve Harley & Cockney Rebel, the Sweet, T. Rex

CROSSOVER GENRES

GLAM METAL

The Darkness, Poison, Twisted Sister

SHOCK ROCK

Alice Cooper, KISS, the Plasmatics

BRITPOP

Oasis–"Cum On Feel the Noize" (Slade) and "Heroes" (David Bowie)

GOTH ROCK

Bauhaus–"Telegram Sam" (T. Rex) and "Ziggy Stardust" (David Bowie)

Goth Metal

||||||||||||||||||||||||||||||||||||||||||||||||||||||||||||||||||||||||||||||||||||||||||||||||||||||||

Despite goth's strong feminine side and the overwhelming whiff of masculinity that trails heavy metal, goth and metal have otherwise made a natural, moody pair. As the frontman for the crossover thrash band Carnivore in the 1980s,[1] Brooklyn native Peter Steele already had experience bridging divides among entrenched rock cliques when he later formed Type O Negative. Draped in overwrought goth vibes, the group's breakthrough third album, *Bloody Kisses*, was an anomaly even amidst the mishmash alternative rock landscape of 1993. The record didn't just conjoin goth and metal energies; it did so while utilizing progressive rock structures and song lengths as well.

Cradle of Filth, as one might pick up from their name, was one of England's rare purveyors of black metal when they started playing together in the early 1990s. Their albums *Dusk and Her Embrace* and *Cruelty and the Beast* welcomed an increasingly goth spirit that helped their music translate across limiting metal genre brackets. A major label jump in the 2000s found them becoming even more approachable. Type O Negative and Cradle of Filth are two early artists in the genre, but even more so than in the United States and UK, gothic metal has found a dedicated audience on the European continent. Musically, goth metal isn't really beholden to goth rock forerunners like Bauhaus, so most any kind of metal band can paint their nails black, put on some tight or flowy black clothes, and wrap themselves in dramatic melancholy.

Key Players: Anathema, Cradle of Filth, Danzig, HIM, Lacuna Coil, My Dying Bride, Paradise Lost, Type O Negative

CROSSOVER GENRES

GOTH ROCK
Alien Sex Fiend, Fields of the Nephilim

INDUSTRIAL METAL AND INDUSTRIAL ROCK
Nine Inch Nails, Skinny Puppy

Goth Rock

Moody rockers who dressed in black like Alice Cooper and Black Sabbath had come before, but it was from certain UK post-punk bands in the late 1970s that gothic rock, or just "goth," took shape. The sullen austerity of their music reflected the country's socioeconomic climate at that time, while a heightened sense of drama and dour melodies mingled with, and sometimes partly replaced, punk's anger.

The first goth bands did not necessarily see themselves as any different from other punk and new wave bands. In his memoir, *Cured*, Lol Tolhurst, former drummer and founding member of the Cure, recalls the time bandleader Robert Smith played him a tape of song ideas that would become their second album, *Seventeen Seconds*. "It was a departure brought on by our exposure to the bleeding edge of new music like Wire and the Banshees," he writes. "However, I felt that more than the Banshees, the real influence was Wire. Their subtly shifting minimal punk soundscapes were far more in line with what we were thinking and doing than the more bombastic drama of the Banshees."[1]

Tolhurst heard in these demos "a glacial sonic landscape that mirrored my own lonely feeling at the time."[2] *Seventeen Seconds* mirrored a lot of other people's loneliness, too. That album, along with the two that followed, *Faith* and *Pornography*, are now commonly referred to by fans as the Cure's goth trilogy, a glowering trio of albums that got darker one by one each year from 1980 to 1982. By that point, they had pushed the bleak mood so far that their next album, *The Top* in 1984, kicked off with an exaggerated laugh.

Tolhurst may have felt Wire was the greater influence, but Robert Smith actually joined Siouxsie and the Banshees temporarily as a live guitarist when the two groups toured together in 1979.[3] Susan Dallion, aka Siouxsie Sioux, and Steven Severin were part of the Sex Pistols' entourage known as the Bromley Contingent. They were even standing behind the Pistols on the set of *Thames Today* when they incited a national moral outrage by swearing during a televised interview with Bill Grundy in 1976. Two years later, they formed their own band and put out their debut album, *The Scream*, which Nancy Kilpatrick's *The Goth Bible* cites as "the first full-length release in the genre of goth."[4]

Also in 1978, in the northwest of London in Northampton, Peter Murphy joined a band formerly called the Craze with Daniel Ash, David J, and Kevin Haskins. They soon changed their name to Bauhaus 1919, and then from there dropped the inaugural year of the famous German art school they named themselves after. Bauhaus came out of the gate with a goth classic, their 1979 debut single "Bela Lugosi's Dead." Four years later, the sorta-cult-classic vampire lust movie *The Hunger*, starring David Bowie and an endless supply of candles and flowing curtains, established its goth bona fides with a Bauhaus performance of "Bela Lugosi's Dead" in the opening sequence, which put a blue-lit and caged Peter Murphy on screen before any of the actual actors.

The four pillars of early goth include the aforementioned the Cure, Siouxsie and the Banshees, Bauhaus, as well as Joy Division. Though the latter's two studio albums, *Unknown Pleasures* and *Closer*, are certainly a crucial part of any goth fan's record collection, Joy Division's drama was not theatrical, and they never got into the hair and makeup that comes with the scene. Indeed, none of the four bands really claimed to be goth. Bauhaus considered themselves a dark glam band, Robert Smith felt the Cure were a pop band, and the Banshees identified with punk.[5]

Many artists that followed in the 1980s, such as Fields of the Nephilim, the Sisters of Mercy, and the Mission, solidified the idea of goth, but the four early progenitors remain central to its identity. In the 1990s, rock also began to lose ground as the dominant musical expression of gothness. The industrial music scene had its admirers of goth bands, and vice versa. That includes Ogre, frontman for Vancouver, British Columbia's Skinny Puppy, who was a professed Bauhaus fan.[6] The hybrid goth-industrial became an identifiable subculture and a common club night theme, giving goths a greater choice of rhythms to dance alone to.

Pioneer Artists: Bauhaus, the Cure, Joy Division, Siouxsie and the Banshees

Key Players: Alien Sex Fiend, All About Eve, Fields of the Nephilim, Gene Loves Jezebel, Killing Joke, the Mission, the Sisters of Mercy

CROSSOVER GENRES

ETHEREAL WAVE
Cocteau Twins, Dead Can Dance

GOTH METAL
HIM, Type O Negative

INDUSTRIAL ROCK
Rammstein, Stabbing Westward

Grindcore

Mick Harris was the drummer in Napalm Death, the band often credited with inventing grindcore, from late 1985 through 1991. In fact, Harris claims to have coined the term, explaining to Albert Mudrian in *Choosing Death* that, "with this new hardcore movement that started to really bloom in '85, I thought 'grind' really fit because of the speed so I started to call it grindcore."[1]

The blast beat, which defines grindcore, requires spasmodic jack-hammering on the snare drum, broken up by spontaneous fills. The beat is primarily what separates it from the other heaviest metals. Though the bands could play their detuned instruments fine, musicianship was not the utmost concern in grindcore, as it all came in a twisted blur. In addition to sharing the blast beat, grindcore and death metal also have vocals in common: deep, growling, and indistinguishable, sometimes described as puking into the mic.

When Napalm Death's debut, *Scum*, finally surfaced, it was, against all odds, an underground hit in the UK, if something of a novelty one. Legendary DJ John Peel found their extreme take on hardcore punk intriguing and played them on his BBC Radio 1 show. He was a particular fan of the track "You Suffer," which famously clocks in at little over one second.[2] Because trends catch on fast on the crowded island of Britain, Napalm Death were not alone for long. There was Extreme Noise Terror from Ipswich, who Harris also played with. Carcass came from Liverpool, and the band became notable for pulling their clinically gruesome (and sometimes hilarious) lyrics and song titles straight from medical dictionaries, which somehow led to its own recognized subgenre within grindcore, goregrind. "Three Swedish bands—General Surgery, Regurgitate, and Necrony—have created music that falls into this genre and have mimicked the song titles and lyrics of Carcass."[3] writes Natalie J. Purcell of goregrind in her book, *Death Metal Music*.

Grindcore wasn't necessarily enamored of the same blood-and-guts imagery that death metal favored; Napalm Death's concerns were more sociopolitical. The buzz around Napalm Death lasted long enough to make them one of the least likely *NME* cover stars of all time in November of 1988. John Peel continued to support the scene that year by being a booster of Carcass' debut, *Reek of Putrefaction*.[4] Many bands in the growing genre were signed to Earache Records, whose profile was raised enough by the media's fascination with grindcore that in 1991 their offices were raided by police after the passing of the UK's Obscene Publications Act.[5] Grindcore made some inroads into the underground hardcore and metal scenes in the United States and Europe, and the UK bands continued to change and swap members through the 1990s, but it was hard to top the initial impact of such an explosive genre.

Key Players: Carcass, Extreme Noise Terror, Napalm Death, Repulsion, Terrorizer

CROSSOVER GENRES

DEATH METAL
Cattle Decapitation, Exhumed

HARDCORE PUNK
Deep Wound, Negative Approach

Groove Metal

Groove metal has been identified as an in-between phase bridging 1980s thrash metal and 1990s nu metal.[1] Like an unwashed friend of funk metal, it bangs its tangled hair in rhythm but doesn't bounce off the walls. Think of White Zombie's "Thunder Kiss '65" and "More Human Than Human." It is ideal music for stomping around.

Arlington, Texas, band Pantera are often cited as one of the originators of the genre. Theirs was a storied leap across metal from glam to groove, captured succinctly by the way their guitarist, the late, great Darrell Abbott, went from "Diamond" to "Dimebag." Securing a major label deal at the same time as their credibility was improving, the band pivoted with their 1990 album, *Cowboys from Hell*. Of the record, Martin C. Strong notes that, "gone was the '80's metal garb and cheesy choruses; check shirts, tattoos, and a brutally uncompromising thrash-based groove had forcibly taken their place."[2]

Key Players: Down, Pantera, Lamb of God, Machine Head, Prong, Sepultura, Soulfly, White Zombie

CROSSOVER TRACKS

FUNK METAL

Faith No More–"Falling to Pieces," Fishbone–"Freddie's Dead,"
Primus–"Jerry Was a Race Car Driver"

HARD ROCK

Aerosmith–"Back in the Saddle Again," Heart–"Barracuda,"
Mötley Crüe–"Dr. Feelgood"

Grunge

Named after their high-school math teacher, Mr. Epp and the Calculations started out, like many teenage bands do, half in the realm of imagination. The Bellevue Christian High School students began designing record sleeves and tour T-shirts well before either milestone was reached.[1] Even after they started rehearsing in real life, they still stayed one step ahead of reality. In the summer of 1981, the band wrote anti-fan letters to magazines under assumed identities about how they'd seen Mr. Epp & the Calculations, and they sucked.[2]

One of the Calculations, Mark McLaughlin (who would soon take the punk name Mark Arm), wrote such a letter to a local fanzine called *Desperate Times*—which began, "I hate Mr. Epp & the Calculations! Pure grunge! Pure noise! Pure shit!"—that included, according to Mudhoney biographer Keith Cameron, "the first published usage of the word 'grunge' in reference to a Seattle band," though he also points out that the term had been used before, citing a Lester Bangs reference to the Count Five's "grungy spunk."[3]

By the 1990s, grunge had become a term applied to bands from all over the world, but those bands were capitalizing on a sound that had developed organically throughout the 1980s in the US Pacific Northwest. Grunge will always be first and foremost associated with Seattle—over twenty-five years later, whenever the Seattle Seahawks are on Monday Night Football, they *still* play grunge songs when cutting to commercials. Locals sigh at this limited view of the city's music, but the record label most associated with that music may not exactly be free of blame.

"Bruce Pavitt, founder of Sub Pop records, began using the word in the April 1988 issue of *The Rocket*," cites Stephen Tow in *The Strangest Tribe*, his book that focuses on the early years of grunge. "Within a few months, local media picked it up. Pavitt could fold his arms and laugh as the international media latched onto grunge to describe *all* music coming out of Seattle."[4] The term may have started as a joke, but not everyone was in on it, and a vital new music genre was shaped by manufactured mystique.

The UK music press caught on before the slower US media did. In 1989, Sub Pop sprang for a plane ticket for *Melody Maker* writer Everett True to come to Seattle and check out the label and the scene.[5] The resulting two-page spread described the band Blood Circus as "minimalist grunge metal," as well as "complete and utter white trash."[6] Such was the tongue-in-cheek tone of the piece, playing up and playing along with the Pacific Northwest's backwater image partly at the behest of Sub Pop.

In the same article, Mudhoney, the best known of the bunch at that point because of the attention paid to their *Superfuzz Bigmuff* EP, were billed as "raging primal grunginess," and "Touch Me I'm Sick" was already deemed a grunge classic. True declared that the music coming out of the city was "trampling gleefully over the grave of punk rock and heavy metal."[7] For all of the article's intentional hyperbole, those observations proved prescient. Other Seattle bands saw more money roll in, but "Touch Me I'm Sick" encapsulated the energy first in a way that no other single song did. Tow asserts that "if grunge did in fact exist as a legitimate style of music, it is arguably best represented"[8] by that song.

It is also true that an unstable combination of punk rock and heavy metal is at the core of what became known as grunge. It was around this time that crossover thrash was bridging the divide between punk and metal, but grunge didn't have the same culture clash hang-ups. This was surely in part because of Seattle's geographic isolation, which previously made for unique post-punk approaches from pre-grunge bands like the Blackouts and the U-Men. Not all Seattle bands were into the same kind of metal, either. Alice in Chains had glam-ish beginnings, Soundgarden were on a Led Zeppelin trip, and Nirvana's 1989 debut, *Bleach*, reflects their early friendship with sludge metal daddies the Melvins.

If grunge had a coming out party, it was probably on June 9, 1989, when Sub Pop put on their first Lame Fest at the Moore Theater in Seattle. The all-local bill had the then little-known band Nirvana—who were a week away from the release of *Bleach*—opening, Mudhoney headlining, and TAD playing in between. None of them were used to playing venues that large at that point, but the show sold out. Emboldened by its success, Sub Pop reprised the event that December with the same lineup at the Astoria Theatre in London.[9] Though attention was turning to the Seattle scene, its pivotal commercial breakthrough, the major label release of Nirvana's all-conquering second album, *Nevermind*, wherein Kurt Cobain laid off the Melvins influence and leaned on classic and college rock, was still well over a year away.

Write-ups of the Moore Theater show invoked the word "grunge,"[10] but it had yet to become a household name. "We didn't say that word in the '80s," former music director of Seattle alternative rock station 107.7 Marco Collins recalls. "When I saw Mudhoney for the first time, Nirvana for the first time, it wasn't in Seattle, it was in San Diego and Mexico, and the word 'grunge' just didn't exist then. It's funny now, you use the G-word up here [in Seattle], and people cringe." As a local in-joke became a worldwide reality, Sub Pop must have wondered if their marketing strategy had been a little too successful. There's a reason why the first major autopsy of the era, Doug Pray's 1996 documentary about the grunge explosion, was called

Hype! The title wasn't Gen-X jadedness coming from an outsider; it succinctly captured how those on the inside felt about the whole thing.

By 1993, grunge had become so big that Pearl Jam could stop making music videos and Nirvana could make an album as abrasive as *In Utero*, and their profiles only raised. *Singles*, Cameron Crowe's fond portrait of the young and the plaid in Seattle, had been successful the year before, and the accompanying soundtrack went platinum. Mudhoney and TAD finally found their way onto major label rosters. More new acts piled on from across America and beyond. Collins felt he was struggling being handed so many records by bands from outside of his city that were creating the exact same sound, often at the impetus of their record labels. On one hand, he understood it; on the other hand, it was frustrating watching so many artists follow trends and swamp the marketplace.

In Seattle, the healing process would be long, and in some ways is still going on. "It's funny," Collins says, recalling a recent conversation with Pearl Jam's Mike McCready, "he said to me, 'Do you remember when you told me you hated my band?'" Collins was taken aback, but McCready assured him that, long ago, in a moment of honesty, he had leveled the accusation that Pearl Jam sounded like Bad Company. "I just couldn't imagine being that much of a dick," Collins says, about a comparison that seems rather harmless today.

Pioneer Tracks: Green River–"Come on Down," Mudhoney–"Touch Me I'm Sick," Mother Love Bone–"Stardog Champion," Soundgarden–"Nothing to Say," the U-Men–"Solid Action"

Key Players: Alice in Chains, Babes in Toyland, the Fluid, Gruntruck, Hammerbox, Hole, L7, Mad Season, the Melvins, Nirvana, Pearl Jam, Screaming Trees, Skin Yard, Stone Temple Pilots, TAD, Temple of the Dog

CROSSOVER GENRES

GARAGE ROCK (PACIFIC NORTHWEST)
The Kingsmen, the Sonics, the Wailers

HEAVY METAL
Black Sabbath, Led Zeppelin, Motörhead

PUNK ROCK (AUSTRALIA)
Radio Birdman, the Saints, the Scientists

Hard Rock

In *The Decline of Western Civilization Part II: The Metal Years*, the middle episode of her observantly insightful rock documentary trilogy, director Penelope Spheeris begins a question to singer Steven Tyler and guitarist Joe Perry of Aerosmith with the assertion that they "are the definitive hard rock band that really set the standards."[1] Spheeris might have reconsidered her words had she heard "I Don't Want to Miss a Thing," but *Armageddon* was a decade away, and there's still merit to her claim. Aerosmith made heavy blues rock, but not quite heavy metal in the darker vein of Sabbath, positioning themselves almost perfectly between the two. They were an American answer to Led Zeppelin: all the sex and drugs but none of the J. R. R. Tolkien novels.

Hard rock is a broad, simplistic label initially applied to late 1960s blues rock and the mainstream rock and early heavy metal that grew out of it in the 1970s: Black Sabbath, Cream, Deep Purple, Heart, Led Zeppelin, Steppenwolf, et al. In those days, one might have preferred blues rock to glam rock, but there was no need to fight about it like mods and rockers on a beach. By the late 1970s and early 1980s, though, between punk's opposition to prog and heavy metal kids arguing with hair metal kids, hard rock began to experience internal strife. Straight-ahead hard rock certainly had its torchbearers through the 1980s, from Joan Jett & the Blackhearts' insta-classic cover of "I Love Rock 'n' Roll" to the posture and thrust of the Cult, but an all-encompassing "hard rock" was starting to look like something of an outdated concept.

Then Guns 'n' Roses came along in 1987 with their debut album, *Appetite for Destruction,* and a genre-crossing hard rock sound with such wide commercial appeal that it almost seemed possible that the multi-platinum record could singlehandedly mend all those fences. As the 1990s began, grunge might have also helped to mitigate the divides in hard rock on a mainstream level, while the underground found common cause with crossover thrash. At that point, however, rock was already being taken to such extremes with metal and industrial and other new "alternative" places, that the term "hard rock" seemed best suited not for the harder bands, but for bands who were the closest to 1970s-era hard rock bands. It now comes up mostly as an award category at the Grammys.

Pioneer Tracks: Cream–"Sunshine of Your Love," Deep Purple–"Smoke on the Water," the Kinks–"You Really Got Me," Link Wray–"Rumble"

Key Players: AC/DC, Guns 'n' Roses, Van Halen, and roughly half of all rock bands in between.

CROSSOVER TRACKS

BLUES ROCK

Bad Company–"Bad Company," Derek and the Dominos–"Layla," Free–"All Right Now"

HEAVY METAL

Black Sabbath–"Iron Man," Judas Priest–"Living After Midnight," Metallica–"Enter Sandman"

PSYCHEDELIC ROCK

The Doors–"Break on Through," Iron Butterfly–"In-A-Gadda-Da-Vida," Jimi Hendrix–"Purple Haze"

Hardcore

Once the accelerated bubblegum of the Ramones caught on, it was only a matter of time before rock and roll was stripped down even further and sped up as fast as it could go. Solos and melodies scraped off, what remained was a simple, aggressive music that spoke directly to the listener's simple, aggressive impulses. Slam dancing was born, a violent progression from punk's hyper but more solitary pogo, which made going to concerts more like a contact sport.

Hardcore, what Steven Blush called a "suburban American response"[1] to punk rock at the end of the 1970s, had more in common with the Oi! and street punk bands an ocean away in Britain than with the more diverse, experimental punk scenes from the US cities those suburbs ringed. Taking a cue from the Sex Pistols, there was almost nothing that hardcore wouldn't rail against, including other kinds of punk, even factions within hardcore itself. Some in Washington, DC, didn't like all the drinking and glue sniffing they saw happening around them and started a straight edge scene. Rivalries developed between hardcore cliques from different spots on the East Coast or towns in Southern California, which would sometimes turn violent.

Hardcore's maps help make its narrative compelling, but as a style of music, it didn't take long for it to run out of terrain. This was always going to happen, given its reductionist nature. The first bands were, and have remained, the most influential: Black Flag and the Germs in LA, Dead Kennedys in San Francisco, Bad Brains and Minor Threat in DC, Agnostic Front and Cro-Mags in New York, and D.O.A. and the Subhumans (not the UK group of the same name) from Canada.

Innovation in the early days was likely to put a band at odds with the purity standards dictated by hardcore hive mind. Restrictions loosened as the decade wore on. Black Flag got slower and heavier, some bands went artsy while others became accessible, and a few DC bands got in touch with their feelings. The post-hardcore era had begun, but most were either still calling it hardcore or something else entirely, like alternative rock. There were, of course, fans who still believed in the power of pure hardcore, and from the late 1980s into the 1990s, that part of the community would, creatively and commercially speaking, do what it could to close ranks.

Tacoma, Washington, is a place with a deeper rock and roll history than many might assume. It is worthy of its shout-out in the Steve Miller Band song "Rock'n Me" simply by being home to influential 1960s garage rock bands like the Sonics and the Wailers. Though the music scene in Tacoma is stuck right between more famous counterparts in Seattle and Olympia, in the 1990s, a band called Botch ensured that Tacoma made an important contribution to the attempted evolution of hardcore.

Botch bassist Brian Cook moved to town in the summer of 1992. After spending his first year in the Pacific Northwest as a sullen, withdrawn teenager, he met future bandmate Dave Knudson during his junior year of high school when he overheard Knudson ask another student in their math class if she knew any bass players. Cook volunteered. There couldn't have been a more appropriate location for the origin of a band who would later coin the term "evil math rock" to describe their own music.

Knudson, a guitarist, had already been practicing with drummer Tim Latona. Cook mentioned that he liked punk, and Knudson said he wanted to cover Dead Kennedys' "Too Drunk To Fuck." Dave Verellen joined on as the vocalist a bit later, but everyone aside from Cook had grown up in the same neighborhood. Knudson and

Latona had a couple of songs already worked out, Cook recalls, so the musical direction was already in place: heavy, angry, mid-tempo songs. "We all started going to shows together and eventually wound up going to see this Seattle hardcore band called Undertow. Stylistically, it wasn't too far from what we were playing, but it was way more raw and direct."

Being in a hardcore band back then meant covering other hardcore songs, and Botch obliged with Earth Crisis and Inside Out tracks. They also looked beyond the walls with a version of the B-52's "Rock Lobster" and a bass-driven interpretation of "O Fortuna" from Carl Orff's *Carmina Burana*. "The whole 'heavy-band-doing-ironic-covers' is a really cringe-worthy concept to me now," Cook admits, but Botch wanted to show that they could draw from a broader swath of music. At this point, their name was spreading in hardcore circles outside the Pacific Northwest. They got the attention of Aaron Turner, whose Hydra Head Records was then based in Boston, and the label released Botch's first full-length record in 1998, *American Nervoso*.

"I have a very clear memory of a band conversation prior to recording our first 7" where we toyed with the idea of dumbing down our music," Cook confesses. Botch considered writing an album like *Lookinglasself* by Snapcase, who were one of the bigger hardcore bands around at the time. Instead of pandering, Botch listened to their instincts and went the opposite route, crossing their fingers that people would catch up sooner or later. "I think our first 7"s still sounded very much in line with the modern hardcore era, but with *American Nervoso*, we felt that we were taking the risk of alienating the hardcore audience, and that was fine by us. By that point, we were more interested in bands like Monorchid and Shellac than we were with whatever Revelation Records was putting out."

As pivotal as *American Nervoso* was for Botch, and as challenging as it was for hardcore, the stakes were raised significantly little more than a year later when they released *We Are the Romans* at the end of 1999. It was more approachable *and* more complex. Their senses of humor (in the song titles) and anger (pretty much everywhere else) were working overtime. *We Are the Romans* operated with a subversive intellectualism too often missing from hardcore at the time. It had fans at shows shouting "Mondrian Was a Liar!" as if they were hurling posthumous accusations at the Dutch painter.

We Are the Romans also raised a valid question about genres and artists who work within them: How far can one band pull a style of music along with them before it snaps back? Botch started out following the rules of hardcore, but did they ultimately catapult themselves into another genre? The terms "metalcore" and "mathcore" follow them around now, but in their time, they were just called hardcore because that was where they came from.

Though some of the foundational bands of hardcore punk turned out to be experimental, somewhere along the line rules were set. The music had to go somewhere, but stray too far and you could wind up in a subgenre with a half-serious name. If hardcore remains one of the most immediately identifiable rock genres, it isn't for lack of trying by groups like Botch.

Pioneer EPs: Black Flag–*Nervous Breakdown* EP, the Germs–*Lexicon Devil* EP, the Middle Class–*Out of Vogue* EP, Teen Idles–*Minor Disturbance* EP

Key Players: Bad Brains, Circle Jerks, D.O.A., Dead Kennedys, the Descendents, the Faith, Government Issue, Hüsker Dü (*Everything Falls Apart*), Minor Threat, Minutemen (*The Punch Line*), Reagan Youth, T.S.O.L., Void, Youth Brigade (*Sound & Fury*)

CROSSOVER GENRES

(1990S PRE-)METALCORE
Botch, Converge, Snapcase

POST-HARDCORE (WASHINGTON, DC)
Fugazi, Jawbox, Shudder to Think

STREET PUNK
Cockney Rejects, the Exploited, Sham 69

Heavy Metal

Heavy metal is one of the first subgenres to come out of the rock and roll expansion of the 1960s. Its influence is embedded in not only the dozens of metal styles that multiplied from the 1980s onward, but other genres as well. It is a music of exertion, pushing instruments, performances, volumes, and sometimes wardrobes to their limits. Anything rock and roll does, heavy metal doubles it: double kick drum pedals, double-necked guitars, double-speed playing.

It has also worked its way into mainstream culture in a way that would have seemed far fetched back in the Satanic Panic days of the 1980s. America didn't turn to Lucifer as some feared, but heavy metal has become normalized. Every American under the age of fifty either had an older brother who was into heavy metal or knows an older brother who was into heavy metal. The original, massively popular *Guitar Hero* video game, released in 2005, was chock-full of classic shredders. The devil horns hand gesture is now thrown by children and adults alike to celebrate even the most mundane pleasures: *"These nachos rock!"*

The first stirrings of heavy metal are heard in Black Sabbath, the Beatles' "Helter Skelter," Led Zeppelin, and "In-A-Gadda-Da-Vida": the dark fields where 1960s rock tuned down and buried flower power. Judas Priest, though, were one of the first to self-identify as heavy metal. "Judas Priest said from day one that we wanted to be known as a heavy metal band," explains the group's legendary singer, Rob Halford, making time for an email interview in the middle of recording Priest's latest album.

Birmingham, England, is a city that lays fair claim to being the birthplace of heavy metal.[1] It is the hometown of both Sabbath and Priest. The wider Midlands region is also metal country, from Led Zeppelin to Def Leppard. Halford remembers the scenes and genres in the Midlands being a mix of authentic blues, progressive rock, and progressive blues rock bands. His regular hangouts in Birmingham were Henry's Blues House and the famous Mothers Club.

Among the artists and albums that inspired his creative thinking in the late 1960s, Halford specifically mentions the Who, Jimi Hendrix, the Beatles' *Sgt. Pepper's Lonely Hearts Club Band*, King Crimson's *In the Court of the Crimson King*, and Janis Joplin's *Pearl*. Judas Priest had been playing in different formations since the start of the 1970s when Halford joined as the band's singer soon before they recorded their debut album, *Rocka Rolla*. For those only aware of Judas Priest hits like "Living After Midnight" and "Breaking the Law," *Rocka Rolla* hardly sounds like the same band as it dips into the blues, progressive rock, and even 1950s rock 'n' roll. Halford notes that having different thinkers—himself, their famed guitarist pairing of K. K. Downing and Glenn Tipton, and bassist Ian Hill—made for limitless ideas, and they let their chemistry lead the way. "We wrote the early songs with total freedom and self-exploration."

Judas Priest didn't become *Judas Priest* overnight; it took them the better part of a decade. As the early heavy metallers that the band felt a kinship with—Zeppelin, Sabbath, Deep Purple—moved on or dropped out in the 1970s, Priest sharpened their sound from *Sad Wings of Destiny* to *Stained Class*, an album that bridges the gap between fans of their darker, more complex earlier material and those who prefer the hit songs that were all over the radio and MTV in the early 1980s.

Halford's operatic, dynamic reach was not just crucial to the character of Judas Priest, but it helped define heavy metal itself, influencing countless metal singers that came after, such as King

Diamond and Iron Maiden's Bruce Dickinson. Halford developed his technique by keeping an open mind and letting loose in jam sessions and rehearsals. Because there was no standard yet, Halford was able to set it. "I sang the way the music moved me. Very few singers were around for me to focus on, as metal was so new."

In the late 1970s, as Judas Priest were hardening their sound, heavy metal solidified as a genre with the advent of the New Wave of British Heavy Metal (NWOBHM). Up until that point, metal was a form of hard rock with roots in other styles that came before. With NWOBHM, metal was now influenced by *earlier* metal. From that point, it was able to turn inward and form a self-referential, self-sustaining core: a molten center of gravity into which any musical style could then be pulled in and reforged in its image.

The number of metal bands throughout Britain suddenly swelled with Iron Maiden, Diamond Head, Saxon, Tygers of Pan Tang, and a slew of others. Records by these groups would find their way across the Atlantic, where they ended up in the hands of eager young metalheads such as Lars Ulrich and James Hetfield, who bonded over them as they wrote Metallica's first songs.[2] Halford felt a connection with NWOBHM and thought it was a great moment for Judas Priest to take in. "To us, it felt like the next obvious step. . . . What we had made was being emulated and improvised upon."

The story of heavy metal explodes in numerous directions from this point, but some aspects of it have remained. Thirty years after Judas Priest rocked the Capital Centre outside Washington, DC, it might not be as easy to find a Zebraman in the parking lot of a metal show, but, unlike so many other labels that artists and fans brush off, heavy metal is one genre that both sides enthusiastically embrace. Why might that be? "Heavy metal is an everyman music," Halford says, "although the roots are in the working class, people that struggle. The messages and volume connect. All these conditions were there from the start and are still with us."

Pioneer Tracks: The Beatles–"Helter Skelter," Black Sabbath–"Paranoid," Iron Butterfly–"In-A-Gadda-Da-Vida," Led Zeppelin–"Communication Breakdown," Steppenwolf–"Born to Be Wild"

Key Players: Alice Cooper, Anthrax, Black Sabbath, Deep Purple, Def Leppard, Iron Maiden, Judas Priest, Metallica, Megadeth, Mötley Crüe, Pantera, Ozzy Osbourne, Rainbow, Scorpions, Van Halen

CROSSOVER TRACKS

HARD ROCK
Blue Öyster Cult–"Godzilla," Guns 'n' Roses–"It's So Easy"

PROGRESSIVE ROCK
Jethro Tull–"Aqualung," King Crimson–"Pictures of a City"

PSYCHEDELIC ROCK
Cream–"Tales of Brave Ulysses," the Jimi Hendrix Experience–"Foxy Lady"

Hypnagogic Pop

"Hypnagogic pop is pop music refracted through the memory of a memory. It draws its power from the 1980s pop culture into which many of the genre's players were born."[1] says writer David Keenan in influential music magazine *The Wire*. Hypnagogic pop is one of those concept genres that sprang fully conceptualized from the brain of its music-journalist creator, but Keenan has experience making music as well, including being a founding member of the underappreciated Glasgow experimental rock band Telstar Ponies. His sympathies for both sides might be why "hypnagogic pop" is a well-meaning, even generous, term.

Hypnagogic pop is music made in the 2000s that comes across as the misremembered sound of 1980s popular music, played on equipment that was either made in that era or designed to sound like it was made in that era, and that also has a mild hallucinatory quality. As new lingo does in the Internet age, the term took off quickly among music sites not long after Keenan's article came out. Soon it was being regularly paired up or conflated with chillwave.

Looking back at Keenan's article, "Childhood's End," however, the term seems to have slipped away from his original intent, as often happens with these things. The music that he was talking about—Ariel Pink, the Skaters, Zola Jesus, Emeralds—doesn't totally line up with the sound of chillwave's major players. The term has since largely fallen out of use, but artists still work with the ideas behind it.

Key Players: Ariel Pink / Ariel Pink's Haunted Graffiti, Ducktails, John Maus, Peaking Lights, Pocahaunted, the Skaters, Zola Jesus

CROSSOVER TRACKS

DREAM POP

Vinyl Williams–"World Soul," Wild Nothing–"Chinatown"

SYNTH-POP

Chromatics–"Kill for Love," M83–"Kim & Jessie"

■   HAVE A SENSE OF HUMOR   ■

Arena Rock/Stadium Rock, Blog Rock, Bubblegum, Butt Rock/Hair Metal, Cock Rock, Crack Rock Steady, Dad Rock, Geek Rock/Nerd Rock, Mope Rock/Sadcore, Pigfuck and Twinklecore, Yacht Rock

Almost as long as people have been formulating ideas about new rock genres with serious intent, they've been cooking up more joking genre names to let out some of the serious air that can surround rock and roll and its taxonomy. Music journalists toss such terms out all the time to color their reviews or relieve boredom. Fans and others, too, can get funny ideas stuck in their heads. Sometimes these ideas catch on, even in a big way, and occasionally they prove to have a durable shelf life in the rock lexicon.

ARENA ROCK/STADIUM ROCK |||||||||||||||||||||||||||||||||||||||||||||||||||||

Everyone has heard of arena rock and could likely come up with the names of at least a few arena rock bands on the spot if asked to do so, but its usefulness as a genre term is pretty much limited to functioning as a backhanded compliment. Arena rock, or stadium rock if you want to dream a bit bigger, is rock and roll that can push the air all the way to the back of large sports venues without drifting off. It certainly has to sound big and loud, but as often as it is direct and anthemic (Boston and Def Leppard), it can also be complex and nuanced (prog rock consistently filled arenas in the 1970s). Between "We Will Rock You" and "Bohemian Rhapsody," Queen covered both bases.

BLOG ROCK |||||||||||||||||||||||||||||||||||||||||||||||||||||||||||||||||||||||||||

Arena rock was aimed at the many fans brought together in one place, while blog rock reached an audience of separate individuals both everywhere and nowhere in particular. In the mid-2000s, the Internet vaunted its own legitimacy by coining a genre term of its own make and support. Blog rock, as the *Guardian* later put it, "referred to music that had gained popularity through MP3 blogs—specifically those giving coverage to the more left-field, less image-obsessed artists largely ignored by the mainstream music press."[1] Declaring a genre based on its means of distribution dates back to at least the 1980s and the rise of terms like indie rock and its antithesis, "corporate rock," but as a way to define actual music, it's pretty much useless. Bands of all shapes and sizes had songs featured on blogs even back then. If anything, it remains most associated with indie rock groups that didn't get big, exemplified by a pair of self-released debuts from blog rock's peak year, 2005: Minnesota's Tapes 'n Tapes record, *The Loon,* and the self-titled album from New York's Clap Your Hands Say Yeah.

BUBBLEGUM

Bubblegum was no joke, but there's a bit of a condescending smirk behind its name. A significant money-making force crafted by anonymous grown-ups and aimed at young teenage audiences in the late 1960s, bubblegum was pop music first and foremost. However, the difference between "rock" and "pop" wasn't as pronounced back then, and many bubblegum hits were performed by bands using rock instrumentation. The genre's crowning achievement, "Sugar, Sugar," was performed by a garage rock band, albeit a fictional cartoon one, the Archies. Close behind it was the Ohio Express' "Yummy Yummy Yummy," the pair of them making for quite the aural toothache.

BUTT ROCK/HAIR METAL

If you grew up in the 1980s and 1990s, chances are that you've used, or at least heard, the term butt rock before. Back then, it was used as a derogatory term for the glam metal that MTV was playing day in and day out, but it could also apply to the wider world of jean-everything hard rock and hesher-friendly metal. As to where the name butt rock specifically comes from, there are of course theories floating around the Internet, but the only conclusive fact is that the term gets funnier the more you think about it. Interestingly, the same kind of music gets its other, more famous nickname from the other end of the body: hair metal. It's no surprise that the most obvious nickname for glam metal—all the members of these bands were required to have huge hair—has proven the most enduring.

COCK ROCK

Since we're already going around the human body, we might as well address cock rock. This label is meant to signify the most manly of all rock bands, the kind that strut and prowl on stage, thrusting their leatherbound groins hither and yon, all the more blatantly so in music videos while holding their guitar necks straight out between their legs. The 1970s and 1980s were the golden years of cock rock, from Mr. Golden God himself Robert Plant in Led Zeppelin all the way to Warrant's tour of tired, sexist cliches, "Cherry Pie."

CRACK ROCK STEADY

Silly as they could appear, cock rockers weren't really known for laughing at themselves. Ska punks, however, typically have a better sense of humor, as evidenced by Crack Rock Steady. The term was coined by the irreverent New York ska punk band Choking Victim, who wrote a song by that name and also used it as the title of their first EP in 1994. The micro-genre essentially belongs to them (when the band broke up at the end of the 1990s, some members formed a new group called Leftöver Crack), but it has also been used as a label for other ska punk bands whose punk side is of the faster, more hardcore-influenced variety.

DAD ROCK

Less cracked out is dad rock, which is rock made by dads, or rock that your dad likes. Popular use of the term dates back to the 1990s, when the British music press used it as a term of derision towards certain

Britpop bands that were a little too in-debt to the 1960s and Paul Weller,[2] though the term has since slipped into wider, more general use. Everyone's dad-rock list will be a little different, but Bob Dylan would have to go somewhere on top. Every dad wishes he could have been the toast of the Greenwich Village folk scene. Also up there would be Dire Straits. Led by Mark Knopfler, the London band's smooth blues rock was refined on their 1985 album, *Brothers in Arms*, after which they continued to kick out easy dad rock jams like their 1992 single "The Bug." Speaking of Knopfler, dads love it when a member of one of their favorite old bands releases a mature solo album. A prime example of that would be former Eagles member Don Henley, whose second solo album from 1984, *Building the Perfect Beast*, kicks off in high-nostalgia mode with the dad rock classic "The Boys of Summer."

GEEK ROCK/NERD ROCK

Just as uncool as dad rock, but proud of it, is geek rock, or, perhaps preferably, nerd rock. In modern use, the terms "nerd" and "geek" aren't quite as interchangeable as they once were. Some time ago, the term "nerd" was reclaimed as a point of pride; to be a nerd about something, be it books or beer or often both, is to be enlightened and obsessive in a charming way. Geeks are still just geeks, though. The plant pot–hatted Ohio new wavers Devo remain the fathers of nerd rock. "I was never cool/In school" began Ben Folds Five's breakout nerd-rallying cry, "Underground," from their self-titled 1995 debut. Weezer sang about playing Dungeons and Dragons in the garage on their self-titled debut from the year before. Soon other alt- and pop punk newcomers like Wheatus and Nerf Herder were following in their footsteps.

MOPE ROCK/SADCORE

While the nerd rockers are happy to be uncool, performers of mope rock are happy to be unhappy. "With the exception of 'twee,' is there any genre coinage more deflating to rock's rebel stance than 'mope rock?'"[3] asks Adam Brent Houghtaling. Most rock bands at least take a shot at writing a sad song here and there, so mope rock artists are designated by their repertoires having a predominance of sad songs. Sometimes referring to it as "Gloom Rock," Houghtaling traces it as far back in rock and roll as "Heartbreak Hotel."[4] Simply between Joy Division and Morrissey, long ago nicknamed the "Pope of Mope," Manchester can easily claim to be the capital of mope rock. Sadcore, too, is essentially another term for the same thing here.

PIGFUCK AND TWINKLECORE

Some of these mock genres say more about the artists making them than the sound of the music itself, but some can get quite specific. Writing for the *Village Voice* in 1987, veteran music critic Robert Christgau came up with the slightly-too-vivid "Pigfuck" as another label for noise rock,[5] a term which Dave Grohl–biographer Paul Brannigan characterized as "a memorably unpleasant turn of phrase which goes some way to evoking the violent, perverse and knowingly obnoxious nature of the music in question."[6] Much cuter is the term "twinklecore," which came around in the early days of the 2010s emo revival.[7] The name refers to the "twinkling" (bursts of bright, clean notes) guitar playing of certain second-generation emo bands in the 1990s such as American Football, as well as the guitar-tapping technique used by math-rock-adjacent bands like Pele and Minus the Bear. Given American Football's elevated status with the emo-revival generation, it makes sense that the twinkling guitar sound would become a signature element.

YACHT ROCK

As the fictional music critic "Hollywood" Steve Huey says right in the beginning of episode 1 of *Yacht Rock*, the web-based video series from the mid-2000s that bestowed upon the world its titular term, "from 1976 to 1984, the radio airwaves were dominated by really smooth music, also known as Yacht Rock."[8] Ostensibly, yacht rock is the soft rock that rich people would listen to while they did cocaine on their fancy boats in the late 1970s and early 1980s: the Doobie Brothers, Hall and Oates, Christopher Cross, Kenny Loggins, Steely Dan, and the like. It was not a real thing until the show's underground popularity made it one, at which point some of the artists saw an unlikely influx of new, young admirers. A world in which the lameness of Hall and Oates was a long-established fact was turned upside down: their "You Make My Dreams" was used for a big choreographed scene in the 2009 indie film *500 Days of Summer,* and they sold out Madison Square Garden in 2016. It goes to show that anyone can change the course of music history, even comedians.

HAVE A SENSE OF HUMOR PLAYLIST

ARENA ROCK / STADIUM ROCK	Led Zeppelin–"Stairway to Heaven" Journey–"Don't Stop Believin'" U2–"Where the Streets Have No Name"
BLOG ROCK	Clap Your Hands Say Yeah–"The Skin of My Yellow Country Teeth" Tapes 'n Tapes–"Insistor" Voxtrot–"Raised by Wolves"
BUBBLEGUM	The Archies–"Sugar, Sugar" The Ohio Express–"Yummy Yummy Yummy" The 1910 Fruitgum Company–"Goody Goody Gumdrops"
BUTT ROCK, COCK ROCK, AND HAIR METAL	Winger–"Easy Come Easy Go" Warrant–"Cherry Pie" Poison–"Nothin' But a Good Time"

CRACK ROCK STEADY	Choking Victim–"Crack Rock Steady" Leftöver Crack–"Crack City Rockers"
DAD ROCK	Bob Dylan–"Tangled Up in Blue" Don Henley–"The Boys of Summer" Dire Straits–"The Bug"
GEEK ROCK / NERD ROCK	Devo–"Jocko Homo" Ben Folds Five–"Underground" Weezer–"In the Garage"
MOPE ROCK / SADCORE AND GLOOM ROCK	The Smiths–"Heaven Knows I'm Miserable Now" The Cure–"Prayers for Rain" Red House Painters–"Things Mean a Lot"
PIGFUCK	Sonic Youth–"Confusion Is Next" The Butthole Surfers–"Human Cannonball" Killdozer–"The Pig Was Cool"
TWINKLECORE	American Football–"Never Meant" Pele–"The Mind of Minolta" Minus the Bear–"Absinthe Party at the Fly Honey Warehouse"
YACHT ROCK	The Doobie Brothers–"What a Fool Believes" Loggins and Messina–"Sailin' the Wind" Christopher Cross–"Sailing"

Indie Folk

The name indie folk suggests a merging of indie rock and folk music, but neither "indie" nor "folk" were very meaningful designations when indie folk took hold. Forget having your records released on an actual independent label; all an artist had to do to be "indie" by the mid-to-late 2000s was not sell as many records as U2. The other side of it was just as easy; all one had to do to be "folk" was play acoustic instruments.

English band Mumford & Sons still get lumped in with indie folk, and they were never indie. "I think the Mumford & Sons entrée required deeply rooted folk-rockers to take sides," says Kim Ruehl. "It was like another big bang in roots music—there had been an explosion a decade earlier with the *O Brother* soundtrack. Then there was a contraction, followed by the Mumford explosion. Suddenly, the traditionalists were split between thinking Mumford were amazing and thinking they were sellouts."

Following in the wake of Mumford & Sons came the Lumineers, the Head and the Heart, Of Monsters and Men, Edward Sharpe and the Magnetic Zeros, and more shouts of "hey!" than one could possibly count. Some of these vaguely folk-rock-ish groups had legitimate roots music chops, says Ruehl, while some were just great pop songwriters who enjoyed playing acoustic instruments. The difference between the two isn't always obvious to the casual listener, so it's easier to toss every band with someone who can play a banjo in it into the indie folk pile.

American folk rock and British electric folk have influenced indie folk artists from both nations. It is arguable that Elliott Smith—

who got his start in Portland, Oregon, playing in the indie rock band Heatmiser—was more "acoustic alt-rock" than he was indebted to folk traditions. However, the hushed side of his solo work bears some resemblance to Nick Drake, and a few of his songs, such as B-side "I Don't Think I'm Ever Gonna Figure It Out," employ American roots-style guitar playing.

The emerging popularity of not just indie rock but also the acoustic singer-songwriter and alt-country in the 1990s set the stage for indie folk in the 2000s. Sam Beam's rustic debut album under the name Iron & Wine, *The Creek Drank the Cradle*, sounded like it was transported from a century prior when it came out in 2002. The following year, M. Ward released his third album, *Transfiguration of Vincent*, and Sufjan Stevens put *Michigan* on the indie folk map with his storyteller's detail and genteel instrumentation.

In 2004, Conor Oberst of Bright Eyes put together a tour with Jim James from My Morning Jacket and M. Ward where they would play one another's material on a night by night rotation. Dubbed "The Monsters of Folk," the tour was a success, but lining up their schedules to write and record an album together proved trickier for the supergroup.[1] When it finally arrived in 2009, the *Monsters of Folk* album was an appropriately self-aware mile marker showing how far the indie folk trend had traveled.

Key Players: Beirut, Edward Sharpe and the Magnetic Zeros, Fleet Foxes, the Head and the Heart, Iron & Wine, the Lumineers, Mumford & Sons, Noah and the Whale, Sufjan Stevens, M. Ward

CROSSOVER TRACKS

ALTERNATIVE COUNTRY

The Avett Brothers–*Mignonette*, Blitzen Trapper–*Wild Mountain Nation*

EMO(CORE)

Bright Eyes–*Fevers and Mirrors*, Dashboard Confessional–*The Places You Have Come to Fear the Most*

INDIE ROCK

Fruit Bats–*Mouthfuls*, Okkervil River–*Don't Fall in Love With Everyone You See*

Indie Pop

To an extent, there have been differences in the way Americans and Brits read "rock" and "pop." For both parties, the two terms were generally interchangeable in the 1960s and into the 1970s, though by the end of the "Me" decade, America was drawing lines, as witnessed in the pitting of rock versus disco. The United States was beginning to see "rock" and "pop" as increasingly separate entities, but in the UK, "pop" could still be indebted to the Beatles and played on guitar, bass, and drums.

In his book on the Stone Roses, John Robb makes recurring reference to the "pure pop"[1] sound of the band's singles and self-titled debut album. Their second single, "Sally Cinnamon," is a simple but charming indie pop tune. "I pop pop pop blow blow bubble gum/You taste of cherryade" went the second verse, the sense of innocence nearly overbearing yet somehow working for them. The song's naif-ish tone fit alongside the music of C86, which had taken off not long before.

Independent guitar pop from the UK in the 1980s, including C86 but also prior to it, is where indie pop begins. It mirrors the advent of indie rock in the United States, and they are essentially two ways of looking at the same phenomenon of independent and/or inexperienced musicians and labels having increased access to what were once the exclusive machinations of the record industry. In both cases, glossy production and glossy magazine pages were both out of the question and unnecessary. Perhaps the only real difference between the two was that the British preferred their rock melodies to be like their chocolate: a little bit sweeter.

Certain bands in the United States did have a taste for indie pop's sugar early on. Calvin Johnson was attending Evergreen State College in Olympia, Washington, in the early 1980s when he sowed the seeds for both his band, Beat Happening, and his label, K Records. Beat Happening's music was intentionally rudimentary and humorous. The band's quirky approach might have gone over Henry Rollins' head when they opened for Black Flag in Olympia,[2] but influential listeners in England caught on to them. In turn, Johnson and his bandmates were turned on to like-minded British groups like Oxford's Talulah Gosh and Glasgow group the Pastels. "The band's sound was an oddity at the time," writes Mark Baumgarten. "Decidedly amateurish, the Pastels' songs featured themes of childhood, a melodic sensibility that harkened back to '60s pop groups, and a lead vocalist who could not sing, at least in the traditional sense. If Beat Happening had a British cousin, the Pastels were it."[3]

Once the term indie pop left the 1980s, it became harder to pin down. It is reasonable enough to call an early 1990s group like the Sundays indie pop, even though their sublime balance of the Smiths and the Cocteau Twins came without a hint of shamble, but the doors have flung so wide open by this point that "sounds like the Pastels" doesn't begin to cover it, though such comparisons probably remain the clearest interpretation.

Pioneer Tracks: Beat Happening–"What's Important," Orange Juice–"Simply Thrilled Honey," the Pastels–"Million Tears," Primal Scream–"The Crystal Crescent," the Vaselines–"Son of a Gun"

Key Players: The Darling Buds, the Field Mice, Heavenly, K Records, the Lightning Seeds, the Lucksmiths, Sarah Records, Talulah Gosh, Velocity Girl

||||||||||||||||||||||||||||||||||||||||||||||||||||||||||||||||||||||||

CROSSOVER GENRES

||||||||||||||||||||||||||||||||||||||||||||||||||||||||||||||||||||||||

BRITPOP

Bis, Catatonia, Comet Gain

CHAMBER POP

Belle & Sebastian, the Divine Comedy, the High Llamas

INDIE ROCK

The Sundays, Teenage Fanclub, the Wedding Present

Indie Rock

To find a concise history of indie rock, one need look no further than the lyrics of "Gimme Indie Rock," a story-in-song released in 1991 by the band Sebadoh. "Gimme Indie Rock" starts by accurately dating the origin of the term back to the early 1980s and namechecking the Velvet Underground and the Stooges, the two 1960s bands no indie rocker can leave off their list of influences. It then goes on to cite characteristics of the genre and name-drops bands identified with them: the looseness of Jon Spencer's pre-blues explosion band, Pussy Galore; Dinosaur Jr.'s use of effects pedals (Sebadoh leader Lou Barlow had previously played bass in Dinosaur Jr.); Thurston Moore's sense of humor and his band Sonic Youth's breaking down of barriers. One of those barriers was that even though by 1991 they had signed to a major label, they were so cool that they got to keep their indie cred in the deal.

The term "indie" wasn't always so loaded. In the early 1980s, it meant what it said: music that was released on independent record labels, or even by the bands themselves, free from the control of corporate record companies. Though it was affiliated with rock, it didn't come pre-attached to any particular style; punk, post-punk, and other kinds of bands could be indie as long as they weren't funded by the Man. Over time, indie rock came to imply the sound of an artist more than the business side of their music. Independence would still be a meaningful qualification for some until the alt-rock gold rush of the 1990s muddled scene politics.

Michael Azerrad's *Our Band Could Be Your Life* profiled thirteen different bands, and one of the criteria by which he chose them was if and when a band's albums were released by a label that benefited from corporate record company distribution.

"Virtually every band did their best and most influential work during their indie years," he says of the groups in his book, "and once they went to a major label, an important connection to the underground community was invariably lost."[1] His assertion isn't simply that the large, scattered network of independent bands, labels, distributors, record shops, zines, and radio stations[2] was socially and economically important. There is also a qualitative judgment in there: It was *creatively* important, and these bands made better music when they were indie bands. This was a commonly held belief in the 1980s and 1990s, but it is a perspective that doesn't get as much vocal support in today's poptimist times.

Azerrad's definition of indie rock starts with Black Flag, Minutemen, Mission of Burma, and Minor Threat, a reminder that the first independent rock music was punk with its DIY ethos.

DIY was still a talking point around indie rock throughout the 1990s, but "indie rock" had also come to identify guitar bands, like Pavement, Superchunk, and Guided by Voices, with certain shared musical traits. The term gradually split in two, with one use effectively meaning "Sebadoh-esque," and the other being a giant umbrella signifying "not corporate rock" that every other new-ish niche rock genre, from post-hardcore to shoegaze, could fit under.[3]

"By the time the word 'indie' came into vogue, its definition was anything but useful," observes Jesse Jarnow in *Big Day Coming*, his book on Yo La Tengo, noting that somewhere in the band could be found "an exact resemblance of some version of the indie archetype."[4] Founded in 1984 by Ira Kaplan, who had been a music critic known for reviewing independent records, and Georgia Hubley, the daughter of independent filmmakers,[5] Yo La Tengo had their indie bona fides established before they played their first note. Jarnow notes that what distinguished the band's musical identity in the vast underground was partly that they were neither hardcore, post-punk, or new wave, and that they "liked the Kinks and folk music too much."[6]

Indie rock is no exception to regional variation. The Research Triangle, in North Carolina, had Superchunk, whose members Laura Ballance and Mac McCaughan started Merge Records in the band's early days (when they were just Chunk) to put out their own 7" singles,[7] and the label grew to become one of the largest independents in the United States. Interestingly, *Our Noise: The Story of Merge Records* notes of indie rock that, "In Chapel Hill, there was an alternative coinage: 'young rock,'"[8] which, sure, that works. Built to Spill were (and still are) something of the standard bearers of Northwest indie rock, and few fans looked at them differently when they moved from independent Seattle label Up Records to the Warner Bros. behemoth for their 1997 album *Perfect From Now On*.

For every successful conversion story such as Built to Spill, who released some of their best work after moving to a major label, there are a dozen cautionary tales. Indie rock was meant to be a refuge from the major label game, another way forward that both artists and their art would ultimately benefit from. The term's journey from punk principle to "sounds like Pavement" is a convoluted one, but going DIY is more practical than ever now that the corporate ogre at the gate isn't what it used to be.

Pioneer Tracks: Buzzcocks—*Spiral Scratch* EP, the Clean—"Anything Could Happen," the Feelies—"Crazy Rhythms," R.E.M.—"Gardening at Night," the Smiths—"Hand in Glove"

Key Players: Broken Social Scene, Built to Spill, Cat Power, Death Cab for Cutie, Dinosaur Jr., the Elephant 6 Collective, Guided by Voices, Helium, Modest Mouse Pavement, Liz Phair, Sebadoh, Spoon, Superchunk, Yo La Tengo

CROSSOVER GENRES

COLLEGE ROCK

Pixies, the Replacements, Throwing Muses

JANGLE POP

10,000 Maniacs, Felt, the Sundays

POST-PUNK

Hüsker Dü, the Minutemen, Mission of Burma

Industrial Metal and Industrial Rock

Industrial music has a lot less to do with rock music than Americans who came of age in the 1990s might think. For that demographic, Nine Inch Nails is likely the first band to come to mind if the term "industrial" comes up. The connection is so ingrained, it is practically inseverable (which drives old school industrial music fans from the 1970s and 1980s nuts).

But in the wired eyes of purists, the rise of Nine Inch Nails was the point at which the canary in the corporate coal mine smelled the cold hard cash and keeled over. S. Alexander Reed's critical history of industrial music, *Assimilate*, lays out the case for how Trent Reznor sullied the intently outsider genre with populist appeals by stepping away from the style's unofficially established limits on harmonic variation and regularly utilizing "compellingly poppy cycles of four chords,"[1] as well as lyrically employing an "I" voice "over three times more often than the industrial norm."[2]

Reed is particularly dismissive of the "rock-plus-synthesizer acts"[3] that got pulled in by Reznor's Jet Ski wake and landed on major labels. Filter, Stabbing Westward, Gravity Kills, and Orgy: These are groups whose names ring *I Love the '90s* bells but whose music "was contextualized as merely another flavor in the 'alternative' stew"[4] on commercial radio. The history of industrial music meant little in this new context, both to these bands and their listeners. All the clanging and grinding was not only artificial (a sin against the first generation of industrial music), but merely ornamental (a sin against the second generation). The dead-end result, then, was where Marilyn Manson and White Zombie intersected with nu metal.[5]

This era, the early to mid-1990s, was the period when industrial music and rock and roll had the most in common. Not that either of them were particularly happy about it, but there were points when the two appeared to be working well together. The amalgamation of industrial music and heavy metal did not begin in 1988 with Al Jourgensen and Ministry, but their third album, *The Land of Rape and Honey*, introduced an organic element to an otherwise synthetic body, as it dug up the corpse of the band's initial new wave identity and set fire to it with heavily distorted guitar just to make sure it was dead. Coming from the other direction was Steve Albini's first band, Big Black, an antagonistic early 1980s post-punk trio with an industrialized edge provided by the use of a drum machine and grim (or grimly humorous) lyrical subject matter.[6]

Those who want to dig back even further for proof of rock's presence in industrial music also point to isolated influences like genre-straddling English band Killing Joke, whose dark streak was embodied by a penchant for resonant, militant percussion and frontman Jaz Coleman's howl. There was certainly an open exchange of ideas between post-punk and industrial music in the early 1980s, but what the artists sought to accomplish, and the processes by which they attempted to do so, were distinct.

In the mid-1970s, multidisciplinary artists Throbbing Gristle, from Northern England, extended their harsh experimentalism into the realm of sound and founded Industrial Records, which gave the genre its name. The first wave of industrial music that they inspired included London's Test Dept. and Berlin's Einstürzende Neubauten, both of whom bashed away on actual industrial refuse like sheet metal, creating a kind of postapocalyptic tribal vibe. The second wave of industrial music solidified around aggressive electronic atmospheres, menacing vocals, and mechanized rhythms that were increasingly geared toward dancing. The music was now taking hold not just in England (Cabaret Voltaire and Nitzer Ebb) and Europe (Front 242 and Die Krupps), but also in Vancouver, Canada (Skinny Puppy and Front Line Assembly), and Chicago, Illinois (the aforementioned Ministry and My Life with the Thrill Kill Kult), where the industrial label and record store Wax Trax! was located.

The long walk that it took for industrial music to get from performance art with power tools to Johnny Cash covering Nine Inch Nails' "Hurt" seems almost inevitable when looked at step by step, even if the trip from point A to point B looks unlikely from a distance. Not everyone may have been thrilled that the two set aside their differences and shacked up for a while, but it produced better results than just what ended up in the buzz bin.

Key Players: Die Krupps, Front 242, Godflesh, KMFDM, Ministry, My Life with the Thrill Kill Kult, Nine Inch Nails, Nitzer Ebb, Revolting Cocks

CROSSOVER GENRES

ALTERNATIVE ROCK
Gravity Kills, Stabbing Westward

NU METAL
Marilyn Manson, Mushroomhead, Static-X

POST-HARDCORE
Big Black, Lard, Pailhead

Jangle Pop

||||||||||||||||||||||||||||||||||||||||||||||||||||||||||||||||||||||||||||||||||||||||||||||||||||||||

It is a generally accepted rock truism that the sound of an electric twelve-string guitar is "jangly," but is it really? In that "jingle jangle morning," Bob Dylan was following a *tambourine* player. A tambourine definitely jangles. On the other hand, there are a few bell-like adjectives that people are fond of using to describe a Rickenbacker.[1] Either way, it's too late. We're stuck with jangle pop, and it gets the job done well enough.

That job is to describe a swath of lo-fi, indie, and melodic rock music that owes some measure of debt to the Byrds and/or is played at mid-tempo with a touch of looseness and space. Jangle pop crosses generations and genres, but the real oil was struck in the 1980s: R.E.M.'s *Murmur*, the Paisley Underground, C86, a number of classic songs by the Smiths, and many other bands from the Railway Children to the Sundays . . . it seemed the well would never run dry. In the past decade, the jangle aesthetic has popped up in scenes from Melbourne, Australia, to the Acela Corridor in the Northeast United States.

Key Players: The Byrds, the dB's, the Go-Betweens, the Housemartins, the Lucksmiths, the Plimsouls, R.E.M., the Railway Children, the Sundays, the Wedding Present

CROSSOVER TRACKS

ALTERNATIVE ROCK

10,000 Maniacs–"Candy Everybody Wants," the Smiths–
"William, It Was Really Nothing"

PAISLEY UNDERGROUND

Game Theory–"Erica's Word," Rain Parade–"Talking In My
Sleep"

Jazz Rock

Noting that it is also referred to as "jazz fusion," Encyclopædia Britannica defines jazz rock as jazz improvisation "accompanied by the bass lines, drumming styles, and instrumentation of rock music, with a strong emphasis on electronic instruments and dance rhythms."[1] In this "jazz-tries-on-rock" interpretation, Miles Davis' *Bitches Brew* is an early touchstone, and bands like the Weather Report and Mahavishnu Orchestra followed soon thereafter. On the other hand, the "rock-tries-on-jazz" perspective sees the style as developing alongside psychedelic and progressive rock, both of which do incorporate improvisation ("Brash and exciting, their music is a wedding of rock and jazz" reads the inside cover of Blood, Sweat & Tears' self-titled second album). These two views are not mutually exclusive, though their boundaries of where and how rock and jazz connect aren't identical.

Jazz rock is also something that can happen when a band's guitarist gets too technically proficient at their instrument. Boston band Karate are one such example. The group's first two albums, *Karate* and *In Place of Real Insight*, fell easily into the indie rock category, and some even identified leader Geoff Farina's raw-but-restrained yell and the band's stop-start rhythms with emocore, which was gaining notoriety in 1996 and 1997 when those records came out. Something was definitely up with Farina's mellower and more intricate guitar playing on their third album, *The Bed Is in the Ocean*, and by the next one, *Unsolved*, it was clear: jazz. Song lengths only got longer from there, and Karate found themselves making indie jazz rock in the new century.

Key Players: Blood, Sweat & Tears, Brand X, Chicago, Electric Flag, the Free Spirits, Mahavishnu Orchestra, Nucleus, the Weather Report

CROSSOVER GENRES

CANTERBURY SOUND
Caravan, Soft Machine

NO WAVE
James Chance and the Contortions, the Lounge Lizards

Kindie Rock

Indie rock for kids was bound to happen. Indie rockers were always going to age out of playing for their peers, start families, and look for ways to keep making music that fit into their new, nightlife-unfriendly schedules.[1]

Children are savvy though, and kindie rock wouldn't fly if it was only geared toward parents looking to trick their spawn into listening to lame old-people music. Thus, the genre is distinguished not only by lyrical content that avoids sex, drugs, and rock and roll, but also by a generally softened approach to melodies and performances. That said, the realm of kindie rock is otherwise stylistically diverse. Early leaders in the genre include They Might Be Giants, whose quirky songs always had youthful appeal, and Dan Zanes of the Del Fuegos.

In Seattle, kindie rock started to take off when Caspar Babypants and the Not-Its! both released debut albums in 2009. Caspar Babypants is the former frontman of the Presidents of the United States of America, Chris Ballew. The Presidents were a much-needed dose of lighthearted rock in the grunge era, and their debut album sold strongly on the back of local-gone-national radio hits like "Peaches" and "Lump." The sly yet innocent sense of humor that defined the Presidents made Ballew's transition to Caspar Babypants completely natural.

Members of the Not-Its! also come from notable 1990s groups. Sarah Shannon was the singer in the Sub Pop band Velocity Girl, and Jennie Helman was in Micro Mini, one of the better bands to come out of Seattle's indie pop reaction to grunge. The Not-Its! don't sound like any one of their former bands in particular, but they land somewhere in a simplified, happy middle, and they are just as likely to step on a fuzz pedal now as they were back in the day.

Key Players: Caspar Babypants, Lisa Loeb, the Not-Its!, Recess Monkey, They Might Be Giants, Dan Zanes

CROSSOVER GENRES

ALTERNATIVE ROCK

The Del Fuegos, the Presidents of the United States of America, Velocity Girl

COMEDY ROCK

The Bonzo Dog Doo-Dah Band, Bowling for Soup, the Rutles

POP PUNK

The Aquabats, the Hippos, Me First and the Gimme Gimmes

Krautrock

"Some people think of 'Krautrock' as any rock groups that played in West Germany in the seventies," explains music writer David Stubbs, "but for me, it comes down to a key group of formal innovators." Stubbs' shortlist includes Kraftwerk, Neu!, Can, Tangerine Dream, Faust, Ash Ra Tempel, Cluster, and Harmonia—all of whose stories he brought to life in his in-depth history of the genre, *Future Days*. Because these artists have been conversationally tied together for ease of reference outside their home country, the impression is one of a conventional scene where all of the major players interact, but convention didn't mingle much with those who made what is also called, more kindly perhaps, *Kosmische Musik*.

Stubbs notes that there was some crossover, as Michael Rother and Klaus Dinger of Neu! played for a time with Kraftwerk, and Rother formed Harmonia with Hans-Joachim Roedelius and Dieter Moebius of Cluster. Aside from exceptions like that, he says, the groups evolved in isolation oblivious to one another and often in commune-style settings. "Can didn't really have very much idea about Faust, for example. It was a case of great minds thinking alike, responding in different ways to the cultural circumstances of post-war Germany."

Not only were the bands geographically spread around West Germany, no two sounded alike. The mechanical, minimal 4/4 "Motorik" beat that so many indie rock bands dabble in today was pioneered by Can drummer Jaki Liebezeit and Dinger of Neu!, both now sadly passed. On the other end, there was the "immaculately structured electronics" of Kraftwerk; the diverse collage approach of Faust, heard in the pounding neo-folk drum circle–ish "It's a Rainy Day (Sunshine Girl)," and the ambient journeys of Tangerine Dream, who often weren't overly concerned with rhythm in the first place.

There were many people, the artists themselves in particular, who weren't happy about being labeled together because they felt it didn't do justice to their individualism. For Stubbs, that right there was the defining characteristic of Krautrock: West German innovation—an innovation impelled by unique historical circumstances—and a rejection of the conventions of British and American rock music. "There is generally a rejection of the verse-chorus structure, in favor of ambience or loops [and] repetition, an inclination towards electronics as a means of expanding the sound palate, and far more emphasis on instrumentation than on vocals and lyrics, which are often deliberately fey and 'weak,' rather than full-throated. Krautrock wasn't about making 'major lyrical statements,' its effects are implicit, generally, mind expanding in a different way."

As it goes with all the coolest artists, bands, and scenes in the history of Western popular music in the twentieth century, hardly anyone was paying attention to West Germany's interpretation of the psychedelic explosion when it was actually happening. Not only did these bright, inventive bands not become a part of their country's mainstream culture in their time, even today younger audiences in Germany haven't so much as heard of these bands. Stubbs quotes guitarist John Weinzierl, a founder of the Munich collective Amon Düül II, who, like Faust, were one of the early West German commune bands—himself quoting the Bible: "A prophet is not without honor except in his own country."

As there was no truly cohesive "scene" to begin with (the music was largely ignored at home, though it gained traction in France and the UK), neither was there an official end to the Krautrock movement. Faust and Ash Ra Tempel rolled to a stop in the mid-1970s. Can went through two different singers from two different countries—Malcolm Mooney from the United States followed by Damo Suzuki from Japan—and then decided to leave the position open until calling it a day (for a while, anyway) with a self-titled album in 1979. By that point, Kraftwerk were already on a rise few could have foreseen at their outset: *Trans-Europe Express* was a critical and underground favorite in 1977, and soon enough they would have legitimate hit singles like "The Model." Tangerine Dream kept at it, too, and released scores of records made with a rotating cast assembled around core founder Edgar Froese until his death in 2015.

Citing the conservative nature of today's mainstream rock and its ceaseless veneration of past greats, Stubbs says that the music these bands made still offers new audiences and musicians a sense of exploration and expansion. "Krautrock was always forward looking. It'll speak to the 2040s, the 2050s, and beyond."

Pioneer Tracks: Amon Düül II–"Phallus Dei," Can–"Yoo Doo Right," Faust–"Why Don't You Eat Carrots?," Kraftwerk–"Ruckzuck," Neu!–"Hallogallo"

Key Players: Ash Ra Tempel, Cluster, Harmonia, Popol Vuh, Tangerine Dream

||||||||||||||||||||||||||||||||||||||||||||||||||||||||||||||||||||

CROSSOVER TRACKS

||||||||||||||||||||||||||||||||||||||||||||||||||||||||||||||||||||

INDIE ROCK

Ciccone Youth (Sonic Youth)–"Two Cool Rock Chicks Listening to Neu," Stereolab–"Wow and Flutter"

POST-PUNK

Joy Division–"She's Lost Control," Public Image Ltd–
"Fodderstompf," the Teardrop Explodes–"Kilimanjaro"

PSYCHEDELIC ROCK

Acid Mothers Temple–"Pink Lady Lemonade," Hawkwind–
"Master of the Universe," Phish–"David Bowie"

Lo-Fi Rock

In his history of Postcard Records, *Simply Thrilled*, music journalist Simon Goddard recounts the story of how Glaswegian indie pop band Orange Juice recorded their first single in "a tiny reel-to-reel bunker hidden at the back of a clothes shop in Strathaven"[1] in 1979. Despite the big ideas that the young lads, joined by Postcard founder Alan Horne, brought to John McLarty Tailors & Outfitters that cold day in December,[2] when they listened back to the tapes, "Falling and Laughing" had the kick drum so high in the mix[3] that it "hiccupped through the A-side like an in-built scratch."[4] There was no money left to try again, so they released the label's first single as it was. Original copies now fetch anywhere between $500 and $1,000 online.[5]

Lo-fi rock is made either by artists who are broke or artists who want to sound like they are broke. Whether or not music is "lo-fi" is determined not by *how* it is played but by *what* it is played on and recorded with. There is, however, a built-in logic loophole by which the music somehow becomes more lo-fi the sloppier it is played; the combined amateurism factor can somehow add value to the product. You don't often hear about great lo-fi metal bands (certain death metal aficionados aside) the way that people go on about the early records of Eric's Trip, Guided by Voices, Pavement, Sebadoh, and the Microphones. Quality digital recording equipment being as affordable as it is nowadays, lo-fi rock could become a lost art, but many still practice it.

Key Tracks: Eric's Trip–"Behind the Garage," Guided by Voices–"I Am a Scientist," the Microphones–"Don't Wake Me Up," Orange Juice–"Falling and Laughing," Pavement–"Box Elder," Sebadoh–"The Freed Pig"

CROSSOVER TRACKS

GARAGE ROCK

The Shaggs–"Philosophy of the World," the Sonics–"Psycho"

INDIE POP

Beat Happening–"Our Secret," Vaselines–"Son of a Gun"

NOISE ROCK

Psychedelic Horseshit–"Endless Fascination," Times New Viking–"Teen Drama"

Math Rock

|||||||||||||||||||||||||||||||||||||||||||||||||||||||||||||||||||||||||||||||||||||||||||||||||||||||||||||||||||||||

"Rather than having something to say, I want to make the listener feel moved," explained guitarist Kozo Kusumoto to Noisey in 2013. "Rather than moving them with beautiful lyrics or an interesting story, we do it with a tight performance and our sound."[1] Kusumoto, with guitarist Nobuyuki Takeda, bassist Jun Izawa, and drummer Akinori Yamamoto, plays in Lite, one Japan's preeminent math rock bands. Japan is one place where math rock has truly thrived. "Meet Tricot, The Japanese Trio Making Math Rock Cool Again"[2] proclaimed a headline on another music site in 2015, but in a scene stocked with Lite, Tricot, toe, Zazen Boys, Uchu Conbini, MOMA, and others, math rock wasn't necessarily in need of a makeover.

Math rock is identified by the use of intricate, agile guitar and bass parts that start and stop along with rhythms that fall outside rock-typical $4/4$ time signatures. As with most other genres, it has identifiable early outliers that predate the term, but math rock got lodged in the independent rock conversation in the 1990s to describe a strain of post-hardcore that was showing off some progressive rock tricks.

As was the case with screamo, it was hard to use the term "math rock" with a totally straight face. Either you couldn't take the term seriously, or you didn't want to be seen taking the term seriously. The music itself, though, was killer: brainy *and* brawny.

Chavez guitarist Matt Sweeney has claimed that the term was coined by a friend who was humorously appraising his previous band, Wider.[3] If the New York band Chavez were math rock, they were perhaps on the indie rock side of the spectrum, relying on vocals and melodies like Matador labelmates Pavement and Yo La Tengo. On the other end were groups that had less use for hooks and singers, many of which were also commonly labeled as post-rock at the time. In his book on Slint's highly influential final album, *Spiderland*, Scott Tennent writes that the record was an influence on math rock, among other 1990s genres.[4]

"Math class is tough!" notoriously declared Teen Talk Barbie in 1992, right around the time that Don Caballero was starting out in Pittsburgh, Pennsylvania. "Math = complicated" was what "math rock" implied, and Don Caballero, with drummer Damon Che as the linchpin, were complicated, right down to their long, ludicrous song titles. "Up until their final studio effort, *American Don*, Che and [guitarist Ian] Williams continued to push and innovate upon an unparalleled brand of energetic, artistic and unpredictable math-rock,"[5] said Pitchfork in 2002, applying the label in a serious manner.

The humor hasn't been entirely drained from math rock, but the term is more legit among its practitioners and fans today than in its early years, even earning a hardcore-based tangent, mathcore— yet another label for the music of bands like Dillinger Escape Plan, Converge, and Botch. Japanese math rock bands compose spritely and playful arrangements, but most often they don't have titles like "Let's Play Guitar in a Five Guitar Band." The ArcTanGent festival in England proudly proclaims itself to be "the world's ultimate music festival for connoisseurs of Math-rock, Post-rock, Noise-rock, Alt-rock, and everything in between."[6] The fact that math rock comes first in that equation shows how much it now amounts to.

Key Players: A Minor Forest, Battles, Chavez, Don Caballero, Lite, Minus the Bear, Slint, Toe

Math Rock Songs (Literal Edition): Drive Like Jehu—"New Math," Haircut One Hundred—"Love Plus One," Modest Mouse—"Never Ending

Math Equation," Radiohead—"2 + 2 = 5," the Violent Femmes—"Add It Up"

CROSSOVER GENRES

EMO(CORE)

Algernon Cadwallader, Joan of Arc, Roadside Monument

INDIE ROCK

Dianogah, Pele, Polvo

POST-HARDCORE

June of 44, Rodan, Shellac

Metalcore

‖‖

Metal and hardcore swore they couldn't stand each other in the the early 1980s only to have a torrid crossover affair later that decade. In the 1990s, their relationship was back on the rocks. Hardcore withdrew into itself, dwelling on its past, and metal was having an identity crisis after being dumped by the mainstream. When it looked as if their differences were irreconcilable, the two started talking again.

In an interview with *Skyscraper* in 1998, Converge vocalist Jacob Bannon and bassist Nate Newton addressed questions about the band's place between hardcore and metal. "We are all totally old-school hardcore kids . . . we grew up on it. But we grew up on metal, too,"[1] said Newton, calling the increasing number of metal-influenced hardcore bands at the time "a natural progression."[2] The Boston group's early records *Petitioning the Empty Sky* (1996) and *When Forever Comes Crashing* (1998) looked for ways to punch up hardcore with metal's technical skills. They also had songs like "The Saddest Day" and "Farewell Note to This City" that could speak to certain emo kids. (A different 1990s metalcore band, Coalesce, from Kansas City, Missouri, also connected with emo when they released a split 7" with, and relinquished a member to, the Get Up Kids.)

Metalcore in the late 1990s and early 2000s was more about hardcore bands coming back to metal on their terms: the thinking person's hardcore of Converge or the more classic crossover of Syracuse's straight edge vegans Earth Crisis. As the 2000s wore on, the perspective shifted to the metal side: headbangers like Killswitch Engage from Massachusetts and Atreyu from Orange County, California. Somehow, groups like Sheffield, England's Bring Me the

Horizon unlocked the commercial potential within the genre. What once was a "will they or won't they?" drama between metal and hardcore has long since settled into a comfortable partnership.

Key Players: All That Remains, As I Lay Dying, Atreyu, Avenged Sevenfold, Bring Me the Horizon, the Devil Wears Prada, Hatebreed, Killswitch Engage, Shadows Fall , Underoath

CROSSOVER GENRES

ELECTRONICORE
Enter Shikari, I See Stars

EMO (THIRD GENERATION)
A Day to Remember, Senses Fail

Mod and the Mod Revival

Rock and roll snuck its way into the mod world when Peter Meaden, then manager for the Who, decided to hitch the fledgling band to mod's wagon in 1964. Mod was a lifestyle revolving around dressing smart, riding vespas, and popping pills. Music was but one part of it, and that part was focused on Motown, soul, and R&B.[1] Booker T. and the M.G.'s "Green Onions" was an anthem. The Who briefly changed their name to the High Numbers and put out the "Zoot Suit"/"I'm the Face" single in an attempt to fit in, but soon afterward they ditched the new name and aggressive approach[2] and still wound up being the quintessential mod band anyway, anyhow, anywhere.

The Kinks also became associated with the mod movement, wearing sharp outfits and occasionally being photographed on scooters. London was the center of the mod scene. Its flagship rock-and-roll bands—the Who, the Kinks, the Small Faces—all came from the capital, as did the Action, while the Creation were from just north of the M25 motorway. Mod spread throughout the UK and then poured over the borders into countries that were still in the thrall of the British Invasion, the United States included. Still, like any youth movement, it was bound to age out sooner or later.

Toward the end of the 1960s, mod went into a lull. The Small Faces came apart not long after recording their finest hour, *Ogdens' Nut Gone Flake*, and the others who were still going had little choice but to evolve. Thematically speaking, the Who went a bit prog. They had released one of the first "concept" albums with *The Who Sell Out*, and then entered their rock opera phase with *Tommy*. It wouldn't be long until the band revisited their early days with their second completed opera, *Quadrophenia*.

The film adaptation of *Quadrophenia*—starring Phil Daniels, future narrator of Blur's "Parklife," and Sting, future composer of "De Do Do Do De Da Da Da"—came out in 1979, six years after the album. By that point, a mod revival was in full swing in England. This time around, the Jam were the clear heirs to the Who's throne. The power trio cut their teeth playing 1950s rock and roll and R&B covers in their hometown of Woking before they stepped into the middle of the punk melee wearing skinny ties instead of safety pins.

Tony Fletcher, a music writer who in his youth was the author of a fanzine called *Jamming*, was one of many kids in the UK who were taken with the notion of a mod revival. In his memoir, *Boy About Town*, he describes listening to the Jam's second single, "All Around the World," for the first time: "Finally, it dawned on me: this was *a punk record made by mods*. Teenage mods. Mods of the 1970s, mods that I hadn't realised until now actually existed, mods that I'd thought were confined to the booklet in *Quadrophenia*."[3] Driving the point home, the band recorded versions of the Who's "So Sad About Us" and the Small Faces' "Get Yourself Together," but perhaps their best-known mod cover was of the Kinks' "David Watts," which was a single from their double-entendre-titled third album, *All Mod Cons*.

The Jam weren't the only band of their generation to be influenced by the Who, but leader Paul Weller and bandmates Rick Buckler and Bruce Foxton brought back the fashion as well—blue, white, and red targets included. Other bands like Secret Affair and the Purple Hearts soon got in on the action, but no other mod revival band achieved the level of commercial and critical success that the Jam did. Interestingly, whereas the Who had gradually moved on from their soul and R&B beginnings, Weller's own songwriting inched closer and closer to soul and R&B until it dominated their final album, *The Gift*. (Also interesting is that Weller and Pete Townshend didn't connect when they first met, though they eventually got on well.)[4]

The revival would be cut short when Paul Weller decided to end the Jam on top in 1982, but the music of mod would come back into style again in the 1990s. In the Britpop years, bands like Blur made a habit of writing Kinks-ian character sketch songs, Menswear put subliminal mod messages in their music videos, and Weller's stalling solo career was suddenly resurgent, earning him the media-given nickname "the Modfather."[5] In their November 19, 1994, issue on "The New Mod Generation," *Melody Maker* even found a few people in nice jackets to pose with some scooters for a cover shoot in an attempt to start a mod revival *revival*.

Pioneer Tracks: Booker T. and the M.G.'s–"Green Onions," the Creation–"Making Time," the Kinks–"David Watts," Small Faces–"What'Cha Gonna Do About It," the Who–"My Generation"

Key Players: The Action, the Chords, the Jam, John's Children, the Lambrettas, the Purple Hearts, Secret Affair

CROSSOVER TRACKS

BRITISH INVASION

The Beatles–"Taxman," the Yardbirds–"For Your Love"

BRITPOP
Blur–"Parklife," Ocean Colour Scene–"The Day We Caught the Train"

PUNK ROCK
The Adverts–"Gary Gilmore's Eyes," the Undertones–"My Perfect Cousin"

MICRO-GENRES

Acapella Hardcore, Acoustic Black Metal, Breakfast Violence, Evil Math Rock and Low Rock, Grebo, New Wave of New Wave, Nintendocore, Romo, Zeuhl

ACAPELLA HARDCORE ||||||||||||||||||||||||||||||||||||||||||||||||||||||||||||||||||||

Sometimes a single band can create, and even name, their own genre. "Did you ever hear of Jud Jud?" Tobias Carroll asks. The band that he is referring to were a mysterious unit that put out two brief records of acapella hardcore. Their name is an onomatopoeia, the sound of a voice mimicking a low and heavy hardcore "breakdown" guitar riff. In the minute-or-so-length songs found on their *Demos* and *No Tolerance for Instruments* EPs from 1998, Jud Jud paid fond, if gently mocking, tribute to every tried-and-true move in the hardcore songbook with either a gruff "jud" or a "waaayyyooowww."

ACOUSTIC BLACK METAL |||||||||||||||||||||||||||||||||||||||||||||||||||||||||||||||||

Carroll then brings up Impaled Northern Moonforest. "They were acoustic black metal, which I think was all recorded when someone was sleeping, so it's acoustic guitars and a guy screaming, but really softly." The signature blast beat drumming of black metal, it turns out, was provided by a guy slapping his legs. The establishment might not want to acknowledge their contribution to music, but you can't fully erase history. "Looks like their Wikipedia page may have been deleted," says Carroll, "but they are still on *Polish* Wikipedia."

BREAKFAST VIOLENCE |||||||||||||||||||||||||||||||||||||||||||||||||||||||||||||||||||

Among other things, Tobias Carroll is something of a leading historian of breakfast violence. Presenting at the 2015 Pop Conference at the Museum of Pop Culture (then called Experience Music Project)

in Seattle, Carroll laid out the story of one of hardcore's least-known, but best-named, subgenres.

As a term, breakfast violence is a play on power violence, the abstract subgenre of hardcore that was primarily based in California in the 1990s. As a scene, it was a limited number of bands from around Washington, DC. There was Mancake (yes: man plus pancake), which featured Jason Hamacher and Shelby Cinca from the post-hardcore band Frodus. Brent Eyestone, founder of Magic Bullet Records, was inspired by Mancake and got in on the action with Waifle (yes: waif plus waffle).

Their onstage antics, too, weren't entirely the same. Waifle were all about throwing cereal at the audience, while Mancake's experience was that the audience would throw the cereal at *them*. Mancake also assumed aliases like Ponan and Reno and dressed up in things like JNCO pants and stilts.[1] All of it was intended to hold up a funhouse mirror to the increasingly self-serious hardcore scene of the 1990s. If a micro-scene predicated on poking fun of its parent scene seems destined to burn out quickly, that assumption is half-right. "It was pretty short-lived," says Carroll. "Waifle actually ended up doing a fair amount. I think Mancake only ever did the one record."

EVIL MATH ROCK AND LOW ROCK

Botch (see the earlier entry on hardcore) was another band with their own genre. They were challenging the conventions of hardcore so thoroughly with the 1999 release of their second album, *We Are the Romans*, they came up with the half-joking term "evil math rock" to describe their music. "We liked stuff like Chavez and Don Caballero and June of '44 and Jesus Lizard," explains Brian Cook, "but we knew we didn't really belong to that microcosm, even though that scene came to inspire us more than, say, Integrity or Strife or whatever bands were really carrying the hardcore torch at the time."

For Botch, "evil math rock" just seemed like the best way to acknowledge their interest in the kind of technical, clever post-hardcore and post-rock of the kind those four bands made, without coming across as if they were jumping on any bandwagon. Another band that came up with their own name for the music they made was Morphine. Led by bassist Mark Sandman, the Boston band featured a baritone saxophone, played by Dana Colley, instead of an electric guitar. The deep, distinct kind of alt-rock that they played across a string of great albums in the 1990s was coined low rock by Sandman, who died of a heart attack on stage in Italy in July 1999.[2]

In the history of British pop music since the birth of rock and roll, the ten-year period from 1986 to 1996, from C86 to Romo (more on that one in a bit), might have been the most fruitful era for generating new genres. Some of the genres were so bound by specific location, or came and went so quickly, or both, that if it wasn't for the determination of the weekly music press, they may not have ever been noticed at all.

GREBO

As with Botch and Morphine, the UK band Pop Will Eat Itself got ahead of the music writers by coming up with a name for their industrial-edged indie rock: grebo. They even reinforced it with a couple of on-brand songs: PWEI's *Poppiecock* 12" in 1986 featured a track called "Oh Grebo I Think I Love You," and the following year their debut album, *Box Frenzy*, came out swinging with "Grebo Guru." It worked a little too well, and soon the term was used to rope together the surprisingly robust late 1980s music scene that was happening in the town of Stourbridge in the West Midlands, which included Ned's Atomic Dustbin and the Wonder Stuff. "We revived this '70s (slang) word for dork or nerd, and the press had to build this movement around it to describe everyone with long hair and a nasty guitar sound," PWEI vocalist Graham Crabb told the *Los Angeles Times* in 1989. "I think Grebo was dead as soon as it started. The English press are always looking for the next new thing."[3]

NEW WAVE OF NEW WAVE

Indeed, by the time Crabb was interviewed by the *Los Angeles Times*, Pop Will Eat Itself had moved toward a more sample-laden, pop-industrial collagist sound, while the Neds and the Wonder Stuff could slot safely into indie and alternative rock as the press dropped grebo for Madchester, baggy, acid house, and the Second Summer of Love. Guitar rock stayed in fashion through the early 1990s with recently minted genres such as shoegaze and grunge, but as the luster started to fade from those, in the fall of 1993, a few writers at *New Musical Express* came up with the New Wave of New Wave,[4] which in hindsight was seen to be a botched first attempt at creating Britpop.

"The NWONW . . . was a frantic, speed-fuelled attempt to launch a handful of bands at the chart and reclaim the guitar baton from America,"[5] writes Steve Lamacq, giving a succinct analysis of the prefab scene in *Going Deaf for a Living*. In its brief existence in ink, the NWONW consisted of basically three English bands: the political punks S*M*A*S*H, the pop punk These Animal Men, and Elastica, who quickly rose above it. It's easy to dismiss it all now, but it's not impossible to see where the idea was coming from: the side of new wave being theoretically revived was the one closer to post-punk, so connections could be made via Elastica's nods to Wire, S*M*A*S*H's aggro rhetoric, and These Animal Men's rough polish and keyboard stabs.

Still, the Britpop movement was fully coming together by the summer of 1994, and the NWONW had to be sacrificed to make page space. By year's end, *Select* magazine was asking Sonya Aurora-

Madan, singer for Echobelly, another band the press tied to the scene before Britpop came along and provided them a more spacious home, "Why did NWONW fail so dismally?" "Because it wasn't real," she said. "The bands existed before people made a scene out of it. . . . We participated because you're riding on a wave and you're going to get attention, but I found the whole thing ironic."[6] The magazine even took a final swipe at it ("perhaps the most hazardous sub-genre of all")[7] in a January 1999 piece rounding up the decade's music and fashion trends called "The '90s: A Warning From History."

NINTENDOCORE

As inventive as the music press can be, it never could have dreamed up Nintendocore. In the late 1990s, two Sacramento, California, high school students named Nick Rogers and Forrest Harding played covers of songs from Nintendo games at a talent show. A fellow student, Spencer Seim, was so into it that he started playing drums for them. Rogers and Harding eventually left the band, but Seim carried on with new members joining him.[8] The Advantage, as they came to be called, used rock instrumentation to play amped up but otherwise impressively faithful covers of the thin, digital tunes heard on 1980s 8-bit console games like *Double Dragon*, *Castlevania*, and *Metroid*.

It was a novel concept, but one with serious intent. "While the tunes have a kitschy nostalgia appeal for listeners who were weaned on the games, the Advantage's approach is respectful, even reverential, toward the original source material, much of it written by classically trained Japanese composers."[9] reported the *New York Times* in a 2004 profile of the band. Less reverent were Southern California's Horse the Band, whose own take on the idea of Nintendocore would come to be more what the genre was ultimately known for: attaching the flimsy sound of vintage video game music to the kind of hyper metalcore that was starting to come into fashion around the time they released their 2003 debut album, *R. Borlax*.

ROMO

Turning back once more to the UK: as Britpop was in full swing, the cover of the November 25, 1995, issue of *Melody Maker* declared something called Romo to be "the future pop explosion!" The paper was effectively predicting a scene's success at a time when it was still working itself out on the dance floor of London club nights like Arcadia and Club Skinny. Music journalists Simon Price and Taylor Parkes went so far as to write a manifesto for the movement[10] before the artists themselves—Plastic Fantastic, Orlando, Dex Dexter, Sexus, Hollywood, Viva, Minty—were quite ready for their close-up.

Romo (short for "Romantic Modernism") was, in part, about elevating and celebrating artifice in pop music. These acts had all clearly spent time refining their look, but the quality of their tunes never had the time to catch up to that of their image. As it took substantial influence from the New Romantics of the early 1980s, much of the music came from synth-pop and electronic music. Romo has even been cast positively as foretelling the arrival of the more famous New York–based electroclash movement, which began a few years after Romo's quick demise.

ZEUHL

Romo played with the concept of fame but never truly found fame for itself, but French musician Christian Vander has spent his long career actively rejecting it. The highly skilled drummer founded the band Magma in 1969, and with it he created a molten blend of progressive rock, jazz, and art rock that was deemed to be so much a subgenre in and of itself that it was given its own name: zeuhl. Not only was the loose-but-forceful music way out there, but also Vander created his own conceptual realm for it to exist in.

"Disgusted by the music industry—and the audience members who attended his pre-Magma shows with Carnaby Street Swingers—Vander largely turned his back on our world and created another more mythological one, which he called Kobaïa," writes Will Romano. Vander even came up with his own language to go along with his new world, Kobaïan, which resembled "a Germanic variant."[11] (Decades later, Icelandic band Sigur Rós would do something similar when they invented "Hopelandic," a mixture of their native tongue and speaking in tongues that bandleader Jónsi Birgisson has famously sang in.) The inscrutable product of a singular mind, zeuhl music would seemingly be impossible for another band to play, even if they wanted to.

MICRO-GENRES PLAYLIST

ACAPELLA HARDCORE	Jud Jud–"High Hat Song"
ACOUSTIC BLACK METAL	Impaled Northern Moonforest–"Nocturnal Cauldrons Aflame Amidst the Northern Hellwitch's Perpetual Blasphemy"
BREAKFAST VIOLENCE	Mancake–"International House of Mancake" Waifle–"Hook, Line, and Sinker"
EVIL MATH ROCK	Botch–"C. Thomas Howell as the 'Soul Man'"
LOW ROCK	Morphine–"Buena"
GREBO	Pop Will Eat Itself–"Grebo Guru" The Wonder Stuff–"It's Yer Money I'm After Baby" Ned's Atomic Dustbin–"Grey Cell Green"
NEW WAVE OF NEW WAVE	S*M*A*S*H–"(I Want to) Kill Somebody" These Animal Men–"You're Always Right" Elastica–"Stutter"
NINTENDOCORE	The Advantage–"Mega Man II-Flash Man" Horse the Band–"Seven Tentacles and Eight Flames"
ROMO	Plastic Fantastic–"Fantastique No. 5" Orlando–"Nature's Hated"
ZEUHL	Magma–"Kobaïa"

Neo-Progressive Rock

Neo-progressive rock, or neo-prog, was a way to refer to bands who made prog rock music in the years after the rise of punk, when prog became a four-letter word. Though first-generation prog-ers like Jethro Tull, Pink Floyd, and Rush were all still making music, a new batch of torchbearers arrived in the UK: groups like Marillion, Twelfth Night, IQ, and Pendragon. The music of neo-prog bands was defined by carrying on the genre's theatrical and symphonic attributes, though often these bands had new synthesizers, not the kind you'd hear on classic 1970s prog records.[1]

For a minute there, it appeared to be a commercially viable movement. Aylesbury balladeers Marillion and their debut, *Script for a Jester's Tear*, were voted best band and album in the *Sounds* magazine reader's poll in 1984.[2] "It didn't—couldn't—last," writes Paul Stump, unsparingly appraising the whole affair. "With their slightly embarrassed adoption of modish mullet haircuts and casual wear (alternated with preposterously cheap theatrical costumes), neo-progressive bands just didn't look quite right, a little like school-pop-group members at class reunions."[3] Were it not limited to that movement, the term "neo-progressive rock" could potentially fit groups like Queensrÿche in the 1980s and 1990s, the post-hardcore prog of the Mars Volta and Coheed and Cambria in the early 2000s, and even Radiohead's "Paranoid Android."

Key Players: IQ, Marillion, Pallas, Pendragon, Twelfth Night

CROSSOVER GENRES

ALTERNATIVE ROCK
Coheed and Cambria, the Mars Volta

PROGRESSIVE METAL
Porcupine Tree, Queensrÿche

Neo-Psychedelia

‖‖

While neo-progressive rock limits itself by latching on to a specific time and place, the term neo-psychedelia is rendered nearly useless by its all-encompassing nature. The label dates back to the days of post-punk, when it was applied to bands who were influenced by psychedelic rock from the 1960s.

It's arguable that psychedelic rock has never fully gone out of style, but the late 1970s was a time when it wasn't particularly trendy. Formed in Cambridge, England, and led by surrealist lyricist Robyn Hitchcock, the Soft Boys were early to go back to that well. They were rewarded with cult status and much posthumous love for their two albums, especially the second, *Underwater Moonlight* from 1980. Liverpool was a hot spot, the birthplace of two more commercially successful, and splendidly named, examples of neo-psychedelia: the Teardrop Explodes and Echo and the Bunnymen, who among other accomplishments gave long overcoats their long overdue rock-and-roll cred. A small but dedicated psychedelic rock revival in England followed in the early 1980s, documented on WEA Records' *A Splash of Colour* compilation. The US was also seeing a resurgence of psychedelic rock at the indie level during this time with the Paisley Underground in Los Angeles.

Psychedelic signatures were all over the left-of-mainstream rock world by the end of the 1980s and have been a perennial presence ever since. Notable individual contributions to pushing psych rock forward have been made by people such as Jason Pierce with Spacemen 3 and Spiritualized or Jonathan Donahue with the Flaming Lips and Mercury Rev, but the more directions in which artists come up with to pull the sound—shoegaze, the Elephant 6 collective that started in the 1990s, freak folk—the less concise the definition of neo-psychedelia becomes.

Key Players: The Black Angels, Dungen, Echo and the Bunnymen, the Flaming Lips, Mercury Rev, the Soft Boys, Spacemen 3, Spiritualized, Super Furry Animals, Tame Impala, the Teardrop Explodes, Temples

CROSSOVER GENRES

FREAK FOLK
Akron/Family, Espers

SHOEGAZE
Swervedriver, the Telescopes

New Rave

Whether you spell it "new," "nu," or "neu," new rave is the same fluorescent detonation in the demilitarized zone between guitar rock and dance music in the mid-2000s. It ascended in 2006, peaked in 2007, and flatlined by 2008, smothered by the same internet-accelerated hype cycle that gave it life.

The story goes that the term was cooked up in late 2005 by Jamie Reynolds of the band Klaxons and Joe Daniel of Angular Recording Corporation,[1] who put out Klaxons' first 7", "Gravity's Rainbow." As Reynolds told *The Guardian* in early 2007, "it started as an in-joke and became a minor youth subculture."[2] *NME*, never far from a trend, whether real or imagined, may have also played a role in its invention[3] and certainly filled some columns with it.

Musically, the high-water mark for new rave was surely Klaxons' brash debut album, *Myths of the Near Future*, which collected the Mercury Prize in 2007 as well as an array of praise from reviewers that ranged from faint to breathless. Aside from the inventors and abandoners of the genre itself, the number of declared or assigned new rave bands barely cracks single digits, and their legacy is of less-than-consistent quality. Sounding like the Rapture covering the Birthday Party's "Zoo Music Girl," Shitdisco's "I Know Kung Fu" holds up okay. Less so Trash Fashion's novelty tune "It's a Rave Dave," but that's probably intentional.

Context is important to understanding new rave's motives. The long shadow cast by the self-serious rock bands of the post-Britpop era still loomed over the UK's pop landscape. One too many listens to Coldplay's *X&Y* and you'd probably be thrilled to hear something called Does It Offend You, Yeah?, too. New rave got too much irony in its diet, but having a self-conscious laugh was part of the point. For some, the music was secondary and the real impact was on the worlds of fashion and youth club culture.[4]

Key Players: CSS, Does It Offend You, Yeah?, Hadouken!, Klaxons, Late of the Pier, New Young Pony Club, Shitdisco, Trash Fashion

||||||||||||||||||||||||||||||||||||||||||||||||||||||||||||||||||||||||||||

CROSSOVER TRACKS

||||||||||||||||||||||||||||||||||||||||||||||||||||||||||||||||||||||||||||

DANCE PUNK
The Faint–"Agenda Suicide," Le Tigre–"TKO"

SYNTH-PUNK
The Screamers–"122 Hours of Fear," the Units–"High Pressure Days"

New Wave

Once it finally got going in 1976, punk rock quickly became too successful for its own good. No amount of amateur musicianship, media establishment scorn, or spitting amongst the audience could derail its momentum. Once punk rock bands started moving serious units, Jon Savage writes in *England's Dreaming*, the "carefully formulated definitions" of punk cooked up by the UK scene's formative Svengalis Malcolm McLaren and Bernard Rhodes were no longer of consequence. "'Punk' was now 'New Wave' and could mean acts as diverse as American visitors Talking Heads, Television or Blondie . . . [who] showed that the illusion of any Punk unity of style or of milieu—either in London or New York—was becoming unsustainable."[1]

There's a gap wider than one of David Byrne's old oversized suits between how the term "new wave" was originally deployed and what it is most understood to mean today, especially in America. In 1977, punk rock became the new wave. When post-punk came along after it, *that* became the new wave. For those that didn't distinguish between punk and post-punk, new wave covered both. For those who wrote about the music or played it on the radio, it was a gentler term under which to slip punk into people's living rooms.[2]

Who *was* new wave and who wasn't was determined by a loose set of standards that didn't have much to do with the actual music. As long as a band didn't play folk, prog, or blues rock and bared some scar of modernity, they were in—and even then there were exceptions. There were rigid rockers like the B-52's, the Cars, and Devo, but also those that found their groove like the Pretenders, Squeeze, and Ian Dury and the Blockheads. There were many who got cerebral with state-of-the-art electronics, and those like Adam and the Ants, Bow Wow Wow, and the Thompson Twins (in their early days) who got physical with tribal drum rhythms.

New wave could indicate many things and, by that same token, meant very little in terms of describing the actual music. Rather than trying to parse out what ABC, INXS, and XTC share in song, it was, and is, easier to remark on other characteristics of the genre like its brash appearance, meaning it remains inextricably tied to the image of the era, the "new wave hairdos" that the Beastie Boys gave a shout-out to in "Girls." Somewhere along the line, the whole genre just became easier to understand as flamboyantly attired bands playing synthesizers on MTV.

A blunt but fair observation was made by first-generation video jockey Martha Quinn in the book *VJ*: "If you ask who summed up the '80s better, U2 or A Flock of Seagulls, I'd have to say A Flock of Seagulls."[3] Such a statement is sure to tickle some as much as it troubles others, but there is a general ring of truth to it. New wave and Quinn's former employer in its early days formed a kind of influential partnership. Later on, MTV's Viacom sister channel VH1 built its reputation on doing everything it could to make sure the decade was remembered as a neon pop-culture paradise through its *I Love the '80s* series (based on the identically named BBC program). Really, it's not hard to argue that the image of a band like the suave Duran Duran in pastel suits crammed on the bow of a sailboat cruising to "Rio" makes for better television than Bono bellowing Latin in "Gloria" on a barge in a dingy Dublin shipyard.

By 1987, MTV was shoving new wave aside to make screen time for less progressive, yet even more superficial, glam metal. However, when audiences finally tired of *those* hair bands, they couldn't wait to start waxing nostalgic about new wave. Performing and recording covers of the multitude of signature songs from that period became a regular pastime for all kinds of artists in the 1990s. Punk bands could get easy cheers by speeding up a new wave favorite. Perhaps connecting with the genre's unabashed sensitive side, emocore came up with some great covers as well.

Still, most of the bands who wrote all those songs didn't experience the same renewed interest. Those few that survived the downturn had to adapt to do so. David Gahan was the only one of the four members of Depeche Mode who didn't play keyboards on their 1981 debut album, *Speak & Spell*, but as they capped off their increasingly sensual, moody decade with the smash *Violator*, real drums, and even guitars, were making increasing appearances. Riding high in the first half of the 1980s and hitting a rough patch in the second, Duran Duran made a rare comeback from new wave in 1993 on the strength of the mature alt-rock ballad "Ordinary World" and its follow-up, "Come Undone."

One thing that the glut of cover versions in the 1990s highlighted was that new wave was the consummate singles genre. One only needs to hear "My Sharona" to get the Knack. Focusing on the short-term single instead of the long-haul album had become an alien concept after the Beatles started releasing full-length records worth playing all the way through, so much so that "AOR," album-oriented rock, became a common industry term.

It would seem that no such spelunking is needed to get to the bottom of new wave, but is that notion worth reconsidering? Sure, many of the groups arrived on set fully made up and ready for the top: Duran Duran, Kajagoogoo, and A Flock of Seagulls all came out of the gate with soon-to-be-big singles already in hand. Still, there were those that had a bit more history behind them. The biggest example was of course New Order and their transition from an entire separate life before that as Joy Division, but others had more to them as well.

The Thompson Twins' debut album, saddled with the clunky title *A Product Of . . . (Participation)*, fits between the post-punk disco of the Athens, Georgia, band Pylon and the echoing dislocated rhythms of Bristol's the Pop Group. Orchestral Manoeuvers in the Dark started out by mingling Kraftwerk with some rock instrumentation on singles like "Electricity" and "Enola Gay." Years after their initial success in the UK, the group finally captured American ears as they settled into stable synth-pop with "So in Love," from their fourth album, *Crush*, in 1985. They would borrow from "So in Love" the following year on "If You Leave," the big single they wrote under a tight deadline for the John Hughes film *Pretty in Pink*, which became OMD's commercial calling card despite their previous life on the cutting edge.

Pioneer Tracks: Adam and the Ants–"Kings of the Wild Frontier," Blondie–"Heart of Glass," Devo–"Whip It," Gary Numan–"Cars," Roxy Music–"Love is the Drug," Talking Heads–"Life During Wartime"

Key Players: A Flock of Seagulls, ABC, the B-52's, the Cars, Culture Club, Depeche Mode, Duran Duran, Devo, Eurythmics, the Human League, Orchestral Manoeuvers in the Dark, the Pretenders, Spandau Ballet, Squeeze, Thompson Twins

CROSSOVER TRACKS

COLLEGE ROCK

INXS–"Don't Change," Modern English–"I Melt With You," the Psychedelic Furs–"Love My Way"

GOTH ROCK

Bauhaus–"The Man With the X-Ray Eyes," the Cure–"In Between Days," Siouxsie and the Banshees–"Peek-A-Boo"

POST-PUNK

Killing Joke–"Eighties," Public Image Ltd–"Rise," Wire–"Map Ref. 41°N 93°W"

New Wave of American Heavy Metal

||||||||||||||||||||||||||||||||||||||||||||||||||||||||||||||||||||||||||||||||||||||||||||||||||||

There are a few snags with the idea of a New Wave of American Heavy Metal. For one, it demands comparison with the New Wave of British Heavy Metal, which was a more easily identifiable wave of new heavy metal bands in the UK around the same time in the late 1970s. There wasn't so much a new wave of metal in America in the 1990s and 2000s as much as there was *more* metal. The typical narrative is that grunge and alternative rock chased heavy metal off the playground in the early 1990s, but sales figures and people who went to ice hockey games back in that era will tell you a different story.

The nu metal craze fueled the idea of a New Wave of American Heavy Metal, and there has been a lot of overlap in use of the two terms. The idea of a New Wave of American Heavy Metal encompasses the alarming rise of metalcore in the 2000s. It can also rope together any and all metal bands on the North American continent from the past thirty years, which is why, in addition to being a clunky tribute acronym (NWAHM), it's not a terribly useful scene label.

Key Players: As I Lay Dying, Avenged Sevenfold, Disturbed, Killswitch Engage, Korn, Lamb of God, Slipknot

CROSSOVER GENRES

NU METAL
Deftones, System of a Down

PROGRESSIVE METAL
Cave In, Coheed and Cambria

New Wave of British Heavy Metal

"The New Wave of British Heavy Metal (or NWOBHM, as it would come to be known) movement was basically pimply-faced seventeen-year-old boys discovering a music that they could call their own," writes guitarist Phil Collen in his memoir, *Adrenalized*. Before joining Def Leppard in 1982, Collen was in what he calls an "extreme glam" band called Girl. Though both bands were considered part of the NWOBHM, Collen claims that neither felt they had much to do with it.[1]

Def Leppard aimed higher than the Sheffield club circuit. Their commercial ambition was right there in their odd but catchy name: an imaginary, hearing-impaired, sub-Saharan predator with the spelling stylized to emulate Led Zeppelin. It's debatable how heavy their metal really was, but they made for an approachable face for the fledgling movement. First recognized in print by writer Geoff Barton in *Sounds* magazine at the end of the 1970s,[2] the preexisting, if scattered, scene that he dubbed the New Wave of British Heavy Metal needed as much momentum as possible if it was going to take off.

Heavy metal came from Birmingham, but the NWOBHM was from all over Blighty. Venom and Raven were from Newcastle. Diamond Head and Witchfinder General hailed from Stourbridge. There was Saxon from Barnsley and the Tygers of Pan Tang from the seaside town of Whitley Bay. Iron Maiden and Girlschool, an all-female band in the scene, were from London—as were Motörhead, who, although they were worshipped by many a NWOBHM fan, predated the scene and were perhaps a little too straightforward hard rock to be classified as part of it.

The New Wave of British Heavy Metal was all about stepping up metal's game. Technical prowess wasn't just admired among fellow players; audiences took note as well, showing their appreciation with the newfound form of metal applause, headbanging.[3] The roots of many subsequent metal genres all trace back to the NWOBHM's innovations in music and presentation. This was the point when heavy metal decided that one of its primary directives going forward was to push the limits: harder, louder, shreddier. Significant as it was, by the mid-1980s, the wave was no longer new and the heavy metal press was thirsty for young blood. The scene had moved on, but it had set the course for some time to come.

Iron Maiden assured their place in the heavy metal hierarchy when they replaced original singer Paul Di'Anno with Bruce Dickinson, who had an operatic delivery that could give Rob Halford a run for his money. The album that Dickinson joined the band for, *The Number of the Beast*, was the beginning of Iron Maiden's prime, the one that put their posters on the bedroom walls of those spotty teenagers. Released in 1982, it was the beginning of a run of albums that could do no wrong, even when they took a prog turn on *Seventh Son of a Seventh Son* in 1988. Aside from Def Leppard, Iron Maiden became the NWOBHM's biggest export, transcending the movement and becoming, like Judas Priest before them, synonymous with heavy metal.

Some of the most influential NWOBHM bands, however, weren't the most successful ones. Diamond Head's commercial achievements never matched their influence, but they were the favorite NWOBHM band of young Southern California heshers Lars Ulrich and James Hetfield. When the two formed Metallica in 1981, they were taking cues from Diamond Head's debut album, *Lightning to the Nations*, and would eventually come to record covers of over half the songs on that record.[4]

Pioneer Tracks: Def Leppard–"Getcha Rocks Off," Fist–"Name, Rank and Serial Number," Iron Maiden–"Running Free," Motörhead–"Motörhead," Son of a Bitch–"Stallions of the Highway"

Key Players: Angel Witch, Diamond Head, Girlschool, Grim Reaper, Raven, Samson, Saxon, Tygers of Pan Tang, Venom, Witchfinder General

CROSSOVER TRACKS

HARD ROCK
Budgie–"Crash Course in Brain Surgery," UFO–"Doctor Doctor"

HEAVY METAL
Deep Purple–"Speed King," Judas Priest–"The Ripper"

SPEED METAL
Flotsam and Jetsam–"Iron Tears," Megadeth–"Mechanix"

No Wave

No Wave was bound to happen. The young artists at the center of the New York City scene were willfully confrontational, and the music they produced was uncontainable, but No Wave was also the logical conclusion of certain ideas at the heart of the punk rock conversation. The setting that nurtured it, downtrodden lower Manhattan in the late 1970s, was a modern urban bohemia that was rare in America, providing untended vacancies for hungry idealists who didn't want the distraction of needing a full-time job to get by.

The actual scope of No Wave has become dwarfed by its afterlife allure. Forty years will do that to a cult classic. Anti-commercial by nature, No Wave wasn't looking for success, despite the outsize personalities and performance antics of prime movers like Lydia Lunch and James Chance. The number of groups in the scene was limited and always shifting, the musicians swapping roles and rotating in and out of gigs. There was Lunch's Teenage Jesus and the Jerks, James Chance and the Contortions, Glenn Branca's Theoretical Girls, Mars, DNA, Daily Life, the Gynecologists, Tone Death, Terminal, and several others that came and went in the few years that No Wave grew away from the light.

Exposure at first was limited, but any external pressure proved detrimental. Much like New York punk had its own *Punk* magazine, No Wave had the fanzine *No*, which was based at NYU and started by bandmates Chris Nelson and Jim Sclavunos.[1] The scene was eventually brought to the attention of Brian Eno, who not long after relocating to New York helmed the *No New York* compilation that collected four songs each from the Contortions, Teenage Jesus and the Jerks, Mars, and DNA. Released in late 1978, No Wave's big break had a kind of fracturing effect on the movement it sought to elevate, and it seems that few involved in making it were completely happy with the final product. Many would continue on—Lunch established a varied solo career; Branca put together his guitar ensembles and other ventures—but by decade's end the micro-eruption was dissipating. The aftershocks, however, both early (Sonic Youth, whose Thurston Moore and Lee Ranaldo played in Glenn Branca and Rhys Chatham's experimental guitar orchestras) and delayed (every other art-damaged band from New York in the past twenty years), were lasting.

Key Players: James Chance and the Contortions, Daily Life, DNA, the Gynecologists, Teenage Jesus and the Jerks, Mars, Theoretical Girls, Tone Death

CROSSOVER GENRES

EXPERIMENTAL ROCK
Boredoms, Sonic Youth, Swans

NOISE ROCK
Big Black, the Jesus and Mary Chain (*Psychocandy*), Scratch Acid

POST-PUNK
The Birthday Party, the Mekons (*The Quality of Mercy is Not Strnen*), the Pop Group

Noise Pop

Taking credit for the term in an NPR piece in 2012, Noise Pop Festival founders Jordan Kurland, Kevin Arnold, and Dawson Ludwig wrote that they coined the label to "define a certain yin and yang of melody and dissonance."[1] Who's on their noise pop playlist? The Velvet Underground, Big Star, R.E.M., Hüsker Dü, the Jesus and Mary Chain, Dinosaur Jr., the Replacements, Sonic Youth, the Lemonheads, and so forth. Alternative rock, basically, and also post-punk, college rock, shoegaze, grunge, post-hardcore, emo, indie rock, post-rock, and, curiously, Primal Scream's C86-defining "Velocity Girl," which is quite lacking in dissonance.

The term was broad enough to sustain a life of its own outside of the festival. In a 2014 piece entitled "When I'm Gone: Why Vivian Girls Mattered," Pitchfork wistfully recalled a "late-00s noise pop boom."[2] The following year, Vice put forth the idea that noise pop "ultimately died"[3] in 2010. In both eulogies, the notion was that a not-entirely-connected cluster of bands from both American coasts from that time period—among them No Age, Wavves, and Dum Dum Girls from the West and the Pains of Being Pure at Heart, Crystal Stilts, and Vivian Girls from the East—had created an actual noise pop scene. Many genres start with a few artists and blow up from there, but noise pop may have done the reverse.

Key Players: Crystal Stilts, Deerhoof, Dum Dum Girls, No Age, the Pains of Being Pure at Heart, Sleigh Bells, Vivian Girls, Wavves

CROSSOVER TRACKS

INDIE ROCK

Best Coast–"Boyfriend," Male Bonding–"Year's Not Long"

NOISE ROCK

The Birthday Party–"Release the Bats," the Jesus Lizard–"Nub"

Noise Rock

||||||||||||||||||||||||||||||||||||||||||||||||||||||||||||||||||||||||||||||||||||||||||||||||||||||||||||

Rock music had the novel idea to make noise desirable with the introduction of guitar distortion in the 1960s. "Surplus sound is a key characteristic of electrified music," writes Paul Hegarty in *Noise/ Music*, "and as the 1960s go on, distortion and feedback, pushing the machinery beyond limits, offers another layer of noise that is both literal and noise in the sense of being unwanted, excess, waste. These noises are quickly used and become techniques."[1] This is how the sound of the Kinks' supposedly slashed guitar amplifiers on "You Really Got Me" came to be re-created en masse by effects pedal manufacturers.

It has been the responsibility of each successive generation of rock music to get under the skin of the old guard. The experimental fringes of punk like the No Wave movement encouraged not simply distortion and volume, but other disturbances such as feedback and atonality. This was picked up on by the next wave of abrasive New York groups like Sonic Youth and Swans. Comparing those two bands in 1985 in the *New York Times*, where he was the first chief pop music critic, Robert Palmer (not the "Addicted to Love" singer of the same name) wrote that "Sonic Youth's new album, *Bad Moon Rising*, also kicks up a fearsome noise, but its palette of sounds and colors is considerably more varied."[2]

In the 2000s, Columbus, Ohio, coughed up a small scene led by Times New Viking and Psychedelic Horseshit that fogged up low-fidelity punk with plumes of feedback, which the latter band dubbed "shitgaze," a pun on shoegaze. Beyond the outskirts of rock lurk the true noise terrorists, often working alone under assumed aliases, such as Japan's prolific Masami Akita (Merzbow), Brooklyn's Margaret Chardiet (Pharmakon), and Britain's Benjamin John Power (Blanck Mass).

Key Players: Big Black, Butthole Surfers, Cows, Girl Band, Health, Lightning Bolt, Melt-Banana, Sonic Youth, Swans, Times New Viking, Unsane

CROSSOVER GENRES

INDUSTRIAL METAL
KMFDM, Ministry

NOISE POP:
No Age, Sleigh Bells

Nu Gaze

Writing for Drowned in Sound in 2009, Nathaniel Cramp, founder of Sonic Cathedral ("the label that celebrates itself," a shoegaze-terminology joke), declared that there was no such thing as nu gaze. "What there is, however, is a renewed interest in all things shoegaze."[1]

To some, however, nu gaze wasn't only a renewed interest in a marginalized genre. British band My Vitriol has been credited with coining the term to describe their own music.[2] The "nu" connection may seem unfortunate to some, but My Vitriol's 2001 debut album does actually include a nu metal song, "C.O.R.," even if it only lasts for forty seconds. The rest of *Finelines* is less brutish, and its collision of the sharp, surging rock popular in the United States at the time with a British melodic sensibility might still be the most apt sound for the nu gaze label.

As the decade went on, use of the term gathered steam, and the idea of it became bigger and less clear. Electronic-based artists like M83 and Ulrich Schnauss entered the conversation, as did a number of bands who were much closer to the *old* gaze. More recently, the Philadelphia band Nothing comes close at times to updating the My Vitriol recipe, but the nu gaze tag has now pretty much fallen out of use.

Key Players: Amusement Parks on Fire, M83, My Vitriol, Nothing, Ulrich Schnauss, Serena-Maneesh, Working for a Nuclear Free City

||||||||||||||||||||||||||||||||||||||||||||||||||||||||||||||||||||||

CROSSOVER TRACKS

||||||||||||||||||||||||||||||||||||||||||||||||||||||||||||||||||||||

POST-METAL

Deafheaven–"Sunbather," Isis–"Altered Course"

SHOEGAZE

Cheatahs–"The Swan," Film School–"Dear Me"

Nu Metal

The free compilation CD that came with the January 1995 issue of *CMJ New Music Monthly* kicked off with Radiohead's "My Iron Lung" and included tunes from a typically diverse college radio–friendly bunch: Massive Attack, the Wolfgang Press, Jewel, and so on. Smack in the middle of the disc, two tracks after "Who Will Save Your Soul," crouched the future of commercial hard rock: "Clown," from Korn's self-titled debut album.

Korn should have been an outlier in the post-grunge rock world of the mid-1990s: the novelty elements in their music—blaring bagpipes and ferociously spitting lyrics from nursery rhymes, in the same song no less—seemed unlikely to endear them to the mainstream. Defying the odds, *Korn* found its audience. Defying logic, twenty years after its release, the album was named the "Most Important Metal Record of the Last 20 Years"[1] by *Rolling Stone* in 2014 (though in 2004 the magazine's *Album Guide* only awarded *Korn* two stars).[2]

Credit has been given to Korn for being the first band labeled "nu metal,"[3] and to *Korn*'s producer, Ross Robinson, as the button-pushing guru of the genre.[4] In *Fargo Rock City*, Chuck Klosterman writes that Korn "fuse the three most obnoxious elements of modern music: the down-tuned throb of metal, the mind-numbing rhythm of rap, and the inaudible howl of hard-core thrash."[5] You can argue with the choice of adjectives, but his observations about genre lineage are spot-on. Korn bassist Fieldy even explained to Klosterman that their "musical history starts with the Red Hot Chili Peppers and early Faith No More."[6]

Appearing to have fun was antithetical to nu metal, which took performative angst to a new level, as seen in the video for Staind's gloomy radio hit "It's Been Awhile," with singer Aaron Lewis hunched in a semi-fetal position, eyes downcast. When they weren't pummeling their own feelings into submission, they were taking their anger out on 1980s pop staples. Nu metal was a genre that accosted dynamic singles like George Michael's "Faith," New Order's "Blue Monday," and Michael Jackson's "Smooth Criminal" and stomped them into one-dimensional caricatures.

Nu metal is often conflated with rap metal. There is overlap between the two, but they are not entirely the same. Nu metal also had a shock rock, glam side. Korn walked it like they talked it, going as far as to write a song named after their favored Adidas tracksuits, but bands like Mushroomhead, Mudvayne, and Slipknot wore Halloween masks or took fashion tips from the Marilyn Manson camp. (Manson himself is sometimes but not always associated with nu metal.)

If many initially benefited from the association, they have also, unfairly or not, had a hard time coming out from underneath it. One such band is Deftones, whose 1995 debut album *Adrenaline* did have traces of nu metal. By *White Pony* and *Deftones*, however, they had moved beyond the genre. They went too rough on their cover of the Smiths' "Please Please Please Let Me Get What I Want," but you can tell singer Chino Moreno was feeling it.

As over the top as nu metal could be, in hindsight, the conditions that allowed it to thrive are more clear. By the end of the 1990s, MTV had given up on whatever adults were left in its audience and was chasing after the polarized concerns of the 12-to-18-year-old crowd. On one side, there was Britney, Christina, and a fleet of manufactured boy bands. What else was supposed to balance that out?

Pioneer Tracks: Coal Chamber–"Loco," Deftones–"Bored," Korn–"Blind," Mushroomhead–"Never Let It Go," Papa Roach–"Orange Drive Palms"

Key Players: Disturbed, Korn, Limp Bizkit, Linkin Park, Mudvayne, Papa Roach, Slipknot, Staind

CROSSOVER TRACKS

FUNK METAL

Faith No More–"We Care a Lot," Rage Against the Machine–"Killing in the Name," Red Hot Chili Peppers–"Fight Like a Brave"

GROOVE METAL

Pantera–"Cowboys From Hell," Sepultura–"Refuse/Resist," White Zombie–"Thunder Kiss '65"

INDUSTRIAL ROCK

Marilyn Manson–"The Beautiful People," Nine Inch Nails–"Down In It," Pigface–"Suck"

Oi!

Oi! came into being via *Sounds* magazine, where it was hyped by writer Garry Bushell, who also played in the Gonads. Bushell was a central figure in the scene, putting together Oi! compilation albums and managing the Cockney Rejects, whose song "Oi! Oi! Oi!" was the lead track on the first of those comps.[1]

Oi! was part of UK punk's second wave, regarded by fans as hard-hitting and working class, but seen as only skin deep by detractors. Oi! punched up the three-chord belligerence of *Never Mind the Bollocks, Here's the Sex Pistols* with choruses that resembled UK football chants; Cockney Rejects even dinged the charts in 1980 with their cover of "I'm Forever Blowing Bubbles," a terrace anthem for East London football club West Ham. This was a time when UK violence surrounding the sport was entering its prime, and the band's overt association with their team invited more trouble than they expected.[2] Football hooligans, it turns out, wouldn't be the worst crowd drawn to the genre.

Decades later, Oi! still can't fully shake the associations it made with the National Front and racist factions that severely limited its commercial appeal. Hersham band Sham 69 broke up before the term was even coined, and others, like London band the Business, pushed back at the right wingers, but not everyone did all they could to distance the music from that element.[3] The controversy and critical dismissal, however, didn't initially travel with the records over to America, where Sham 69's two-minute rallying cries spoke to hardcore's stripped-down aggression and anti-fashion sense.[4]

Key Players: The 4-Skins, the Business, Cockney Rejects, Sham 69

CROSSOVER GENRES

HARDCORE
D.O.A., Minor Threat

STREET PUNK
The Exploited, UK Subs

The Paisley Underground

"With all due modesty and respect," Steve Wynn recalls of the Paisley Underground, "I was kind of at the center of it all—mostly because I was working at Rhino Records as the indie music buyer." In the early 1980s, Wynn was living in Los Angeles and playing guitar with different people. The band he would lead through the rest of the decade, the Dream Syndicate, came together around the time he met musicians Susanna Hoffs and Vicki Peterson, who were then calling themselves the Bangs. Wynn had ordered the first Salvation Army single and was giving Hoffs and Peterson tips on pressing their own. "It only made sense that we would start doing shows together, since we were kind of an island in the midst of an LA scene that wasn't that geared towards '60s- or garage rock–influenced music."

Born in 1960, Steve Wynn was reared on the Beatles, the Who, and Creedence Clearwater Revival. Those glory days of rock have been enshrined in the public consciousness for so long that it's hard to imagine a world in which their relevance would feel negligible—but Los Angeles in the early 1980s was just such a world. At the same time that the Dream Syndicate were starting out, Mötley Crüe and their ilk were marauding around the city. Not only were the 1960s long gone, but the 1970s were dead, too.

In that shallow pool, it was brave to look back at the deep end. The Dream Syndicate, the Bangs, and their friends in the Three O'Clock and the Rain Parade stood out in their shared love of classic psychedelia. The story goes that Michael Querico of the Three O'Clock came up with the name Paisley Underground. Wynn confirms this, though he doesn't remember exactly when he first heard it used. "I always liked that name and thought it gave some kind of context and center to what we were doing. Look, as good as all of the bands were, it really helped that we came out together and built some kind of a scene. It made it easier to book shows, get press, and have people in other cities pay attention."

As the summer of 1982 wound down, the Dream Syndicate recorded their first LP, releasing it shortly thereafter in the fall. *The Days of Wine and Roses* now sounds ahead of its time, not behind it. The band, which then also included bassist/vocalist Kendra Smith, guitarist Karl Precoda, and drummer Dennis Duck, knew they had done something special. Wynn notes that it isn't easy, especially for new groups, to translate the live show into a recording, but he thinks the low budget and speed at which they made *The Days of Wine and Roses* worked in their favor. "I was working at Rhino the day it came out, and it was a thrill to place it high on the new release racks in the store—the perks of being an employee in a hip and influential store."

By its nature, the Paisley Underground stayed tight-knit in its hometown, but word was leaking out, and the Dream Syndicate began to be covered by magazines like *Creem* that Wynn had grown up reading. They started playing out in cities like San Francisco and Austin. They found that cities like New York, Chicago, Boston, and Atlanta got what they were doing, but others didn't as much. The indie underground didn't have the kind of resources to unite and spread the word nationally the way that, say, MTV would soon be able to do. The Bangs would become the band in the scene to make the most of that particular resource after they became the Bangles and signed to Columbia Records. No less than Prince became enamored with the concept of the Paisley Underground, famously giving his "Manic Monday" to the Bangles, helping them on their way to the global recognition they would reach with "Walk Like an Egyptian."

Major labels came calling as the 1980s moved along. The Dream Syndicate released *Medicine Show* on A&M Records in 1984, Rain Parade put out *Crashing Dream* on Island the following year, and the Bangles hit the big time the year after that. The attention was deserved, but it meant more obligations. "The scene died in 1983," Wynn states frankly. "That's when we all got record deals, national and international press, and started to tour constantly." Those developments were all good and necessary he says, but it meant that the days of playing shows and hanging out together, influencing one another's music, were a thing of the past. Aside from public perception, the scene had dissipated. "I tried to keep up on what my buddies were doing, but you can see that we all started to sound much less alike as time went on. No surprise and not a bad thing."

At decade's end, the four bands at the center of the Paisley Underground had all broken up. Beginning with *Kerosene Man*, Wynn released a number of solo albums throughout the 1990s and beyond. The scene's legend lingered on, the 2000s saw its own breed of retro-revolutionaries, and, perhaps given the manageable size of their clique, the original bands even came together for a benefit concert in 2013. Happy to see all the bands for the most part still active and healthy, Wynn recalls everyone getting along and glad to see one another—no small feat among rock lifers. "The thing that struck me that night was that all four of the bands were as good, or actually better, than they were before. And that all of us were having a great time together, and there wasn't a single problem child in the bunch. Those were two really special and memorable nights for me. I hope we can do it again someday."

Pioneer Tracks: The Bangles—"Hero Takes a Fall," the Dream Syndicate—"The Days of Wine and Roses," the Rain Parade—"This Can't Be Today," the Salvation Army–"She Turns To Flowers," the Three O'Clock–"Jet Fighter"

Key Players: All of the above, Green on Red, the Long Ryders, Opal

||||||||||||||||||||||||||||||||||||||||||||||||||||||||||||||||||||||||||||||||

CROSSOVER TRACKS

||||||||||||||||||||||||||||||||||||||||||||||||||||||||||||||||||||||||||||||||

INDIE ROCK

Game Theory–"Date with an Angel," the Green Pajamas–"Kim the Waitress," the Revolving Paint Dream–"Flowers in the Sky"

POST-PUNK

The dB's–"Black and White," the Feelies–"Crazy Rhythms," the Soft Boys–"I Wanna Destroy You"

PSYCHEDELIC ROCK

The Byrds–"Eight Miles High," Pink Floyd–"See Emily Play," Quicksilver Messenger Service–"Who Do You Love (Part 1)"

Pop Punk

A full account of pop-minded punk would have to include the Ramones, the Clash, Buzzcocks, Hüsker Dü, and more, but the modern notion of pop punk sprang from California in the mid-1990s. Pop punk was the prozac that mainstream rock needed after the sudden end of Nirvana with Kurt Cobain's suicide. The order of the words here is significant: pop punk prioritized melody over velocity. Speed and simplicity were part of it; otherwise, it wouldn't be punk. Greater accessibility, although still a crime in the eyes of some, was on the agenda.

Green Day didn't just jump in at the right time out of nowhere. The band had been active in the Bay Area since the late 1980s and were on their second album, *Kerplunk*, when their sizeable indie-level sales caught the attention of the majors, and Warner Bros scooped them up for their third. "It's timing really," said Billie Joe Armstrong of Green Day to *Punk Planet* in 2000, for a story that delved into the aftermath of the US punk boom of 1994. "A lot of people were getting bored with slower, drudgy, introverted music that was going on, then we came out."[1]

In the first weeks of 1994, *Dookie* set off the second big rock-and-roll gold rush of the 1990s. California was used to gold rushes, but punks throughout the state, and across the country, steeled themselves for being on the giving or receiving end of the inevitable cries of "sellout!" The hurling of such accusations was further complicated when the Offspring's *Smash* (also their third) made waves that summer on the strength of the unavoidable "Come Out and

Play." *Smash* was released on Epitaph Records, a well-regarded independent punk label started in 1980 by Bad Religion guitarist Brett Gurewitz.

Some of the most significant pop punk releases of 1994 were on Epitaph. In addition to the Offspring, the label also put out two other significant breakthroughs that key year, Rancid's *Let's Go* and NOFX's *Punk in Drublic*. One notable Cali-punk breakthrough that *didn't* come out on the label that year was Bad Religion's own. After seven albums and over a decade of doing it themselves, the LA punk mainstays went with Atlantic for *Stranger Than Fiction*.

By the end of 1994, alternative rock playlists were flooded with fast, catchy songs from Golden State punk bands. Long hair was out, singing with an affected British accent was in. They didn't all go platinum, but the boundless appetite for more brought attention that might not have otherwise come to oldtimers like the Descendents (and their spinoff, All), the Mr. T Experience, and the Vandals, and newcomers like Face to Face. The wave also swept up pop punk bands from outside of California such as Screeching Weasel (Illinois), Hagfish (Texas), and MxPx (Washington).

Pop punk was everywhere for a couple of years, until focus shifted around the time Green Day took a first acoustic stab at maturity with "Good Riddance (Time of Your Life)," its lyrics destined to be quoted in high school graduation speeches for eternity. Fortunately, San Diego area band Blink 182 soon swept in, with a sense of humor raised on NOFX's album titles and an earnest side gleaned from emo, and kept the California dream alive.

Pioneer Tracks: Buzzcocks—"Ever Fallen in Love (With Someone You Shouldn't've)," the Dickies—"Banana Splits," the Descendents—"Hope," the Ramones—"Blitzkrieg Bop," the Undertones—"Teenage Kicks"

Key Players: Blink 182, the Bouncing Souls, Good Charlotte, Green Day, Fall Out Boy, the Mr. T Experience, MxPx, the Offspring, Screeching Weasel, Sum 41

CROSSOVER GENRES

ALTERNATIVE ROCK

Imperial Teen, the Rentals, that dog.

EMO(CORE)

Alkaline Trio, the Get Up Kids, Saves the Day

GRUNGE

The Fastbacks, Supersuckers

Post-Britpop

In his book on the Britpop scene, writer John Harris concludes that the "most potent legacy" of the genre was not the work of bands who thrived on artistic flair, but rather the "vision of Noel Gallagher, perched alone on a stool, playing 'Wonderwall' while the assembled thousands sang along."[1] The term "post-Britpop" has since become shorthand for safe, guitar-centric UK bands who achieved their greatest commercial success roughly between 1997 and 2005. The "post" prefix dooms the era to designated driver status, soberly popping *Let it Be* in the car stereo and escorting Britpop home from its big party.

Prime among post-Britpop precursors is Radiohead's *The Bends*, which you can hear more than a few traces of in Coldplay's early material. One can also hear the promise in Britpop-adjacent alternative rock like Manic Street Preachers' soaring *Everything Must Go* and two debut albums from bands who hung on the sides of the hype train, Mansun (*Attack of the Grey Lantern*) and Longpigs (*The Sun Is Often Out*). Where it all ended up was a bit more traditionalist.

"The first post-Britpop group to achieve similar success to Blur and Oasis were Travis,"[2] writes Harris about the band who dared to ask "Why Does It Always Rain On Me?" That Glaswegian group had been kicking around for some time by then, as had Welsh bands Stereophonics and Catatonia, both of whom get tossed on the post-Britpop pile. Catatonia, in particular, had released some charming singles and the album *Way Beyond Blue* at Britpop's peak in 1996; they just happened to be more successful a couple of years later. Some see Travis' second album, *The Man Who*, as setting up the future success of Coldplay's debut, *Parachutes*, which might also make them responsible for Starsailor and the like.

Key Players: Catatonia, Coldplay, Doves, Elbow, Embrace, Gay Dad, Idlewild, JJ72, Keane, Snow Patrol, Starsailor, Stereophonics, Travis

||||||||||||||||||||||||||||||||||||||||||||||||||||||||||||||||||||||||||||||||||||

CROSSOVER TRACKS

||||||||||||||||||||||||||||||||||||||||||||||||||||||||||||||||||||||||||||||||||||

ALTERNATIVE ROCK

Longpigs–"On and On," Manic Street Preachers–"A Design for Life," the Verve–"The Drugs Don't Work"

BRITPOP

Gene–"Where Are They Now?," Oasis–"Wonderwall," Suede–"The Wild Ones"

Post-Grunge

Like post-Britpop in the UK, the idea of post-grunge in the United States is that of the comedown after a major cultural moment. The term, which wasn't in use when the music it describes was being made, can either be used as a wide angle lens through which to view the messy state of American commercial rock music in the second half of the 1990s or, in tighter focus, an apt enough label for all of the humorless dude bands who put Bush's *Sixteen Stone* on a diet and sang like they had Eddie Vedder stuck in their throats.

The latter interpretation of post-grunge is the most useful, as rock music from this time that wasn't directly in debt to one Seattle band or another is better understood within the context of either its own distinct genre (pop punk, ska revival, etc.) or the "alternative" catchall. It can still be hard to keep your Fuels and Tonics straight, but isolating "post-grunge" to bands like Creed and Puddle of Mudd makes it easier to poke fun at, with the easiest target of all, of course, being Nickelback.

Key Players: 3 Doors Down, Bush, Creed, Days of the New, Fuel, Nickelback, Our Lady Peace, Puddle of Mudd, Seven Mary Three, Silverchair, Tonic

CROSSOVER TRACKS

GRUNGE

Candlebox–"Far Behind," Stone Temple Pilots–"Plush"

NU METAL

Linkin Park–"In the End," Staind–"It's Been Awhile"

Post-Hardcore

"I always thought 'post-hardcore' was almost like an afterthought," says Jon Bolling. "I don't think bands like Jawbox, Shudder to Think, and Fugazi, coming out of DC, initially were called post-hardcore." However, the tag does make sense in the way that members of those groups had roots in the capital's hardcore scene. Washington, DC, is a prominent setting for the stories of both hardcore and post-hardcore, and much of that has to do with its continuity and the recurring roles of certain musicians.

Minor Threat had been at the forefront of the city's hardcore scene in the early 1980s, and frontman Ian MacKaye, after his brief but fortuitous spell in Embrace, joined up with Guy Picciotto and Brendan Canty from Rites of Spring, as well as bassist Joe Lally, and formed Fugazi in 1987. Michael Azerrad describes how the band "jettisoned the trappings (and traps) of hardcore," fusing punked up sing-alongs with "sinuous funk and reggae beats."[1] Not all post-hardcore bands would outwardly share Fugazi's interest in reggae, but their start-stop rhythms became a distinct tic of the genre. Jawbox and Shudder to Think were part of the same close-knit scene and put out records on MacKaye's Dischord label. Jawbox singer/guitarist J. Robbins had also played with the early 1980s hardcore band Government Issue. They would eventually be joined by others like the high-concept hardcore soul revue the Nation of Ulysses and the wired and influential Hoover.

Washington, DC, was not the only place where bands were liberating hardcore punk from its limitations. San Diego was the home of Drive Like Jehu, led by vocalists/guitarists Rick Froberg and John

Reis, who had previously played together in a band called Pitchfork in the late 1980s. Together for two albums in roughly five years (*Drive Like Jehu* in 1991 and their major label debut/swansong, *Yank Crime*, in 1994), Drive Like Jehu perfected an adrenalized art punk that always sounded an inch away from spinning out of control, even on a song like "Luau," which rode the same steady riff for nearly ten minutes. Not long after Drive Like Jehu started making waves, San Diego's post-hardcore scene swelled with the founding of Gravity Records and similarly careening Clikatat Ikatowi and Antioch Arrow.

All the way north up the coast, Olympia, Washington, was known for Beat Happening and riot grrrl, but it was also the home of a dissonant trio called Unwound, who communicated in cryptic dream-journal entries. Discussing the band's debut album recorded in 1992, Unwound biographer David Wilcox writes that "a good chunk of the record belongs specifically to the post-hardcore landscape of the time, broadly defined by Nation of Ulysses on the east coast and the burgeoning Gravity Records scene on the west," and that, in relation to the grunge scene the media was focused on at the time, Unwound were "something darker, angrier, and noisier."[2]

Post-hardcore is a genre with clearly identified roots but only loosely defined results. Hardcore had reduced punk rock to its base elements, and post-hardcore was free to rebuild on its foundation without blueprints. Punk had also been so influential that it seemed like every other alternative rock band that came after had at least a trace of it in their music. Other subgenres in the 1990s, such as emocore and screamo, were and are considered part of the bigger post-hardcore picture. At its most basic, the tag is shorthand for "clearly owns a few Fugazi records."

"It's funny," Bolling says, "when I would interview bands, I'd say 'you guys are punk' or 'you're post-punk,' and a lot of bands at the time that fit into the post-hardcore thing said 'no, we're a rock band.'" Assigning genre tags grew into a regular pastime in music culture in the 1990s. Sometimes it was done for the fun of conversation; other times it was taken seriously. The more specific the terms became, however, the more likely it was that bands would fit the description of more than one.

There wasn't an overwhelming demand for music writers to differentiate between every artist, but how many times could they be expected to write "so-and-so are a punk band" without wanting to get a little creative? Using the term "post-hardcore" was a way to efficiently give the sonic footprint of bands like the Nation of Ulysses, Unwound, and Quicksand without defining them too narrowly. Still, it was never going to be sufficient for everyone. "You start writing about something," Bolling recalls, "and then all of a sudden it's not emocore anymore, it's math rock or something." Though he recognized its futility, he didn't mind using the terms because there was enough of a net positive in helping listeners determine what they were interested in.

Post-hardcore's breakout moment came in the mid-1990s when major labels snapped up most (save for the staunchly independent Fugazi) of the genre's headliners: Drive Like Jehu, Jawbox, Shudder to Think, and the New York–based Helmet and Quicksand. Though punk had long-standing issues with the idea of selling out, the albums these five bands released on majors were exceptional and, in some cases, their best. The downside was that they were now competing in an overcrowded marketplace, and it was easy to get lost in the shuffle.[3]

Pioneer Tracks: Big Black–*Atomizer*, Bitch Magnet–*Star Booty* EP, Fugazi–*Fugazi* EP, Scratch Acid–*Just Keep Eating*, Squirrel Bait–*Skag Heaven*

Key Players: At the Drive-In, Bitch Magnet, Drive Like Jehu, Fugazi, Girls Against Boys, Helmet, Hoover, Jawbox, the Jesus Lizard, Lungfish,

Lync, the Nation of Ulysses, Quicksand, Refused, Shellac, Shudder to Think, Thursday, Unwound

|||||||||||||||||||||||||||||||||||||||||||||||||||||||||||||||||||||||||||

CROSSOVER TRACKS

|||||||||||||||||||||||||||||||||||||||||||||||||||||||||||||||||||||||||||

EMO(CORE)
Boys Life–*Boys Life*, Giants Chair–*Red and Clear*, Texas is the Reason–*Texas is the Reason* EP

HARDCORE
The Faith and Void–*Faith/Void Split*, Government Issue–*You*, Naked Raygun–*Throb Throb*

NOISE ROCK
Lowercase–*Kill the Lights*, Mclusky–*Mclusky Do Dallas*, Young Widows–*Old Wounds*

Post-Metal

Unlike other "post-" genres, post-metal isn't about what comes *after* metal. The term is meant to identify metal bands from the late 1990s onward that shared traits with post-rock. "I think the unfurling of rock and metal music into these longer structures was almost an inevitable development," says Jack Chuter, author of *Storm Static Sleep.* "I think it was a big mixture of people seeing what was going on from post-rock and taking inspiration from that. But also, with a band like Neurosis, it's probably a bit more ambiguous as to how they got there." He adds that influences as disparate as folk music and the time-stretching slowness of doom metal also shaped post-metal.

ISIS was the first band Chuter heard who fell in the post-metal bracket and is still one of the first that people think of in connection with the term. The Boston-based band led by Hydra Head Records founder Aaron Turner began playing together in the late 1990s. Their debut album, *Celestial*, drifted unnoticed by most post-rock fans, but in 2002, their second, *Oceanic*, pulled those listeners in. The following year they toured with Scottish post-rockers Mogwai, their fandom of each other mutual.

Russian Circles are another band who have shown the potential of post-metal. "Russian Circles was a happy accident," explains Brian Cook, who was playing in his second band, These Arms Are Snakes, when he started getting together with guitarist Mike Sullivan and drummer Dave Turncrantz. Russian Circles were in Seattle recording their new album with Matt Bayles (the go-to guy in the Northwest for heavy, dynamic rock music who recorded both Botch and These Arms Are Snakes), and Cook filled in on the sessions. The favor turned out to be a nice change.

The creative process in Russian Circles allowed the three of them to try out different variations of their songs, finding ways to get everyone excited even when they weren't the focus of attention. There was a significant difference in the way it made Cook play his instrument. The priority was no longer to keep busy on the fretboard, but to find textures and interplay that kept things interesting. Over twenty years of playing music, Cook has been in one band that defied the rules of hardcore, and another that helped establish the rules (or lack thereof) of post-metal. "For me, each band has been a part of an evolution of some sort of personal catharsis. The older I get, the less I feel the need to constantly bludgeon people with sound, but there is something about brute auditory force that still excites me."

Pioneer Tracks: Botch–"Man the Ramparts," Godflesh–"I Wasn't Born to Follow," ISIS–"Relocation Swarm," Neurosis–"Lost"

Key Players: Agalloch, Boris, Cult of Luna, Jesu, Nadja, Palms, Pelican, Rosetta, Russian Circles, Sanhet

CROSSOVER GENRES

ALTERNATIVE METAL
System of a Down, Tool

EXPERIMENTAL METAL
Neurosis, Voivod

POST-ROCK
Mogwai, This Will Destroy You

Post-Punk

In the UK, punk rock was given nary more than a year or two before some started calling it out in 1977 for not having effected wide-scale revolution in the music industry and society itself. The Sex Pistols and the Clash had put out their debut albums, and yet Pink Floyd were still out there with their giant floating pig. There wasn't much anarchy to speak of, and bloated arena rock had not keeled over and died as it was supposed to have.

Post-punk was a schism in the punk rock movement of the 1970s. There were those who felt that punk had to draw lines and adhere to a strictly defined form of the music. There were others who rejected the idea of defining it. The former was determined to rebuke rock's status quo, while the latter sought rebellion on more methodological terms. To the oi-sters and street punks, it was a style. To the post-punks, it was an approach.

Symbolic of the newly forming rift was when—again, in 1977—Howard Devoto abandoned his role as frontman for one of Manchester's premier punk groups, Buzzcocks, to form Magazine, who made use of such sacrilegious things as keyboards and tempo changes. In fact, Magazine's 1978 debut album, *Real Life*, wasn't without a few art rock tics, albeit kept in check. They would hardly be the only ones: This Heat and John Lydon's post-Pistols band Public Image Ltd were stretching their abrasive ruminations out to *Kosmische* lengths. Up in the North, Joy Division and Gang of Four were stripping the warm flesh from rock, exposing its nervous system and mechanical function.

Simon Reynolds even writes of "a sense in which post-punk *was* 'progressive rock,'[1] albeit one revitalized in a punk fashion. "It was a particular kind of 'art rock' to which post-punk pledged allegiance, though," he explains. "Not prog's attempt to merge amplified electric guitars with nineteenth century classical instrumentation and extended compositions, but the minimal-is-maximal lineage that runs from the Velvet Underground to Krautrock and the more intellectual end of glam."[2]

Jamaican music was also a significant influence. Gina Birch, who would form the Raincoats in 1977 in London with Ana da Silva, was moved by the passion of the Sex Pistols and Subway Sect, but it was ultimately the Slits who made her go out and buy a bass guitar. "It felt like these bands were ours," she says, "the performance, those songs, they were representing and articulating on my behalf." Reggae, dub, ska, and even the double bass of jazz musician Cecil McBee were influences on Birch's playing.

The origin story of American punk, inasmuch as the generally accepted timeline begins in the mid-1970s in New York City, has an almost opposite creative trajectory. Punk rock in Manhattan was the unpolished glam of the New York Dolls, the spiny jams of Television, the urban surrealist poetry of Patti Smith, the stiff funk and growing eclecticism of Talking Heads. The Ramones were but one side of it, yet when they traveled to London in 1976, though faster and dirtier, they validated the city's preexisting pub rock scene and cemented the notion of punk as a three-chord bash.

From Pere Ubu in Cleveland to X in Los Angeles, many of the first punk bands across the United States were coming from an avant-garde approach. It was only after the UK sold America back a simplified model of punk rock (which was then stripped even further and called hardcore) that the UK found a need for any such "post-punk" or "new wave" designations. Punk was thus reduced to humorless brute force, and post-punk either got with the new wave–

pop program or settled for the margins. Even John Lydon started writing radio-friendly songs in the 1980s like "Rise" and "Seattle."

But what if that wasn't what post-punk was at all? "I think that you can really define 'post-punk' to a scene in Brooklyn in 1999–2000, the millennial cusp," says Colin Newman, "people, outliers, who were referencing bands like Wire and Gang of Four." Newman has at least some say in what post-punk is, given that his band Wire are credited with helping to create it. Newman's reading of post-punk begins with postmodernism spreading into the conversation about every art form in the 1980s, and, with that, the addition of "post" to categories of music like "post-rock."

"People were always looking to apply new labels," says Birch. "Journalists tried 'new wave' for ages, but that's definitely been sidelined for 'post-punk' now. At the time, I don't remember post-punk being used that much." As fans of their early influential records *The Raincoats* and *Odyshape* can attest, the Raincoats weren't particularly interested in genre, but just knew what they hated: poseurs, pomp rock, and the Stranglers ("an affront to punk!").

Newman remembers groups like Joy Division and Cabaret Voltaire having high regard for Wire in the beginning, and that these were the kind of bands who were looking forward, as opposed to what he saw as the retro direction the Clash were taking. "The Clash were turning into a sort of latter-day Rolling Stones almost. They wanted to be a big rock band, clearly. Wire didn't really have any aspirations to be a rock band *per se*. It's ultimately personal. You can make connections, but we were also not spearheading a movement, I don't think."

"We knew punk was coming already in 1975, because a lot of music had become quite boring," he says. The psychedelic and progressive rock that had once been exciting was stagnating. In London, a new generation of what was called pub rock, bands who defined themselves as small groups playing small venues, "real music" as it were, was coming up. Punk rock had gone the same way by the following year, and post-punk moved quickly as well. By 1978, Wire could see the shift away from punk in the audience right in front of them. Instead of dressing up in the general punk rock look, people were starting to come to the gigs looking like Wire. Newman says that, unlike their second and third albums, *Pink Flag* was widely available in the States and became very influential in the hardcore movement, of which they knew nothing about in Britain. "I didn't really know anything about American hardcore, probably until the '90s. I mean, who was interested in punk rock at the end of the '70s? Nobody. Punk rock was out! There was nothing more old than punk rock."

As decidedly and proudly rudimentary as hardcore punk was in the late 1970s and early 1980s, it, too, would eventually realize it had larger creative ambitions. Los Angeles band Black Flag began with the basic template from which hardcore was built, but in between their 1981 debut *Damaged* and their delayed second album in 1984, *My War*, they were flirting heavily with heavy metal. In his Sonic Youth biography, *Goodbye 20th Century*, David Browne writes how the double LP, "a symbol of all that was overstuffed and ponderous about rock . . . had been partially redeemed by postpunk"[3] in the form of Hüsker Dü's *Zen Arcade* and Minutemen's *Double Nickels on the Dime*—both released the same year as *My War*. Credible punk bands releasing such sprawling records opened the door for Sonic Youth to do the same with *Daydream Nation* four years later. Browne uses the term "post-punk" to describe two American bands who are often now referred to as "post-hardcore," which shows how the terminology applied to punk-related music has shifted.

Newman recounts a conversation he had with producer Mike Thorne in 1979 after they had finished the third of Wire's famed first three albums. He asked Thorne if he could have seen the band that ultimately made *154* in the one that started with *Pink Flag*.

Absolutely, Thorne responded. "People saw it in us, without a doubt. The person who signed Wire to EMI was the guy who'd signed Pink Floyd. People were saying Wire were like the Pink Floyd of punk. 'You're not going to understand anything they're doing right now, and they're going to sell a billion records in ten years' time.'" That sounded like a plan to Newman, but it wasn't the plan that EMI stuck with. "I think by the time they got to *154* they were thinking, 'Yeah, that's not going to really happen, is it?' The world had changed as well."

Pioneer Tracks: Magazine–*Real Life*, Pere Ubu–*The Modern Dance*, Public Image Ltd–*Public Image (First Issue)*, Television–*Marquee Moon*, Wire–*Pink Flag*

Key Players: A Certain Ratio, Cabaret Voltaire, the Fall, the Feelies, Gang of Four, Joy Division, Kleenex/LiLiPUT, the Mekons, Mission of Burma, the Pop Group, the Raincoats, Scritti Politti, Siouxsie and the Banshees, the Slits, Swell Maps, Television Personalities, This Heat, Young Marble Giants

CROSSOVER TRACKS

ART ROCK (LATE 1990S/EARLY 2000S UK)
*Campag Velocet–*Bon Chic Bon Genre*, Clinic–*Internal Wrangler*, *Regular Fries–*Accept the Signal*

NEW WAVE
Devo–*Q: Are We Not Men? A: We Are Devo!*, Talking Heads–*More Songs About Buildings and Food*, XTC–*White Music*

---

*Sometimes referred to as "Skunk Rock"

POST-PUNK REVIVAL

Liars–*They Threw Us All In a Trench and Stuck a Monument On Top*, the Rapture–*Out of the Races and Onto the Tracks* EP, Yeah Yeah Yeahs–*Machine* EP

Post-Punk Revival

||||||||||||||||||||||||||||||||||||||||||||||||||||||||||||||||||||||||||||||||||||||||||||||

From the late 1990s through the mid-2000s, there were two trends in rock that rose to prominence together. They were both presented as the pretty young things on the block, but they were also both retro-sensible movements that would come to be labeled revivals: the garage rock revival and the post-punk revival.

If the garage rock revival had its home base in Detroit, the post-punk revival was headquartered in New York City. Whether by accident or shrewd decision making, the Strokes' 2001 debut album, *Is This It*, brought together garage rock simplicity and production values with post-punk blasé and an acceptably light measure of louche, which allowed them to mingle freely at either party. It is that band's crossover appeal that likely leads to some conflation between the two revivals, which otherwise are rooted in identifiably different sounds.

Shortly before *Is This It* came out, the Rapture released their *Out of the Races and Onto the Tracks* EP. Less than a year later, word of mouth about their new 12" single, "House of Jealous Lovers," raised expectations around the band considerably. It was one of the first releases from DFA Records, the label started by British producers Tim Goldsworthy and James Murphy, who was also getting his LCD Soundsystem up and running at the time.

As the Rapture and DFA were drawing up plans to get the indie kids dancing, Interpol cultivated a quasi-mysteriousness in their matching black suits. Joining *White Blood Cells* and *Is This It* on college dorm-room shelves everywhere, their 2002 debut album, *Turn on the Bright Lights*, was post-punk on protein shakes. Pulled along by a rhythm section loaded with killer snaking bass lines, Paul Banks delivers his vocals with an Ian Curtis–lite intonation, and the overall momentum was (and still is) enough to distract from how silly the lyrics could get.

As the 2006 documentary *Kill Your Idols* points out, a few bands from this time were also bearing traces of No Wave. Liars, led by Angus Andrew (an Australian who had been going to school in LA before moving to New York), put out their first album, *They Threw Us All in a Trench and Stuck a Monument on Top*, in the fall of 2001. Liars wore their scuffed-up, gum-soled, dance-punk shoes well for the majority of the record, up until the thirty-minute looping closer, "This Dust Makes That Mud," which revealed their true experimental intentions.

Yeah Yeah Yeahs went in the opposite direction. After a slow rollout with two abrasive EPs in two years for the independent Chicago label Touch & Go Records, the band stepped up in the spring of 2003 with their accessible and well-reviewed major label debut album, *Fever to Tell*. Frontwoman Karen O didn't smooth too much edge off her vocals, but she did get her Chrissie Hynde on with everyone's favorite, "Maps." That fall, the Rapture's *Echoes* finally arrived with shards of downtown nightlife and Public Image Ltd's *Metal Box* in its hands, cherry-picking from the danceable parts of post-punk.

Soon came sophomore efforts from the Strokes and Interpol, with the latter noticeably lightening up a bit on *Antics*. As the Libertines—Britain's answer to the Strokes, garbed in Queen's Guard jackets and armed with poetry chapbooks—were self-imploding, Birmingham band Editors and London's Bloc Party came through with zeitgeist-seizing debuts.

Key Players: Bloc Party, Editors, Franz Ferdinand, the Futureheads, Interpol, LCD Soundsystem, Liars, the Libertines, Radio 4, the Rapture, the Strokes, Yeah Yeah Yeahs

CROSSOVER GENRES

DANCE PUNK
Death from Above 1979, the Faint, Moving Units

GARAGE ROCK REVIVAL
Black Lips, the (International) Noise Conspiracy, the Kills

POST-PUNK
Gang of Four, Joy Division, Public Image Ltd

Post-Rock

||||||||||||||||||||||||||||||||||||||||||||||||||||||||||||||||||||||||||||||||||||||||||||||||||||||||||||||||||||||||||||||||||

Simon Reynolds may not have been the first person to write down "post-rock," but in 1994 he did give the term its first definition. His concept was one in which bands made music using "rock instrumentation for non-rock purposes." In Europe, London was the unsurprising focal point (Stereolab, Seefeel), and East London, in particular, caught Reynolds' attention, being the stomping grounds of both Bark Psychosis and Disco Inferno. Young and hungry, fueled by art and angst at the end of the 1980s, the two bands created a kind of *post*-post-punk, starting out at the end of one thing as much as at the conception of another. Graham Sutton's Bark Psychosis pushed anger and ambience to extended lengths, and Ian Crause's Disco Inferno looped guitar lines like samples and used samplers like instruments.

The contemporaneous American parallel had no centralized location, but one of its more notable homes was Chicago. There, a new label called Thrill Jockey became a hub for experimental locals like Tortoise and the Sea and Cake, as well as out-there artists from elsewhere like Trans Am. It was usually outsiders who drew this connection, as post-rock back then was not a scene or a style, but a hypothesis with substantial, if scattered, evidence. These bands all produced notably different results, but their formulas shared contrarian impulses, textures of Krautrock, insights from jazz, and a willingness to go out on a limb.

Somewhere in between the May 1994 issue of *The Wire* and the end of the decade, a major rift formed, stretching the definition of post-rock in a way that included music that didn't comport with what had been its fundamental principle. As albums by Slint, Mogwai, and Sigur Rós became many people's base understanding of the genre, post-rock's transition toward "rock instrumentation for *epic* rock purposes" was well underway. It is those bands, and others with enigmatic names like Godspeed You! Black Emperor, Do Make Say Think, and Explosions in the Sky, who create grandiose rise-and-fall rock, who best represent the modern understanding of the genre. Not surprisingly, those folks dislike the term just as much as the Thrill Jockey bands do.

"It's such a loaded term," says Jack Chuter, "and it's almost got a manifesto embedded within it, which I don't think a lot of bands felt that they were consciously striving for. 'Post-rock' suggests that they're courageously stepping beyond the boundaries of rock music and entering this new frontier of music. That grandiosity . . . I don't think people wanted that attributed to what they were doing."

Chuter chose to begin *Storm Static Sleep* on two trails with two bands: Talk Talk in his home country and Slint in the United States. Precocious as they were mysterious, Slint were a band creatively daring beyond their years who came from a hardcore scene in Louisville that was artsier than outsiders would likely expect from Kentucky in the late 1980s. Their role as granddaddies to introspective atom smashers like Mogwai (who in their early days named a song "Slint") is well established in post-rock lore.

Less historically presumed, in America at least, has been the post-rock influence of Talk Talk, who were often remembered most for "It's My Life" (reinforced by No Doubt covering it in 2003) until their final album, *Laughing Stock*, was reissued in 2011. In 2012, *Spirit of Eden* and *The Colour of Spring* were reissued, at which point a new generation of savvy listeners had been thoroughly informed of leader Mark Hollis' genius and the artistic limb that Talk Talk were out on. Full of space and rich in revisitable detail, those records, as Chuter's book points out, were influential on Do Make Say Think[1] and others.

Chuter reckons the point of fracture in post-rock terminology was in the mid-1990s, when Reynolds stopped inducting new artists into the category and when other journalists started to apply it to bands like the often-instrumental Glaswegian band Mogwai. Released in 1997, their first official album, *Young Team*, is practically the reset button on the genre. This is not the band's fault. They were admirers of Slint, Labradford, Trans Am, and Flying Saucer Attack, but they didn't have a clue what post-rock was.[2] They were a band, Chuter says, who didn't have all of the forward drive of rock music, but were still very much rooted in it.

Then came Sigur Rós, the Icelandic band whose sophomore effort, *Ágætis byrjun*, was your local bookseller's favorite album of 2001. Somehow their idiosyncratic ambient rock caught on, and soon they were lending their songs to a Tom Cruise movie and having their music imitated in numerous commercials. Explosions in the Sky would also be widely imitated in the 2000s. The Austin, Texas, quartet had been steadily gathering true believers and critical praise with their "sad, triumphant"[3] instrumental rock for several years when they were tapped to do the soundtrack for the movie *Friday Night Lights* in 2004. Sports documentaries and football highlight reels looking for emotional gravity will to this day still whip out some approximation of "Your Hand in Mine." Cinematic by nature, post-rock proved ideal for soundtracks: Explosions in the Sky and Mogwai have made a habit of doing them.

In terms of pop-culture infiltration, post-rock may have hit a peak in the 2000s, but Mogwai, Sigur Rós, Explosions, and others have more or less kept the fans they've gathered, even as they've moved on from the genre's trademark *"wait for it . . ."* buildups. "I think the whole crescendo thing got really tired from everyone hearing and playing it," says Chuter. While the excitement of waiting for those inevitable tidal waves of noise to crash took a while to wear off, eventually they became too predictable. "What I really liked is, in the late '00s, you started to hear bands consciously teasing away from that. There's almost a quite deliberate subversion of those dynamics to wrench themselves out of that up-down formula."

Perhaps post-rock is a term that has served two ultimately well-meaning purposes but at this point has outlived its usefulness. Even so, the word is not likely to go away soon. "A couple years back, when I was fully engaged with post-rock and going to events like Arc-TanGent, I felt that there was something really crucial about this music for people. It wasn't just one genre that they liked. Obviously, everyone likes a bit of everything, but you get the impression with post-rock fans that it almost matches the hyperbolic scale of the music, their love and adoration for this stuff. They speak in such extreme life-or-death terms about this music and the impact it has on them."

Pioneer Tracks: Bark Psychosis–*Hex*, Disco Inferno–*Open Doors, Closed Windows*, Slint–*Spiderland*, Stereolab–*Peng!*, Talk Talk–*Spirit of Eden*

Key Players: Aerial M/Papa M (David Pajo), Do Make Say Think, Explosions in the Sky, Gastr del Sol, Godspeed You! Black Emperor, June of 44, Labradford, Mogwai, Mono, Sigur Rós, Thee Silver Mt. Zion Memorial Orchestra (and variations), Tortoise, Trans Am

|||||||||||||||||||||||||||||||||||||||||||||||||||||||||||||||||||||||||

CROSSOVER TRACKS

|||||||||||||||||||||||||||||||||||||||||||||||||||||||||||||||||||||||||

EXPERIMENTAL ROCK

Grails–*Take Refuge in Clean Living*, Piano Magic–*Popular Mechanics*, Tarentel–*From Bone to Satellite*

POST-PUNK

Dif Juz–*Huremics* EP, the Ex–*Tumult*, This Heat–*This Heat*

SLOWCORE

Bedhead and Macha–*Macha Loved Bedhead* EP, the For Carnation–*The For Carnation*, Low–"Do You Know How to Waltz?"

Power Metal

Once the new wave of British heavy metal (NWOBHM) had made its way into the minds and record collections of aspiring metal musicians in places like California and New York, it was time for US bands to step their game up. Power metal was a growth spurt for American heavy metal in the early 1980s. The young, pre-mustachioed Metallica were huge NWOBHM fans, and they feel those influences with earnest American grit. Their 1983 debut album, *Kill 'Em All*, flipped the bird to operatic vocals and ushered in the era where an angry yelling dude was good enough. Preferable, even.

Metallica were at the head of the pack, but plenty of others were also pushing the bass up and weighing the tone down. Power metal was heavier and snarlier than Judas Priest or even Iron Maiden. Ultimately, the term "power metal" proved to be a quickly dated snapshot along the way to thrash metal matriculation. However, in more recent years, a modified understanding of what "power metal" means has come into the dialogue. The term is now often used to refer to a largely European-based scene that gets its operatic rocks off on D&D fantasy themes. Influential on this side of power metal are a clutch of German metal acts who rose to prominence in the 1980s, such as Helloween, Blind Guardian, and Rage. Their angle of winking escapism has been developed over the years into one of power metal's major selling points.

Key Players: Accept, Armored Saint, Blind Guardian, Dio, Dragonland, Helloween, Kamelot, Manowar, Nocturnal Rites, Omen, Power Quest, Sabaton, Stratovarius

CROSSOVER GENRES

NEW WAVE OF BRITISH HEAVY METAL
Grim Reaper, Saxon

SYMPHONIC METAL
Dark Moor, Nightwish

Power Pop

"Groundbreaking" may not be the first word one would associate with Cheap Trick, but there are two rock-and-roll inventions patented by the quartet from Rockford, Illinois: being "big in Japan" and power pop. If the term "power pop" wasn't coined specifically to describe their music, it might as well have been. Cheap Trick own it. "Surrender," "I Want You to Want Me," "Dream Police": game, set, match.

Some will tell you that the Memphis pop prodigy Alex Chilton and his band Big Star invented it[1] with their *#1 Record* in 1972, which does predate Cheap Trick by a year or two. Tom Petty and the Heartbreakers' "American Girl" is a power pop contender from their self-titled 1976 debut album. In Britain, "power pop" was one of the new fads being bandied about in the music press as they looked for the next big thing after punk. British radio and television presenter, and an *NME* writer early in his career, Stuart Maconie recalls in his memoir that in the late 1970s, "Punk was sweetening into new wave and power pop."[2] Colin Newman also remembers that back then his band Wire had been called "power pop," before anyone gave them the post-punk label that has since stuck to them.

Originally busting out of Bellingham, Washington, in the late 1980s with Cure-style haircuts on their heads and XTC records under their arms, the Posies are the other serious challenger for the power pop crown. In fact, so serious about it were Jon Auer and Ken Stringfellow that the two core members of the Posies *actually joined Big Star.* Point made, and the Posies' melodic guitar rock certainly had the chops, but did they deliver "Beatlesque melodies with the might of Kiss or [Ted] Nugent"[3] quite like Cheap Trick?

Key Players: Big Star, Cheap Trick, the Knack, the Posies, Teenage Fanclub

CROSSOVER TRACKS

NEW WAVE
The Cars–"Just What I Needed," Squeeze–"Up the Junction"

SOFT ROCK
Fleetwood Mac–"Go Your Own Way," Peter Frampton–"Show Me the Way"

Powerviolence

Powerviolence is a puzzlingly named satellite genre orbiting hardcore. Though not exactly redundant, there's something a bit superfluous about "power" (i.e., as opposed to *weak* violence?), whether you choose to write it out attached to the violence as a compound word or keep them separated as "power violence." The origin of the term is generally credited to guitarist Matt Domino of the late 1980s hardcore band Infest. Eric Wood, himself an influential powerviolence practitioner, was in the practice room with Domino at the time, playing together in the band Neanderthal.[1]

Living near each other in Southern California, these first powerviolence bands shuffled members. Arising from the shuffle at the turn of the 1990s was Man Is the Bastard, also featuring Wood, who was one of the band's two bassists and vocalists. Man Is the Bastard are both exemplary and unique among powerviolence bands by virtue of their low-end heavy sound and the incorporation of member Henry Barnes' homemade sonic contraptions.[2] Their early tracks like "Skull Crusher" give the gist of what powerviolence did with hardcore, warping it with dark noise and tempo shifts that come with almost jazz-like unpredictability to break up the blast beats, but still keeping it all to within a couple of minutes or less. As with other kinds of hardcore, sociopolitically charged lyrics were common, if not clearly enunciated.

A record label central to powerviolence was Slap a Ham Records, based in the Bay Area and run by Chris Dodge, who also played bass in the appropriately named Spazz. Slap a Ham put out records throughout the 1990s by all of the aforementioned groups, as well as Crossed Out, Capitalist Casualties, and others.

Key Tracks: Capitalist Casualties–"Violence Junkie," Crossed Out–"Crutch," Infest–"Where's the Unity?," Man Is the Bastard–"Skull Crusher," Spazz–*Spazz7*"

CROSSOVER GENRES

HARDCORE
The Locust, Nails

SCREAMO
The Blood Brothers, Orchid (Massachusetts)

Progressive Metal

||||||||||||||||||||||||||||||||||||||||||||||||||||||||||||||||||||||||||||||||||||||||||||||||||||||||||

Progressive rock and heavy metal were a natural pair from the beginning. The first song on King Crimson's first album from 1969, "20th Century Schizoid Man," is proto–heavy metal, a lurching cousin of Black Sabbath's "War Pigs." Rush brought it heavy in the first half of the 1970s with early Rust Belt radio hits like "Working Man" before they turned progressive. Jethro Tull even won the very first Grammy for Best Hard Rock/Metal Performance Vocal or Instrumental in 1989—a notorious moment always painted as an ignorant snub of Metallica.

"Are You Ready For 'Neo-Classic' Rock?" implored the cover of the November 2005 issue of *Alternative Press*, alerting readers to the brainy nature of that month's cover stars, Coheed and Cambria. Coheed and Cambria stood out in the 2000s for wearing their classic prog rock influences with pride, but others before them, like Tool and Sweden's Meshuggah, had also broken from the pack with progressive song structures and themes. Though that "neo-classic" tag avoids using the *p*-word up front to keep from scaring the magazine's teenage punk and metalhead readership away, inside the issue, band leader Claudio Sanchez is less coy about calling his music "progressive rock," and the article makes mention of their stage sets and supplementary graphic novels. "Elaborate and progressive as the music is, it's only part of the band's appeal," explains writer DX Ferris. "Every Coheed tune is a chapter of an expanding science-fiction epic."[1]

Key Players: Coheed and Cambria, Dream Theater, Gojira, Meshuggah, Nevermore, Opeth, Porcupine Tree (*In Absentia*), Queensrÿche, Tool

CROSSOVER GENRES

ALTERNATIVE METAL

System of a Down, Type O Negative

PROGRESSIVE ROCK

King Crimson, Rush

Progressive Rock

|||||||||||||||||||||||||||||||||||||||||||||||||||||||||||||||||||||||||||||||||||||||||||||||||||||||||||||||||||||||||||||||||||

"I've never had a problem with the term 'progressive rock' as it was applied from 1969 for the next few years," recalls Ian Anderson, the legendary leader of Jethro Tull. "But of course it became shortened to 'prog rock' or just 'prog' as a genre, which embraced a certain disdain for the overly elaborate, self-indulgent music that came out of that prog-rock era. I'm thinking of Genesis and Emerson, Lake and Palmer, and Yes as the main offenders, but of course, there were many others."

Anderson's distinction between "progressive" and "prog" is an interesting take on a genre that has been celebrated and maligned in equal measure. As the music became longer and more grandiose, the term shortened and cut to the quick. Cheered on by arenas full of fans and left to their own devices by record company overseers, progressive rock bands in the first half of the 1970s pushed the music to such conceptual and structural extremes that those who continue to attempt to match or surpass it are still the exception, not the rule. It was the height of achievement for rock until suddenly it wasn't, but did the overinflated prog balloon pop on its own accord, or was it really punk that came along and stuck it with a safety pin?

"The textbook definition of progressive rock prescribes an artistic approach to music . . . that developed, initially in Britain, in the late 1960s and continued into the 1970s, which sought to fuse rock with different musical styles, usually of distinctly European origin—from classical to folk,"[1] writes Will Romano. In its early years, progressive rock was primarily driven by British bands who formed in the mid-to-late 1960s: the Moody Blues from Birmingham, Jethro Tull from Blackpool, and the majority from in and around London—Pink Floyd, King Crimson, Yes, Genesis, and Emerson, Lake and Palmer. North American progressive rock didn't find the same level of notoriety until bands like Kansas and Styx from the United States and Rush from Canada came on the scene in the mid-1970s.[2] Frank Zappa's *Freak Out!* and the Beach Boys' *Pet Sounds* are the pre-prog exceptions, both released in 1966 a year before the Beatles' *Sgt. Pepper's Lonely Hearts Club Band* and now regarded as harbingers of the rock concept album.

Jethro Tull's debut album, *This Was*, was informed by blues and jazz but still reached for something different. Anderson points out that Jethro Tull's first guitarist, Mick Abrahams, who only appears on *This Was*, was "very much a blues and R&B kind of guitar player" who didn't have any interest in folk or classical music. "The songs that I started writing in the summer of 1968 weren't really resonating with him," he remembers. Around the end of that October, they parted ways, and Jethro Tull started down the path toward progressive rock.

Despite his fondness for and familiarity with the blues, to Anderson, the idea of making a career out of what felt like "borrowed" music didn't sit right. "I didn't feel I had the credentials," he says. "I was not black. If I heard myself speak, I was not American. I felt my respect and love for that music form meant that I didn't want to go out there and be an imitator. I didn't feel right about that at all. It felt like I was stealing something."

To arrive at the music he felt more comfortable in, Anderson listened to everything that was around him. "I carefully filtered out country and western and Hawaiian guitar music, but pretty much everything else was something that I would pay attention to and see if it worked for me to incorporate. I suppose the folk music and classical music of Northwestern Europe would be the driving force from the second album onwards." It's not that he abandoned the blues completely; he just felt that if he was going to make music that involved the blues scale, it had to have a different life of its own beyond twelve-bar blues.

Around this time, Anderson felt aligned with the music of rock bands like Cream, Blind Faith, and Jimi Hendrix, and also Pentangle (who were on the progressive end of electric folk) and players like Roy Harper, Bert Jansch, and Al Stewart. He notes two earlier signposts to forging his own musical path, *Sgt. Pepper* and Pink Floyd's *The Piper at the Gates of Dawn*, which he sees as the origins of what a couple years later would begin to be called "progressive."

Progressive rock's initial creative and commercial boom began around 1969, which was the year of Pink Floyd's *Ummagumma*, Jethro Tull's *Stand Up*, King Crimson's landmark debut *In the Court of the Crimson King*, and other first albums from Yes and Genesis. Though it certainly wasn't beloved by all rock fans, by 1970, the genre was to some, as Paul Stump writes, "the music of the future—to a sizeable minority, the new classical music."[3] Four years on, the movement had largely peaked. Yes had gone from writing some of prog's most enduring songs like "Roundabout" and "Long Distance Runaround" to creating Exhibit A for the prosecution of the genre's overindulgence: the four-song double album *Tales from Topographic Oceans*.

Noting that complexity for the sake of itself doesn't make music good, Anderson says he tries to find a balance between music that is sufficiently detailed and elaborate enough to keep himself entertained, but without leaving his audience behind by making it too clever for its own good. But it wasn't just the music that progressive rock stretched past previous limits of potential. The storylines behind some of progressive rock's biggest records, like those of Genesis' *The Lamb Lies Down on Broadway* and Yes' *Tales from Topographic*

Oceans, were sometimes more off-the-cuff than one would expect from such an ambitious bunch.

In the end, all the technological advancements and pyrotechnics that enabled progressive rock to become such a spectacle for eyes and ears also began to weigh it down.[4] King Crimson split, Jethro Tull explored folk rock, and others wandered off. Still, the arrival of punk rock didn't spell the immediate demise of progressive rock. In 1977, there was room for both *Never Mind the Bollocks, Here's the Sex Pistols* and Pink Floyd's *Animals*, as well as Rush's *A Farewell to Kings* and Yes' *Going for the One*. Though many of prog's main proponents found new ways forward in the 1980s, the neo-progressive rock movement arrived to try to revitalise the form. King Crimson came again, and went again, and came yet again. Jethro Tull was awarded that infamous Grammy. Prog was down, but not out.

Pioneer Albums: The Beatles–*Sgt. Pepper's Lonely Hearts Club Band*, the Moody Blues–*Days of Future Passed*

Key Players: Emerson, Lake and Palmer, Genesis, Gentle Giant, Jethro Tull, Kansas, King Crimson, Pink Floyd, Procol Harum, Rush, Soft Machine, Yes

CROSSOVER TRACKS

INDIE FOLK

The Decemberists–*Picaresque*, Fleet Foxes–*Crack-Up*, Sufjan Stevens–*Illinois*

PROGRESSIVE METAL

Dream Theater–*Images and Words*, Queensrÿche–*Operation Mindcrime*, Tool–*Lateralus*

PSYCHEDELIC ROCK

The Doors–"The End," the Jimi Hendrix Experience–"1983 . . . (A Merman I Should Turn To Be)," the Mothers of Invention–*We're Only in It for the Money*

Proto-Punk

||||||||||||||||||||||||||||||||||||||||||||||||||||||||||||||||||||||||||||||||||||||||||||||||||||||||||||||

Proto-punk is the search for a breadcrumb trail no one intentionally left behind. Its use as a label is an attempt to answer how punk happened. It can refer to an influence on punk that predates the genre (the Velvet Underground), a band whose style "predicted" punk (the Sonics), or both (the Stooges). The usual suspects here are MC5, the Modern Lovers, the New York Dolls, and a variable handful of others.

The old cliche that one day in 1976 punk fell out of the sky and all of a sudden we weren't in Kansas anymore—or listening to Kansas anymore—still lingers, but it has been gradually chipped away by re-examination of all the evidence to the contrary. *Punk* magazine cofounder Legs McNeil and writer Gillian McCain's benchmark oral history *Please Kill Me*, first released in 1996, traces punk back to the Velvet Underground in 1965.[1] Lester Bangs also gave credit to "La Bamba," the raw West Coast garage rock bands of the 1960s, and the Kinks' "You Really Got Me."[2]

Key Players: MC5, the Modern Lovers, the New York Dolls, Rocket from the Tombs, the Sonics, the Stooges, the Velvet Underground

||||||||||||||||||||||||||||||||||||||||||||||||||||||||||||||||||||||||||
CROSSOVER GENRES
||||||||||||||||||||||||||||||||||||||||||||||||||||||||||||||||||||||||||

GARAGE PUNK
The Gories, the Mono Men

SURF ROCK
Dick Dale, the Trashmen

Psychedelic Folk

Psychedelic folk is a general term for folk-style music made under the influence of psychedelic elements. The label can apply to the acid folk groups of the late 1960s, the freak-folk regeneration of the 2000s, and a number of individuals and outsider micro-scenes in between. Britain's electric folk movement also gets filed under psychedelic folk, though the two were not quite the same, as Jeanette Leech points out, characterizing electric folk as "an important parallel development."[1]

Acid folk and rock music took some of the same drugs, but they also had musical connections. In their prime, the Incredible String Band, psychedelic folk's Scottish flagship, had considerable success with rock audiences. So too did another Scottish musician, Donovan, whose 1968 hit "Hurdy Gurdy Man" had a heavy beat and sinister psychedelic guitar slashes, in contrast to the cheerier nature of his previous pop tunes like "Sunshine Superman" and "Mellow Yellow." Despite having friends in high places, as Leech writes, "None of the acid- and psychedelic-folk bands signed by record companies in the wake of the Incredible String Band sold many records."[2]

One exception to that rule would be the hippie duo Tyrannosaurus Rex, which Marc Bolan formed in the late 1960s with the bongo-beating Steve Peregrin Took after Bolan's first attempts at a rock career didn't pan out. Though Bolan's fanciful mystic folk had the ear of supporters like John Peel, the audience for it soon plateaued, and Bolan turned his attention back to a heavier sound on the duo's fourth album, *A Beard of Stars*, soon after which he had his glam rock awakening.

Key Players: Comus, Donovan, the Holy Modal Rounders, the Incredible String Band, Pearls Before Swine, Tyrannosaurus Rex

||||||||||||||||||||||||||||||||||||||||||||||||||||||||||||||||||||||||
CROSSOVER TRACKS
||||||||||||||||||||||||||||||||||||||||||||||||||||||||||||||||||||||||

FREAK FOLK
Bowerbirds–"In Our Talons," Vetiver–"Been So Long"

PSYCHEDELIC ROCK
The Charlatans (US)–"Time to Get Straight," Love–"Bummer in the Summer"

Psychedelic Rock

||||||||||||||||||||||||||||||||||||||||||||||||||||||||||||||||||||||||||||||||||||||||||||||||||||||||||||||||||||||||||||

December 4, 1965: the Grateful Dead perform for the first time at one of Ken Kesey's early Acid Test parties in San Jose, California. June 18, 1967: Jimi Hendrix lights his guitar on fire on stage at the Monterey Pop Festival. May 19, 1990: Phish perform at the Upper Dining Hall at St. Paul's School in Concord, New Hampshire.[1]

That last one might not be immediately recognizable as a significant date in the history of psychedelic rock, but a technicolor torch of sorts was passed that day. Among the students in the audience was a teenage John Colpitts, who would later become known as Kid Millions, drummer of the mind-opening band Oneida. "They were virtuosic and entertaining," Colpitts remembers.

It is nearly impossible to overstate the impact that psychedelic drugs have had on rock music. In the summer of 1965, the Beatles put out the soundtrack to their proto–stoner comedy movie *Help!*, and within a year, *Revolver* arrived bearing the LSD-laced "Tomorrow Never Knows." In early 1967, they were in Abbey Road recording their psychedelic period peak, *Sgt. Pepper's Lonely Hearts Club Band*, while Pink Floyd were down the hall summoning *The Piper at the Gates of Dawn*. This was Syd Barrett's Floyd, the only Floyd that still really matters to some critics and fans. In his famous profile of Barrett, Nick Kent writes that his songwriting was "the quintessential marriage of the two ideal forms of English psychedelia—musical rococo freak-outs joining together with Barrett's sudden ascent into the lyrical realms of ye olde English whimsical loone, wherein dwelt the likes of Edward Lear and Kenneth Grahame."[2]

California was a sunnier setting for the acid-dropping set, and the Bay Area, with bands like Quicksilver Messenger Service and Jefferson Airplane, was the home base of American psychedelic rock. No band was perhaps more central to its development there than the Grateful Dead, who early in their career were something of the house band for Kesey's storied Acid Tests in 1965 and 1966. Around the band grew an offbeat fanbase called Deadheads, some of whom were dedicated to recording the group's live performances. Through this, the Grateful Dead's music became, as Jesse Jarnow writes, "the dominant psychedelic ritual in the United States"[3] by way of the massive network of tape trading that sprang up amongst fans.

Psychedelic rock was an attempt at re-creating through music the effects of certain drugs on human perception, but the listening experience of psychedelic rock wasn't dependent on taking them. David Henderson writes about what Jimi Hendrix was trying to do with music around the time of his second album, *Axis: Bold as Love*, "It was not about LSD or any hallucinogenic—he was the drug, he was the high . . . He saw his music as a living life-form that had the potential to give people a direct feeling, a direct understanding—that would open their eyes to cosmic powers by simply directly experiencing his music."[4] The development of progressive rock in the years immediately following the psychedelic rock boom, in part, took the stretched song lengths and instrumental virtuosity of the genre and imposed precise structures and detailed concepts on them—still *out there* yet requiring a more sober mind.

The feeling remained in the exploratory music of the prog rock bands, space rockers like Hawkwind, 1970s soul and funk, the wild outfits of glam rock, and guitar solos of early heavy metal. Throughout all these developments, the Grateful Dead never stopped. Yet every generation deserves their own heroes, and that is the role that Phish slowly grew into when they came out of the hippie-friendly college town of Burlington, Vermont, in the 1980s. "Phish's music is a new kind of psychedelic, one for individuals raised in suburban captivity," writes Jarnow. "Though the band's roots in the Dead and the Allman Brothers and Frank Zappa and classic rock are clearly audible, the music transforms into something else with an intricate internal language."[5]

At the time of his first Phish concert, Colpitts had missed out on punk. His guides were the classic rock radio station WPDH in Poughkeepsie, New York, and his friend Bobby Matador. The two graduated from American psychedelic rock staples to finding out about Germany's own countercultural *Kosmische Musik*. Moving to New York City later in the 1990s, Matador and Colpitts found that the city "was actually a terrible place for rock music," the celebrated 2000s scene not yet in place. In that decade, Oneida released a number of albums that experimented with psychedelic rock ideas, and Colpitts has since come to have a reach into the ecosystems of academic composition, jazz and improvisation, and "the so-called indie music scene," but has reservations about all of them.

Colpitts compares those reservations to the unconflicted feeling of going to see the Grateful Dead perform in the 1980s: "I think the most connection I felt was walking around outside a Dead concert at Foxborough or Albany. I was walking around and thinking, 'wow look at all these strange people.' I would smile directly at people, and they would smile back at me. Why? I don't know. It was as if I could reach back and touch a fantasy of the '60s. The peace and love and benevolent fantasy of it all. Of course the '80s Dead was the darkest time. Everyone was doing hard drugs. I bought a ticket from a complete wasted person who might not have realized they were selling me my miracle ticket. But I was just bopping along."

Pioneer Tracks: the Beatles—"Tomorrow Never Knows," the Jimi Hendrix Experience—"Purple Haze," Pink Floyd—"See Emily Play," Jefferson Airplane—"White Rabbit," the Grateful Dead—"The Golden Road (To Unlimited Devotion)"

Key Players: The 13th Floor Elevators, Big Brother and the Holding Company, Blue Cheer, the Byrds, Country Joe and the Fish, Cream, the Doors, Moby Grape, Quicksilver Messenger Service, Santana, the Steve Miller Band, Traffic, the Yardbirds, the Zombies

CROSSOVER GENRES

KRAUTROCK
Amon Düül II, Ash Ra Tempel, Can

PAISLEY UNDERGROUND
The Bangles, the Dream Syndicate, the Three O'Clock

PROGRESSIVE ROCK
King Crimson, the Moody Blues, Yes

Psychedelic Soul

Psychedelic soul refers to a time in the late 1960s when soul music was taking some influence, and some drugs, from psychedelic rock. Some of the artists attributed with creating psychedelic soul, notably Sly and the Family Stone and Parliament-Funkadelic (P-Funk), would go on to set funk up for its heyday in the 1970s. In that regard, psychedelic soul can be seen as having taken audiences to the bridge between soul and funk, paying James Brown at the toll booth.

"My soul has been psychedelicized!" sang the Chambers Brothers on their 1968 hippie-beckoning hit, "Time Has Come Today," instantly recognizable in its opening seconds for Lester Chambers' ticking clock cowbell, though its lengthy wander veers closer to Pink Floyd than P-Funk. Psychedelic soul didn't spend too long on the fringe. The following year, even a well-established act like the Temptations was getting in on the action with "Psychedelic Shack."

"It's not quite soul, not quite rock & roll," writes Dave Marsh about Sly and the Family Stone's music, "but an epiphanous ritual that operates on its own terms." Crediting Sly Stone and his band with causing a revolution in soul music that "ended the domination of the sweet soul sound" of Stax, Motown, and Muscle Shoals, Marsh also claims that after the short but significant psychedelic soul movement, "the great bulk of disco and funk rock simply worked off variations of Sly and the Family Stone's innovations."[1]

Key Players: The Chambers Brothers, Parliament-Funkadelic, Sly and the Family Stone, the Undisputed Truth

CROSSOVER TRACKS

FUNK ROCK

Mother's Finest–"Baby Love," War–"Why Can't We Be Friends?"

PSYCHEDELIC ROCK

The Doors–"Soul Kitchen," Carlos Santana–"Soul Sacrifice"

Psychobilly

||||||||||||||||||||||||||||||||||||||||||||||||||||||||||||||||||||||||||||||||||||||||||||||||||||||||||||||||||||||||||||||||||||||

"This isn't an absolute rule," says Jim Heath, aka the Reverend Horton Heat, "but I think that psychobilly is largely punk rock with an upright bass." Between rockabilly and its spikier offshoot, psychobilly, the main difference is the influence of punk on the latter, which dictates the speed and attitude in which it is played. And indeed, the fast-slapping technique used by the upright bass player, Heath notes, is key.

Heath has never considered the Reverend Horton Heat to be a psychobilly band, but the implication of the song "Psychobilly Freakout," from their 1990 debut album, *Smoke 'Em If You Got 'Em,* followed them wherever they went. Claims were made that they invented psychobilly. The band themselves denied such proclamations, but that didn't matter to some folks on the other side of the Atlantic, where psychobilly largely originates from. "When we started showing up in Europe, these big psychobilly guys wanted to kick our ass. 'You didn't invent psychobilly, so we're going to beat you up now.' I said, 'I know, I know, I know. I never said that.'"

Heath points to British band the Meteors, who started playing in 1980, as one of the early psychobilly bands, attributing the growth of that style partly to the idea that rockabilly never really died out in England. The Stray Cats, for instance, moved from New York to the UK because there was a greater platform for their sound there. Meteors leader P. Paul Fenech sang about sci-fi and horror subject matter, which gave the genre a point of lyrical fixation.[1] Exaggerated fashion and makeup became psychobilly identifiers and were taken to their logical conclusion by the Welsh band Demented Are Go.

Punked-up rockabilly does have its own history in America. The Cramps carved out their rockabilly niche at CBGB's back in the heady days of punk in 1970s New York. Their debut album, *Songs the Lord Taught Us*, featured songs with titles like "I Was a Teenage Werewolf" and "Zombie Dance," themes that match up with the goth side of European psychobilly. There was a goth influence on the 1990s wave of psychobilly bands as well, which included Tiger Army from California, led by Nick 13, who seems to have named himself in the numerical pop-punk style so prevalent in that era. Tiger Army's music would turn ambitious enough to become divisive,[2] but others have been happy to tweak but not trouble the tried-and-true methods of psychobilly.

Key Players: The Cramps, Demented Are Go, Flat Duo Jets, Guana Batz, the Meteors, Nekromantix, Reverend Horton Heat, Tiger Army, Zombie Ghost Train

CROSSOVER GENRES

COWPUNK
The Blasters, the Gun Club, Nashville Pussy

PUNK BLUES
The Immortal Lee County Killers, the Jon Spencer Blues Explosion, Laughing Hyenas

ROCKABILLY
The Paladins, the Polecats, the Stray Cats

Pub Rock

||||||||||||||||||||||||||||||||||||||||||||||||||||||||||||||||||||||||||||||||||||||||||||||||||||||||||||||||||||||||||||||||||||||||||

Like pub grub, pub rock is simple hearty fare: backbeat meat and potatoes, sonic bangers and mash. It was not a new style of rock and roll, but a purposeful return to its late 1950s and early 1960s roots. Though some of the more notable acts managed to make it into the studio to cut records for posterity, the genre, as the name suggests, was predominantly a live movement that took place in pubs and other small venues in Britain's capital and outlying areas. Some of the more notable London spots that nurtured the ragtag scene, like the Hope & Anchor in Islington and Dingwalls in Camden, are still open in one form or another.

In its heyday, the first half of the 1970s, pub rock's innovation came not in its sound, but its presence. Going against prevailing glam and prog trends of flashy outfits and polished performances, pub rock bands were intentionally rough around the edges. "Most of the early Pub Rock groups were content to play rehashed R&B and Country," Jon Savage observes. "The only sign of anything new was a group called Kilburn and the High Roads, which featured the men-acing, twisted performances of polio victim Ian Dury. . . . However, the breakthrough of Dr Feelgood, who electrified the metropolis with razor-sharp performances, tightened up R&B into a menacing mesh."[1]

Pub rock, if nothing else, was the first retaliation against the dominant commercial rock of its day. In addition to Dury, it was also where future punk and new wave stars like Joe Strummer (the 101ers), Elvis Costello (Flip City), and Nick Lowe (Brinsley Schwarz)[2] cut their teeth. The movement was supplanted by punk rock, but on records like *Never Mind the Bollocks, Here's the Sex Pistols*, echoes of pub rock riffs come out from underneath the filth and the fury. Despite being localized by its own nature, pub rock still was an important step backward toward the future.

Key Players: The 101ers, Brinsley Schwarz, Dr. Feelgood, Ducks Deluxe, Eddie and the Hot Rods, Kilburn and the High Roads

CROSSOVER TRACKS

NEW WAVE

Elvis Costello–"Waiting for the End of the World," Nick Lowe–"So It Goes"

PUNK ROCK

The Sex Pistols–"Pretty Vacant," the Stranglers–"Something Better Change"

Punk Blues

Punk blues is good for when you want a side of anger with your sorrow or your sadness served up fast. Given that the blues is the foundation of rock music, it isn't surprising that it should work its way so naturally into punk's subconscious. Punk blues can take different shapes. It occurs when bands write fast songs with blues riffs, but it can also happen when punks play the blues or come up with songs that are blues-like. Social Distortion's 1996 single "I Was Wrong," for example, with its "me against the world" stance, is blues from the punk perspective.

One finds blues influenced by punk less frequently, but one example is Bob Log III, who plays the blues with punk flair. Since the early 1990s, Bob Log III has had a long career as a one-stuntman band bringing salty blues-lick stompers like "Boob Scotch" (which is about exactly what it sounds like) to blues impurists everywhere. One group who managed to spill both blues in their punk and punk in their blues is, of course, the Jon Spencer Blues Explosion. Though their rough-edged eclecticism swallowed more than just those two genres, their fiery streak of albums in the 1990s was punctuated by the one they made with the underappreciated blues lifer R. L. Burnside, *A Ass Pocket of Whiskey*.

Key Players: Bob Log III, Boss Hog, the Chrome Cranks, the Delta 72, Doo Rag, the Jon Spencer Blues Explosion, Social Distortion

CROSSOVER GENRES

GARAGE ROCK REVIVAL
The Black Keys, the White Stripes

PSYCHOBILLY
Flat Duo Jets, the Meteors

Punk Jazz

Punk and jazz might seem like they come from different sides of the tracks, but, as NPR has pointed out, they "do have elements in common—the most important being attitude."[1] According to Tad Friend in his *New Yorker* piece on the Lounge Lizards leader John Lurie, the New York saxophonist "wore a Borsalino fedora and old suits and painted expressionist album covers and picked up girls at the Mudd Club and snorted coke at the Palladium with Steve Rubell and Rick James."[2] That is indeed both punk *and* jazz. The Lounge Lizards' distinctly downtown sound was regarded as one way in which the two can intersect.

The genre may not take a pure fifty-fifty hybrid form, but the influence and spirit of jazz pops up in punk. New York was a town big enough for more than one punk-jazz saxophonist, with James Chance and the Contortions and John Zorn's Naked City approaching the combination from the more abrasive No Wave camp, which shared jazz's principle of free improvisation. The Netherlands' classification-dodging band the Ex have shown jazz inclinations. Since "jazz" for many rock fans just means "the presence of a saxophone," that would also qualify Chicago art-punk band Sweep the Leg Johnny, who hit their manic peak in 2000 with the sharp, progressive *Sto Cazzo!*

Key Players: James Chance and the Contortions, the Ex, the Lounge Lizards, Naked City, Nomeansno, the Pop Group, Sweep the Leg Johnny

CROSSOVER TRACKS

ALTERNATIVE ROCK
Morphine–"Honey White," Sonic Youth–"I Love Her All the Time"

PROTO-PUNK
MC5–"Starship," the Stooges–"LA Blues"

Punk Rock

Punk rock was conceived when the young John Lydon, as he recalled, "gyrated like a belly dancer"[1] in Malcolm McLaren's Sex boutique in London as he sang along with Alice Cooper's "I'm Eighteen." Punk rock was invented in the basement of the Art Garden gallery and frame shop in Forest Hills, Queens, by four mischief makers who all took on the same family name.[2] Punk rock burst out of Iggy Pop's chest like *Alien* when he smeared peanut butter on himself while being held aloft by the audience at the Cincinnati Pop Festival in 1970.

Punk rock began when the Sonics howled about psychos and witches instead of love and good times. Punk rock sparks flew when kids watching *Blackboard Jungle* started ripping up theater seats as "Rock Around the Clock" began to play. Punk rock started down its path when Robert Johnson sold his soul to the Devil at the crossroads.

Punk rock spit its first gob when Baudelaire pissed off French society with *Les Fleurs du Mal*. Punk rock was discovered when Leif Erikson found America and then Columbus swooped in five hundred years later and took the credit. Punk rock fermented when Jesus turned water into wine. That was punk as fuck.

"As we all know, primitivism was one of punk's founding principles," writes Carola Dibbell in a piece on the Slits for the *Boston Phoenix* in 1981. "The idea was that with sophistication rock had lost its soul and that by investing brutally simple forms with feeling (or energy) some kind of magic would occur, and it did. But the structure's limited, so where you do go when you start repeating yourself?"

Citing a handful of prominent punk bands who either broke up or grew up when faced with punk rock's inherent limitations, Dibbell notes how the Slits went primitive. "Rather than build formally on the idea of freedom-within-limits, they pursued the venerable bohemian idea of pure self-expression."[3]

It has been noted often that punk's revolutionary reputation is undercut by how dependent on history it was. Punk bands would be lauded for severing ties with the past while at the same time covering 1960s hits like "(I'm Not Your) Stepping Stone." More surprising would be how wide punk's own influence would become. JJ Wandler recalls a time seeing the Dream Syndicate play live. Frontman Steve Wynn told the audience that the band came up in Los Angeles at the same time as hardcore punks Black Flag, and the first songs they wrote were their best attempt to emulate them. "All the things that shape our musicality and shape our psyche are what come out when we play music," Wandler says. "So even though they wanted to play like Black Flag and be punk rock, they ended up being the Dream Syndicate."

The ideas behind punk rock go beyond musical parameters: Do it yourself, get back to basics, make the most out of what little you have. Oh, and don't sell out. That was a very important rule, at least in the 1990s. Not so much in the 1970s, when the Sex Pistols famously made a sport out of jumping around major labels, and others like the Clash saw no conflict with signing to one. Not now, either, when bands are lucky to make any money at all and licensing songs for television advertisements is considered a big break, not a crime.

"Punk" is a word that represents both a style of music and an ideological approach to making it, and those two facets have been at odds with each other from nearly the beginning. The view of punk as a style—loud and fast, three chords, no solos—ultimately led certain factions of the movement toward a different kind of conformity. In contrast, a philosophy of "anything goes" is by its nature going to bump up against the very notion of genre, which must set at least some parameters. How far can the traditionalists go without losing the spirit, and how far can the free thinkers take it without abandoning the sound? And how do listeners, each allowed their own opinion of what punk really means, navigate it all?

"I think it got to this really weird point of like, 'is a genre your musical lineage, or is a genre just what you're playing?'" Tobias Carroll says, bringing up two post-hardcore bands from New York City, Quicksand and Texas is the Reason. Both had members who had played in prior groups that were entrenched in the city's hardcore scene, but also had been listening to things like shoegaze and Britpop and wanted to make broader music that reflected that. There was also the Swedish band Refused and their influential 1998 album *The Shape of Punk to Come* ("Hey, you can use sequencers!") and San Diego's the Locust ("Hey, you can use a keyboard!").

"At the same time," says Carroll, "I also remember the late '90s having the 1988-style hardcore revival where bands were very consciously writing hardcore songs that sounded like they were ten years old." Hearing new bands who sounded like old Youth of Today records was cool at first, but then it turned into ten bands doing the same thing, then fifty, and they were all using the same font. The period Carroll describes was just another nostalgic wave in a genre that has been selling the future and singing the past almost from day one.

Pioneer Tracks: The Damned—"New Rose," Death—"Rock 'n' Roll Victim," the Dictators—"California Sun" (cover), the Ramones—"Blitzkrieg Bop," the Sex Pistols—"Anarchy in the UK"

Key Players: Black Flag, Blondie, Buzzcocks, the Clash, the Dead Boys, Generation X, the Jam, the Patti Smith Group, Richard Hell and the Voidoids, Stiff Little Fingers, the Stranglers, Talking Heads, Television, UK Subs, Wire, X, X-Ray Spex

CROSSOVER TRACKS

GARAGE ROCK
The Kingsmen–"Louie Louie," the Sonics–"Strychnine," Them–"Gloria"

PROTO-PUNK
The Modern Lovers–"Roadrunner," the New York Dolls–"Personality Crisis," the Stooges–"I Wanna Be Your Dog"

ROCK AND ROLL
Chuck Berry–"Johnny B. Goode," the Crickets–"I Fought the Law," Paul Revere and the Raiders–"(I'm Not Your) Steppin' Stone"

Queercore

Thinking about what could substantiate riot grrrl as a music genre, *Girls to the Front* author Sara Marcus points to lyrics that touch on gender politics, noting how that might be the same thing that would make queercore a genre. "That would probably be the only thing you can say to unite all queercore musicians, that their lyrics at some point touch on the politics of queer sexuality."

Musically, queercore traces back to 1980s hardcore punk. San Francisco had Pansy Division, who wrote accessible pop-punk songs—being from the Bay Area in the 1990s, after all—about gender, sexuality, and relationships from a nonheteronormative perspective. God Is My Co-Pilot came from New York City with a similar lyrical perspective but a more free-flowing, noisy sound, collaborating with experimental saxophonists John Zorn and Jim Sauter, guitarist Elliott Sharp, and Jad Fair of Half Japanese.[1]

In the Northwest, Donna Dresch fronted the Portland-based Team Dresch, whose racing indie rock was captured on albums like *Personal Best* that were released on Dresch's own Chainsaw Records, which also put out two killer early records by art-minded duo the Need in the late 1990s, among many others. The region also boasted the queercore band with the longest name and the shortest, craziest songs: Behead the Prophet, No Lord Shall Live. The musical definition of queercore continues to expand as new artists from Gravy Train!!!! to Lesbians on Ecstasy add to its growing voice.

Key Players: The Butchies, God Is My Co-Pilot, Limp Wrist, the Need, Pansy Division, Team Dresch, Tribe 8

||||||||||||||||||||||||||||||||||||||||||||||||||||||||||||||||||||||||||||
CROSSOVER GENRES
||||||||||||||||||||||||||||||||||||||||||||||||||||||||||||||||||||||||||||

INDIE ROCK
The Hidden Cameras, Longstocking

PUNK ROCK
The Dicks, Extra Fancy

Raga Rock

The term "raga rock" was coined in the midst of rock music's dalliance with Indian music in the mid-1960s, coinciding with the early days of psychedelic rock. The most high-profile proponent was George Harrison, who famously studied the sitar with the master of the instrument, Ravi Shankar. Harrison was introduced to Shankar's music by David Crosby in 1965,[1] and the quiet Beatle was soon incorporating the sitar into "Norwegian Wood (This Bird Has Flown)," which appeared on *Rubber Soul* at the end of the year.

Slight impressions of Far Eastern sounds were also heard in the Kinks' "See My Friends," the Byrds' "Eight Miles High," and the Rolling Stones' "Paint It Black."[2] It seems that by that point Harrison was granted one raga rock song per Beatles album, with "Love You To" on *Revolver* and "Within You Without You" on *Sgt. Pepper's Lonely Hearts Club Band*. The influence would continue to mark Harrison's music, and raga rock lingered in the air for a while after the Summer of Love. A flash of sitar even appears in the middle of the Jackson 5's "Never Can Say Goodbye."

When Britpop revived everything from the 1960s that it could, raga rock was given its due by Kula Shaker with their singles "Tattva" and "Govinda." Completing the circle in a way, the UK indie band Cornershop, led by Midlands-born Tjinder Singh, covered "Norwegian Wood (This Bird Has Flown)" on their breakthrough 1997 album *When I Was Born for the 7th Time*, singing the lyrics in Punjabi.[3]

Key Tracks: The Beatles–"Norwegian Wood (This Bird Has Flown)," the Byrds–"Eight Miles High," Traffic–"Paper Sun," the Yardbirds–"Heart Full of Soul"

CROSSOVER TRACKS

BRITPOP

Cornershop–"Norwegian Wood (This Bird Has Flown)" (the Beatles), Kula Shaker–"Govinda"

ELECTRIC FOLK

Donovan–"Hurdy Gurdy Man," the Incredible String Band–"The Half-Remarkable Question"

Rap Metal

The journey of rap metal begins on the same trail blazed by its older brother, rap rock. Public Enemy and Anthrax's "Bring the Noise" was the rap metal equivalent of Aerosmith and Run-D.M.C.'s rap rock pioneering "Walk This Way," and, when it came out, it offered exciting potential to those eager to hear how the two genres could work together. They weren't the first rap artist and metal band to collaborate; another forerunner was Sir Mix-a-Lot, often deemed a one-hit wonder for the immortal "Baby Got Back." Mix's 1988 debut, *Swass*, featured fellow Pacific Northwesterners Metal Church ripping it up on the track "Iron Man."

High-profile pairings like these brought rap metal to wider audiences, but it would be groups that mixed the two styles within their own music that became the model. The group that would most successfully implement and build on that model, subsequently shaping rap metal to come, was Rage Against the Machine. You can't blame a band for those that borrow from them, but at least one Rage Against the Machine member, bassist Tim Commerford, has expressed a measure of guilt for it, having once apologized via *Rolling Stone* for inspiring Limp Bizkit.[1]

Some of that guilt may have first come to the surface when Commerford famously swung up in the scaffolding on stage at the MTV Video Music Awards in 2000, as the pride of Jacksonville took to the podium to whine about being the most hated band in the world while accepting their award for Best Rock Video. Repeatedly looking back at Commerford but never seeming to recognize a member of a band he purportedly loved, truer words surely never came to

Durst when he said into the mic, "This guy is rock 'n' roll, he should be getting the award."

Pioneer Tracks: Anthrax and Public Enemy—"Bring the Noise," Beastie Boys—*Licensed to Ill,* Sir Mix-a-Lot—"Iron Man"

Key Players: Biohazard, Body Count, Dog Eat Dog, Downset., Hed PE, Limp Bizkit, Linkin Park, P.O.D., Rage Against the Machine

CROSSOVER GENRES

NU METAL
Deftones, Korn

RAP ROCK
311, Kid Rock

Rap Rock

"[T]he riffs-and-rhymes formula that powered 'Walk This Way' remains the blueprint for most rap-rock,"[1] opined the *New York Times* in the year 2000, a strange time when teenyboppers and goateed gas-station attendants with Ibanez guitars competed for the hearts, minds, and ears of America's youth. Back then, rap metal was all over the airwaves, and the term was used more or less interchangeably with rap rock. Now that everyone has had time to heal, it is easier to see how one is more of a blanket term that includes the other.

Rock and rap music had been dabbling in one another years before "Walk This Way" came along. Blondie's winking "Rapture" appeared on their *Autoamerican* album and became a number one hit about men from Mars who just can't stop eatin' cars when released as a single in early 1981. The Clash took some inspiration from the nascent hip-hop movement as well on their song "The Magnificent Seven." In kind, hip-hop made increasing use of rock record samples.

Ignoring the boundaries that many saw between the two styles, the Beastie Boys remade themselves from minor hardcore punks into a commercially viable rap act that used a lot of rock samples and even had the guitarist from Slayer play on "No Sleep 'Til Brooklyn." After their hip-hop cred was set with *Paul's Boutique*, they let their old punk urges loose on album tracks like "Time for Livin'" and "Heart Attack Man." Then came "Sabotage," the first single from their 1994 album *Ill Communication*, one of the most successful meldings of rap and rock up to that point.

The rap rock that followed in that decade may not have always lived up to the promise of "Sabotage," but it was still reaching further into the world of pop music than ever before. Rage Against the Machine did it right. Beck found "Where It's At." The band 311 had their designated rapping guy. Sugar Ray got a designated record-scratching guy. Everlast got a second life out of "What It's Like." The possibilities are still there even if the results may vary.

Pioneer Tracks: Aerosmith and Run-D.M.C.–"Walk This Way," Blondie–"Rapture," the Clash–"The Magnificent Seven"

Key Players: 311, the Beastie Boys, Crazy Town, Everlast, Faith No More, Kid Rock, Red Hot Chili Peppers

CROSSOVER GENRES

ALTERNATIVE ROCK
Black Grape, Luscious Jackson

RAP METAL
Body Count, Cypress Hill–*Skull & Bones*

Reggae Rock

IIIIIIIIIIIIIIIIIIIIIIIIIIIIIIIIIIIIIIIIIIIIIIIIIIIIIIIIIIIIIIIIIIIIIIIIIIIIIIIIIIIIIIIIIIIIIIIIIIIIIIIIIIIIIIIIIIIIIIIIII

In a sense, reggae played the part of both pop and rock music in its home country, Jamaica. It took a bit of time to catch on in America and Europe, but when those territories finally bit, they bit hard. The influence trickled in slowly through the early 1970s via some of the biggest names in rock: Eric Clapton's cover of "I Shot the Sheriff," Led Zeppelin's "D'yer Mak'er," the Rolling Stones' "Hey Negrita." The soulful outlaw appeal spoke to many a punk rocker, and the easy vibe spoke to less aggressive types. Reggae rock is a fairly simple formula, occurring whenever reggae's defining rhythm and bass style makes its way into what would otherwise be a considered a rock song.

Does this mean that the Police were actually pioneers of something? Kinda! "Sting, Godfather of Reggae Rock" may not be a commonly used phrase, but respect is due. Their third ever single, "So Lonely," stitched a reggae verse onto a faster power pop chorus, as had the Clash's "(White Man) In Hammersmith Palais." Two singles later, "Walking on the Moon" melded the two styles even more successfully. It wasn't the only mode in which the Police played, but reggae was integral to their initial sound.

If other bands have since done it with greater authenticity, the Police were still surely the most commercially successful at it, though the 1990s rolled crossover joints with Sublime's "Santeria" and 311's "All Mixed Up," and passed it on to more recent groups like Pepper and Iration.

Key Players: 311, Iration, Pepper, the Police, Slightly Stoopid, Sublime

CROSSOVER TRACKS

HARD ROCK

Led Zeppelin–"D'yer Mak'er," the Rolling Stones–"Hey Negrita"

NEW WAVE

Elvis Costello–"Watching the Detectives," the Pretenders–
"Private Life"

Riot Grrrl

The riot grrrl movement encompassed a lot more than the music that came out of it, but the few bands who made it constituted one of the most vital and socially significant scenes in rock music. Riot grrrl sprang out of Olympia, Washington, in the early 1990s. The small state capital and its famously free-spirited Evergreen State College were already known for a DIY-indie community and Calvin Johnson's K Records when poet-turned-singer Kathleen Hanna, an Evergreen student, formed the band Bikini Kill in 1990 with fellow students Tobi Vail (drums) and Kathi Wilcox (bass). Vail soon recruited a friend, Billy Karren, to join as a guitarist.[1]

Around the same time, two hundred miles south of Olympia in another college town, Eugene, two University of Oregon students, Molly Neuman and Allison Wolfe, were piecing together the first issue of their *Girl Germs* zine. They also talked about being in a band together, and their bluff was called when Johnson invited them to play a gig in Olympia with Bikini Kill, and so Bratmobile became a reality. The two bands, whose connections with the other Washington would give them both a kind of dual citizenship in Olympia's indie world and DC's political punk community, were soon to become the musical arm of a multifaceted feminist movement.

An important method of communication and networking for the movement was the writing and self-publishing of zines. In early July 1991, when both bands were based in DC for the summer, Hanna, Neuman, Wolfe, and their friend Jen Smith printed copies of a small but significant new zine they had collaborated on. Marcus writes of the occasion, "They had decided to put out one issue per week for the rest of the summer, so they'd have something to pass out at shows, a way to make connections with other girls who lived in DC. They named the zine *Riot Grrrl*: a blend of Jen's 'girl riot' and the growling 'grrrl' that Tobi had recently made up as a jokey variation on all the tortured spellings of 'womyn/womon/wimmin' feminists liked to experiment with."[2]

Bikini Kill and Bratmobile were friends and central players in the riot grrrl community, but their music wasn't uniform. Both played guitar-based music with punk energy, but they achieved different results. The addition of one more band to the scene made pinning down a "riot grrrl sound" even more complicated. Heavens to Betsy, the duo of future Sleater-Kinney leader Corin Tucker and Tracy Sawyer, had watched both Bikini Kill and Bratmobile with admiration,[3] but their songs would swing between punk release and the Northwest indie rock manner of building mood and tension. Three different bands, three different voices, and other groups like Huggy Bear and Excuse 17 would soon arrive as well.

Does the music of riot grrrl stand as one genre? "I am not sure that I'd agree that there was a sound," Marcus says. There would be female vocals, of course, but that isn't exactly musically specific. Another characteristic might be the use of electric guitars, but that would exclude a group like Tattle Tale, the acoustic/folk duo of Jen Wood (who later went solo) and Madigan Shive (who went on to start Bonfire Madigan) formed in Seattle in the early 1990s when the two were teenagers. Marcus thinks that Shive would want to preserve Tattle Tale's place in riot grrrl, and that if one is talking about the scene as a community, then Lois Maffeo—the Olympia-based singer/songwriter who went by just Lois on her albums for K Records in the 1990s—also qualifies.

The community came to have a notably strained relationship

with the press in the 1990s, seeing the obvious value in spreading the word but also understanding how their movement could be co-opted. *Sassy* magazine was a sincere source of support, but others in the media misrepresented the scene just as they feared. Sometimes they weren't even sure who was actually in it. "Another part of the problem with the press was of nomenclature," writes *Girl Power* author Marisa Meltzer. "There was little differentiation between riot grrrl bands and bands who simply had women in them . . . there were plenty of bands, like L7 or Babes in Toyland, who were like-minded and also from the punk community but didn't use the term to describe their music or philosophy."[4]

"I feel like the construction of riot grrrl as a music genre, as opposed to a kind of political thing that involves music, happens retrospectively," said Marcus. This gradual morphing of a political movement into a music genre designation in the general public's perception was something that Marcus tried to undo with *Girls to the Front*. It is also one of the first things she preemptively addresses when she speaks about riot grrrl to classrooms.

That any of these students would regard riot grrrl as a "style" of music is not so much their own fault for misunderstanding as it is the result of how knowledge changes shape over time as it is passed down through so many hands. "Certain cultural artifacts have more staying power and more cultural durability than other artifacts," Marcus notes. "Music, especially [with] the digitization of music, happens to have a much greater durability than the other elements of riot grrrl culture. I love that the music has survived so robustly."

Part of that durability is, of course, accessibility. It takes much less time to pull up a Bratmobile song on YouTube or Spotify than it does to track down and get a hold of a copy of *Girl Germs*. This is where the *Alien She* exhibition provided a valuable experience when it traveled around the United States between 2013 and 2016. The "first exhibition to examine the lasting impact of Riot Grrrl on artists and cultural producers working today,"[5] it was curated by Astria Suparak and Ceci Moss, featured work by artists such as Miranda July and Ginger Brooks Takahashi, and had regional music curators that included Wolfe and Donna Dresch of Team Dresch. At the exhibition's stay at the artist-run gallery Vox Populi in Philadelphia in the spring of 2014, for example, there were walls of zines from the era that one could sit down and read front to back.

Flipping through some of those zines, when music did come up—it was but one of many subjects written about—it would often be punk, punk-adjacent, or at least punk in the DIY sense. Bikini Kill, who received a bit more attention in the mainstream music press, were also perhaps the closest of the initial riot grrrl groups to a more straightforward punk rock sound. These reasons might be why the use of "riot grrrl" as a genre term usually implies punk roots. "Of course riot grrrl came out of punk, but even the boundaries of punk are complicated," Marcus points out, citing the lyrics of "Punk Means Cuddle" by Tsunami. "There's a band that would have been identified as indie pop, or indie rock, claiming punk for itself."

Of the bands *Girls to the Front* focuses on, Bikini Kill and Heavens to Betsy are two that Marcus sees younger fans gravitating toward, if perhaps only for the reason that their frontwomen went on to greater notoriety with Le Tigre and Sleater-Kinney, respectively. Marcus herself had a strong affinity for the UK's preeminent riot grrrl band Huggy Bear, whose music is overdue for revisitation by critics and audiences. "In fact," she says, "the band that I joined in 1995 was more indebted to Huggy Bear than anybody else."

Key Players: Bikini Kill, Bratmobile, Excuse 17, Heavens to Betsy, Huggy Bear, Lois, Tattle Tale

CROSSOVER TRACKS

GRUNGE

Babes in Toyland–"Bruise Violet," Hole–"Olympia," L7–"Shove"

POST-PUNK

Bush Tetras–"Too Many Creeps," Kleenex–"Ain't You," the Slits–"Shoplifting"

QUEERCORE

The Need–"Majesty," Team Dresch–"She's Amazing," Tribe 8–"Butch in the Streets"

Rockabilly

|||||||||||||||||||||||||||||||||||||||||||||||||||||||||||||||||||||||||||||||||||||||||||||||||||||||||||||||||||||||||||||||||||

"Listen man, I gotta tell you something," says Dallas-born, generation-spanning musician Jim Heath, pausing mid-question. "I'm not a person who likes to toot my own horn, but I don't know where the term 'rockabilly' would be without Reverend Horton Heat."

Heath is talking specifically about the *term*, but it's fair to say his impact on the music itself since the 1980s has been substantial. The Reverend Horton Heat have been around for over three decades, and in that time, they have released eleven albums to date. He was present for the big rockabilly revival of the late 1970s and early 1980s, but unlike every other artist who was a part of that musical fling, Heath has stayed committed, keeping rockabilly breathing wherever he goes.

Rockabilly in its original time, the 1950s, was essentially one and the same with rock and roll. Elvis Presley's first single, "That's All Right," and the label that put it out, Sun Records, are key points of origin for both, though the two genres have precedents that date back further. Even after dealing Elvis over to the major label RCA-Victor in order to stay afloat, Sun Records in the mid-to-late 1950s boasted a roster that featured Carl Perkins, Jerry Lee Lewis, Roy Orbison, and Johnny Cash, all artists who are central to the early history of rock and rockabilly. Though the term "rockabilly" had been tossed around here and there in the 1950s, only after people became accustomed to the rock-and-roll sprawl of the 1960s could they look back on "Blue Suede Shoes," "Folsom Prison Blues," and the many musicians that had stayed true to the sound of those records and really identify the music as something distinct.

Peter Guralnick writes that rockabilly's purity comes from its preservation in the time between the release of "That's All Right" in 1954 and the various career declines of Elvis, Perkins, Lewis, and Gene Vincent.[1] The music was rock 'n' roll that either refused to grow or stayed true to its roots, depending on how you see it. By the 1960s, it had reached Europe—influencing Britain and France's answers to Elvis, Vince Taylor and Johnny Hallyday respectively—but it had run out of gas at home. Rockabilly rusted in the driveway until the Clash covered Taylor's "Brand New Cadillac," the Cramps sped up and freaked out rockabilly until it was psychobilly, and Brian Setzer's Stray Cats found international success.

Rockabilly is now regarded as a time-tested American tradition, but when Heath was starting out, first in high school bands and then as a hired-gun guitarist, they were making it up as they went along. Heath's own experience is that the term "rockabilly" wasn't in the common rock vocabulary the way it is now until the early 1980s. He recalls a few other players from the Dallas area that were into it, like T. Tex Edwards, Homer Henderson, and Ted Roddy, all of whom helped steer Heath beyond the normal. "I played quite a few gigs backing up old rockabilly guys. They don't mind being called 'rockabilly,' but they would tell me, 'Rockabilly wasn't really something that we called this music. Back then, we just called it rock 'n' roll. Sometimes, we'd call it hillbilly bop.' Different bands would have different names for it."

In Heath's estimation, Robert Gordon of Tuff Darts, a band in the CBGB's circle of the mid-1970s, was one of the first to make it a scene, and everyone that followed, from Shakin' Stevens to Levi and the Rockats, from the Stray Cats to the Blasters, owes a lot to him. It was at the famous Hot Klub in Dallas that Heath saw the Blasters for the first time. Between that band, the Paladins, the Stray Cats, and some others, a friend of Heath's dubbed the moment "the Great

Rockabilly Scare of '83." The momentum built until they were playing nationally by 1989. Everywhere they went, promoters would line Heath up with interviews with music writers. In those first years, he recalls, the first question he was asked was "What is rockabilly?"

"They didn't know. Every club we played, we would come up there with [an] upright bass, and they'd go, 'How many songs do you use the cello on?' They would try to talk us out of it. They'd say, 'This isn't going to sound good. You guys got to play electric bass tonight.' We don't even have an electric bass."

Then there was the time that a music writer insisted that Elvis Presley wasn't rockabilly, to which Heath replied by telling them to go listen to "Mystery Train" and "Baby, Let's Play House" and reconsider.

As much as they were preachers, they were also teachers. It took persistence on their part, but the Reverend Horton Heat began to break through. Sometimes there would already be little rockabilly scenes in certain towns, especially in Los Angeles, where one of the city's foundational punk bands, X, had an unabashed rockabilly guitarist, Billy Zoom.

Of all the record labels that the Reverend Horton Heat could have ended up on, it's delightfully counterintuitive that their first three albums were put out by a record label based 2,000 miles northwest of Dallas that was building its reputation on bands like Nirvana and Mudhoney. How did they end up on Sub Pop? "It's kind of a cool story."

Having played some of the same rooms as bands on their roster, the Reverend Horton Heat were on the label's radar. At one point, they drove all the way up from LA for their first gig in Seattle, only to find out that there was no gig, and the guy who said he set it up was gone. There they were, stuck with nothing to do and hardly any money to their name, when they were given the chance to play a short five-song set at the end of a show on Saturday night. They agreed and ended up winning the packed crowd over with a rendition of "Psychobilly Freakout" that turned bloody when Jimbo Wallace broke a bass string and tried to rip it off with his bare hand, putting a giant gash in his finger.

"I stopped and I looked over at him like, 'Are you okay?' There was blood everywhere, just spurting out. He looks at the crowd, and he takes his hand and makes a cross across his eyes and down the middle of his face. A blood cross. People had this shocked look on their face, and he looked at me and just said, 'Go.' I went up to the microphone: 'It's a psychobilly freakout!' We kept playing." People from Sub Pop saw it all from near the front row, and a record deal followed shortly after.

"You know, man, I honestly just think that rockabilly was the kicking dog of all music. It became that about the time the Beatles went psychedelic. The Beatles started out playing a lot of rockabilly songs, they covered Carl Perkins and rockabilly guys. If you listen to songs like 'Memphis' and '30 Days' by Chuck Berry, it's more of a rockabilly type of a sound. Labels don't necessarily tell the whole story, but they get you in the ballpark."

Pioneer Tracks: Bill Flagg—"Go Cat, Go," Bill Haley and the Saddlemen—"Rocket 88," Carl Perkins—"Blue Suede Shoes," Curtis Gordon—"Rompin' and Stompin'," Elvis Presley—"That's All Right"

Key Players: Johnny Cash, Eddie Cochran, Dale Hawkins, Ronnie Hawkins, Buddy Holly, Johnny Horton, Charlie Feathers, Wanda Jackson, Sleepy LaBeef, Alis Lesley, Jerry Lee Lewis, Janis Martin, the Rock and Roll Trio, Gene Summers, Gene Vincent

||||||||||||||||||||||||||||||||||||||||||||||||||||||||||||||||||||||||||||||||

CROSSOVER TRACKS

||||||||||||||||||||||||||||||||||||||||||||||||||||||||||||||||||||||||||||||||

ALTERNATIVE ROCK

The Replacements–"I Will Dare," the Smiths–"Rusholme Ruffians," Social Distortion–"Ring of Fire" (Johnny Cash)

COUNTRY ROCK

The Bottle Rockets–"Manhattan Countryside," Creedence Clearwater Revival–"Bad Moon Rising," NRBQ–"Me and the Boys"

PUNK ROCK

The Clash–"Brand New Cadillac" (Vince Taylor), the Fall–"Container Drivers," X–"I Must Not Think Bad Thoughts"

Rock in Opposition

To the uninitiated ear, all progressive rock sounds artsy and out there. For those well-versed in lengthy improvisations played in difficult time signatures, there is a difference between prog rock and its unofficial leftist fringe, sometimes called avant-prog. Henry Cow were part of the latter.[1] Formed by guitarist Fred Frith and multi-instrumentalist Tim Hodgkinson at Cambridge University in 1968, their line-ups and compositions were experimental and loose in structure. Frith once composed a song based on the Fibonacci Sequence,[2] which is all one might need to know to decide if Henry Cow is going to be their kind of band.

Rock in Opposition was at birth a coalition of Henry Cow and four other bands: Etron Fou Leloublan, Samla Mammas Manna, Stormy Six, and Univers Zero, all of whom were from different European countries. Membership in the group required taking two vows: to remain independent and not sign with a commercial record company and to keep high standards in their songwriting.

They were not sworn to uphold a dedication to making any one style of music, but "Rock in Opposition" eventually came to be used as a term to describe the music of the bands who were in RIO, most likely because it was a lot easier than trying to describe their sounds any other way. As for the organization itself, Rock in Opposition kicked around for a mere two years[3] before succumbing to the fact that it was a self-made union of unconventional musicians trying to fight the powers that be.

The Players: Etron Fou Leloublan, Henry Cow, Samla Mammas Manna, Stormy Six, Univers Zero

CROSSOVER GENRES

ART ROCK
Art Bears, Massacre, Skeleton Crew (Fred Frith's post–Henry Cow groups)

PROGRESSIVE ROCK
Camel, Gentle Giant

San Francisco Sound

||||||||||||||||||||||||||||||||||||||||||||||||||||||||||||||||||||||||||||||||||||||||||||||||||||||||||||||||||||||||||||||||||||||||||||||||

Like an old hippie caricature, the term "San Francisco Sound" stays fixed in its prime, refusing to acknowledge the 1960s ended. The connection between the San Francisco Sound and psychedelic rock is obvious, but they aren't entirely the same. San Francisco's psychedelic rock wasn't pure; it was laced with blues, country, folk music, and more. Jerry Garcia spent the early 1960s playing bluegrass before forming a jug band with Bob Weir and Ron McKernan, who afterward became the Grateful Dead in 1965. The Charlatans, one of the city's psychedelic rock initiators, spent their 1965 temporarily fleeing to Virginia City, Nevada, where they picked up an Old West motif and brought country and folk back with them.

The rest of the pieces fell into place in 1966. That was the year that Janis Joplin provided Big Brother and the Holding Company an inimitable blues singer and Grace Slick left the Great Society for Jefferson Airplane, bringing "White Rabbit" and "Somebody to Love" along with her. Joplin and Slick remain two of the San Francisco Sound's most recognized voices and faces, while most of the male musicians in the scene tend to blur together. As the Monterey Pop Festival rang in the Summer of Love and Haight-Ashbury became the hippest intersection in the country, newcomers from the city like Sly and the Family Stone, Santana, and the Steve Miller Band added to the San Francisco Sound.

Despite how the story is usually told, not everyone at the time was enamored with what the City by the Bay had to offer. "Among the velvet-trousered denizens of the Scotch of St James," the late British music critic Ian MacDonald writes, making reference to the famous Swinging London nightclub, "the feeling was that the vaunted San Francisco Sound was strictly Amateur Hour. The tiny shriek of treble-boosted Gibson guitars squeezed through cheap fuzz boxes and heaps of small speakers, the fret-squeaking rumble of overdriven Fender basses, the hectoring voices of earnest white college kids raring to change the world."[1]

Music critic Ellen Willis goes as far as to question how much they even wanted to be a part of the rock world at all. "San Francisco and its environs have never been hospitable to rock and roll," she writes in 1973, offering a kind of proto–hot take, though one with a valid point behind it: "The fabled acid-rockers were folkies at heart, and so were their fans."[2] Willis backs this up with an anecdote from John Fogerty about hippie scenesters in the city wanting to drop the word "rock" for "head music." No less contrary a directive should have been expected from the command center of counterculture.

Key Players: Big Brother and the Holding Company, the Charlatans (US), Country Joe and the Fish, the Grateful Dead, Jefferson Airplane, Moby Grape, Quicksilver Messenger Service, Santana, Sly and the Family Stone, the Steve Miller Band

CROSSOVER GENRES

CALIFORNIA SOUND
The Beach Boys, the Byrds, the Eagles

JERSEY SHORE SOUND
The Gaslight Anthem, Southside Johnny, Bruce Springsteen

TULSA SOUND
J. J. Cale, Eric Clapton, Leon Russell

"Screamo has it worse," Tom Mullen immediately replies when asked which rock genre might be more misunderstood than emo. Screamo is a light-hearted name for an intense strain of post-hardcore. The term was not originally intended to denote a separate genre, but to convey exactly what you'd expect: emo with screaming in it. Though emo and screamo came to take on connotations that separated them, in the early 1990s, the styles were more closely related. If the second wave of emocore took the hardcore of the first-generation bands and dialed the speed and anger down a bit, screamo dialed them *up*.

Bay Area band Portraits of Past were only together for a couple of years in the mid-1990s, but their first, only, and posthumous album, referred to as *01010101*, gradually attained revered status on the West Coast. Still Life, a band from Moorpark, California, also showed up early and too often get overlooked. Ebullition Records, based in Goleta, California, put out records by both Portraits of Past and Still Life and was central to West Coast hardcore and emocore as the publisher of the zine *HeartattaCk*, which extensively covered the scene. Further south, Gravity Records had bands like Antioch Arrow and Clikatat Ikatowi who played a faster, rougher version of the kind of artfully chaotic post-hardcore that fellow San Diegans Drive Like Jehu were making.

Screamo solidified itself as a genre in the late 1990s, when a small wave of bands from the Northeast—like Orchid from Amherst, Massachusetts, and Saetia from New York—propagated the style. Around the same time in the Seattle area, the Blood Brothers were beginning to turn one of post-hardcore's latest inventions, the "auxiliary screaming guy" (a kind of back-up vocalist whose job it was to scream different lines behind whatever the lead vocalist was singing/shouting about), on its head, replacing the frontman role with *two* auxiliary screaming guys. Screamo still came across as a nickname to some, but the joke had been repeated so many times that many were now taking it seriously—or as seriously as they could.

Screamo became re-conflated with emo at the hands of the third wave. At first, the results weren't so bad (Alexisonfire), sometimes they were even quite good (Thursday), but the returns quickly diminished (the Used). What was left in the underground became more experimental, like City of Caterpillar, which featured former members of Virginia screamo band Pg. 99.[1] Mullen estimates that screamo was ruined by 2005 or so. "Yes, the word changes. Yes, the term morphs . . . [but] just because it's a little chuggy and you're screaming . . . it's not screamo."

Pioneer Tracks: Antioch Arrow–"Ain't My Day," Drive Like Jehu–"If It Kills You," Heroin–"Leave," Portraits of Past–"Bang Yer Head," Still Life–"Empty Cage"

Key Players: The Blood Brothers, Circle Takes the Square, City of Caterpillar, Clikatat Ikatowi, Orchid, Pg. 99, Saetia

CROSSOVER GENRES

EMO(CORE)
Cap'n Jazz, Moss Icon, Rites of Spring

METALCORE
Alexisonfire, Silverstein, the Used

POST-HARDCORE
Hoover, Thrice, Thursday

Shock Rock

||||||||||||||||||||||||||||||||||||||||||||||||||||||||||||||||||||||||||||||||||||||||||||

"It took another late-night discussion to find a reason to execute Alice," writes Alice Cooper bassist Dennis Dunaway in his memoir, *Snakes! Guillotines! Electric Chairs!*, recalling the band's process of plotting out the stage show for their Love It to Death tour. "During 'The Ballad of Dwight Fry,' a sadistic nurse was to get strangled by her tormented inmate when he escaped from his straitjacket. The mock murder would be punished by a mock execution, followed, ultimately, by a mock resurrection."[1]

Alice Cooper were an unlikely bunch to become the band that would elevate shock rock from sideshow to center stage. A quintet of jocks and truants from Cortez High School in Phoenix, Arizona, they began as a British Invasion–inspired group named the Spiders. In the late 1960s, they moved to Los Angeles where they hit the town and connected with Frank Zappa, releasing two albums on his Straight record label that were quirky to a fault. Then came fate in the form of producer Bob Ezrin, the single "I'm Eighteen," and their dark, theatrical turn on their third album, *Love It to Death*. The tour that followed would become famous for its drama, detail, and simulated violence—chopping up baby dolls, sitting in fake electric chairs, and wearing real boa constrictors. Alice Cooper had exhausted themselves by 1975, having been compelled to outdo the gore and costumes of previous stage shows with every new tour.

Alice Cooper put together the howls, face paint, and fire of Screamin' Jay Hawkins, Screaming Lord Sutch, and the Crazy World of Arthur Brown.[2] They were not the first rock band to wear costumes, but they put everything they could think of into an over-the-top whole of menacing vaudeville, held together with some pretty great riffs by guitarist Glen Buxton. An intentionally warped reflection of their times, Alice Cooper went from second-run psychedelic rock to being ahead of the pack, a precursor to punk, glam metal, and more. Their tight-fitting leather and spandex stage wear appeared shiny and new on Hollywood hair metal bands a decade later. Slash from Guns 'n' Roses, like Cooper before him, had an affinity for giant pet snakes.

The 1980s would bring into question what shock rock really was. LA heavy metal band W.A.S.P. stood on arena stages next to giant skulls and wore exploding codpieces, which was enough to rile up the Parents Music Resource Center (PMRC), but to others must have seemed as safely theatrical as Cooper's beloved *West Side Story*. More disturbing were the notorious lengths that punk performer GG Allin would go to in order to test the limits of his much smaller club audiences. His music was unremarkable, but his lyrics and behavior had few peers in depravity. A troubled product of a troubled upbringing, and an Alice Cooper fan in his youth, Allin took the line between outlaw performer and actual outlaw and relieved himself all over it.

Metal troupe GWAR, from Virginia, combined wild costumes with gross-out subject matter, while also stirring a bent sense of humor into the foul stew. Clad in foam and rubber suits that made them appear to be alien S&M gladiators, they became fodder for MTV News segments in the early 1990s. Marilyn Manson came after Alice Cooper's rock-theater throne with his Dead to the World tour in 1996 and 1997. At one point deep into the show, gesticulating from a mock neo-Nazi podium with no eyebrows, Manson distinctly called to mind not Cooper, but Bob Geldof's portrayal of Pink in the film adaptation of *The Wall*.

By the 2000s, plenty of bands still tried to be offensive, but so much blood, be it fake or real, had already been spilled that the sight of nu metal bands in masks failed to really shock.

Pioneer Tracks: The Crazy World of Arthur Brown—"Fire," Screamin' Jay Hawkins—"I Put a Spell on You," Screaming Lord Sutch—"Jack the Ripper"

Key Players: Alice Cooper, GG Allin, GWAR, KISS, Marilyn Manson, W.A.S.P.

CROSSOVER GENRES

BLACK METAL
Marduk, Mayhem, Rotting Christ

HEAVY METAL
The Genitorturers, King Diamond/Mercyful Fate, Lizzy Borden

PUNK ROCK
Dwarves, the Misfits, the Tubes

Shoegaze

Before he started Food Records with former Teardrop Explodes keyboardist David Balfe, Andy Ross wrote for the UK music weekly *Sounds* under the name Andy Hurt. One night, he went to go see Moose, an indie band from London, play a gig when he noticed singer/guitarist Russell Yates had a habit of looking down at the stage while playing. In writer Ian Gittins' "Shoegaze: An Oral History" piece for the former music website Wondering Sound, Ross recalled, "A week later, I met up for lunch with two *NME* journalists, Steve Lamacq and Simon Williams, and I said, 'Look, this scene with Slowdive, and all those other bands—how about we call it shoegazing?'"[1]

This was not the first time a British music journalist had tried to come up with a name for this new style of rock that used heavy amounts of delay and reverb to achieve a hazy, dream-like quality, accompanied by understated vocals delivering impressionistic lyrics. Tying this assortment of bands—who seemed united in an appreciation of the ethereal qualities of the Cocteau Twins, the hallucinogenic "glide guitar" of My Bloody Valentine, and the squall of early Jesus and Mary Chain—together was proving tricky. Steve Sutherland, then deputy editor at another UK music weekly, *Melody Maker*, had already pushed "The Scene That Celebrates Itself" under the notion that all of the groups regularly socialized together.[2]

"None of the bands involved at the time felt that much affiliated with each other," Rachel Goswell, of Slowdive, recalls. During those years, she lived in Slowdive's hometown of Reading, roughly forty miles west of London. On occasion, she would go out in the city and perhaps see a member of Lush or Blur out and about in Camden, but, she says, "I think it was predominantly press created, the scene. Obviously we toured a lot with Ride in the end, and we got on really well with them. Swervedriver were one of my favorite bands at the time. We all loved the Valentines. . . . I think we did one gig with the Cocteau Twins."

Goswell acknowledges that these bands being largely from neighboring parts of England played a part in them being lumped together. In a *Melody Maker* article from September 1992, titled, a tad preemptively, "Whatever Happened to Shoegazing?," the members of Moose described the scene as all the bands who "came from that gap between Swindon and London."[3] "The only other band of note that came out of Reading was Chapterhouse," Goswell remembers, "and they were doing Stooges covers."

The term "shoegaze" did get one thing right: Some of them did have to look down at their feet quite often. "I think it was just about wanting to create a beautiful wall of sound, and that's not really possible with one pedal," says Goswell. "Christian [Savill, Slowdive guitarist] got ridiculous about the pedals—eighteen pedals, I think. You know, once you buy one pedal, you just want more and more and more. I don't play much guitar, so I just kind of come in occasionally and add a little bit of noise here and there. I've just got four pedals now. Very basic, travel light."

Creation Records, already home to My Bloody Valentine, would become one of the two most prominent labels for shoegaze artists, with label boss Alan McGee signing up Ride, Swervedriver, and Slowdive. "As teenagers the ultimate dream was to be on Creation," says Goswell, "and we were really lucky to have the opportunity." She remembers Slowdive were almost catapulted into the weekly music press as their self-titled debut EP was welcomed with fanfare in

NME, *Melody Maker*, and *Sounds*. The other notable label was 4AD, headed by Ivo Watts-Russell, which boasted Lush, Pale Saints, and the Cocteau Twins.

It was only a matter of time before the British music press turned on its own creation. "The worst part was waiting for the backlash, because we knew it would come," Goswell remembers.

Some of the qualities that drew attention to the first bands in the scene were now liabilities for those coming up in their wake. Ride, who had been one of the more favored shoegaze bands since their initial EPs came out in 1990, never really accepted the tag, and came out in 1992 with "Leave Them All Behind," an eight-minute single announcing the band's intention to stay ahead of the pack. The album that followed, *Going Blank Again*, cleared away the blurriness of their earlier records.

Some of the up-and-comers suddenly wanted to distance themselves. In the aforementioned *Melody Maker* feature, Damon Albarn of Blur, whose first single, "She's So High," bore a few shoegazing traits, said of the scene that, "It had nowhere else to go . . . it's become a cliché now, that 'We're trying to do something different' line."[4] Blur would soon become one of those bands who tried to "do something different" with each album and became massively successful by doing so.

Blur would experience some of their own early critical backlash, but they rode the shoegaze wave well, getting on and off at the right times. Catherine Wheel, a band from a coastal town in the county of Norfolk and led by Rob Dickinson (cousin of Bruce Dickinson, singer for Iron Maiden), did much the same from their 1992 debut, *Ferment*, to their next album, *Chrome*.

In 1994, Ride released *Carnival of Light*, a critical and commercial disappointment after their early peaks. Two years later, at the height of Britpop, which might have provided an opportunity for revitalization, the band announced their breakup in advance of their album *Tarantula*. *Melody Maker* writer Neil Kulkarni, for one, reveled in their demise in his review of the record, which ran under the headline "Eight-Legged Snooze Machine." Admitting a lack of objectivity up front with his account of a freshman year at college where the cool kids were into Ride and he was alone in his dorm room listening to Jane's Addiction and Public Enemy, he finds vindication in the assertion that "'Tarantula' is Ride's swan song and is as dull as you expect, or as irrelevant as you think, depending on your age."[5]

In his memoir, Alan McGee humorously shoulders some of the blame for Ride's change of direction, recalling, "If anything, it went wrong for Ride when I started playing them Byrds and Beatles records. . . . I think they'd have sold more over the long term if they hadn't changed their sound so drastically—perhaps I could have got another five shoegazing albums out of them."[6] *Tarantula* was deleted by Creation Records a mere week after its release. The prior year, both Slowdive and Swervedriver were dropped by Creation within a week after they released their latest albums. Chapterhouse and Pale Saints were both done by 1996. Swervedriver regrouped and released one more album with another label before the end of the 1990s, while some members of Slowdive reconfigured as Mojave 3.

For all the premature endings, it wasn't the end. Shoegazing had taken a small foothold in the United States early on, in the form of bands like Swirlies and Lilys. Kurt Heasley formed Lilys in Washington, DC, in the late 1980s, and their 1992 debut album, *In the Presence of Nothing*, copped impressively from the My Bloody Valentine playbook. As Emma Anderson points out to Gittins, "In the US, where Lush did reasonably well, shoegazing was never a negative term."[7] More new shoegaze bands started forming in places scattered around America. The Pacific Northwest was fertile ground for shoegazing, growing the High Violets, Voyager One, the Melody Unit, and more. There were bands in the 2000s that incorporated shoegaze elements into their sound, if not as faithfully to classic guidelines, like Longwave and Black Rebel Motorcycle Club.

In more recent years, Slowdive, Ride, Lush, Swervedriver, and other first-generation shoegaze bands have reunited, released new music, and gone on tour, playing bigger venues than they did back in the day. "It's nice to see how it has gone full circle, and it's now an accepted genre of music," says Goswell. "I think that's what really still flabbergasts me a little bit, that it's actually a genre. I still find it odd. It's amazing, and it's a lovely thing that all these younger bands have come along. Then you've got dream pop, nu gaze . . . it's a little bit mind-blowing to see how it's developed over the years and how it is a positive."

Pioneer Tracks: Cocteau Twins–"Sugar Hiccup," the Jesus and Mary Chain–"Just Like Honey," My Bloody Valentine–"You Made Me Realise," Siouxsie and the Banshees–"Melt!," Sonic Youth–"Beauty Lies in the Eye"

Key Players: Adorable, Blur (*Leisure*), the Boo Radleys (*Everything's Alright Forever*), Catherine Wheel (*Ferment*), Chapterhouse, Curve, Lilys, Lush, Moose, Pale Saints, Ride, Slowdive, Swervedriver, Swirlies, the Telescopes

CROSSOVER TRACKS

CHILLWAVE

Memoryhouse–"When You Sleep" (My Bloody Valentine), the Radio Dept.–"Heaven's On Fire"

SLOWCORE
Galaxie 500–"Blue Thunder," Red House Painters–"Katy Song"

SPACE ROCK
Flying Saucer Attack–"Feedback Song," Spiritualized–"Let It Flow"

Ska Punk

In *Gimme Something Better*, an oral history of Bay Area punk, Schlong guitarist Gavin MacArthur recalls opening for Operation Ivy: "The place went totally crazy.... I'd listened to a few ska things, and of course I listened to punk. That was the first band I heard that combined the two."[1] Forming in Berkeley in 1987, Operation Ivy were only together for a couple of years, but their influence and popularity grew posthumously. Op Ivy patches on JanSport backpacks were ubiquitous in American high schools in the 1990s. "The first year Op Ivy came out," remembers Lookout! Records founder Larry Livermore, "we sold 2,000 the whole year. And in '95 we were selling 2,000 a week. Of a band that had been broken up for six years."[2]

The 2 Tone scene in Britain was an obvious influence on Operation Ivy, who went so far as to update the label's black-and-white Walt Jabsco mascot for its own purposes, giving it a more aggressive punk makeover. Ska punk, in fact, is a bit of a misnomer. The 2 Tone genre had already found the middle ground between ska and punk. What American ska punk found was the middle ground between *2 Tone* and punk: one part ska to two parts punk.

Ska punk was largely a Californian venture at first, but not entirely. In the same year that Operation Ivy broke up, Boston's the Mighty Mighty Bosstones released their debut album, *Devil's Night Out*, a spontaneous grab bag of 2 Tone with chugga-chugga rock and other era-appropriate touches. Back in Berkeley, Tim Armstrong of Op Ivy spent a couple weeks putting ska punk band Dance Hall Crashers together before landing in Rancid, whose 1993 self-titled debut was decidedly all punk and no ska.

Armstrong must have been feeling the itch watching other Southern California groups like Reel Big Fish, Voodoo Glow Skulls, and No Doubt pick up what he had put down. Rancid's third album, . . . *And Out Come the Wolves*, arrived in the summer of 1995 with a prominent ska punk single, "Time Bomb," which fell in heavy rotation on alt-rock radio with No Doubt's "Just a Girl" and Sublime's "Date Rape." Soon enough, bands like Goldfinger were tossing short ska breaks into punk songs, and the Mighty Mighty Bosstones finally struck the royal oil of commercial success that they had been working toward with *Let's Face It* in 1997, just in time before the ska punk bubble burst.

Key Players: Dance Hall Crashers, Fishbone, the Mighty Mighty Bosstones, No Doubt, the O.C. Supertones, Operation Ivy, Reel Big Fish, Save Ferris, Skankin' Pickle, Voodoo Glow Skulls

||||||||||||||||||||||||||||||||||||||||||||||||||||||||||||||||||||

CROSSOVER GENRES

||||||||||||||||||||||||||||||||||||||||||||||||||||||||||||||||||||

2 TONE
The Beat, Madness, the Specials

POP PUNK
Goldfinger, Less Than Jake, the Suicide Machines

Skate Punk

For a few generations now, skateboarding and punk rock have been twin keys to suburban teenage liberation, and skate punk is whatever punk rock records skateboarders are listening to *en masse*. In the early 1980s, this meant more aggressive stuff like Southern California hardcore, while in the 1990s, skaters' tastes went more pop punk, which was also, not coincidentally, largely a product of Southern California. Skate punk is whatever is cool in SoCal because that's where 85 percent of all skateboarders live.

Digging up the soundtracks to old skater movies like *Thrashin'* and *Gleaming the Cube* doesn't really give a clear picture of skate punk's origins. The former has Circle Jerks and Fear, but also Meat Loaf and Fine Young Cannibals, while the latter has the Dickies and some very dated hired tunes. "Who's playing the Warped Tour this year?" used to be a quick and easy question to find out what bands were skate punk back in the day. Honestly, skaters probably shouldn't even listen to punk anymore because that was their parents' music.

Key Players: Agent Orange, Face to Face, FIDLAR, JFA, Lagwagon, MxPx, NoFX, Pennywise, Rich Kids on LSD, Wavves

CROSSOVER GENRES

POP PUNK
Green Day, Screeching Weasel

SURF ROCK
Laika and the Cosmonauts, Man or Astro-man?

Skiffle

|||||||||||||||||||||||||||||||||||||||||||||||||||||||||||||||||||||||||||||||||||||||||||||||||||||||||||||||||||||||||||||

The 140-character definition of skiffle, longtime folk-punk singer-songwriter Billy Bragg explains to a full house of dedicated fans in the rare-book room upstairs at the Strand Book Store in New York City, is "English schoolboys playing Lead Belly's repertoire."[1]

Skiffle is a word that means different things in the United States and Britain, Bragg says. It is a "pre-rock" genre and, like rock 'n' roll, it started in America, with roots stretching back to the New Orleans–centric trad jazz movement of the late 1930s. Bragg's story of skiffle begins in Chicago, where in African American neighborhoods, it was slang for the music you would hear at rent parties. Somewhere between there, a couple decades of overly stringent musicians' union stipulations between the United States and UK, and the end of post-WWII rationing in Britain in 1954, skiffle became "a subgenre of American roots music played exclusively by British people."

Historical context, Bragg emphasizes, is important to understanding why skiffle took off the way it did. The end of rationing saw the sales of clothing, cosmetics, and music increase dramatically. There was also a sudden leap in the presence of American culture. The film *Blackboard Jungle* was shown in theaters in 1955, and people went just to hear Bill Haley's "Rock Around the Clock" play in the beginning sequence, as it was the first time real rock 'n' roll was heard in Britain. At the end of that same year, Glasgow-born musician Lonnie Donegan released a single of "Rock Island Line," a railroad folk song that Lead Belly had recorded in the 1930s. Donegan became "the first Brit to get in the charts playing a guitar."

The guitar had not been a familiar instrument in British culture, but after "Rock Island Line" and the end of rationing, annual sales of guitars in the UK soared. Skiffle was even more DIY than punk because these kids were making their own instruments. Joining the guitar was an upright bass that was created out of a tea chest (like a washtub bass in the United States), and washboard was also commonly played in what's estimated to be thousands of skiffle groups across the UK, some of which had future leaders of the British Invasion among their ranks. Skiffle was all the rage from 1956 until 1958, when it was superseded by rock 'n' roll. In that regard, it is comparable to the first generation of rockabilly in the United States, which was nearly as short-lived and supplanted by the same forces.

Key Players: Lonnie Donegan, the Quarrymen, the Rattlesnakes, Rory Storm and the Hurricanes

CROSSOVER GENRES

BEAT BOOM
The Beatles, the Hollies, the Searchers

ROCK 'N' ROLL
Chuck Berry, Bill Haley and the Comets, Elvis Presley

ROCKABILLY
Eddie Cochran, Carl Perkins, Gene Vincent

Slowcore

"At one point, some label asked 'how can you describe your music?,' and we said something like 'loud music you can sleep to,'" recalls Matt Kadane. Along with his brother Bubba, Kadane has spent more than twenty-five years in two bands: Bedhead, who formed in Dallas in the early 1990s, and then the New Year, which in some ways picked up where Bedhead left off in 1998. "Whenever we played live, we tried to be as loud as we could be without destroying the integrity of the music. We thought that in a good way it was soporific to some degree. . . . Slow doesn't necessarily mean quiet, but it did carry with it those connotations. The vocals were always quiet, I'll admit that."

Slowcore was an unofficial contrarian movement in 1990s rock. It had no center, as its most prominent artists came from opposite corners: Codeine in New York City; Red House Painters in San Francisco; Low in Duluth, Minnesota; and Bedhead in Dallas—four cities that form a crooked diamond across the map of the lower forty-eight. Of those bands, who were actually quite different from one another save for the down tempos and temperaments, Codeine were the first and still perhaps most apparent example of slowcore.

Distorted and downtempo, Codeine's music is hardcore with two lead feet. The "core" in slowcore would ultimately not come to indicate a derivation of hardcore, but the other kind of usage in which "core" implies a core element of the music: cuddlecore, sadcore, etc. Their debut album, *Frigid Stars*, felt alone in its orbit when the preeminent grunge label, Sub Pop, picked it up in 1991.[1] Codeine were coming to an end in 1994, by which time Red House Painters had cemented their reputation among the sullen with a few sprawling records; Low released *I Could Live in Hope*, a debut that was like an intimate counterpart to Codeine without the self-defense of noise; and Bedhead finally put out their first album, *WhatFunLifeWas*.

Kadane took issue with the slowcore label, particularly because Bedhead's music was more varied than the tag indicates. He remembers his dad being a fan of the Beatles, the Ramsey Lewis Trio, Willie Nelson, and Waylon Jennings. He and Bubba, older by two and a half years, started finding their own music in the late 1970s. "Not that I'm proud of the decisions that we made, because I was nine and he was eleven, and we liked Styx and terrible bands like that, but we also got into stuff that we continued to like: the Clash, the Who, and the Jam." Later, MTV was often on in the background, but they also sought out records by the Factory bands from Manchester. Another significant influence on Bedhead were Talk Talk, whose *Spirit of Eden* was the album that taught the Kadane brothers how to slow down.

When Bedhead became official in 1991, their dynamic, space-sensitive sound was something of an anomaly. Kadane notes that they didn't know many other bands doing what they were doing. "We didn't play our first show out of Texas until 1994, and that was in Germany."

WhatFunLifeWas was followed by *Beheaded* in 1996 and *Transaction de Novo* in 1998, which "felt at the time more like a return to form in some ways, after having made a pretty consistently slow record in the middle." Bedhead officially came to a halt in 1998, not long after *Transaction de Novo* was released. Their transition to the New Year was fairly seamless, as many of the New Year's early songs were written when Bedhead was still around. The New Year records have arrived on a patient schedule, with *Newness Ends*, *The End Is Near*, and *The New Year* coming out in four-year intervals from 2000 to 2008, at which point they didn't release another until *Snow* in 2017. Other slowcore alumni have remained active as well, Low and Mark Kozelek particularly so.

Pioneer Tracks: American Music Club–"Asleep," Codeine–"D," Galaxie 500–"Tell Me," Red House Painters–"24," Talk Talk–"I Believe In You"

Key Players: Bedhead, Codeine, Ida, Low, Red House Painters, Spain

CROSSOVER TRACKS

ALTERNATIVE ROCK
Cranes–"Cloudless," Mazzy Star–"Fade Into You," Mojave 3–"Love Songs on the Radio"

INDIE ROCK
Idaho–"Happy Times," Karate–"Gasoline," Pedro the Lion–"The Longest Winter"

POST-ROCK
The For Carnation–"Moonbeams," Mogwai–"CODY," Slint–"Washer"

Sludge Metal

The differences between doom, stoner, and sludge metal can be as tricky to grasp as a fistful of mud, but the imagery of the last might just be what keeps it alive.

As shocking as it is that a logging town like Aberdeen, Washington, in the 1980s could produce a band as huge as Nirvana, it is almost more shocking that nearby Montesano had already produced a band as significant as the Melvins to befriend and influence them. The soggy isolation of Grays Harbor County allowed them room to follow their weirder impulses without any fear of scene rejection, but it also didn't keep them from reaching an audience and reacting to other scenes. "In their first punk phase, they played faster-than-light hardcore," writes Michael Azerrad. "Then, when everyone began doing the same, they played as slow as they possibly could, just to piss everybody off. And to really piss them off, they injected heavy metal into the mix."[1]

The title of their debut full-length album from 1987, *Gluey Porch Treatments*, denoted the abrasive, adhesive mixture contained therein. The cavernous plodding opener "Eye Flys" used drums to build a mood, not a rhythm. The Melvins weren't ones to stick in one mode for too long. The record alternated between outcast hardcore bursts and the slower material, but it was always thick and heavy. Those hardcore-punk spasms that the Melvins would mix into otherwise dirgelike songs remain, in fact, one of the more tangible indicators of the difference between sludge and doom metal.

Key Players: Acid Bath, Buzzov·en, Corrupted, Crowbar, Eyehategod, Down, Grief, the Melvins

|||||||||||||||||||||||||||||||||||||||||||||||||||||||||||||||||||||||||||||||||

CROSSOVER TRACKS

|||||||||||||||||||||||||||||||||||||||||||||||||||||||||||||||||||||||||||||||||

GRUNGE

Alice in Chains–"Sludge Factory," Soundgarden–"Slaves and Bulldozers"

STONER METAL

Bongzilla–"Gateway," High on Fire–"The Yeti"

Soft Rock

Soft rock is a large, cozy blanket concept used to designate rock music that is largely devoid of sex and aggression, or light pop music played on rock instruments. There is ample evidence pointing to the 1970s as the true glory days of soft rock. One need look no further than America, Bread, and Chicago: the ABCs of soft rock. The alphabet keeps running with the Doobie Brothers, the Eagles, Fleetwood Mac, and so on. Shag carpets, the economy, guitar bands—soft was the way to be in the 1970s.

The 1980s and 1990s are not without their case, however. The decade of greed was generous with soft rock: REO Speedwagon, Mike and the Mechanics, some big Foreigner hits, and the ongoing career of Billy Joel, to name a few. As the alternative revolution raged on outside the castle in the 1990s, Bryan Adams and Sting battled over the soft rock throne. As for today, they don't really make 'em like "Fields of Gold" anymore, which is almost kind of a shame.

Key Players: America, Bread, Chicago, Christopher Cross, the Doobie Brothers, the Eagles, Fleetwood Mac, Billy Joel, REO Speedwagon, Sting

CROSSOVER TRACKS

ALTERNATIVE ROCK
Counting Crows–"Mr. Jones," the Wallflowers–"Sixth Avenue Heartache"

NEW WAVE
The Pretenders–"Back on the Chain Gang," Tears for Fears–
"Everybody Wants to Rule the World"

POST-BRITPOP
Keane–"Everybody's Changing," Travis–"Writing to Reach You"

Sophisti-Pop

Sophisti-pop is a term devised in recent years that helps fans of artists like Destroyer to bond over their fondness for the mature melodies of Prefab Sprout's pebble-smooth second album, *Steve McQueen* (*Two Wheels Good* in the United States). It enables the drawing of connections between bands who have otherwise been parked in either the post-punk or new wave lot.

On one end, you had Aztec Camera's "Oblivious" and Scritti Politti's "The 'Sweetest Girl,'" agile but unhurried early 1980s singles put out on the storied indie labels Postcard and Rough Trade, respectively. On the other, there were those that tread into the realm of "adult contemporary," which in the age of yacht rock acceptance has lost much of the stigma that once surrounded it. One of the most notable among those were the Blue Nile, who, like Aztec Camera, were also from Scotland, making the country a minor sophisti-pop hub. The Blue Nile weren't afraid to studiously polish their albums or to only release a new one once or twice a decade, two habits that became their reputation.

Key Players: ABC, Aztec Camera, the Blue Nile, Destroyer, Prefab Sprout, Scritti Polliti, the Style Council

||||||||||||||||||||||||||||||||||||||||||||||||||||||||||||||||||||||||

CROSSOVER TRACKS

||||||||||||||||||||||||||||||||||||||||||||||||||||||||||||||||||||||||

JANGLE POP

The Go-Betweens–"Streets of Your Town," the Lightning Seeds–
"Pure"

NEW WAVE

Joe Jackson–"Steppin' Out," Ultravox–"Vienna"

Southern Rock

In the realm of Southern rock, things aren't often what they first appear to be. A fluid shuffling of blues and country priorities in rock music, kin to country rock but with more room to groove and improvise, on the surface, Southern rock reads as simple-leaning and rootsy, but musically, it was more forward-thinking than it is often credited with being. Though the genre got rolling at the end of the 1960s, the Southern rock sound is, for the most part, conspicuously absent of psychedelic rock influence. Still, the members of these bands were considered hippies in the South, liberal not just with the length of their hair but also their attitudes toward many other things.

Some have seen "Southern rock" as a marketing ploy cooked up by outsiders to sell records. A marketing ploy, yes, but not one cooked up by outsiders. According to Scott B. Bomar's book *Southbound,* it was Mo Slotin, an underground journalist in Atlanta, who came up with the term. Capricorn Records, the premier Southern rock record label founded in 1969 and based in Macon, Georgia, then ran with the term, making buttons that said "Capricorn Records Supports Southern Rock" on them.[1]

If Southern rock reimagined the timeline of American rock and roll with the influence of the British Invasion erased from it, considering that a significant portion of rock's foundation was laid below the Mason-Dixon Line, it would only be fair that the South was not thrilled to have the blues sold back to them by the likes of the Rolling Stones. That wasn't necessarily the case, however. Duane and Gregg Allman's early combo, the Allman Joys, had mop-top haircuts and copped the same beat-boom moves that every other guitar band in the mid-1960s did,[2] and they surely weren't the only Southern rockers with Beatles LPs on the shelf back in their childhood bedrooms.

Lyrically made for the moment, musically "The South's Gonna Do It Again" is lodged in the 1950s, not the 1970s. A twangy echo of "Rock Around the Clock," with boogie-woogie piano and country fiddle providing the appropriate flair, as an attempted anthem for the genre, it doesn't quite capture the potential of the present. On the other hand, the real all-but-official anthem, Lynyrd Skynyrd's "Sweet Home Alabama," attempted to be clever and left itself wide open to misinterpretation. The band would later downplay the song's perceived counter attack to Neil Young's "Southern Man."[3]

After a long season in the sun, blemished by the tragic deaths that befell both the Allmans and Skynyrd, Southern rock began to fall out of popular favor at the end of the 1970s in the face of disco (though Wet Willie joined that craze), heavy metal (though Molly Hatchet were already on the cusp of that one), and other newfangled directions that rock was moving. One major exception, a group who not only survived but thrived, was ZZ Top, who, being from Texas, were always a bit left of the Southern rock center. The randy trio grabbed the implements of new wave—drum machines, synthesizers, and pop-songwriting formulas—and built the massively successful 1983 album *Eliminator*, which enlightened new MTV viewers everywhere about the magic of "Legs."

Pioneer Tracks: The Band—"Caledonia Mission," Canned Heat—"Going Up the Country," the Grateful Dead—"Viola Lee Blues," Lonnie Mack—"Memphis"

Key Players: The Allman Brothers Band, Barefoot Jerry, Black Oak Arkansas, the Charlie Daniels Band, Eric Quincy Tate, the Georgia Satellites, Lynyrd Skynyrd, the Marshall Tucker Band, Molly Hatchet, Wet Willie, ZZ Top

||||||||||||||||||||||||||||||||||||||||||||||||||||||||||||||||||||||||||||||
CROSSOVER GENRES
||||||||||||||||||||||||||||||||||||||||||||||||||||||||||||||||||||||||||||||

BLUES ROCK
Alabama Shakes, the Fabulous Thunderbirds, Stevie Ray Vaughan and Double Trouble

COUNTRY ROCK
The Kentucky Headhunters, the Outlaws, Hank Williams Jr.

INDIE ROCK
Band of Horses, My Morning Jacket, Okkervil River

Space Rock

||||||||||||||||||||||||||||||||||||||||||||||||||||||||||||||||||||||||||||||||||||||||||||||||||||||||||||||||

There are two ways to be a space rock band. One, the band's sprawling, atmospheric rock conveys the feeling of being in outer space. Two, the band writes songs about being in outer space.

The Verve in their early days were an example of the first kind of space rock. Their lengthy singles "Gravity Grave" and "She's a Superstar" were stoned and stargazing jams. The title of their first album, *A Storm in Heaven*, says it all. Their cavernous sound was largely due to Nick McCabe's inimitable guitar playing. As the band pursued more traditional songcraft on subsequent albums, McCabe's otherworldly explorations were reined in, but his stamp remained crucial to their character.

Hawkwind are the kings of the second kind of space rock. Formed in London at the end of the 1960s, Hawkwind are famous for kicking Lemmy out of the band, and thus we have them to thank for Motörhead. From *In Search of Space* in 1971 to *Space Bandits* in 1990, most of their albums have sci-fi related titles. Their best-known song, "Silver Machine," is about taking a ride in said machine to the "other side of the sky." Hawkwind were always going on about outer space, so much so that they deserve their space rock crown, even if their brand of hard rock could just as easily be categorized as psychedelic or progressive.

Key Tracks: Hawkwind—"Silver Machine," the Jimi Hendrix Experience— "Third Stone from the Sun," Pink Floyd—"Set the Controls for the Heart of the Sun," the Verve—"A Man Called Sun"

CROSSOVER TRACKS

ALTERNATIVE ROCK

Cave In–"Innuendo and Out the Other," Failure–"Another Space Song"

AMBIENT ROCK

Hammock–"Turning into Tiny Particles . . . Floating Through Empty Space," Sigur Rós–"Svefn-g-englar"

PROGRESSIVE ROCK

Eloy–"The Light from Deep Darkness," Gong–"Fohat Digs Holes in Space"

Speed Metal

The headbanger's arms race that followed the New Wave of British Heavy Metal (NWOBHM) moved so fast that the dialogue around it could barely keep up. Back then, speed metal was a commonly used term. Today, it has been mostly replaced in the conversation by thrash metal, which captures not just the pursuit of "faster," but "harder" as well.

"The San Francisco metal scene was quite different from L.A., and many of the early speed metal bands gained their first foothold there,"[1] writes David Konow, reflecting on the stomping grounds of Metallica, Exodus, college radio station KUSF, and "Metal Mondays" at the Old Waldorf club in the early 1980s. This is part of the origin story of speed metal, which also happens to be the origin story of thrash metal, and Konow notes the interchangeability of the two terms.[2] Others see speed metal as a subset of thrash, with speed metal being cleaner and more about showing your chops.

Heavy metal linguistics now tends to identify speed metal as a layover on the way from the NWOBHM to thrash metal. Grindcore, death metal, and black metal all pulled ahead of thrash metal in the bpm race, so speed metal was no longer the best at what it was named for, making it irrelevant as a brand.

Key Players: Anthrax, Anvil, Exciter, Megadeth, Metal Church, Metallica, Overkill, Raven, Slayer, Testament

CROSSOVER GENRES

D-BEAT
Anti Cimex, Discharge, the Varukers

NEW WAVE OF BRITISH HEAVY METAL
Diamond Head, Iron Maiden, Saxon

POWER METAL
Accept, Armored Saint, Helloween

Stoner Metal

Ozzy Osbourne's ode to marijuana, "Sweet Leaf," appeared on Black Sabbath's *Master of Reality* in 1971 and sealed the deal between stoners and heavy metal, but stoner metal as a genre unto itself didn't fully arrive until the 1990s. Although slow and heavy like doom metal, unafraid to take gnarly turns like sludge metal, and capable of rambling on for extended periods of time like drone metal, there is one quality that distinguishes stoner metal from its brethren: a more potent influence of psychedelic rock.

Sleep, a trio from San Jose, California, showed their green thumb on their 1992 album, *Sleep's Holy Mountain*, and a few years later, they started to work on *Dopesmoker*. All of their ideas went into one single song that, in the process of recording, came out in different versions at different lengths on either side of an hour. For a long time, the record wasn't officially released, though one version that made its way out of the vaults in 1999 was a trim 52 minutes in length and retitled *Jerusalem*.

There is also another strain of stoner metal that doesn't follow the early Black Sabbath sonic template but makes up for it by wearing a love of smoking weed on its ripped sleeves. This is where Madison, Wisconsin, vocal cord–damaging pot monsters Bongzilla come in. Even better, or worse, is the death metal band Cannabis Corpse, a collaboration of members from other metal bands who makes grass-themed puns out of the atrocious titles of Cannibal Corpse songs. At any speed, stoner metal is proof that one person's harsh realm is another's positive vibrations.

Key Players: Acid King, Belzebong, Black Sabbath, Bongripper, Bongzilla, Cannabis Corpse, Electric Wizard, Goatsnake, Goblin, High on Fire, Sleep, Weedeater

|||||||||||||||||||||||||||||||||||||||||||||||||||||||||||||||||||||||||
CROSSOVER TRACKS
|||||||||||||||||||||||||||||||||||||||||||||||||||||||||||||||||||||||||

DESERT ROCK / STONER ROCK
Fu Manchu–"The Wasteoid," Kyuss–"Green Machine"

SLUDGE METAL
Buzzov·en–"Weeding," the Melvins–*Stoner Witch*

Stoner Rock

Fu Manchu guitarist Scott Hill always associated the term "stoner rock" with the Grateful Dead. He does not like the Grateful Dead. "I do not like any type of hippie shit! I first heard that term applied to us in an interview we did while we were on tour and in Austin, Texas. The interviewer told us we were stoner rock. I didn't really pay much attention to it. It does not really bother me. Call us whatever you like."

Hill feels that Fu Manchu's background in hardcore and punk, from the early days when they were called Virulence, keeps them apart from stoner rock, which strikes him as something that would lack aggression. "I know some people who get really stoned, and they have a lot of energy, and then there's people I know who get really stoned, and they can't move from the couch."

Somewhere along the line stoner rock was linked to desert rock, but it encompasses more than that. A stylistic specificity hardens when the genre is hammered down into stoner metal, but, really, stoner rock can be whatever rock-music stoners tend to listen to. Hence, Hill's association of the term with the Grateful Dead. The Dead weren't the first bunch of musicians to get stoned, but they certainly made a whole thing out of it.

Key Players: Black Sabbath, Blue Öyster Cult, Dead Meadow, Fu Manchu, Kyuss, Monster Magnet, Nebula, Saint Vitus, Sleep, Wolfmother

CROSSOVER GENRES

PSYCHEDELIC ROCK
The Doors, the Grateful Dead, Phish

SPACE ROCK
Hawkwind, Pink Floyd, Spacemen 3

STONER METAL
Electric Wizard, Goatsnake, High on Fire

Straight Edge

Washington, DC, became the birthplace of straight edge when Minor Threat released their self-titled debut EP in 1981. *Minor Threat* was eight songs and barely nine minutes long, and smack in the middle of it was "Straight Edge," a forty-five-second polemic against the fab four of punk substance abuse: speed, dope, 'ludes, and glue. Frontman Ian MacKaye was taking a moment to assert his personal stance against the use of recreational drugs at shows and in day-to-day life[1] and may or may not have been actively trying to alienate a sizeable segment of the hardcore world.

Straight edge would become one of the most significant facets of Minor Threat's legacy. The idea and attitude behind the song caught on, and punks throughout the United States who were keen on sobriety began to outwardly express their allegiance to the lifestyle by drawing black Xs on the backs of their hands. This self-branding trend had also started in the nation's capital, where clubs would keep the under-twenty-one attendees from being served booze by identifying them with the very visible Sharpie mark.[2] Straight edge had a huge impact on punk culture, but musically it was pretty much like regular ol' glue-sniffin' hardcore, aside from the obvious differences in personal politics and lyrical subject matter.

Key Players: 7 Seconds, Champion, Good Clean Fun, Gorilla Biscuits, Minor Threat, Ten Yard Fight

CROSSOVER TRACKS

HEAVY METAL
Ozzy Osbourne–"Suicide Solution," Rainbow–"Drinking with the Devil"

PUNK ROCK
Black Flag–"Six Pack," Jawbreaker–"Kiss the Bottle"

Street Punk

Not to be confused with "gutter punk," a term that refers to actual homeless punk kids, street punk was a name for certain segments of Britain's second punk rock wave in the early 1980s. In a reversal of post-punk's anything-goes ethos, what qualified as punk was narrowed back down, much in the way that American hardcore whittled away any frivolity. Bands like GBH, the Exploited, UK Subs, and Cockney Rejects exemplified the style: guitar chords few, fast, and frayed; drum beats speedy and simple; vocals shouted more than sung. Some groups, GBH among them, even had more than a touch of Motörhead in their sound,[1] forecasting the punk-metal crossover still to come.

This was the point where punk culture really discovered its aptitude for conformity, but out of that came the identity by which it is still generally known today. The mohawk hairstyle and studded leather jackets became the uniform, and a roughed-up, blunt-tongued take on the metallic pub rock of the Sex Pistols became the default setting from which to rebuild the genre in the image of itself. Street punk was also meant to refer specifically to those with working class credentials, which were also something of a requirement to join this generation in the UK.[2]

Key Players: Blitz, Cockney Rejects, the Exploited, GBH, One Way System, Sham 69, UK Subs

||||||||||||||||||||||||||||||||||||||||||||||||||||||||||||||||||||||||||||||||

CROSSOVER GENRES

||||||||||||||||||||||||||||||||||||||||||||||||||||||||||||||||||||||||||||||||

CROSSOVER THRASH
Discharge, English Dogs

OI!
Angelic Upstarts, the Business

Sunshine Pop

||||||||||||||||||||||||||||||||||||||||||||||||||||||||||||||||||||||||||||||||||||||||||||||||||||||||

Made entirely of members of the Dedrick family, the Free Design came from a small village in western New York state and released their first record, *Kites Are Fun*, in 1967. Their music sounded like the Cowsills had picked up some jazz and prog rock records, but weren't dabbling in any chemicals harder than sugar, maybe caffeine. The innocently named *Kites Are Fun* was reissued in Japan by the now-defunct Trattoria label in 1994 and in the United States by Light in the Attic Records in 2003. In between, the polyglot pop band Stereolab released an EP called *The Free Design*, thus cementing the Dedrick family's outsider-cool status.

Sunshine pop is another way of reframing certain music from the age of flower power that would otherwise be classified as pop, soft rock, folk rock, or, in some cases, even a more artful kind of bubblegum. Between the late 1960s and early 1970s, there was no shortage of musical acts writing light, upbeat songs about sunshine, rainbows, flowers, incense and peppermints, and other sorts of pleasant things. In shorter supply back then were genres, so all of these groups had to wait years for sunshine pop to be invented before they could join hands under their own banner.

As the example of Trattoria and the Free Design shows, the value of the more forgotten sunshine pop groups may have in effect been retaught to America and Europe by Japan. There, the Shibuya-kei scene in the 1990s, which nurtured artists such as Pizzicato Five and Cornelius (the musical alias of Keigo Oyamada, who ran Trattoria), took inspiration from such records. The groups often cited as the major instigators of the style—the Beach Boys, the Mamas and the

Papas, the 5th Dimension[1]—never strayed too far from public awareness, but others like the Millennium and Roger Nichols & the Small
Circle of Friends[2] have surely benefited a little bit from the belated
recognition.

Key Players: The 5th Dimension, the Beach Boys, the Free Design, the
Mamas and the Papas, the Millennium, Roger Nichols & the Small Circle
of Friends

CROSSOVER GENRES

BUBBLEGUM
1910 Fruitgum Company, the Lemon Pipers

INDIE POP
Loney Dear, Stereolab

Surf Rock

Defining surf rock as "any instrumental or vocal music with beach or surfing themes,"[1] a prominent side of the surf-music craze of the early 1960s, writer Kent Crowley pulls no punches in addressing how the Beach Boys were first regarded by Southern California's original surf rock bands: as the scene's first major infiltrators. "Surf guitarists began to resent their transformation of this loud, raw, driving guitar music into a vehicle for pitch-perfect jazz harmonies."[2] The surfers themselves were no more stoked, as their catchy songs entreating everyone to come along surfing with them—even though most of the Beach Boys didn't actually surf—were crowding their waves with unwanted newcomers.

One of the biggest problems that both camps had was how the Beach Boys were hard-selling the culture. Surfers were all about playing it cool, and so were surf rock musicians. Until the Beach Boys arrived, surf songs were mostly instrumental, their force and flow meant to approximate the thrill of riding a wave. The lack of vocals made surf rock an ideal backdrop to the action, a soundtrack for the surfing life. It also allowed for the musical innovations that surf rock led to, such as giving rock guitar a role in percussion as well as melody.[3]

Played pretty much exclusively on Fender guitars and amps that were given surf rock's trademark "wet" sound via cranking up the reverb tank, the music's instrumental nature provided a suitable platform for innovations in both tech and technique. Dick Dale, the King of the Surf Guitar, gave the genre one of its most identifiable markings, the double-picking guitar style, borrowed from how the Middle Eastern oud is played. It worked so well on his careening rendition of the ancient folk song "Miserlou" that it became integral to his sound and that of other surf musicians.[4]

Surf rock's precursors—the Ventures' cover of "Walk, Don't Run," the Fireballs' "Bulldog," and early Link Wray singles like "Rumble" and "Rawhide"—were instrumental hits, and many of the most identifiable tunes of surf rock's two-year heyday from 1962 to 1964 were as catchy as those of any vocal group at the time. They are songs you know by heart even if you don't know their names: Dale's "Miserlou" and "Let's Go Trippin'," the Bel-Aires' "Mr. Moto," the Chantays' "Pipeline."

The Beach Boys crashed the party with the unremarkable single "Surfin'" in late 1961, followed by the much improved "Surfin' Safari" backed with "409" in early 1962, which capitalized on the similar "hot-rod rock" craze. They would duplicate the surf-and-turf-platter approach the following year with "Surfer Girl" backed with "Little Deuce Coupe," by which point they had also released "Surfin' U.S.A." and a barrel of other album tracks with "surf" somewhere in the title. The year 1963 brought more overt hits: the Surfaris' "Wipe Out" and the Trashmen's "Surfin' Bird."

The genre's two-year run in the pop culture spotlight wasn't the end, however. Surf rock became the sound of spy movies, Dick Dale was deemed a heavy metal guitar innovator, and every era in rock since has had its revivalists, from Jon & the Nightriders in the 1980s to Man or Astro-man? in the 1990s. The Clinton years were especially kind to surf rock. The *Pulp Fiction* soundtrack is the obvious example of that, of course, but it also made more subtle appearances. For one, indie rock band Modest Mouse referenced surf rock, not just lyrically in "Head South," but also in the pluck and bridge-bending sigh that has been a signature of leader Isaac Brock's guitar playing.

Pioneer Tracks: The Fireballs–"Bulldog," the Ventures–"Walk, Don't Run," Link Wray–"Rawhide"

Key Players: The Beach Boys, the Bel-Airs, the Challengers, the Chantays, Dick Dale and His Del-Tones, Jan and Dean, Jon & the Nightriders, the Surfaris, the Trashmen

CROSSOVER TRACKS

ALTERNATIVE ROCK

Man or Astro-man?–*Is It . . . Man or Astro-man?*, Shadowy Men on a Shadowy Planet–"Having an Average Weekend," Southern Culture on the Skids–"Make Mayan a Hawaiian"

INDIE ROCK

The Allah-Lahs–"Tell Me (What's On Your Mind)," Modest Mouse– "Interstate 8" and "Head South," Wavves–"King of the Beach"

PUNK ROCK

Agent Orange–"Miserlou," the Ramones–"Rockaway Beach," Surf Punks–"My Beach"

Symphonic Metal

Grandiose as the name suggests, symphonic metal bolsters traditional heavy metal instrumentation with the sounds of an orchestra, either real or emulated via synthesizer. One of the genre's compelling distinctions is that the bands tend to have female singers with operatic vocal capabilities, hence some referring to it as 'operatic metal.'

Swiss band Celtic Frost are sometimes cited as a precursor to the development of symphonic metal in the late 1990s. Their albums *To Mega Therion* and *Into the Pandemonium* featured opera singers[1] and classical music bombast in the 1980s. Taking their name from one of those Celtic Frost albums, the Swedish band Therion are often credited with inventing symphonic metal as their sound morphed over time from their death metal beginnings. In fact, "symphonic," like "technical," is something that can be slapped in front of any metal genre, as long as someone plays some keyboard strings and sings poems about nature and/or elves over it, even death metal.

The European continent is where most of the heavy hitters of symphonic metal come from: Rhapsody of Fire from Italy, Nightwish from Finland, and the Netherlands have been a particular hot spot, offering Epica, After Forever, and Within Temptation. Those last three are noted for combining "female vocals with death growls, in a style that is commonly referred to as 'Beauty and the Beast' vocals." Cookie Monster, eat your heart out.

Key Players: After Forever, Delain, Edenbridge, Epica, Haggard, Leaves' Eyes, Nightwish, Rhapsody of Fire, Therion, Within Temptation, Xandria

CROSSOVER GENRES

BLACK METAL
Carpathian Forest, Dimmu Borgir

FOLK METAL
Eluveitie, Turisas

Synth-Pop

Synth-pop is exactly what it sounds like: pop music with synthesizers in it. In any given synth-pop song, the synthesizer can be one of the melodic instruments, all of the melodic instruments, or even the *only* instrument. Some of it falls into the realm of rock music (if a given band uses rock instrumentation), and some of it doesn't. The music is often great, and in the 1980s in particular it was an important counter to the macho rock of that decade, but the term itself fails to escape the vagueness of "new wave," as it now applies to pretty much any popular or indie music that leans on synthesizers made before, during, or after that era.

You've waited long enough for a truly controversial opinion, so here it goes: "Jump" by Van Halen is the best synth-pop song of all time. People spend so much time either going on about how great "Eruption" is or laughing at clips of David Lee Roth's isolated vocal tracks that Van Halen doesn't get enough credit for its contribution to synth-pop history. "Jump" is a high-kicking, spandex-suited, pop mega hit (played by a rock band), and from start to finish, that big brassy Oberheim OB-Xa[1] doesn't quit.

Key Players: Depeche Mode, Thomas Dolby, Duran Duran, Erasure, Eurythmics, Frankie Goes to Hollywood, the Human League, Giorgio Moroder, New Order, Gary Numan, Orchestral Manoeuvres in the Dark, Pet Shop Boys, Soft Cell, Thompson Twins

CROSSOVER TRACKS

DANCE PUNK
The Killers–"Smile Like You Mean It," LCD Soundsystem–
"Tribulations"

PROGRESSIVE ROCK MEETS THE 1980S
Genesis–"Invisible Touch," Yes–"Owner of a Lonely Heart"

Synth-Punk

|||||||||||||||||||||||||||||||||||||||||||||||||||||||||||||||||||||||||||||||||||||||||||||||||||||||||||||||||||||||||||||||||

Same as its pop cousin, synth-punk plays punk rock with synthesizers, or it puts synthesizers in punk rock. Leading the charge were Suicide, the comic-reading New York City duo of Alan Vega and Martin Rev, who pitched some legendarily confrontational live battles in the original punk era despite only being armed with a keyboard and a drum machine.

Asserting that synth-punk is an American product, writer Justin Farrar states in his "A (Not At All Definitive) Guide to American Synth-Punk" piece for Red Bull Music Academy that synth-punk bands preferred "integrating their futurist tendencies (automated marching beats, robotic intonations) with the very rock-and-roll tradition through which so many of us Americans came of age."[1] The article also cites Devo, the Screamers, Chrome, and the aforementioned Suicide as the "Big Four" of the genre, but the question lingers as to whether it lasted beyond a few bands in the 1990s, like Six Finger Satellite.

Key Players: Chrome, Devo, the Screamers, Suicide

CROSSOVER TRACKS

INDIE ROCK

Jonathan Fire*Eater–"Give Me Daughters," Six Finger Satellite–"Coke and Mirrors"

POST-PUNK

The Associates–"Party Fears Two," Magazine–"Definitive Gaze"

Thrash Metal

Before frontman James Hetfield set his lyrical sights on the evils of war, the evils of the criminal justice system, and going insane, Metallica were on the time-honored mission to rock out for the sake of rocking out, praising their audience for "thrashing all around" in the chorus of debut album cut "Whiplash." Except that they were going to rock out harder and faster than anyone had before.

American heavy metal bands had two options in the early 1980s, which were shaped by the opposing forces of the New Wave of British Heavy Metal (NWOBHM) and the dawning of MTV. It was time to either toughen up or hire a hairstylist. Those who had the looks that kill focused on making videos that would instantly place them in living rooms across the country. Those who had the riffs that slay honed them underground and began a slow climb to mainstream recognition.

"The word 'thrash' originally came from the hardcore scene," explains Dan Lilker, a founding member of both Anthrax and Nuclear Assault, in the documentary *Get Thrashed!* "Hardcore bands were playing fast, and metal bands got influenced by it, thus you have thrash metal."[1] The documentary traces the genre back to three geographically separate but concurrent points of origin. There was Los Angeles, Metallica's birthplace and Slayer's stomping grounds. San Francisco was the home of Exodus (which featured future Metallica guitarist Kirk Hammett), and where the young Metallica moved to join new bassist Cliff Burton. New York City thrash metal was led by Anthrax and Overkill.

What separated thrash metal from heavy metal as it was known up to that point? Not-so-great singing, for one, with the big exception of Anthrax frontman Joey Belladonna, who could actually hit the notes as traditional metal had required. Hetfield took the mic for Metallica because someone had to do it and someone better never worked out. Dave Mustaine, leader of Megadeth and former Metallica guitarist, had a bit more range to his voice but wasn't known for his singing. Tom Araya of Slayer would let out a demon wail here and there, but otherwise went with the mean growl that became the default setting for thrash metal vocalists.

As the 1980s wore on and thrash metal became more widely recognized, Metallica, Megadeth, Anthrax, and Slayer were deemed the "Big Four" of the genre. (Every genre gets a "Big Four" now, but this one was real.) Slayer were the only one of the four who were into putting pentagrams and goat heads on their record covers, which put them at the vanguard of not just thrash metal but also death metal, but others made breakthroughs elsewhere. Anthrax took an interest in hardcore punk, which led to the Stormtroopers of Death side project that helped spawn crossover thrash.

Heavy metal has historically drawn more loyalists than tourists, and thrash metal inspired some of the most rabid fandom yet seen. If their numbers were limited, they still made themselves heard. Dedication to the scene was a serious matter. In old interviews with thrash metal musicians and young fans, both seem a bit overly concerned with potential "poseurs" infiltrating their ranks. The lengths of proving one's loyalty extended to the dress code. The thrash metal wardrobe featured an interesting quirk: a jean vest made by ripping the sleeves off a jean jacket worn *over* a leather jacket—this, despite the genre being based in two California cities with mild-to-warm climates.

Having temporarily exhausted their creative resources on the

NWOBHM, there were plenty of thrash metal fans in the UK, but not so many bands. Thrash metal had a huge underground following in Germany, which produced bands such as Sodom, Destruction, and Kreator. Other bands considered part of the international thrash metal movement are Celtic Frost from Switzerland, Sepultura from Brazil, Mortal Sin from Australia, and Voivod from Canada.

The summit of Mount Thrash was reached with the Clash of the Titans tour. Famous festivals that catered to the same crowd already existed as individual events, but this was a portable experience that ran from 1990 to 1991. Megadeth, Slayer, and Anthrax all took part in the North American leg of the tour, leaving Metallica the only ones to skip out on the Big Four's coronation. In the world of metal, delineated and debated like no other rock genre, it was a rare moment of nearly universal consensus that these bands be deemed figureheads, though why the tour wasn't called *Thrash* of the Titans is anyone's guess.

Some see this as the movement's last hurrah before tastes in rock changed, but Metallica's "Black Album" came out a month before *Nevermind* did; they were already done with thrash metal. The other three more or less kept doing what they did best. The media moved on, but fans remained. New thrash metal today wants to stay true to the glory days, but those glory days were all about new breakthroughs. Brandon Stosuy notes that some new thrash bands want to pay homage to the old and others want to keep pushing it. "One of the things I always joked about when I was doing the Show No Mercy column with Pitchfork is that every time I'd interview a band, they'd be like, '*yeah, our next album is our heaviest album to date.*'"

Pioneer Tracks: Anthrax—"Soldiers of Metal," Exodus—"Bonded by Blood," Megadeth—"Rattlehead," Metallica—"Hit the Lights," Slayer—"Black Magic"

Key Players: Anvil, Celtic Frost, Death Angel, Destruction, Exciter, Kreator, Metal Church, Mortal Sin, Nuclear Assault, Overkill, Possessed, Sepultura, Sodom, Testament, Voivod

||||||||||||||||||||||||||||||||||||||||||||||||||||||||||||||||||||||||||||

CROSSOVER GENRES

||||||||||||||||||||||||||||||||||||||||||||||||||||||||||||||||||||||||||||

CROSSOVER THRASH

Municipal Waste, Stormtroopers of Death, Suicidal Tendencies

HARDCORE

Agnostic Front, Cro-Mags, Void

NEW WAVE OF BRITISH HEAVY METAL

Diamond Head, Iron Maiden, Saxon

Tropicália

Music was one facet of the short-lived Tropicália movement, which also encompassed visual art, theater, poetry, and more, and the psychedelic rock dripping into Brazil in 1967 was one element in the mix, which included homespun styles such as samba and bossa nova. In the United States, psychedelic rock was partly a rejection and retreat from square society; in Brazil, it became a part of a celebratory creative stance against government oppression.

A vibrant and eclectic reaction to the stifling dictatorship that had planted itself in power in 1964, the initial Tropicália movement lasted for little more than a year before the junta came after it. For daring to claim artistic freedom and be influenced by Western popular music, leading scene figures Gilberto Gil and Caetano Veloso were briefly imprisoned in December 1968, put under house arrest for four months, and then exiled to London for three years before being granted the right to return.[1]

Before Gil and Veloso were banished to the center of the Swinging Sixties, a few Tropicália landmarks managed to get released. Veloso's 1968 self-titled solo debut was a spark for the movement, followed that year by two more eponymous records, Gil's second album and the debut from Os Mutantes, the São Paulo trio of singer Rita Lee and Baptista brothers Arnaldo and Sérgio Dias. That same active year, all three came together along with Tom Zé and Gal Costa on the collaborative scene-sealing record *Tropicália: ou Panis et Circencis*.

The most out-there of all, Os Mutantes weren't always received well in their homeland at first,[2] but they were also never kicked out of it. They persisted, and as the 1970s began, they pursued their psychedelic rock side further on the albums *A Divina Comédia ou Ando Meio Desligado* and *Jardim Elétrico*. A generation later, Os Mutantes were inspiring artists like Beck on his 1998 album *Mutations*.[3] Returning home in 1972, Gil and Veloso put out new records, *Expresso 2222* and *Transa*, respectively, testaments to Tropicália's resilience.

Key Players: Os Brazões, Gal Costa, Rogério Duprat, Gilberto Gil, Os Mutantes, Caetano Veloso, Tom Zé

CROSSOVER TRACKS

ALTERNATIVE ROCK
Beck–*Mutations*

POST-ROCK
Tortoise–"Gigantes"

PSYCHEDELIC ROCK
Chicano Batman–*Cycles of Existential Rhyme*

Twee

A quick way to explain twee to someone is to remind them of that scene in *High Fidelity* when Rob and Dick, played by John Cusack and Todd Louiso, are quietly enjoying Belle & Sebastian's "Seymour Stein" in the record shop, when Jack Black's character, Barry, storms in the door. Pale, timid Dick visibly gulps as Barry proceeds to ogreishly rip the tape out of the stereo. The irony being, of course, that he replaces it with a cassette of Katrina and the Waves' "Walking on Sunshine," which is pretty damn twee in its own right.

Twee is an aesthetic built around themes of playfulness, innocence, and sentimentality, but in reference to rock music, it is most strongly associated with indie pop bands from the 1980s. In that context, twee functions as a kind of distinct level of indie pop that is more light and jangly than the rest. Bristol-based Sarah Records was a safe harbor for twee in that decade, home to the short-lived Talulah Gosh and the band they became right after, Heavenly, as well as groups like the Field Mice from London and Even As We Speak from Sydney, Australia.

Writing for Pitchfork in 2005, Nitsuh Abebe traced twee back to Television Personalities, the post-punk band started by Dan Treacy in the late 1970s. Identifying their lighthearted approach as a punkish rejection of punk, Abebe says their 1981 debut album, . . . *And Don't the Kids Just Love It*, had the sound of a "trio of 10-year-olds . . . together in a basement," letting out their "vulnerable voices and rudimentary guitar figures"[1] on even serious subject matter. Marc Spitz's book on the subject followed twee all the way back to the end of WWII, but in terms of rock music, he pinpointed pre-punk influences from the Kinks, Nick Drake, and Jonathan Richman and the Modern Lovers.[2]

Glasgow's Belle & Sebastian were never really twee like some declared them to be, but their first few albums put them in the conversation as inheritors of a hometown tradition that dated back at least to 1981 and the release of Glaswegian director Bill Forsyth's beloved and quite twee second film, *Gregory's Girl* (which featured Clare Grogan, then the eighteen-year-old singer from Altered Images). The city unintentionally launched something of a two-pronged twee attack in 1996: there was Belle & Sebastian's gentle campaign, but also the storming of Top of the Pops by the twee punk trio Bis ("average age 18," helpfully noted the show) with their charming if repetitive early 7" single, "Kandy Pop." The 1990s also gifted the world with cuddlecore, which in the form of groups like acoustic duo the Softies was arguably the last pure twee genre, though there's been plenty of twee-adjacent indie pop since then.

Key Players: Beat Happening, Belle & Sebastian, the Darling Buds, Even As We Speak, Field Mice, Heavenly, Talulah Gosh, Television Personalities, Tiger Trap, the Vaselines

||||||||||||||||||||||||||||||||||||||||||||||||||||||||||||||||||||||||||||

CROSSOVER TRACKS

||||||||||||||||||||||||||||||||||||||||||||||||||||||||||||||||||||||||||||

CUDDLECORE
Cub–*Come Out Come Out*, the Softies–*It's Love*, Tullycraft–*Old Traditions, New Standards*

INDIE POP

Bis–*The Secret Vampire Soundtrack* EP, Camera Obscura–
Underachievers Please Try Harder, The Boy Least Likely To–*The
Best Party Ever*

POST-PUNK

Altered Images–*Pinky Blue*, Orange Juice–*You Can't Hide Your
Love Forever*, Young Marble Giants–*Colossal Youth*

TRANSLATIONS

Anadolu Pop, CanRock, Celtic Metal, Celtic Rock, Coldwave, Group Sounds, Gypsy Punk, Idol Metal/Kawaii Metal, Italian Occult Psychedelia, Latin Alternative, Neue Deutsche Härte, Neue Deutsche Welle, Ostrock, Pinoy Rock, Sufi Rock, Viking Metal

ANADOLU POP

Globalization in the twenty-first century has brought such major changes to media and cultural access that it can be difficult to remember how significant of a role geography has played in the development of popular music history up until the past twenty years or so. Historically, a crossroads on the map would often be a musical crossroads, and Turkey, once home to the Ottoman Empire which connected the Middle East and Eastern Europe, was one such example.[1] In the 1960s, Turkey's growing fondness for American rock and roll of the 1950s and British Invasion bands began to seep into its traditional folk music, a process accelerated by, of all things, a popular song contest called Altin Mikrofon (Golden Microphone) set up by a major national newspaper called *Hürriyet* in 1965. Writing for *The Wire* in 2011, Daniel Spicer notes that it was keyboard player Murat Ses that gave this unique music its name, Anadolu Pop, "the definitive term to describe this synthesis of Western pop and Anatolian folk (that is, music originating in the Asian part of Turkey)."[2] Toward the end of the 1960s, the era's wave of psychedelic rock music arrived from Western Europe and swept up Anadolu pop with it, resulting in rich and unique records from groups like Moğollar, Bunalim, Üç Hürel, and many others.

CANROCK

To audiences outside of North America, distinctions between US and Canadian rock music probably don't seem very significant.

Within the United States, your average citizen on the street likely doesn't know (or doesn't care) that the Guess Who, Bachman-Turner Overdrive, Cowboy Junkies, k.d. Lang, and four-fifths of the Band come from Canada. There are those for whom such distinctions justifiably matter, however, including hopefully at least a few Canadians. CanRock addresses this need. The term can really be applied to notable Canadian rock music from any time, such as the 2000s indie rock boom in Toronto and Montreal, but it is perhaps most tied to the somewhat less cool era of Bryan Adams and Loverboy in the 1980s.

It would also be appropriate to use in regards to Canadian bands who have a special connection with the nation's psyche. Chief among those would be the Tragically Hip, whose importance to Canadian culture, rooted in frontman Gord Downie's uniquely poetic lyrics, is almost impossible to overstate. It took a little time for this bond to solidify. As Bob Mersereau writes in his *History of Canadian Rock 'N' Roll*, "There's a long list of video-ready, generic CanRock bands from the mid-'80s who had a lot easier time getting signed than the Tragically Hip."[3] Downie and the Hip were persistent, right up until Downie's passing from brain cancer in October 2017. His diagnosis did not inspire defeat but rather a full band tour in 2016 and solo albums in both 2016 and 2017. His death was met by a nation in mourning, including a genuinely moving televised tribute from Prime Minister Justin Trudeau.

CELTIC METAL/CELTIC ROCK

A far smaller land with no less a musical presence is Ireland, which has contributed more than its fair share per square mile to rock and roll. In addition to the Van Morrisons, U2s, Frames, and Ashes of the mainstream rock market, the sound of the Emerald Isle's folk heritage has been absorbed into both Celtic metal and Celtic rock. Celtic metal is in essence a particular branch of folk metal that draws specifically from Gaelic folk music style and instrumentation and also mythology. Cruachan, a Dublin band that first started playing in the early 1990s and released their debut album, *Tuatha na Gael*, in 1995, are often credited with being one of the first Celtic metal bands. Celtic rock dates back a ways further than Celtic metal, to the Ireland group Horslips and also Runrig, who hail from another green island: Scotland's Isle of Skye. Active since the mid-1970s, Runrig have released more than a dozen albums of songs that deliver modern rock stitched with bagpipes, accordions, keyboards, and Scottish Gaelic lyrics.

COLDWAVE

While Runrig was paying partial tribute to their country's ancient past, down south and across the English Channel, there was a crop of bands embracing the technologically driven new. Coldwave is a term that has come to differentiate European—primarily French, Belgian, Dutch, German, and Italian—post-punk music of the late 1970s and 1980s from the post-punk music that came out of the UK. Pieter Schoolwerth, owner of the American indie label Wierd Records, described coldwave as "a guitar-driven form of 'Wave Music' that was early on quite informed by the icy razor blade guitar sound and high-end heavy drum-tracking of the legendary producer Martin Hannett who created Manchester's Factory Records sound."[4] The term originated from French journalists describing the sound of the band Marquis de Sade as "*La Vague Froide.*" Schoolwerth also lamented that the decision of these groups to sing in their native languages, coupled with the fact that they were often based outside of major cities, meant that few at the time were ever heard in the US and UK.

The first rock-and-roll bands from the West to inspire young musicians in the Land of the Rising Sun were the instrumental groups of the late 1950s and early 1960s. This led to the *Eleki Buumu*, the

"Electric Guitar Boom" that was brought to Japan by groups like Britain's the Shadows and Tacoma, Washington's the Ventures, who subsequently became one of the bestselling foreign bands in Japan.[5]

GROUP SOUNDS

Given its name by musician and actor Yuzo Kayama on live television as he was hosting his own talk show,[6] Group Sounds followed the *Eleki Buumu*, which began as the Japanese interpretation of the beat boom but came into its own with groups like the Mops, the Spiders, the Jaguars, the Golden Cups, and the Tigers. Adhesion to formula was important to Group Sounds' success, but some artists stood out, such as the Mops, who were one of the first to incorporate less polished garage and psychedelic rock elements, leading them to create what musician and author Julian Cope cites as "some of the most urgently deranged and euphorically disruptive music of the entire Group Sounds era."[7] Though the Mops didn't continue on for long after the next trend turnover, their rebellions set up the next generation, deemed "New Rock,"[8] embodied by the freewheelin' heavy psychedelic approach of the Flower Travellin' Band.

GYPSY PUNK

For all its old world allusions, gypsy punk is actually a modern American product, and surely there's something appropriate about that. "Few bands embody the idea of culture-juggling twenty-first-century globalism better than Gogol Bordello," observed the *New York Times* in April 2002, noting how for an upcoming performance at the Whitney Museum, the band would be delivering their "revved-up Gypsy songs, Russian-language punk meltdowns and satirical pantomimes about Soviet border police" with fiddle and accordion as well as guitar and drums. It was Gogol Bordello leader Eugene Hütz who came up with the term "Gypsy punk cabaret" to describe the "raucous, sweaty, tuneful and recklessly vibrant" music he and his bandmates from Russia, Ukraine, and Israel were making.[9] No sound so enlivening stays the property of one band for long, and soon other groups such as Kultur Shock, Balkan Beat Box, and DeVotchKa were stomping their feet to sped-up Eastern European rhythms as well.

IDOL METAL/KAWAII METAL |||||||||||||||||||||||||||||||||||||||||||||||||||||||||||||||||||||||

Circling back to Japan for music that has little history and a questionable depth of seriousness, idol metal, also known as kawaii metal, is nonetheless highly amusing if you have the stomach for it. A highly avoidable collision of hyper-polished, hyper-pink, teenybopper-oriented J-pop and ear-shredding heavy metal guitars, idol metal is, depending on how you look at it, either everything *right* or everything *wrong* with modern disregard for genre boundaries. Idol metal caught America off guard in 2014 when its most famous band, Babymetal—whose three dolled-up singers, Moa Kikuchi, Yui Mizuno, and Suzaka Nakamoto, didn't appear to be your typical middle-school metalheads—came to the States to promote their self-titled debut album with live performances attended by both committed fans and curiosity seekers.[10]

ITALIAN OCCULT PSYCHEDELIA |||||||||||||||||||||||||||||||||||||||||||||||||||||||||||||||||||||

Significantly more obscure and yet certainly less bizarre than other genres is a branch of Italian rock music referred to as Italian occult psychedelia. In some sense a celebration of twentieth-century cultural heritage, this recently coined genre bends Italian psychedelic rock and post-punk in the direction of the familiar sounds and atmospheres of the nation's most famous visionaries, such as composer Ennio Morricone and film director Federico Fellini.[11] Rome band Heroin in Tahiti are one such example of the genre, with their 2012 album *Death Surf* coming across at times like a goth reimagining of a Spaghetti Western soundtrack. In 2016, Italian record label

Boring Machines celebrated its tenth anniversary with the help of the Thalassa Italian Occult Psychedelia Festival.[12]

LATIN ALTERNATIVE

Looking back to the late 1990s, many American alternative rock fans from that time surely recall the buzz around names like Café Tacvba, Soda Stereo, and Aterciopelados. This was the time of the big commercial push behind Latin alternative (known also by the term Rock en Español) in the United States. In his book, *Rock en Español: The Latin Alternative Rock Explosion*, writer Ernesto Lechner notes how the late nineties was an important and transformative moment for Latin rock. Speaking of the growth of these groups from Mexico, Argentina, and many places in between, Lechner writes that "the sounds of rock, punk, hip-hop, and electronica were present in their work, but there was also the refreshing appearance of a new element. These musicians had grown up listening to their parents' record collection of Latin American popular music: boleros, bossa nova, salsa, cumbias, and syrupy Latin pop."[13] To pop music fans, the Latin Explosion of the late 1990s was all about big names like Ricky Martin, Jennifer Lopez, Enrique Iglesias, and Marc Anthony, but their rock counterparts were having an equally important moment, if one measured less by album sales than by artistic achievement.

NEUE DEUTSCHE HÄRTE

Those who picked up the soundtrack to the David Lynch film *Lost Highway* in 1997 were presented with a star-studded track list that featured the likes of David Bowie, Lou Reed, Nine Inch Nails, the Smashing Pumpkins, and Marilyn Manson. By the end of it, however, many were probably left wondering, *"Who the hell are Rammstein?"* This was the Neue Deutsche Härte, or a new wave of hard German music. Taking their name for the Ramstein air base in West Germany where an air show tragedy occurred in the late 1980s, the band had been around for a few years before their dark, industrial-tinged songs found favor in an American market that was learning to love nu metal. The success of their second album, *Sehnsucht*,[14] gave their countrymen like Megaherz a fighting chance.

NEUE DEUTSCHE WELLE

A decade before the Neue Deutsche Härte was the Neue Deutsche Welle, the New German Wave. This was the specifically German version of the coldwave that came over France and Belgium: rooted in post-punk and enamored with electronic instruments and goth ambience. *Assimilate* author S. Alexander Reed points to the electronic dance sound of Dusseldorf groups Die Krupps and Deutsche-Amerikanische Freundschaft as formative for the wave. "The independent hits from Germany's synth-driven underground were making money and receiving attention abroad, especially in the UK, where in 1980 alone the *New Musical Express* named German songs 'Single of the Week' three times." Reed writes that successes such as those gave hope to the underground independent scene, but that ultimately, "wide commercial popularity remained beyond the reach of artists who had shaped West Germany's experimental and industrial awaking between 1978 and 1981."[15]

OSTROCK

Wide commercial popularity in the Western world was entirely out of the question for purveyors of Ostrock, rock and roll from East Germany before the country's reunification. Successful as they may have been on their side of the Iron Curtain, names such as the Puhdys, City, Karat, and the Klaus Renft Combo still don't ring many bells in North America, and they even lost their appeal at home after the Berlin Wall came down. The Puhdys, however, did recover their popularity in the long run.[16] In fact, many Ostrock groups proved to have surprisingly long lifespans even through dips in popularity, with many having come together at different ends of the 1970s and carrying on well after the fall of Communism.

PINOY ROCK ||||||||||||||||||||||||||||||||||||||||||||||||||||||||||||||||||||||||||||||||||||||||||||

In the Philippines, Pinoy rock is something akin to Group Sounds, Ostrock, and Latin alternative all rolled into one. It covers the whole gamut of rock music that has come from that nation of more than 7,000 islands, from the 1970s to present day. The garage rocking "Juan Dela [*sic*] Cruz Band started it all in the '70s," declares an article from the *Philippine Star* from 2011, "then the Manila Sound period produced the likes of Hotdog and VST."[17] Manila Sound groups like Hotdog and the APO Hiking Society sung in both Filipino and English. There may be more than one "golden age" for Pinoy rock, but the 1990s were surely boom years. In this era, the famous Club Dredd in Manila played host to bands such as Eraserheads, the Youth, and Parokya ni Edgar. After these alt-rock parallel boom years, the *Star* notes that the Pinoy rock scene was delivered a blow all too familiar to American rock fans, as "a new wave of foreign-sounding and 'emo' groups dominated the mid-2000s."[18]

SUFI ROCK ||||||||||||||||||||||||||||||||||||||||||||||||||||||||||||||||||||||||||||||||||||||||||||||

More than 3,000 miles away from the Philippines, across numerous seas, gulfs, and bays, is Pakistan, where Sufi rock largely originates from. Sufi rock does what the name implies, mixing rock and roll with the sounds of Islamic-based sufi music, played on traditional instruments such as a reed flute known as the ney. Reporting on the first New York Sufi Music Festival in 2010, Jon Pareles took in more traditional performances from the likes of Rafaqat Ali Khan and Ghaus Box Brohi, but also modern twists from the electrified Dari duo Zeb and Haniya, as well as the Mekaal Hasan Band, who "plugged in with reggae, folk-rock and a tricky jazz-rock riff."[19] From the capital city of Lahore in the Punjab province of Pakistan, guitarist Mekaal Hasan formed the group in 2000, which now claims to be the only band of its kind to feature members from both Pakistan and India,[20] a symbolic olive branch between the two nations. The Mekaal Hasan Band are open-minded in the spirit of the present, but also present in the spirit of the past, their lyrics sometimes quoting 900-year-old devotional poetry, as Pareles noted of their festival performance.

VIKING METAL

Reconnecting with a different kind of faith and way of life are the Scandinavians who play Viking metal. Norway and Sweden provided fertile frozen ground for black metal in the 1990s, and Norwegian black metal quickly distinguished itself from other forms of extreme metal by way of its lyrical fixations on pre-Christian Norse heritage. Though the genre's name might bring to mind the costumes and carousing of pirate metal, Viking metal can actually be quite a serious affair to those who play it. That said, Amon Amarth frontman Johan Hegg did in fact play a Viking warrior in the 2014 historical adventure film *Northmen: A Viking Saga*. Amon Amarth formed in the early 1990s in Tumba, Sweden, and have since released ten albums full of death metal songs about Viking history and mythology. They are far from alone in this endeavor, as Viking metal, distinguished mostly by its thematic and lyrical concerns, overlaps with not just black metal, but other subgenres such as folk metal, modern power metal, and symphonic metal, all of which afford many an opportunity to go berserk.

TRANSLATIONS PLAYLIST

ANADOLU POP	Moğollar–"Dağ Ve Çocuk" Bunalım–"Başak Saçlım" Üç Hürel–"Sevenler Ağlarmış"
CANROCK	The Guess Who–"American Woman" Bryan Adams–"Run to You" Loverboy–"Working for the Weekend" The Tragically Hip–"Nautical Disaster"
CELTIC METAL	Cruachan–"Maeve's March" Waylander–"Born to the Fight"
CELTIC ROCK	Runrig–"Loch Lomond" Horslips–"King of the Fairies"
COLDWAVE	Marquis de Sade–"Conrad Veidt" KaS Product–"So Young but So Cold" Die Form–"Zoophilic Lolita"
GROUP SOUNDS	The Spiders–"Dynamite" The Golden Cups–"Hey Joe" (cover) The Mops–"To My Sons"
GYPSY PUNK	Gogol Bordello–"Immigrant Punk" Kultur Shock–"Sarajevo" DeVotchKa–"The Clockwise Witness"
IDOL METAL / KAWAII METAL	Babymetal–"Gimme Chocolate!!" Doll\$Boxx–"Monopoly" Aldious–"Dominator"
ITALIAN OCCULT PSYCHEDELIA	Heroin in Tahiti–"Death Surf" Father Murphy–"A Purpose" Mamuthones–"The First Born"

LATIN ALTERNATIVE	Soda Stereo–"De Música Ligera" Los Fabulosos Cadillacs–"Matador" Café Tacvba–"Las Flores" Aterciopelados–"Bolero Falaz"
NEUE DEUTSCHE HÄRTE	Rammstein–"Rammstein" Megaherz–"Gott Sein"
NEUE DEUTSCHE WELLE	Die Krupps–"Wahre Arbeit, Wahrer Lohn" Deutsche-Amerikanische Freundschaft–"Der Mussolini"
OSTROCK	The Puhdys–"Lebenszeit" Karat–"Der Blaue Planet"
PINOY ROCK	Eraserheads–"With a Smile" The Youth–"Tao Po" Parokya ni Edgar–"Your Song"
SUFI ROCK	Zeb and Haniya–"Bibi Sanam Janem" The Mekaal Hasan Band–"Chal Bulleya"
VIKING METAL	Bathory–"Valhalla" Amon Amarth–"Thor Arise" Enslaved–"In Chains Until Ragnarok"

War Metal

Ian Christe identifies a "war metal offshoot of Scandinavian black metal" perpetuated by the war-themed groups like Zyklon-B and Niden Div. 187. A decade later, the website Invisible Oranges described war metal as "a blasphemous, violent black/death metal hybrid so extremely fast, raw, and chaotic that it often borders upon grind."[1] The violent, chaotic mess of the latter kind of war metal comes from the genial nation of Canada, where the band Conqueror rained down their destruction. Their 1999 debut album, *War Cult Supremacy*, takes the already ragged and burnt edges of grindcore and black metal and hysterically stomps on their ashes. Conqueror's guerrilla racket was made by two people: drummer James Read and guitarist Ryan Förster. The duo was very temporary, but they made their mark.

Read went on to form Revenge, Förster joined long-running Vancouver metal band Blasphemy, and in 2013, they reunited to form the "war-metal supergroup" Death Worship and a few years later released their *Extermination Mass* EP.[2] War metal essentially belongs to Read, Förster, and those whom they have collaborated with. But once a new metal genre has been unleashed, there is no stopping it, and the scorched earth implications of war metal have been too alluring for metalheads to leave in peace.

Key Players: Conqueror, Death Worship, Revenge

CROSSOVER GENRES

DEATH METAL
Bloodbath, Death

GRINDCORE
Carcass, Napalm Death

Youth Crew

Youth crew was a subsection of hardcore punk in the mid-to-late 1980s centered in New York City and the Northeast. It positioned itself as an unflashy, positive-minded alternative to the spiked hair and substance abuse commonly associated with the punk rock lifestyle in the 1980s. Drug free, booze free, and meat free, the barrier to entry kept the poseurs away and made the bonds between the committed all the stronger. So did the choice to dress like jocks. Youth crew borrowed from the belief system of DC's straight edge scene and the sound of hardcore bands from out West, taking lessons from the likes of Black Flag's *Damaged* and 7 Seconds' *The Crew*.

Connecticut band Youth of Today formed in 1985 and gave the scene its name with the B-side of their "Can't Close My Eyes" 7" single that year. "Youth of Today and other bands from the late eighties 'youth crew' era took their straight edge message across the United States, Europe, and other parts of the world,"[1] writes Brian Peterson in *Burning Fight*. When Youth of Today broke up in 1990 (the band would reform twenty years later), frontman Ray Cappo formed the band Shelter, who drew strong opinions for their dedication to Cappo's newfound Hare Krishna beliefs,[2] which led to some labelling Shelter's music, and that of the first bands signed to his new label, Equal Vision (before its focus was expanded a couple of years later), as Krishnacore. The youth crew scene was not entirely above poking fun at itself, however, as the band Crucial Youth did with their lyrics.

Gorilla Biscuits formed in 1987 when the New York youth crew scene still had momentum behind it. Interviewed on the *Going Off*

Track podcast in early 2017, former member Walter Schreifels, who went on to form post-hardcore bands Quicksand in the 1990s and Rival Schools in the 2000s, recalled how dressing like a jock in the punk world was a "rebellion within that rebellion,"[3] but all scenes run their course. A victim of his own success, Schreifels described how his experience evolved into "playing to a room full of people that think the same things and act the same way and look the same, and I don't like it that much actually."[4]

Key Players: Chain of Strength, Gorilla Biscuits, Judge, Youth of Today, Warzone

CROSSOVER GENRES

POST-HARDCORE
CIV, Quicksand, Rival Schools

STRAIGHT EDGE
7 Seconds, Minor Threat, Uniform Choice

EPILOGUE

Somewhere in the course of reading this book you may have begun to suspect that among the scores of rock genres out there, there is not one where everyone can agree about everything. This book is one music lover's attempt to draw a map of the many kinds of rock music out there. In the discourse around almost every genre, you'll find at least some disagreement. Sometimes you'll find a lot. Differences of opinion can and do occur on the level of detail, general parameters, or even what to call a genre.

Some argue against the idea of genre altogether. Many artists understandably push against having their art categorized. Others have accepted or even embraced genre as part of their identity, notably in the worlds of heavy metal, punk, and rockabilly. Being tied to a movement can have its benefits, but also its perils. If a movement takes off, the rising tide can lift all boats. However, when the water inevitably drifts back out, some of those boats can be left high and dry. The sense of identity that a movement might provide at first can become a hindrance if and when the artist grows tired of that identity—or worse, when fans grow tired of it.

No scene or genre has one determining voice. John Lydon and Patti Smith could possibly have much different takes on the true meaning of punk rock, and who would argue with either? Still, the drive to articulate and define rock music, to dance about architecture (as goes the famous Elvis Costello quote), continues as it has done since the 1960s. This book has aimed to assemble a range of voices and from there try to hone in on where there is correlation of perspective and where perception diverges.

In the course of putting this together, some long-held suspicions were more or less confirmed, but one minor revelation was to see how genres with longevity and historical recognition behind them, such as folk rock from the 1960s, could be just as cooked-up and contentious in their creation as lesser fads that quickly came and went. Whether a genre grows organically or is manufactured doesn't necessarily determine its staying power. All the artificial needs to become authentic is time. Chillwave was hot one summer and cold the next, lauded and then dismissed in the same publications, but don't be surprised if in ten years time young music fans talk about it with the same sense of legitimacy as we do shoegaze now.

Decades of rapid technological development in communication, recording, musical equipment, and instruments has much to do with the exponential proliferation of rock genres from the 1960s to the 2000s. All of that technology presses forward unabated, but at the time of this writing, it feels like it has been years since a truly new rock genre has been thrust into the spotlight for scrutiny. The Internet and the ease of home recording has resulted in more people making and writing about rock than ever, yet the music press in this decade has been mostly content with filing guitar groups under one or more preexisting genres.

One could chalk this up to there now being so many writers for so many outlets covering so many artists at the same time that any attempt at media consensus on a new genre is futile. This could be a factor, but not a full explanation, because it doesn't account for all the new styles of hip-hop and electronic music that have been named and widely recognized in the same time. Has the genre-coining torch been passed? Possibly. It could also be that conversation around rock music has changed its priorities or is taking a breather. There are, as we've seen, already so many genres out there, and Information Fatigue Syndrome is real. Perhaps once everyone is caught up, we can go back to coming up with new names again.

In the meantime, if guitar bands in this decade have all been working in existing genres, they've been doing a swell job refining and building on them. Modern garage and psychedelic bands have kept the music vital, even if it's more left of the mainstream than it was in the 1960s. Post-punk, too, cuts a vigorous figure, and its angles and affectations have bled into everything around it. Emo and pop punk have fared better in this decade than they have since their heydays in the 1990s. In all of the above and more, genre mixing and matching has been welcomed by audiences. Recently, a friend spoke highly of an on-the-rise band by describing them as "emo, but with 20 percent math rock." He was, appropriately enough, very clear about that percentage.

Other genres have returned in less obvious forms. Thanks to the visual emphasis of the Internet and social media, glam has worked its way into everything from major pop stars to minor label indie acts who smear a bit of color on their face or wear something eye-catching in their band photos. Glam rock predicted a music world where sound and vision would be of equal importance to a musician's presence, and here we now are. People are watching music as much as they are listening to it, and technology has made it so that anyone with an iPhone, some editing software and a spare weekend can make a more interesting music video than so many of those big-budget afterthoughts from the 1980s and 1990s.

Progressive rock and new wave both made powerful arguments for the usefulness of synthesizers in guitar-based music, arguments that then went widely unheeded in the 1990s. As early as 2000, though, Radiohead's *Kid A* made it clear that electronic music was becoming an unavoidable influence. A rock band with at least one member committed to a keyboard, sampler, or other kind of electronic gadgetry is now as common as having a saxophone player was in the 1950s. (In fact, the saxophone has recently had something of its own indie renaissance in rock music, but we'll see if that lasts.) The intermingling of analog and digital will only become more common. The possibilities that it opens up are too numerous to ignore, and have become important to keeping up with the times.

That said, keeping up with the times might be more optional than ever. From the late 1960s onward, generations of music journalists have written about the greater concept of rock and roll as its own kind of entity, a crucial quicksilver orb of cultural energy, and the most relevant musicians of the day were the ones pushing up against its evershifting standards of sound, fashion, consumption and attitude. Yet it was only about thirty years after "Rock Around the Clock" that this once rebellious form of popular music got its own institution with the Rock & Roll Hall of Fame and started reflecting on its heritage. Some of the biggest rock bands of the past twenty years have been those that evoke the music's past. Recognition of genre is, in a way, its own act of reflection, but across countless bedrooms, sweaty practice spaces, and scuffed up stages lurks the potential of new manifestations of rock's energy itching to leave a mark.

ACKNOWLEDGMENTS

I am forever thankful to Erin Wicks and Amy Baker for believing in this book. Their vision, knowledge, and enthusiasm make them ideal editors. A huge thanks as well to Mary Gaule and Sarah Haugen.

This book would not have been possible without the wise guidance and unflagging encouragement of friend and agent David Halpern. Kathy Robbins, Lisa Kessler, and Janet Oshiro at The Robbins Office also have my deepest gratitude, as does the sharp-eyed Jess Hoops.

If not for Alex Littlefield's astute early reads of the proposal for this book, it might still be a vague idea for something called *Daddy, What Was Chillwave?*

I am truly grateful to the people who agreed to be interviewed for this book, lending it their time, stories, and expertise: Ian Anderson, Gina Birch, Jon Bolling, Tobias Carroll, Jack Chuter, Marco Collins, John Colpitts, Brian Cook, Rachel Goswell, Melissa Giannini, Rob Halford, John Haughm, Jim Heath, Scott Hill, Matt Kadane, David Kilgour, Damon Krukowski, Sara Marcus, Tom Mullen, Stuart Murdoch, Colin Newman, Kim Ruehl, Brandon Stosuy, David Stubbs, Doug Van Pelt, JJ Wandler, and Steve Wynn.

Many thanks also to the people who helped make some of those interviews happen: Jayne Andrews, Russell Beresford, Caroline

Borolla, Jacob Daneman, Anne Leighton, Stephanie Marlow, Fiona Morrison, Shirley O'Loughlin, Rachel Silver, Chris Stone, Tom Wojcik, and Martin at Dammerung Arts.

I would also like to thank these fine folks for the opportunities, support and friendship they've extended: Matt Conner, Suzanne Dottino, Thomas Hannan, Vivian Hua, Celia Johnson, Janice Potter, Maria Gagliano Scalora, Lauren Snyder, Jeff Wilson, and Sarah Zupko.

Dianna and Fred raised me in a home with music always on in the background, and never stopped me from watching too much MTV at an impressionable young age. Larissa played the Smiths loudly enough for me to hear it through the bedroom wall. You're the best, guys.

The love, support, and patience of Jessica and Elliott kept me going throughout all of this. They are all the motivation I could ask for. *Team hug.*

ENDNOTES

Introduction
1. Elijah Wald, *How the Beatles Destroyed Rock 'n' Roll* (New York: Oxford University Press, 2009), 170.
2. Steve Lamacq, *Going Deaf for a Living* (London: BBC Worldwide Ltd, 2000), 80.
3. Ian Christe, *Sound of the Beast* (New York: HarperCollins, 2004), 140.
4. Adam Brent Houghtaling, *This Will End in Tears* (New York: Harper-Collins, 2012), 17.
5. Tristan Kneschke, "On Wandering the Paths of a Spotify Analyst's Mad Music Map," Pop Matters, February 9, 2017, www.popmatters.com.
6. Houghtaling, *This Will End in Tears*, 17.

2 Tone
1. *Two Tone Britain*, directed by Jason Collier (UK: Channel 4, 2004), documentary.
2. George Marshall, "Dawning of a New Era," in *The Two Tone Story* (Lockerbie, Dumfriesshire, Scotland: S. T. Publishing, 2011).
3. Marshall, "Dawning of a New Era," in *The Two Tone Story*.
4. Marshall, "Gangsters," in *The Two Tone Story*.

Acid Rock
1. Tom Shroder, "'Apparently Useless': The Accidental Discovery of LSD," *Atlantic*, September 9, 2014, www.theatlantic.com.
2. Jesse Jarnow, *Heads* (Boston: Da Capo Press, 2016), 18–19.

Alternative Country
1. Tom Mullen, *Washed Up Emo*, podcast, "Episode 7 - The Promise Ring's Davey von Bohlen and Dan Didier," January 28, 2012.

Alternative Metal

1. Mark Yarm, *Everybody Loves Our Town* (New York: Crown Archetype, 2011), 174–176.
2. Jason Heller, "Loud Love: Soundgarden and the Heyday of Alternative Metal," Noisey, August 26, 2016, www.noisey.vice.com.
3. Christe, *Sound of the Beast*, 225.

Alternative Rock

1. Scott Schinder, ed., *Rolling Stone's Alt-Rock-A-Rama*, "Introduction" by Scott Schinder (New York: Bantam Doubleday Dell, 1996), xv.
2. Scott Schinder, ed., *Rolling Stone's Alt-Rock-A-Rama*, "Gimme Danger: The Stooges Saga" by James Marshall (New York: Bantam Doubleday Dell, 1996), 77.

Anarcho Punk

1. Ian Glasper, *The Day the Country Died* (London: Cherry Red Books, 2006), 9.
2. Harry Sword, "Essex Has a Much More Radical History Than You'd Think," Vice, May 31, 2016, www.vice.com.
3. Chuck Eddy, "Crust Never Sleeps: 8 Anarcho Punk Essentials," Spin, February 22, 2012, www.spin.com.
4. Eddy, "Crust Never Sleeps," 2012.

Art Punk

1. Robert Christgau, "Avant-Punk: A Cult Explodes...and a Movement Is Born," *Robert Christgau* (website), www.robertchristgau.com, originally appeared in *The Village Voice*, October 24, 1977.

Art Rock

1. David Marchese, "The (Presumably) True Story Behind Martin Shkreli and That Wu-Tang Album," Vulture, July 11, 2017, www.vulture.com.

America, America

1. *Afro-Punk*, directed by James Spooner (USA: Image Entertainment, 2003), documentary.
2. Amanda Petrusich, *It Still Moves* (New York: Faber and Faber, 2008), 5.
3. Petrusich, *It Still Moves*, 8.
4. Barney Hoskyns, *Hotel California* (Hoboken: John Wiley & Sons, 2006), 1.
5. Hoskyns, *Hotel California*, 150.
6. David Reyes and Tom Waldman, *Land of a Thousand Dances* (Albuquerque: University of New Mexico Press, 1998), XV.
7. Reyes and Waldman, *Land of a Thousand Dances*, 19.
8. Reyes and Waldman, *Land of a Thousand Dances*, 122.

9. *Los Punks*, directed by Angela Boatwright (USA: Vans Off the Wall, 2016), documentary.

10. David N. Meyer, *Twenty Thousand Roads* (New York: Villard Books, 2007), 193.

11. Meyer, *Twenty Thousand Roads*, XI.

12. Meyer, *Twenty Thousand Roads*, 366–367.

13. Peter Doggett, *Are You Ready for the Country* (New York: Penguin Books, 2000), 449.

14. Doggett, *Are You Ready for the Country*, 446.

15. Robert Palmer, "Young Bands Make Country Music for the MTV Generation," *The New York Times*, June 10, 1984.

16. Jon Pareles, "Heartland Rock: Bruce's Children," *The New York Times*, August 30, 1987.

17. Dan Caffrey, "Where We Live: The Jersey Shore Sound," Consequence of Sound, January 13, 2009, www.consequenceofsound.net.

18. Byron Coley, "The Wire 300: Byron Coley commemorates one of the New Weird America's founding fathers," *The Wire*, February 2013, www.thewire.co.uk.

19. Petrusich, *It Still Moves*, 239.

20. Martin C. Strong, *The Great Rock Discography*, 6th ed. (Edinburgh: Canongate Books Ltd, 2002), 243.

21. Rebecca Chaouch, "Taqwacore: Punk Piety For Young Muslim Rebels," *Huffington Post*, November 24, 2014, www.huffingtonpost.com.

22. "What Is Trop Rock?," Trop Rock Music Association (website), www.troprock.org.

Baggy and Madchester

1. Phil Saxe, "A Brief History of the Twisted Wheel," *Size?*, July 21, 2013, www.blog.size.co.uk.

2. John Robb, *The Stone Roses: The Reunion Edition* (London: Ebury Press, 2012), 270.

3. John Robb, *The North Will Rise Again* (London: Aurum Press, 2010), 321.

4. Shaun Ryder, *Twisting My Melon* (London: Corgi, 2012), 192.

5. Dave Haslam, *Manchester, England* (London: Fourth Estate, 2000), 181.

6. Haslam, *Manchester, England*, 175.

7. Peter Hook, *The Haçienda* (New York: HarperCollins, 2014), 157–158.

8. Hook, *The Haçienda*, 148–149.

Baroque Pop

1. Bob Stanley, "Baroque and a Soft Place," *Guardian*, September 21, 2007, www.theguardian.com.

2. Simon Reynolds, *Retromania* (New York: Farrar, Straus and Giroux, 2011), 151.

3. Mark Hertsgaard, *A Day in the Life* (New York: Delacorte Press, 1995), 156.
4. Andrew Grant Jackson, *1965* (New York: Thomas Dunne Books, 2015), 41.
5. Bob Stanley, *Yeah! Yeah! Yeah!* (New York: W.W. Norton, 2015), 186.

Beat Boom

1. Gareth Murphy, *Cowboys and Indies* (New York: Thomas Dunne Books, 2014), 129.
2. Freddie and the Dreamers, "I'm Telling You Now," *The Merv Griffin Show*, December 1965, live performance.

Black Metal

1. Christe, *Sound of the Beast*, 42.
2. Christe, *Sound of the Beast*, 273–280.

Blues Rock

1. Keith Richards, *Life* (New York: Little, Brown and Company, 2010), 29, 35.
2. Keith Richards, *Life*, 79.
3. John McMillian, *Beatles Vs. Stones* (New York: Simon & Schuster, 2013), 37.
4. Richards, *Life*, 81.
5. Anthony DeCurtis and James Henke, eds., *The Rolling Stone Illustrated History of Rock & Roll* (New York: Random House, 1992), 344–345.
6. DeCurtis and Henke, *The Rolling Stone Illustrated History of Rock & Roll*, 407–408.
7. Steven Hyden, *Your Favorite Band is Killing Me* (New York: Back Bay Books, 2016), 62–63.

Boogie Rock

1. "Style Sheets: Boogie Woogie," Jazz in America (website), www.jazzin america.org.

British Invasion

1. Bill Harry, *The British Invasion* (Surrey: Chrome Dreams, 2004), 7.
2. Harry, *The British Invasion*, 22–23.
3. Harry, *The British Invasion*, 23.
4. Harry, *The British Invasion*, 24–25.

Britpop

1. "The Beatles see the Rolling Stones perform for the first time," The Beatles Bible, www.beatlesbible.com.
2. Luke Haines, *Bad Vibes* (London: Windmill Books, 2010), 89–90.
3. Steve Lamacq, *Going Deaf for a Living* (London: BBC Worldwide, 2000), 189.
4. *Live Forever*, directed by John Dower (UK: BBC, 2003), documentary.
5. Alex James, *Bit of a Blur* (London: Little, Brown, 2007), 117.

6. *Britpop Now*, directed by Geraldine Dowd (UK: BBC2, 1995), TV special.

7. Louise Wener, *Just for One Day* (London: Ebury Press, 2011), 238.

8. John Mullen, "Jarvis Cocker: The abdicated king of Britpop," *Select*, January 1999, 54.

9. John Harris, *Britpop!* (Cambridge, MA: Da Capo Press, 2004), 261.

10. Tim Burgess, *Telling Stories* (London: Viking, 2012), 102.

C86

1. Bob Stanley, *Yeah! Yeah! Yeah!* (New York: W.W. Norton, 2015), 438.

2. Alan McGee, *Creation Stories* (London: Pan Books, 2014), 64.

3. Marc Spitz, *Twee* (New York: HarperCollins, 2014), 165.

Canterbury Sound

1. Will Romano, *Mountains Come Out of the Sky* (Milwaukee: Backbeat Books, 2010), 97–98.

Celtic Punk

1. James Fearnley, *Here Comes Everybody* (Chicago: Chicago Review Press, 2014), 86.

Chillwave

1. Tom Cheshire, "Invent a new genre: Hipster Runoff's Carles explains 'chillwave,'" *Wired*, March 30, 2011, www.wired.co.uk.

2. Nitsuh Abebe, "Why We Fight: Chillin' in Plain Sight," Pitchfork, July 22, 2011, www.pitchfork.com.

3. Tom Hawking, "What Did Chillwave Mean, Anyway?," Flavorwire, April 27, 2012, www.flavorwire.com.

Christian Punk

1. Andrew Beaujon, *Body Piercing Saved My Life* (Cambridge, MA: Da Capo Press, 2006), 60–61.

2. Beaujon, *Body Piercing Saved My Life*, 62.

Christian Rock

1. Neil McCormick, *Killing Bono* (New York: Pocket Books, 2004), 123.

2. Beaujon, *Body Piercing Saved My Life*, 24.

3. Darryl Smyers, "Michael Sweet of Stryper: 'We Have Always Thrown Bibles and We Always Will.'," *Dallas Observer*, May 17, 2012, www.dallasobserver.com.

4. Beaujon, *Body Piercing Saved My Life*, 41.

College Rock

1. MTV, "R.E.M. Wins Video of the Year at the 1991 VMAs - MTV Classic," aired September 5, 1991, on MTV, YouTube video, November 18, 2016.

Comedy Rock

1.   Richie Unterberger, *Urban Spacemen and Wayfaring Strangers* (San Francisco: Miller Freeman Books, 2000), 109-110.

Country Rock

1.   Hoskyns, *Hotel*, 57.
2.   Doggett, *Are You Ready for the Country*, 38.
3.   Doggett, *Are You Ready for the Country*, 156.
4.   Doggett, *Are You Ready for the Country*, 385.

Crossover Thrash

1.   *Get Thrashed: The Story of Thrash Metal*, directed by Rick Ernst (USA: Sony Pictures Home Entertainment, 2006), documentary.

Crust Punk

1.   Ian Glasper, *Trapped in a Scene* (London: Cherry Red Books, 2010), 185.
2.   Ian Glasper, *The Day the Country Died* (London: Cherry Red Books, 2006), 198.

Cuddlecore

1.   Rose Apodaca Jones, "Cute. Real Cute: The Look Is Dainty, but Cuddle Core Followers Are Brashly Telling the World They'll Grow Up the Way They Please," *Los Angeles Times*, June 28, 1995.
2.   Jones, "Cute. Real Cute," 1995.

D-Beat

1.   Brian Roe, "Brian Roe - D Beat - The original - Brian Roe," YouTube video, October 20, 2012.
2.   Ian Glasper, *Burning Britain* (London: Cherry Red Books, 2004), 167.

Dance Punk

1.   John Morthland, ed., *Mainlines, Blood Feasts and Bad Taste: A Lester Bangs Reader* (New York: Anchor Books, 2003), 247.
2.   Morthland, *Mainlines, Blood Feasts and Bad Taste*, 247.

Darkwave

1.   Martin Aston, *Facing the Other Way* (London: The Friday Project, 2013), 173.
2.   Aston, *Facing the Other Way*, 177–178.

Deathcore

1.   James Alvarez, "Interview: Despised Icon Revitalize & Reform for 'Beast,'" *New Noise*, November 8, 2016, www.newnoisemagazine.com.
2.   Dom Lawson, "The Rise and Rise of Deathcore: That Genre That Refuses to

Die," Metal Hammer, August 15, 2016, loudersound.com/metal-hammer
.com.

3. Sergeant D, "The Evolution of Deathcore: A Framework for Analysis,"
    Metal Sucks, August 15, 2011, www.metalsucks.net.

Death Metal
1. David Konow, *Bang Your Head* (New York: Three Rivers Press, 2002), 228.

Digital Hardcore
1. Todd Hansen, "Atari Teenage Riot interview," AV Club, July 23, 1997,
    www.avclub.com.
2. "Alec Empire Interview": 'People Are Organized But Political Music Is Not
    Really Being Made.'," Indymedia Ireland, December 28, 2006, www.indy
    media.ie.

Doom Metal
1. Aniruddh "Andrew" Bansal, "An In-depth Conversation with Saint Vitus
    Guitarist Dave Chandler," Metal Assault, May 12, 2012, metalassault.com.
2. Christe, *Sound of the Beast*, 345.

Dream Pop
1. Simon Reynolds, "'Dream-Pop Bands Define the Times in Britain," *New
    York Times*, December 1, 1991.

Drone Metal
1. Invisible Oranges staff, "Interview: Dylan Carlson (Earth)," Invisible Or-
    anges, April 29, 2011, www.invisibleoranges.com.

Dunedin Sound
1. Greg Beets, "20 Questions with David Kilgour," *Austin Chronicle*, May 30,
    2012, www.austinchronicle.com.
2. Scott Plagenhoef and Ryan Schreiber, eds., *The Pitchfork 500* (New York:
    Touchstone, 2008), 56.
3. Jesse Jarnow, *Big Day Coming* (New York: Gotham Books, 2012), 69.
4. Jarnow, *Big Day Coming*, 256.
5. Jarnow, *Big Day Coming*, 257.

Dressing Up
1. Dorian Lynskey, "Amanda Palmer: 'If he were my boyfriend, I'd break up
    with him,'" *Guardian*, April 19, 2006, www.theguardian.com.
2. Lynskey, "Amanda Palmer," 2006.
3. Darryl Smyers, "Valor Kand of Christian Death: 'I Have an Issue with Peo-
    ple Assuming What Jesus Looked Like,'" *Dallas Observer*, September 5,
    2013, www.dallasobserver.com.

4. Smyers, "Valor Kand of Christian Death," 2013.

5. *Lost Anarchy*, "Tales from the Blakside: Gothabilly, Deathrock, and Horrorpunk," YouTube video, May 27, 2014.

6. Plagenhoef and Schreiber, *The Pitchfork 500*, 22.

7. Josh Hart, "Interview: Dani Evans and Christopher Bowes of Alestorm," Guitar World, June 9, 2011, www.guitarworld.com.

8. Draco and the Malfoys (website), www.evilwizardrock.com/.

9. Rachel Humphries and ABC News Business Unit, "Harry Potter 'Wrockers' Conjure Musical Magic," ABC News, July 13, 2007, abcnews.go.com.

Electric Folk

1. Rob Young, *Electric Eden* (New York: Farrar, Straus and Giroux, 2010), 160.

2. Joe Boyd, *White Bicycles* (London: Serpent's Tail, 2006), 184–185.

3. Young, *Electric Eden*, 349.

4. Jeff Perlah, "Ritchie Blackmore's Renaissance: From Deep Purple to Medieval Folk Rock," Newsweek, January 7, 2017, www.newsweek.com/ritchie-blackmore-deep-purple-rainbow-blackmores-night-539420.

5. Alexis Petridis, "'I like tights - and very pointy shoes,'" *Guardian*, June 17, 2005, www.theguardian.com/music/2005/jun/17/worldmusic.folk.

6. Rob Young, *Electric Eden* (New York: Farrar, Straus and Giroux, 2010), 239.

Emo(core)

1. Tom Mullen, *Washed Up Emo*, podcast, "Episode 80 – Mike Kinsella," October 18, 2016.

2. Andy Greenwald, *Nothing Feels Good* (New York: St. Martin's Press, 2003), 14–15.

Ethereal Wave

1. "ethereal," Oxford English Dictionary, www.oed.com.

2. Martin Aston, *Facing the Other Way* (London: The Friday Project, 2013), 86.

Experimental Rock

1. Hertsgaard, *A Day in the Life*, 171.

2. Hertsgaard, *A Day in the Life*, 219.

Folk Rock

1. Richie Unterberger, *Turn! Turn! Turn!* (Milwaukee: Backbeat Books, 2002), 28.

2. Unterberger, *Turn! Turn! Turn!*, 32.

3. Unterberger, *Turn! Turn! Turn!*, 134.

4. Unterberger, *Turn! Turn! Turn!*, 134.

5. Unterberger, *Turn! Turn! Turn!*, 144–145.

6. Unterberger, *Turn! Turn! Turn!*, 231.

Freak Folk

1. Jeanette Leech, *Seasons They Change* (London: Jawbone Press, 2011), 261.

Freakbeat

1. Simon Reynolds, *Shock and Awe* (New York: Dey Street Books, 2016), 31.
2. Richard Norris, "20 best: UK psych records ever made," *FACT*, March 11, 2012, www.factmag.com.

Funk Metal

1. Joel McIver, *Nu-Metal* (London: Omnibus Press, 2002), 11.
2. McIver, *Nu-Metal*, 11.

Funk Rock

1. George Clinton, *Brothas Be, Yo Like George, Ain't That Funkin' Kinda Hard on You?* (New York: Atria Paperback, 2017), 73.

Garage Punk

1. Mark A. Nobles, *Fort Worth's Rock and Roll Roots* (Charleston: Arcadia Publishing, 2011), 32.
2. Michael Hann, "10 of the Best: Garage Punk," *Guardian*, July 30, 2014, www.theguardian.com.

Garage Rock

1. DeCurtis and Henke, *The Rolling Stone Illustrated History of Rock and Roll*, 357.
2. Peter Blecha, *Music in Washington* (Charleston: Arcadia Publishing, 2007), 85.
3. Joe Carducci, *Rock and the Pop Narcotic*, revised edition (Los Angeles: 2.13.61, 1994), 291.
4. Carducci, *Rock and the Pop Narcotic*, 291–292.

Garage Rock Revival

1. Benjamin Nugent, "Music: White Lies and the White Stripes," *Time*, June 16, 2001.

Glam Metal

1. Tommy Lee and Anthony Bozza, *Tommyland* (New York: Atria Books, 2004), 73.
2. Konow, *Bang Your Head*, 271.

Glam Rock

1. Reynolds, *Shock and Awe*, 2–3.
2. Reynolds, *Shock and Awe*, 10.

3. David Bowie, *Moonage Daydream* (New York: Universe Publishing, 2005), 11.
4. Bowie, *Moonage Daydream*, 11.
5. Bowie, *Moonage Daydream*, 11.
6. Ace Frehley, *No Regrets* (New York: Gallery Books, 2011), 97.
7. Lesley-Ann Jones, *Mercury* (New York: Touchstone, 2011), 109.

Goth Metal

1. Christe, *Sound of the Beast*, 178–179.

Goth Rock

1. Lol Tolhurst, *Cured* (New York: Da Capo Press, 2016), 109.
2. Tolhurst, *Cured*, 109.
3. Tolhurst, *Cured*, 107.
4. Nancy Kilpatrick, *The Goth Bible* (New York: St. Martin's Press, 2004), 81.
5. Kilpatrick, *The Goth Bible*, 81.
6. S. Alexander Reed, *Assimilate* (New York: Oxford University Press, 2013), 176.

Grindcore

1. Albert Mudrian, *Choosing Death* (Port Townsend, WA: Feral House, 2004), 35.
2. Mudrian, *Choosing Death*, 124.
3. Natalie J. Purcell, *Death Metal Music* (Jefferson, NC: McFarland & Company, 2003), 23-24.
4. Mudrian, *Choosing Death*, 132–134.
5. Mudrian, *Choosing Death*, 180.

Groove Metal

1. Doc Coyle, "Hidden Gems: Rediscovering the '90s Post-Thrash Groove Metal Scene," VH1, August 12, 2015, www.vh1.com.
2. Strong, *The Great Rock Discography*, 781.

Grunge

1. Keith Cameron, *Mudhoney* (Minneapolis: Voyageur Press, 2014), 11–12.
2. Cameron, *Mudhoney*, 16.
3. Cameron, *Mudhoney*, 16.
4. Stephen Tow, *The Strangest Tribe* (Seattle: Sasquatch Books, 2011), xiv.
5. Mark Yarm, "'Going Out of Business Since 1988!,'" *Northwest Passage*, originally published in *Blender*, July 2008, www.revolutioncomeandgone.com.
6. Everett True, "Sub Pop: Seattle: Rock City," *Melody Maker*, March 18, 1989, 26–27.

7.   True, "Sub Pop: Seattle: Rock City," 26–27.

8.   Tow, *The Strangest Tribe*, xiv.

9.   Jessica Letkemann, "Sub Pop Rock City: The Story of the First Sub Pop Lame Fest," *Northwest Passage*, www.revolutioncomeandgone.com.

10. Michael Azerrad, *Come As You Are* (New York: Broadway Books, 1993), 110.

Hard Rock

1.   *The Decline of Western Civilization Part II: The Metal Years*, directed by Penelope Spheeris (USA: New Line Cinema, 1988), documentary.

Hardcore

1.   Steven Blush, *American Hardcore*, 2nd ed. (Port Townshend, WA: Feral House, 2010), 14.

Heavy Metal

1.   David Bentley, "Midlands Rocks! How Birmingham's Industrial Heritage Made It the Birthplace of Heavy Metal," *Birmingham Post*, June 4, 2013, www.birminghampost.com.

2.   *Some Kind of Monster*, directed by Joe Berlinger and Bruce Sinofsky (USA: Paramount Pictures, 2004), documentary.

Hypnagogic Pip

1.   David Keenan, "Childhood's End," *The Wire*, 306, August 2009, 26.

Have a Sense of Humor

1.   Tim Jonze, "Blog Rock Is Born," *Guardian*, June 13, 2011, www.theguardian.com.

2.   John Robb, *The Nineties* (London: Ebury Press, 1999), 139.

3.   Houghtaling, *This Will End in Tears*, 16.

4.   Houghtaling, *This Will End in Tears*, 7.

5.   Robert Christgau, "Township Jive Conquers the World," *Robert Christgau* (website), www.robertchristgau.com, originally published in *The Village Voice*, March 3, 1987.

6.   Paul Brannigan, *This Is a Call* (Cambridge, MA: Da Capo Press, 2011), 103.

7.   Marah Eakin, "All the Kids Are Listening to Twinklecore?," AV Club, October 8, 2012, www.avclub.com.

8.   J. D. Ryznar, Lane Farnham, Hunter Stair, *Yacht Rock*, episode 1: "What a Fool Believes," Channel 101, June 26, 2005, web series.

Indie Folk

1.   Matt Fink, "Monsters of Folk: Averting Disaster," *Under the Radar*, October 1, 2009, www.undertheradarmag.com.

Indie Pop

1. Robb, *The Stone Roses*, 267.
2. Mark Baumgarten, *Love Rock Revolution* (Seattle: Sasquatch Books, 2012), 93.
3. Baumgarten, *Love Rock*, 122–123.

Indie Rock

1. Michael Azerrad, *Our Band Could Be Your Life* (New York: Back Bay Books, 2002), 5.
2. Azerrad, *Our Band Could Be Your Life*, 3.
3. Andrew Earles, *Gimme Indie Rock* (Minneapolis: Voyageur Press, 2014), 4–5.
4. Jarnow, *Big Day Coming*, 7.
5. Jarnow, *Big Day Coming*, 5–6.
6. Jarnow, *Big Day Coming*, 6.
7. John Cook, Mac McCaughan, and Laura Ballance, *Our Noise* (Chapel Hill: Algonquin Books of Chapel Hill, 2009), 23.
8. Cook et al., *Our Noise*, 21.

Industrial Metal and Industrial Rock

1. Reed, *Assimilate*, 258.
2. Reed, *Assimilate*, 260.
3. Reed, *Assimilate*, 279.
4. Reed, *Assimilate*, 279.
5. Reed, *Assimilate*, 279.
6. Reed, *Assimilate*, 250–251.

Jangle Pop

1. Steve LaBate, "Jangle Bell Rock: A Chronological (Non-Holiday) Anthology . . . from The Beatles and Byrds to R.E.M. and Beyond," *Paste*, December 18, 2009, www.pastemagazine.com.

Jazz Rock

1. "Jazz-rock," *Encyclopaedia Britannica*, www.britannica.com.

Kindie Rock

1. ChrisB, "Imaginary Interview: The Not-Its," Three Imaginary Girls, August 31, 2009, www.threeimaginarygirls.com.

Lo-Fi Rock

1. Simon Goddard, *Simply Thrilled* (London: Ebury Press, 2014), 91.
2. Goddard, *Simply Thrilled*, 92.
3. Goddard, *Simply Thrilled*, 94.
4. Goddard, *Simply Thrilled*, 102.
5. Orange Juice, "Falling and Laughing," Postcard Records, UK, February 1, 1980, vinyl, 7", 45rpm. Value per Discogs, www.discogs.com, July 4, 2017.

Math Rock

1. Daniel Robson, "Mike Watt Loves Japanese Math Rockers Lite and So Do We," Noisey, August 27, 2013, www.noisey.vice.com.
2. Patrick St. Michel, "Meet Tricot, The Japanese Trio Making Math Rock Cool Again," Fader, October 24, 2015, www.thefader.com.
3. Matt LeMay, "Chavez," interview, Pitchfork, December 8, 2006, www.pitchfork.com.
4. Scott Tennent, *Spiderland* (New York: Continuum International Publishing Group, 2011), 3.
5. Brad Haywood, "Bellini—Snowing Sun," album review, Pitchfork, October 13, 2002, www.pitchfork.com.
6. ArcTanGent Music Festival website, http://www.arctangent.co.uk.

Metalcore

1. Peter Bottomley, "Converge," *Skyscraper* 2, summer 1998, 29.
2. Bottomley, "Converge," 29.

Mod and the Mod Revival

1. DeCurtis and Henke, *The Rolling Stone Illustrated History of Rock and Roll*, 396.
2. DeCurtis and Henke, *The Rolling Stone Illustrated History of Rock and Roll*, 396.
3. Tony Fletcher, *Boy About Town* (London: William Heinemann, 2013), 71.
4. Paolo Hewitt, *Paul Weller: The Changing Man* (London: Transworld Publishers, 2008), 199–202.
5. Daniel Rachel, *The Art of Noise* (New York: St. Martin's Press, 2013), 162–163.

Micro-Genres

1. Tobias Carroll, "The Secret History of Breakfast Violence," Red Bull Music Academy Daily, May 29, 2015, www.Daily.redbullmusicacademy.com.
2. *Morphine: Journey of Dreams*, directed by Mark Shuman (USA: 2014), documentary.
3. Mike Boehm, "Pop Will Eat Itself, the Band, to Dish Up New Kitchen-Sink Look Tonight at Coach House," *Los Angeles Times*, October 12, 1989, www.articles.latimes.com.
4. Harris, *Britpop!*, 98.
5. Lamacq, *Going Deaf for a Living*, 131.
6. Adam Higginbotham, "The Think Tanks: Sonya Aurora-Madan Out of Echobelly on Women of the Year, Fame, and, Ah, Quite a Lot of Drugs by the Sound of It," *Select*, January 1995, 57.
7. Ian Harrison, Emma Morgan, and Sam Upton, "The '90s: A Warning From History," *Select*, January 1999, 50.
8. Marc Weingarten, "Resurrecting the Riffs, A Nintendo Rock Band," *New York Times*, April 29, 2004, www.nytimes.com.

9.   Weingarten, "Resurrecting the Riffs, A Nintendo Rock Band."
10. Reynolds, *Shock and Awe*, 614.
11. Will Romano, *Prog Rock FAQ* (Milwaukee: Backbeat Books, 2014), 123–124.

Neo-Progressive Rock
1.   Stonebeard et al, "Neo-Prog: A Progressive Rock Sub-genre," ProgArchives .com, revised April 2009, www.progarchives.com.
2.   Paul Stump, *The Music's All That Matters* (Chelmsford, UK: Harbour Books, 2010), 258.
3.   Stump, *The Music's All That Matters*, 262–263.

New Rave
1.   Laura Martin, "New Rave 10 Years On: A Joke or Britain's Last Great Youth Movement?," *Independent*, February 29, 2016, www.independent.co.uk.
2.   Peter Robinson, "The Future's Bright . . .," *Guardian*, February 3, 2007, www.theguardian.com.
3.   Martin, "New Rave 10 Years On," 2016.
4.   Clive Martin, "It's Not Over Yet: Remembering New Rave, Ten Years Later," Vice, February 24, 2016, www.vice.com.

New Wave
1.   Jon Savage, *England's Dreaming* (New York: St. Martin's Press, 2001), 333.
2.   Jonathan Bernstein and Lori Majewski, *Mad World* (New York: Abrams Image, 2014), 10.
3.   Nina Blackwood Mark Goodman, Alan Hunter, and Martha Quinn with Gavin Edwards, *VJ: The Unplugged Adventures of MTV's First Wave* (New York: Atria Books, 2013), 126.

New Wave of British Heavy Metal
1.   Phil Collen and Chris Epting, *Adrenalized* (New York: Atria Books, 2015), 37.
2.   Christe, *Sound of the Beast*, 33.
3.   Christe, *Sound of the Beast*, 37.
4.   Christe, *Sound of the Beast*, 44.

No Wave
1.   Byron Coley and Thurston Moore, *No Wave* (New York: Abrams Image, 2008), 42.

Noise Pop
1.   Kevin Arnold, Jordan Kurland, and Dawson Ludwig, "The Mix: 100 Essential Noise Pop Songs," NPR Music, June 25, 2012, www.npr.org.
2.   Jenn Pelly, "When I'm Gone: Why Vivian Girls Mattered," Pitchfork, March 3, 2014, www.pitchfork.com.

3. Zachary Lipez and Drew Millard, "The Definitive Guide to Hipster Music Genres," Vice, December 14, 2015, www.vice.com.

Noise Rock
1. Paul Hegarty, *Noise/Music* (London: Continuum International Publishing Group, 2007), 60.
2. Robert Palmer, *Blues & Chaos* (New York, Scribner, 2009), 427.

Nu Gaze
1. Nathaniel Cramp and Gary Wolstenholme, "Shoegaze Week: 'There's No Such Thing as Nu-Gaze' by Sonic Cathedral," Drowned in Sound, April 20, 2009, www.drownedinsound.com.
2. Steven Morgan, "Whatever Happened to My Vitriol?," Drowned in Sound, October 26, 2016, www.drownedinsound.com.

Nu Metal
1. Christopher R. Weingarten, "Korn's 1994 Debut LP: The Oral History of the Most Important Metal Record of the Last 20 Years," *Rolling Stone*, December 11, 2014, www.rollingstone.com.
2. Nathan Brackett and Christian Hoard, eds., *The New Rolling Stone Album Guide*, 4th ed. (New York: Fireside, 2004), 467.
3. Joel McIver, *Nu-Metal* (London: Omnibus Press, 2002), 12.
4. McIver, *Nu-Metal*, 23.
5. Chuck Klosterman, *Fargo Rock City* (New York: Scribner, 2003), 243.
6. Klosterman, *Fargo Rock City*, 242.

Oi!
1. Glasper, *Burning Britain*, 278–286.
2. Glasper, *Burning Britain*, 286.
3. Glasper, *Burning Britain*, 289.
4. Blush, *American Hardcore*, 15.

Pop Punk
1. Kyle Ryan, "The Crash," *Punk Planet* 39, September/October 2000, 72.

Post-Britpop
1. Harris, *Britpop!*, 369.
2. Harris, *Britpop!*, 369.

Post-Hardcore
1. Azerrad, *Our Band Could Be Your Life*, 391–392.
2. David Wilcox, *Unwound: Kid is Gone* (Chicago: The Numero Group, 2013), 22.
3. Eric Grubbs, *Post* (Bloomington, IN: iUniverse, 2008), 66.

Post-Punk

1. Simon Reynolds, *Rip It Up and Start Again* (London: Faber and Faber, 2005), xx.
2. Reynolds, *Rip It Up and Start Again*, xxi.
3. David Browne, *Goodbye 20th Century* (Cambridge, MA: Da Capo Press, 2009), 176.

Post-Rock

1. Jack Chuter, *Storm Static Sleep* (London: Function Books, 2015), 148.
2. Chuter, *Storm Static Sleep*, 140–141.
3. Andrew Dansby, "Explosions in the Sky Is Still That 'Sad Triumphant Rock Band,'" *Houston Chronicle*, June 13, 2012, www.houstonchronicle.com.

Power Pop

1. Stanley, *Yeah! Yeah! Yeah!*, 307.
2. Stuart Maconie, *Cider with Roadies* (London: Ebury Press, 2004), 122.
3. Brackett and Hoard, eds., 157.

Powerviolence

1. James Knight, "Eric Wood from Man Is the Bastard," Vice, September 30, 2008, www.vice.com.
2. Knight, "Eric Wood from Man Is the Bastard," 2008.

Progressive Metal

1. DX Ferris, "Tales from Fantagraphic Oceans," *Alternative Press* 208, November 2005, 190.

Progressive Rock

1. Romano, *Mountains Come Out of the Sky*, 2.
2. Romano, *Mountains Come Out of the Sky*, 151.
3. Stump, *The Music's All That Matters*, 59.
4. Stump, *The Music's All That Matters*, 177.

Proto-Punk

1. Legs McNeil and Gillian McCain, *Please Kill Me* (New York: Grove Press, 2016), 3.
2. DeCurtis and Henke, *The Rolling Stone Illustrated History of Rock and Roll*, 357.

Psychedelic Folk

1. Leech, *Seasons They Change*, 85.
2. Leech, *Seasons They Change*, 105.

Psychedelic Rock

1. "Tour Archives—May 19, 1990," Phish.com, www.phish.com/tours/dates/sat-1990-05-19-upper-dining-hall-st-pauls-school/.
2. Nick Kent, *The Dark Stuff* (Cambridge, MA: Da Capo Press, 2002), 104.
3. Jarnow, *Heads*, 66.
4. David Henderson, *'Scuse Me While I Kiss The Sky* (New York: Atria Books, 2008), 223.
5. Jarnow, *Heads*, 211.

Psychedelic Soul

1. DeCurtis and Henke, *The Rolling Stone Illustrated History of Rock and Roll*, 435.

Psychobilly

1. Kenneth Partridge, "Where to Start with Psychobilly," AV Music, April 20, 2015, www.music.avclub.com.
2. Partridge, "Where to Start with Psychobilly."

Pub Rock

1. Savage, *England's Dreaming*, 81.
2. Doggett, *Are You Ready For The Country*, 436.

Punk Jazz

1. Matt Fleeger, "Five Ways Jazz Can Be Punk," NPR, September 10, 2012, www.npr.org.
2. Tad Friend, "Sleeping with Weapons," *New Yorker*, August 16, 2010, www.newyorker.com.

Punk Rock

1. John Lydon, *Rotten* (New York: Picador, 2008), 74.
2. Alex Vadukul, "His Brother's Keeper: A Ramones Tour of Queens," *New York Times*, April 13, 2016, www.nytimes.com.
3. Evelyn McDonnell and Ann Powers, eds, *Rock She Wrote* (New York: Cooper Square Press, 1999), 303–304.

Queercore

1. Philip Montoro, "Remembering God Is My Co-Pilot," *Chicago Reader*, October 29, 2015, www.chicagoreader.com.

Raga Rock

1. Mark Paytress, *History of Rock* (Bath, UK: Parragon, 2011), 81.
2. Paytress, *History of Rock*, 81.

3. Jon Dennis, "Beatles Cover Versions: 10 of the Best," *Guardian*, October 1, 2014, www.theguardian.com.

Rap Metal

1. Jason Newman, "Rage Against the Machine Bassist: 'I Apologize for Limp Bizkit,'" *Rolling Stone*, September 29, 2015, www.rollingstone.com.

Rap Rock

1. Kelefa Sanneh, "Rappers Who Definitely Know How to Rock," *New York Times*, December 3, 2000, www.nytimes.com.

Riot Grrrl

1. Sara Marcus, *Girls to the Front* (New York: Harper Perennial, 2010), 52.
2. Marcus, *Girls to the Front*, 80–81.
3. Marcus, *Girls to the Front*, 95.
4. Marisa Meltzer, *Girl Power* (New York: Faber and Faber, 2010), 31.
5. *Alien She*, art exhibit, curated by Astria Suparak and Ceci Moss, Miller Gallery, Carnegie Mellon University, September 21, 2013–February 16, 2014, www.millergallery.cfa.cmu.edu/exhibitions/alienshe/.

Rockabilly

1. DeCurtis and Henke, *The Rolling Stone Illustrated History of Rock and Roll*, 67–68.

Rock in Opposition

1. Romano, *Prog Rock FAQ*, 252.
2. Romano, *Prog Rock FAQ*, 255.
3. Romano, *Prog Rock FAQ*, 252.

San Francisco Sound

1. Ian MacDonald, *The People's Music* (London: Pimlico, 2003), 156.
2. Ellen Willis, *Out of the Vinyl Deeps* (Minneapolis: University of Minnesota Press, 2011), 190–191.

Screamo

1. Jason Heller, "Ambient Apocalypse: How City of Caterpillar Encompassed an Era," Noisey, May 20, 2016, www.noisey.vice.com.

Shock Rock

1. Dennis Dunaway and Chris Hodenfield, *Snakes! Guillotines! Electric Chairs!* (New York: Thomas Dunne Books, 2015), 183.
2. Reynolds, *Shock and Awe*, 116–117.

Shoegaze

1. Ian Gittins, "Shoegaze: An Oral History," Wondering Sound, February 13, 2015, www.wonderingsound.com.
2. Gittins, "Shoegaze: An Oral History."
3. Paul Lester, "Whatever Happened to Shoegazing?," *Melody Maker*, September 12, 1992, 6–7.
4. Lester, "Whatever Happened to Shoegazing?," 7.
5. Neil Kulkarni, "Eight-Legged Snooze Machine," *Melody Maker*, March 9, 1996, 37.
6. McGee, *Creation Stories*, 131–132.
7. Gittins, "Shoegaze: An Oral History."

Ska Punk

1. Jack Boulware and Silke Tudor, eds., *Gimme Something Better* (New York: Penguin Books, 2009), 344.
2. Boulware and Tudor, *Gimme Something Better*, 332.

Skiffle

1. All direct quotes in this section from Billy Bragg's "Billy Bragg on Skiffle" presentation at the Strand Book Store, New York, NY, July 22, 2017.

Slowcore

1. Jason Heller, "Reconsidering Codeine, a '90s Band Frozen in Time," AV Music, May 25, 2012, www.music.avclub.com.

Sludge Metal

1. Azerrad, *Come As You Are*, 25–26.

Southern Rock

1. Scott B. Bomar, *Southbound* (Milwaukee: Backbeat Books, 2014), 152.
2. Bomar, *Southbound*, 26–27.
3. Bomar, *Southbound*, 109.

Speed Metal

1. Konow, *Bang Your Head*, 232.
2. Konow, *Bang Your Head*, 232.

Straight Edge

1. Mark Andersen and Mark Jenkins, *Dance of Days* (New York: Akashic Books, 2009), 91.
2. Andersen and Jenkins, *Dance of Days*, 92.

Street Punk
1.   Glasper, *Burning Britain*, 47.
2.   Glasper, *Burning Britain*, 9.

Sunshine Pop
1.   Reynolds, *Retromania*, 152.
2.   Reynolds, *Retromania*, 168.

Surf Rock
1.   Kent Crowley, *Surf Beat* (Milwaukee: Backbeat Books, 2011), 7.
2.   Crowley, *Surf Beat*, 66.
3.   Crowley, *Surf Beat*, 90.
4.   Crowley, *Surf Beat*, 97–99.

Symphonic Metal
1.   Christe, *Sound of the Beast*, 197.

Synth-Pop
1.   Dan Orkin, "Which Synth Was It? A Closer Look at 5 Classic Tracks," Reverb, March 16, 2015, www.reverb.com.

Synth-Punk
1.   Justin Farrar, "A (Not At All Definitive) Guide to American Synth-Punk," Red Bull Music Academy Daily, April 23, 2013, www.Daily.redbullmusic academy.com.

Thrash Metal
1.   Ernst, *Get Thrashed*.

Tropicália
1.   Robin Denselow, "Gil and Caetano Are Imprisoned," *Guardian*, June 15, 2011, www.theguardian.com.
2.   Matthew Trammell, "Os Mutantes's Psychedelic Subversion," *New Yorker*, February 27, 2017, www.newyorker.com.
3.   Gerald Marzorati, "Tropicalia, Agora!," *New York Times*, April 25, 1999, www.nytimes.com.

Twee
1.   Nitsuh Abebe, "Twee as Fuck: The Story of Indie Pop," Pitchfork, October 24, 2005, www.pitchfork.com.
2.   Spitz, *Twee*, 77, 89, 189.

Translations

1. Milo Miles, "'Turkish Freakout': A Musical Turkish Delight," NPR, October 18, 2011, www.npr.org.
2. Daniel Spicer, "The Primer: Turkish Psychedelia," *The Wire* 334, December 2011, 42.
3. Bob Mersereau, *The History of Canadian Rock 'N' Roll* (Milwaukee: Backbeat Books, 2015), 234.
4. Kev Kharas, "Shiver into Existence: Cold Waves and Minimal Electronics," The Quietus, June 29, 2010, www.thequietus.com.
5. Julian Cope, *Japrocksampler* (London: Bloomsbury, 2008), 74–75.
6. Cope, *Japrocksampler*, 82–83.
7. Cope, *Japrocksampler*, 90.
8. Cope, *Japrocksampler*, 120.
9. Ben Sisario, "'Gypsy Punk Cabaret,' a Multinational," *New York Times*, April 14, 2002, www.nytimes.com.
10. Brad Nelson, "Babymetal Review: Pop Fans and Headbangers United in Awe," *Guardian*, November 5, 2014, www.theguardian.com.
11. Fabio Pasquarelli, "Italian Occult Psychedelia - New Scene of Post Punk Trip Weirdness from Italy," Louder Than War, July 30, 2013, www.louderthanwar.com.
12. Rudi Abdallah, "LISTEN: Italian Occult Psych Fest Mixtape," The Quietus, March 31, 2016, www.thequietus.com.
13. Ernesto Lechner, *Rock en Español* (Chicago: Chicago Review Press, 2006), x.
14. Strong, *The Great Rock Discography*, 856.
15. Reed, *Assimilate*, 95–96.
16. AFP, "It's the End for East Germany's Most Successful Band the Puhdys," *National*, December 3, 2014, www.thenational.ae.
17. Jelai L. Tarosa, "Pinoy Rock Scene Not Dead," *Philippine Star*, October 10, 2011, www.philstar.com.
18. Tarosa, "Pinoy Rock Scene Not Dead."
19. Jon Pareles, "Songs of the Saints, with Love, from Pakistan," *New York Times*, July 21, 2010, www.nytimes.com.
20. "About Us," Mekaal Hasan Band official website, www.mekaalhasanband.com.

War Metal

1. Kim Kelly, "Microgenres: War Metal - A Primer," Invisible Oranges, February 21, 2012, www.invisibleoranges.com.
2. Noisey Staff, "Listen to the Bestial Debut from War Metal Supergroup Death Worship," Noisey, February 16, 2017, www.noisey.vice.com.

Youth Crew

1. Brian Peterson, *Burning Fight* (Huntington Beach, CA: Revelation Records, 2009), 59.
2. Peterson, *Burning Fight*, 357.
3. Jonah Bayer et al, *Going Off Track*, podcast, "Episode 240—Walter Schreifels," January 11, 2017.
4. Bayer et al, *Going Off Track*, "Episode 240."

BIBLIOGRAPHY

Andersen, Mark and Mark Jenkins. *Dance of Days: Two Decades of Punk in the Nation's Capital*. New York: Akashic Books, 2009.

Aston, Martin. *Facing the Other Way: The Story of 4AD*. London: The Friday Project, 2013.

Azerrad, Michael. *Come As You Are: The Story of Nirvana*. New York: Broadway Books, 1993.

Azerrad, Michael. *Our Band Could Be Your Life: Scenes from the American Indie Underground 1981–1991*. New York: Back Bay Books, 2002.

Baumgarten, Mark. *Love Rock Revolution: K Records and the Rise of Independent Music*. Seattle: Sasquatch Books, 2012.

Beaujon, Andrew. *Body Piercing Saved My Life: Inside the Phenomenon of Christian Rock*. Cambridge, MA: Da Capo Press, 2006.

Bernstein, Jonathan, and Lori Majewski. *Mad World: An Oral History of New Wave Artists and Songs that Defined the 1980s*. New York: Abrams Image, 2014.

Blackwood, Nina, Mark Goodman, Alan Hunter, Martha Quinn, and Gavin Edwards. *VJ: The Unplugged Adventures of MTV's First Wave*. New York: Atria Books, 2013.

Blecha, Peter. *Music in Washington: Seattle and Beyond*. Charleston: Arcadia Publishing, 2007.

Blush, Steven. *American Hardcore: A Tribal History*. 2nd ed. Port Townshend, WA: Feral House, 2010.

Bomar, Scott B. *Southbound: An Illustrated History of Southern Rock*. Milwaukee: Backbeat Books, 2014.

Boulware, Jack, and Silke Tudor, eds. *Gimme Something Better: The Profound, Progressive, and Occasionally Pointless History of Bay Area Punk from Dead Kennedys to Green Day*. New York: Penguin Books, 2009.

Bowie, David. *Moonage Daydream: The Life and Times of Ziggy Stardust*. New York: Universe Publishing, 2005.

Boyd, Joe. *White Bicycles: Making Music in the 1960s*. London: Serpent's Tail, 2006.

Brackett, Nathan, and Christian Hoard, eds. *The New Rolling Stone Album Guide: Completely Revised and Updated Fourth Edition*. New York: Fireside, 2004.

Brannigan, Paul. *This Is a Call: The Life and Times of Dave Grohl*. Cambridge, MA: Da Capo Press, 2011.

Browne, David. *Goodbye 20th Century: A Biography of Sonic Youth*. Cambridge, MA: Da Capo Press, 2009.

Burgess, Tim. *Telling Stories*. London: Viking, 2012.

Cameron, Keith. *Mudhoney: The Sound and the Fury from Seattle*. Minneapolis: Voyageur Press, 2014.

Carducci, Joe. *Rock and the Pop Narcotic: Testament for the Electric Church*. 2nd ed. Los Angeles: 2.13.61, 1994.

Christe, Ian. *Sound of the Beast: The Complete Headbanging History of Heavy Metal*. New York: HarperCollins, 2004.

Chuter, Jack. *Storm Static Sleep: A Pathway Through Post-Rock*. London: Function Books, 2015.

Clinton, George, and Ben Greenman. *Brothas Be, Yo Like George, Ain't That Funkin' Kinda Hard On You?* New York: Atria Paperback, 2017.

Coley, Byron, and Thurston Moore. *No Wave: Post-Punk. Underground. New York. 1976–1980*. New York: Abrams Image, 2008.

Collen, Phil, and Chris Epting. *Adrenalized: Life, Def Leppard, and Beyond*. New York: Atria Books, 2015.

Cook, John, Mac McCaughan, and Laura Ballance. *Our Noise: The Story of Merge Records, the Indie Label that Got Big and Stayed Small*. Chapel Hill: Algonquin Books of Chapel Hill, 2009.

Cope, Julian. *Japrocksampler: How the Post-War Japanese Blew Their Minds on Rock 'n' Roll*. London: Bloomsbury, 2016.

Crowley, Kent. *Surf Beat: Rock 'n' Roll's Forgotten Revolution*. Milwaukee: Backbeat Books, 2011.

DeCurtis, Anthony, and James Henke, eds. *The Rolling Stone Illustrated History of Rock & Roll: The Definitive History of the Most Important Artists and Their Music*. New York: Random House, 1992.

Doggett, Peter. *Are You Ready for the Country: Elvis, Dylan, Parsons and the Roots of Country Rock*. New York: Penguin Books, 2000.

Dregni, Michael, ed. *Rockabilly: The Twang Heard 'Round the World*. Minneapolis: Voyageur Press, 2011.

Dunaway, Dennis, and Chris Hodenfield. *Snakes! Guillotines! Electric Chairs! My Adventures in the Alice Cooper Group*. New York: Thomas Dunne Books, 2015.

Earles, Andrew. *Gimme Indie Rock: 500 Essential American Underground Rock Albums 1981–1996*. Minneapolis: Voyageur Press, 2014.

Fearnley, James. *Here Comes Everybody: The Story of the Pogues*. Chicago: Chicago Review Press, 2014.

Fletcher, Tony. *Boy About Town*. London: William Heinemann, 2013.

Frehley, Ace, Joe Layden, and John Ostrosky. *No Regrets: A Rock 'n' Roll Memoir*. New York: Gallery Books, 2011. ·

Glasper, Ian. *Burning Britain: The History of UK Punk 1980–1984*. London: Cherry Red Books, 2004.

Glasper, Ian. *The Day the Country Died: A History of Anarcho Punk 1980–1984*. London: Cherry Red Books, 2006.

Glasper, Ian. *Trapped in a Scene: UK Hardcore 1985–1989; Frontline Reports from the Hardcore Punk Underground*. London: Cherry Red Books, 2009.

Goddard, Simon. *Simply Thrilled: The Preposterous Story of Postcard Records*. London: Ebury Press, 2014.

Greenwald, Andy. *Nothing Feels Good: Punk Rock, Teenagers, and Emo*. New York: St. Martin's Press, 2003.

Grubbs, Eric. *Post: A Look at the Influence of Post-Hardcore 1985–2007*. Bloomington, IN: iUniverse, 2008.

Haines, Luke. *Bad Vibes: Britpop and My Part in Its Downfall*. London: Windmill Books, 2010.

Harris, John. *Britpop! Cool Britannia and the Spectacular Demise of English Rock*. Cambridge, MA: Da Capo Press, 2004.

Harry, Bill. *The British Invasion: How the Beatles and Other UK Bands Conquered America*. Surrey: Chrome Dreams, 2004.

Haslam, Dave. *Manchester, England: The Story of the Pop Cult City*. London: Fourth Estate, 2000.

Hegarty, Paul. *Noise/Music: A History*. London: Continuum International Publishing Group, 2007.

Henderson, David. *'Scuse Me While I Kiss the Sky: Jimi Hendrix; Voodoo Child*. New York: Atria Books, 2008.

Hertsgaard, Mark. *A Day in the Life: The Music and Artistry of the Beatles*. New York: Delacorte Press, 1995.

Hewitt, Paolo. *Paul Weller: The Changing Man*. London: Transworld Publishers, 2008.

Hook, Peter. *The Haçienda: The Inside Story of Britain's Most Notorious Nightclub*. New York: HarperCollins, 2014.

Hoskyns, Barney. *Hotel California: The True-Life Adventures of Crosby, Stills, Nash, Young, Mitchell, Taylor, Browne, Ronstadt, Geffen, the Eagles, and Their Many Friends*. Hoboken: John Wiley & Sons, 2006.

Houghtaling, Adam Brent. *This Will End in Tears: The Miserabilist Guide to Music*. New York: HarperCollins, 2012.

Hyden, Steven. *Your Favorite Band Is Killing Me: What Pop Music Rivalries Reveal About the Meaning of Life*. New York: Back Bay Books, 2016.

Jackson, Andrew Grant. *1965: The Most Revolutionary Year in Music*. New York: Thomas Dunne Books, 2015.

James, Alex. *Bit of a Blur*. London: Little, Brown, 2007.

Jarnow, Jesse. *Big Day Coming: Yo La Tengo and the Rise of Indie Rock*. New York: Gotham Books, 2012.

Jarnow, Jesse. *Heads: A Biography of Psychedelic America*. Boston: Da Capo Press, 2016.

Jones, Lesley-Ann. *Mercury: An Intimate Biography of Freddie Mercury*. New York: Touchstone, 2011.

Kent, Nick. *The Dark Stuff: Selected Writings on Rock Music*. Cambridge, MA: Da Capo Press, 2002.

Kilpatrick, Nancy. *The Goth Bible*. New York: St. Martin's Press, 2004.

Klosterman, Chuck. *Fargo Rock City: A Heavy Metal Odyssey in Rural North Dakota*. New York: Scribner, 2003.

Konow, David. *Bang Your Head: The Rise and Fall of Heavy Metal*. New York: Three Rivers Press, 2002.

Lamacq, Steve. *Going Deaf for a Living: A DJ's Story*. London: BBC Worldwide, 2000.

Lechner, Ernesto. *Rock en Español: The Latin Alternative Rock Explosion*. Chicago: Chicago Review Press, 2006.

Lee, Tommy, and Anthony Bozza. *Tommyland*. New York: Atria Books, 2004.

Leech, Jeanette. *Seasons They Change: The Story of Acid and Psychedelic Folk*. London: Jawbone Press, 2011.

Lydon, John. *Rotten: No Irish, No Blacks, No Dogs*. New York: Picador, 2008.

MacDonald, Ian. *The People's Music*. London: Pimlico, 2003.

Maconie, Stuart. *Cider with Roadies*. London: Ebury Press, 2004.

Marcus, Sara. *Girls to the Front: The True Story of the Riot Grrrl Revolution*. New York: Harper Perennial, 2010.

Marshall, George. *The Two Tone Story: Lockerbie, Dumfriesshire*. Scotland: S.T. Publishing, 2011.

McCormick, Neil. *Killing Bono*. New York: Pocket Books, 2004.

McDonnell, Evelyn, and Ann Powers, eds. *Rock She Wrote: Women Write about Rock, Pop, and Rap*. New York: Cooper Square Press, 1999.

McGee, Alan. *Creation Stories: Riots, Raves and Running a Label*. London: Pan Books, 2014.

McIver, Joel. *Nu-Metal: The Next Generation of Rock & Punk*. London: Omnibus Press, 2002.

McMillian, John. *Beatles Vs. Stones*. New York: Simon & Schuster, 2013.

McNeil, Legs, and Gillian McCain. *Please Kill Me: The Uncensored Oral History of Punk*. New York: Grove Press, 2016.

Meltzer, Marisa. *Girl Power: The Nineties Revolution in Music*. New York: Faber and Faber, 2010.

Mersereau, Bob. *The History of Canadian Rock 'N' Roll*. Milwaukee: Backbeat Books, 2015.

Meyer, David N. *Twenty Thousand Roads: The Ballad of Gram Parsons and His Cosmic American Music*. New York: Villard Books, 2007.

Morthland, John, ed. *Mainlines, Blood Feasts and Bad Taste: A Lester Bangs Reader*. New York: Anchor Books, 2003.

Mudrian, Albert. *Choosing Death: The Improbable History of Death Metal & Grindcore*. Port Townsend, WA: Feral House, 2004.

Murphy, Gareth. *Cowboys and Indies: The Epic History of the Record Industry*. New York: Thomas Dunne Books, 2014.

Nobles, Mark A. *Fort Worth's Rock and Roll Roots.* Charleston: Arcadia Publishing, 2011.

Palmer, Robert. *Blues & Chaos: The Music Writing of Robert Palmer.* New York, Scribner, 2009.

Paytress, Mark. *History of Rock: The Definitive Guide to Rock, Punk, Metal, and Beyond.* Bath, UK: Parragon, 2011.

Peterson, Brian. *Burning Fight: The Nineties Hardcore Revolution in Ethics, Politics, Spirit, and Sound.* Huntington Beach, CA: Revelation Records, 2009.

Petrusich, Amanda. *It Still Moves: Lost Songs, Lost Highways, and the Search for the Next American Music.* New York: Faber and Faber, 2008.

Plagenhoef, Scott, and Ryan Schreiber, eds. *The Pitchfork 500.* New York: Touchstone, 2008.

Purcell, Natalie J. *Death Metal Music: The Passion and Politics of a Subculture.* Jefferson, NC: McFarland & Company, 2003.

Rachel, Daniel. *The Art of Noise: Conversations with Great Songwriters.* New York: St. Martin's Press, 2013.

Reed, S. Alexander. *Assimilate: A Critical History of Industrial Music.* New York: Oxford University Press, 2013.

Reyes, David, and Tom Waldman. *Land of a Thousand Dances: Chicano Rock 'n' Roll from Southern California.* Albuquerque: University of New Mexico Press, 1998.

Reynolds, Simon. *Retromania: Pop Culture's Addiction to Its Own Past.* New York: Farrar, Straus and Giroux, 2011.

Reynolds, Simon. *Rip It Up and Start Again: Post-Punk 1978–1984.* London: Faber and Faber, 2005.

Reynolds, Simon. *Shock and Awe: Glam Rock and Its Legacy, from the Seventies to the Twenty-First Century.* New York: Dey Street, 2016.

Richards, Keith. *Life.* New York: Little, Brown and Company, 2010.

Robb, John, *The Nineties: What the F**k Was That All About,* London: Ebury Press, 1999.

Robb, John. *The North Will Rise Again: Manchester Music City (1977–1996).* London: Aurum Press, 2010.

Robb, John. *The Stone Roses: The Reunion Edition.* London: Ebury Press, 2012.

Romano, Will. *Mountains Come Out of the Sky: The Illustrated History of Prog Rock.* Milwaukee: Backbeat Books, 2010.

Romano, Will. *Prog Rock FAQ: All That's Left to Know About Rock's Most Progressive Music.* Milwaukee: Backbeat Books, 2014.

Ryder, Shaun. *Twisting My Melon.* London: Transworld Publishers, 2012.

Savage, Jon. *England's Dreaming: Anarchy, Sex Pistols, Punk Rock, and Beyond.* New York: St. Martin's Press, 2001.

Schinder, Scott, ed. *Rolling Stone's Alt-Rock-A-Rama: An Outrageous Compendium of Facts, Fiction, Trivia, and Critiques of Alternative Rock.* New York: Bantam Doubleday Dell, 1996.

Schwenke, Elmar. *Ostrock! Popmusik in der DDR.* Gudensberg-Gleichen: Wartberg Verlag, 2010.

Snider, Dee. *Shut Up and Give Me the Mic: A Twisted Memoir*. New York: Gallery Books, 2012.

Spitz, Marc. *Twee: The Gentle Revolution in Music, Books, Television, Fashion, and Film*. New York: HarperCollins, 2014.

Stanley, Bob. *Yeah! Yeah! Yeah! The Story of Pop Music from Bill Haley to Beyoncé*. New York: W.W. Norton, 2015.

Strong, Martin C. *The Great Rock Discography*. 6th ed. Edinburgh: Canongate Books Ltd, 2002.

Stubbs, David. *Future Days: Krautrock and the Birth of a Revolutionary New Music*. Brooklyn: Melville House, 2015.

Stump, Paul. *The Music's All That Matters*. Chelmsford, UK: Harbour Books, 2010.

Taylor, Neil. *Document and Eyewitness: An Intimate History of Rough Trade*. London: Orion Books, 2010.

Tennent, Scott. *Spiderland*. New York: Continuum International Publishing Group, 2011.

Tolhurst, Lol. *Cured: The Tale of Two Imaginary Boys*. New York: Da Capo Press, 2016.

Tow, Stephen. *The Strangest Tribe: How a Group of Seattle Rock Bands Invented Grunge*. Seattle: Sasquatch Books, 2011.

Unterberger, Richie. *Turn! Turn! Turn! The '60s Folk-Rock Revolution*. Milwaukee: Backbeat Books, 2002.

Unterberger, Richie. *Urban Spacemen and Wayfaring Strangers: Overlooked Innovators and Eccentric Visionaries of '60s Rock*. San Francisco: Miller Freeman Books, 2000.

Wald, Elijah. *How the Beatles Destroyed Rock 'n' Roll: An Alternative History of American Popular Music*. New York: Oxford University Press, 2009.

Wener, Louise. *Just for One Day: Adventures in Britpop*. London: Ebury Press, 2011.

Willis, Ellen. *Out of the Vinyl Deeps: Ellen Willis on Rock Music*. Minneapolis: University of Minnesota Press, 2011.

Yarm, Mark. *Everybody Loves Our Town: An Oral History of Grunge*. New York: Crown Archetype, 2011.

Young, Rob. *Electric Eden: Unearthing Britain's Visionary Music*. New York: Farrar, Straus and Giroux, 2010.

INTERVIEWS

Ian Anderson
Gina Birch*
Jon Bolling
Tobias Carroll
Jack Chuter
Marco Collins
John Colpitts*
Brian Cook*
Rachel Goswell
Melissa Giannini
Rob Halford*
John Haughm*
Jim Heath
Scott Hill*

Matt Kadane
David Kilgour*
Damon Krukowski*
Sara Marcus
Tom Mullen
Stuart Murdoch
Colin Newman
Kim Ruehl*
Brandon Stosuy
David Stubbs*
Doug Van Pelt
JJ Wandler
Steve Wynn*

*via email

ABOUT THE AUTHOR

Ian King is a music writer and publishing professional who has contributed to *Nylon*, *Slice* magazine, *The Line of Best Fit*, *PopMatters*, *Vol. 1 Brooklyn*, as well as other music media. He lives in Brooklyn, New York, with his wife and their son.